First World War
and Army of Occupation
War Diary
France, Belgium and Germany

30 DIVISION
Headquarters, Branches and Services
Commander Royal Engineers
11 January 1915 - 24 March 1919

WO95/2320/1

The Naval & Military Press Ltd
www.nmarchive.com
Published in association with The National Archives

Published by

The Naval & Military Press Ltd

Unit 10 Ridgewood Industrial Park,

Uckfield, East Sussex,

TN22 5QE England

Tel: +44 (0) 1825 749494

www.naval-military-press.com

www.nmarchive.com

This diary has been reprinted in facsimile from the original. Any imperfections are inevitably reproduced and the quality may fall short of modern type and cartographic standards.

© **Crown Copyright**
Images reproduced by permission of The National Archives, London, England, 2015.

Contents

Document type	Place/Title	Date From	Date To
Heading	Commander Royal Engineers		
Heading	30th Division Divl Engineers C.R.E. Nov 1915-Apr 1919		
Heading	H.Q. 30th Div C.R.E. Vol. I Nov 15		
War Diary	Larkhill	07/11/1915	07/11/1915
War Diary	Havre	08/11/1915	08/11/1915
War Diary	Pont Remy	09/11/1915	09/11/1915
War Diary	Ailly Le	09/11/1915	09/11/1915
War Diary	Haut Clocher	17/11/1915	17/11/1915
War Diary	Flesselles	17/11/1915	28/11/1915
War Diary	Fienvilliers	28/11/1915	30/11/1915
Miscellaneous	Historical Record of The 30th Divisional		
War Diary	War Office London, S.W.	11/01/1915	11/01/1915
Miscellaneous	War Office London, S.W.	29/09/1914	29/09/1914
Miscellaneous	Royal Engineers. Divisional Engineers.		
Miscellaneous	Recruits-Royal Engineers.		
Miscellaneous	Royal Engineers.		
Miscellaneous	Extract from letter dated 10th May, 1915, from Chairman, Manchester City Battalions. Appendix II.		
Diagram etc			
Diagram etc	Appendix IV		
Diagram etc	Appendix V		
Miscellaneous	Appendix VI General Officer Commanding-in-Chief.	13/06/1915	13/06/1915
Miscellaneous	30th Divisional (County Palatine) Engineers.		
Miscellaneous	Appendix VIII	04/10/1915	04/10/1915
Miscellaneous	Field Company		
Miscellaneous	Divisional Signal Company		
Miscellaneous	Divisional Engineers.		
Heading	CRE 30th. Division Vol 2		
War Diary	Fienvillers	01/12/1915	05/12/1915
War Diary	Le Meillard	07/12/1915	21/12/1915
War Diary	Acheux	22/12/1915	27/12/1915
War Diary	Le Meillard	27/12/1915	30/12/1915
War Diary	Chipilly	30/12/1915	31/12/1915
Heading	30th Divisional Engineers War Diary C.R.E. 30th Division January 1916		
War Diary	Chipilly	01/01/1916	29/01/1916
Heading	30th Divisional Engineers War Diary C.R.E. 30th Division. February 1916		
War Diary	Chipilly	01/02/1916	26/02/1916
Heading	30th Divisional Engineers War Diary C.R.E. 30th Division March 1916		
War Diary	Chipilly	01/03/1916	20/03/1916
War Diary	Montigny	24/03/1916	24/03/1916
War Diary	Daours	28/03/1916	28/03/1916
War Diary	Ailly-Sur-Somme	31/03/1916	31/03/1916
Heading	30th Divisional Engineers War Diary C.R.E. 30th Division. April 1916		
War Diary	Ailly Sur Somme	01/04/1916	30/04/1916

Heading	30th Divisional Engineers C.R.E. 30th Division. May 1916		
War Diary	Etinehem	01/05/1916	31/05/1916
Heading	30th Divisional Engineers. War Diary C.R.E. 30th Division June 1916. For Engineers Preparations & Instructions For The Attack See Appendix "A" To July Diary.		
War Diary	Etinehem	01/06/1916	23/06/1916
War Diary	Dugouts 1/2 Mile East Bray	23/06/1916	30/06/1916
Heading	30th Divisional Engineers War Diary C.R.E. 30th Division. July 1916. Appendices.		
War Diary	Dugouts Near Bray	01/07/1916	04/07/1916
War Diary	Etinehem	05/07/1916	07/07/1916
War Diary	Etinehem And Copse Valley	08/07/1916	13/07/1916
War Diary	Corbie	14/07/1916	19/07/1916
War Diary	Billon Copse	20/07/1916	30/07/1916
War Diary	Citadel	31/07/1916	31/07/1916
Miscellaneous	O.C. 200th Field Coy, R.E. Appendix A	20/06/1916	20/06/1916
Miscellaneous	Arrangements for Provision of R.E. Stores during Operations.	20/06/1917	20/06/1917
Miscellaneous	In Avenue Just North of Maricourt Chateau on Maricourt-Montauban Road	20/06/1917	20/06/1917
Miscellaneous	Talus Boise. (Square A.15.a.2.8.)	20/06/1916	20/06/1916
Miscellaneous	List of Stores at Divisional R.E. Dump, Bray, at commencement of active operations. Square L.15.b. (Bray-Albert Road).	20/06/1916	20/06/1916
Miscellaneous	Pontoon Wagon Loads	20/06/1916	20/06/1916
Miscellaneous	Roads	20/06/1916	20/06/1916
Miscellaneous	Water Supply	20/06/1916	20/06/1916
Miscellaneous		21/06/1916	21/06/1916
Miscellaneous	Disposition of R.E's and Pioneers	21/06/1916	21/06/1916
Miscellaneous	Instructions to the O.C. 200th Field Company, R.E.	21/06/1916	21/06/1916
Miscellaneous	Instructions to the O.C. 201st Field Company, R.E.	21/06/1916	21/06/1916
Miscellaneous	Instructions to the O.C. 202nd Field Company, R.E.	21/06/1916	21/06/1916
Miscellaneous	Instructions for the O.C. 238th Army Troops Coy. R.E.	21/06/1916	21/06/1916
Miscellaneous	Instructions for O.C. Section detailed to Command party to form "Strong Points" With 21st Infantry Brigade	21/06/1916	21/06/1916
Miscellaneous	Instructions for O.C. Section detailed to Command party to form "Strong Points" With 89th Infantry Brigade	21/06/1916	21/06/1916
Miscellaneous	Instructions for O.C. Section 200th Field Company detailed for road-making party.	21/06/1916	21/06/1916
Miscellaneous	Instructions for the forward Communication Trench Parties	21/06/1916	21/06/1916
Miscellaneous	Instructions for the Communication Trench Maintenance Parties.	21/06/1916	21/06/1916
Miscellaneous	List "A"	21/06/1916	21/06/1916
Miscellaneous	Strong Point-Party; 21st Infantry Brigade.	21/06/1916	21/06/1916
Miscellaneous	Strong Point-Party; 89th Infantry Brigade.	21/06/1916	21/06/1916
Miscellaneous	201st Field Company, R.E.	21/06/1916	21/06/1916
Miscellaneous	Road Party (a)	21/06/1916	21/06/1916
Miscellaneous	List "S" Road Party (b).	21/06/1916	21/06/1916
Miscellaneous	C.R.E's No. 1944	26/06/1916	26/06/1916
Miscellaneous	Water Truck Party.	26/06/1916	26/06/1916
Miscellaneous	Appendix "J" To O.O. 19		
Miscellaneous	Account Of R.E. Operations From Morning 1st July to Mid-day 2nd July, 1916	02/07/1916	02/07/1916

Miscellaneous	Account Of Operations (Technical Troops) 8th to 13th July, 1916 Appendix C	16/07/1916	16/07/1916
Miscellaneous	Note re Work Done by Technical Units During The Period 20th-29th July and During the Operations 29th 30th July	01/08/1916	01/08/1916
Heading	30th Divisional Engineers C.R.E. 30th Division August 1916		
War Diary	Citadel	01/08/1916	01/08/1916
War Diary	Hallencourt	02/08/1916	03/08/1916
War Diary	Busnes	04/08/1916	11/08/1916
War Diary	Bethune	12/08/1916	31/08/1916
Heading	30th Divisional Engineers War Diary C.R.E. 30th Division September 1916		
War Diary	Bethune	01/09/1916	19/09/1916
War Diary	Doullens	19/09/1916	20/09/1916
War Diary	Vignacourt	21/09/1916	30/09/1916
Heading	30th Divisional Engineers War Diary C.R.E. 30th Division. October 1916		
War Diary	Vignacourt	01/10/1916	04/10/1916
War Diary	Buire	04/10/1916	11/10/1916
War Diary	Fricourt Chateau	11/10/1916	21/10/1916
War Diary	Ribemont	22/10/1916	25/10/1916
War Diary	Pas	26/10/1916	30/10/1916
War Diary	Bavincourt	31/10/1916	31/10/1916
Miscellaneous	Disposition of R.E. and Pioneers		
Miscellaneous	30th Division Operation Order No. 40. Appendix "B"	11/10/1916	11/10/1916
Miscellaneous	Disposition of R.E. & Pioneers. Appendix 'C' to War Diary		
Miscellaneous	Extract from 30th Division Operation Order No. 42, dated 17th October, 1916 Appendix "D"		
Heading	30th Divisional Engineers War Diary C.R.E. 30th Division November 1916		
Heading	30th. Divisional Engineers War Diary Volume 13. November, 1916		
War Diary	Bavincourt	01/12/1916	30/12/1916
Heading	30th Divisional Engineers War Diary 30th Division C.R.E. December 1916		
Heading	Headquarters, 30th Divisional Engineers War Diary For The Month Of December, 1916 Volume 14		
War Diary	Bavincourt	01/12/1916	31/12/1916
Heading	30th Divisional Engineers, War Diary Volume 15, January, 1917		
War Diary	Bavincourt	01/01/1917	07/01/1917
War Diary	Lucheux	07/01/1917	28/01/1917
War Diary	Berneville	28/01/1917	28/02/1917
Heading	30th Divisional Engineers. War Diary. Volume 17. March, 1917		
War Diary	Berneville	01/03/1917	24/03/1917
War Diary	Bretencourt	24/03/1917	31/03/1917
Heading	Headquarters 30th Divisional Engineers. War Diary Volume 18 April 1917		
War Diary	Bretencourt	08/04/1917	08/04/1917
War Diary	Blairville	08/04/1917	08/04/1917
War Diary	Pommier	12/04/1917	12/04/1917
War Diary	Achicourt	19/04/1917	19/04/1917
War Diary	Neuville Vitasse	25/04/1917	25/04/1917

War Diary	Roellecourt	30/04/1917	30/04/1917
Miscellaneous	Arrangements for R.E. Stores. Appendix A		
Miscellaneous	Table "A"		
Miscellaneous	O.C. 200th Field Co. R.E. Appendix A.1.		
Miscellaneous	Appendix B	04/04/1917	04/04/1917
Miscellaneous	Disposition of R.E. and Pioneers.		
Miscellaneous	Instructions To O.C. 200th Field Coy. R.E.	04/04/1917	04/04/1917
Miscellaneous	Instructions To O.C. 201st Field Coy. R.E.	04/04/1917	04/04/1917
Miscellaneous	Instructions To O.C. 202nd Field Coy. R.E.	04/04/1917	04/04/1917
Miscellaneous	Instructions to The O.C. 11th South Lancs Pioneers.	04/04/1917	04/04/1917
Miscellaneous	Arrangements for Provision of R.E. Stores During Active Operations.	04/04/1917	04/04/1917
Miscellaneous	Roads	04/04/1917	04/04/1917
Miscellaneous		06/04/1917	06/04/1917
Miscellaneous	Report On Work Carried Out By The Technical Troops During Operations From 8th To 12th April 1917 Appendix C	08/04/1917	08/04/1917
Operation(al) Order(s)	Orders By C.R.E., 30th Division. Appendix D	21/04/1917	21/04/1917
Miscellaneous	Report On Operations of Technical Troops From 19-4-1917 To 29-4-1917	19/04/1917	19/04/1917
Miscellaneous	Short Account Of Employment Of R.E. And Pioneers During Past Operations 18th March To 22nd March 1917	18/03/1917	18/03/1917
Heading	Headquarters, 30th Divisional Engineers. War Diary. Volume 19. May 1917 Vol 19		
War Diary	Roellecourt	01/05/1917	01/05/1917
Heading	Headquarters 30th Divisional Engineers. War Diary. Volume 20. June 1917 Vol 20		
War Diary	Brandhoek Reninghelst	01/06/1917	15/06/1917
Heading	Headquarters 30th Divisional Engineers. War Diary. Volume 21. July 1917 Vol 21		
War Diary	Reninghelst	01/07/1917	01/07/1917
War Diary	Nordauques.	07/07/1917	07/07/1917
War Diary	Steenvoorde	19/07/1917	19/07/1917
War Diary	H.27.b. 65.7	24/07/1917	24/07/1917
Operation(al) Order(s)	Operation Order No. 1 BY Lt. Col. G.W. Denison, D.S.O., R.E., C.R.E. 30th Division.		
Miscellaneous	Disposition of R.E. and Pioneers on "Z" Day. Appx A	11/07/1917	11/07/1917
Miscellaneous	The following are the arrangements for the supply of R.E. Stores and Tools during the forthcoming operations. Appendix B	11/07/1917	11/07/1917
Miscellaneous	Appendix 1		
Miscellaneous	C.R.E. No. 2991/6	18/07/1917	18/07/1917
Miscellaneous	Appendix		
Heading	Headquarters 30th Divisional Engineers. War Diary. August 1917 Volume 22		
Miscellaneous	Headquarters 30th Divisional Engineers.	03/09/1917	03/09/1917
Miscellaneous	Work Carried Out by the technical troops 30th division During Active Operations From 31-7-17 To 3-8-17	31/07/1917	31/07/1917
Operation(al) Order(s)	Operation Order No. 2. By Lieut. Col. G.W. Denison. D.S.O.H.E. C.R.E. 30th Division.	20/08/1917	20/08/1917
Miscellaneous	March Table Of Technical Troops.	20/08/1917	20/08/1917
Heading	Headquarters 30th Divisional Engineers. War Diary. Volume 23. September 1917		
War Diary	Dranoutre	01/09/1917	01/09/1917

Type	Description	Date From	Date To
Operation(al) Order(s)	Operation Order No. 3 By Lieut-Col. G.W. Denison, D.S.O. R.E. C.R.E., 30th Division. Appendix "A"	01/09/1917	01/09/1917
Miscellaneous	Table To Accompany C.R.E. Operation Order No. 3		
Operation(al) Order(s)	30th Divisional Engineers Order No. 4. Appendix "B"	18/09/1917	18/09/1917
Miscellaneous	O.C. 200th Field Coy. R.E. Appendix "C"	30/09/1917	30/09/1917
Miscellaneous	Working Party Table		
Heading	Headquarters 30th Divisional Engineers. War Diary. Volume 24 October 1917		
War Diary	Dranoutre	00/10/1917	00/10/1917
Heading	Headquarters 30th Divisional Engineers. War Diary. Volume 25. November 1917		
War Diary	Dranoutre	01/11/1917	01/11/1917
War Diary	Goldfish Chateau H.11.a. 8.1	14/11/1917	14/11/1917
War Diary	Westoutre	24/11/1917	24/11/1917
Miscellaneous	O.C. 200th Field Coy. R.E.	17/11/1917	17/11/1917
Operation(al) Order(s)	South Div. Order No. 6	23/11/1917	23/11/1917
Heading	Headquarters 30th Divisional Engineers. War Diary. Volume 26. December 1917		
War Diary	Westoutre	01/12/1917	01/12/1917
Operation(al) Order(s)	30th Divisional Engineers Order No. 6. Appendix 1	01/12/1917	01/12/1917
Miscellaneous	30th Divisional Engineers Order No. 7. Appendix 1	09/12/1917	09/12/1917
Operation(al) Order(s)	30th Divisional Engineers Order No. 8. Appendix 1	17/12/1917	17/12/1917
Operation(al) Order(s)	30th Divisional Engineers Order No. 9 Appendix 1	27/12/1917	27/12/1917
War Diary		02/12/1917	24/12/1917
Heading	Headquarters 30th Divisional Engineers. War Diary. Volume 27. January 1918		
War Diary	Westoutre	01/01/1918	01/01/1918
War Diary	Ham.	19/01/1918	19/01/1918
Operation(al) Order(s)	30th Divisional Engineers Order No. 10. Appendix A	02/01/1918	02/01/1918
Heading	Headquarters 30th Divisional Engineers. War Diary. Volume 28. February 1918		
War Diary	Ham.	04/02/1918	23/02/1918
War Diary	Dury.	26/02/1918	26/02/1918
War Diary	Dury.	23/02/1918	23/02/1918
War Diary	War Diary Headquarters. Royal Engineers, 30th Division. March 1918		
Heading	Headquarters 30th Divisional Engineers. War Diary. Volume 29-March 1918		
War Diary	Dury.	01/03/1918	21/03/1918
War Diary	Ham.	22/03/1918	22/03/1918
War Diary	Ercheu.	22/03/1918	24/03/1918
War Diary	Solente	24/03/1918	25/03/1918
War Diary	Roieglise	25/03/1918	25/03/1918
War Diary	Hangest-En-Santerre.	26/03/1918	26/03/1918
War Diary	Quesnel Hangest-En-Santerre. Braches.	27/03/1918	27/03/1918
War Diary	Rouvrel Estree	28/03/1918	30/03/1918
War Diary	St. Valery-Sur-Somme	31/03/1918	31/03/1918
War Diary		21/03/1918	21/03/1918
Heading	Appendices "A" And "B"		
Operation(al) Order(s)	30th Divisional Engineers Order No. 11. Appendix "A"	18/03/1918	18/03/1918
Miscellaneous	Report On Operations Of 30th Divisional R.E. From 21-3-18 To 31-3-18	01/04/1918	01/04/1918
Heading	War Diary of Headquarters, 30th Divisional Engineers. From 1st April 1918. To 30th April 1918 (Volume 30.)		
War Diary	St. Valery-Sur-Somme	01/04/1918	01/04/1918
War Diary	Proven	02/04/1918	07/04/1918

War Diary	Canal Bank	08/04/1918	12/04/1918
War Diary	Elverdinghe Chateau	13/08/1918	16/08/1918
War Diary	Moonta Camp. Sheet 28 G.16.c.4.O.	18/04/1918	19/04/1918
War Diary	Catterick Camp Sheet 28. G.11.d.5.4	20/04/1918	25/04/1918
War Diary	Broxeele Sheet 27. G.23.b.1.9	26/04/1918	27/04/1918
War Diary	Chateau at P. 2. C. 5.3. (Sheet 27.)	28/04/1918	30/04/1918
Operation(al) Order(s)	Appendix A 30th Divisional Engineers Order No. 12	06/04/1918	06/04/1918
Miscellaneous	Appendix B. 30th Divisional Engineers Order No. 13	11/04/1918	11/04/1918
Miscellaneous	Appendix C (a)		
Miscellaneous	Appendix C (B)		
Miscellaneous	Appendix C (C)		
Miscellaneous	Appendix C (d)		
Miscellaneous	Appendix D	23/04/1918	23/04/1918
Miscellaneous	Instructions for Work on The Watou-Caestre Line North of the Steenvoorde-Abeele Road.	29/04/1918	29/04/1918
Diagram etc			
Miscellaneous	List of Awards to N.C.Os. & Men of The 30th Divisional Engineers During April Appendix F		
Heading	War Diary of Headquarters, 30th Divisional Engineers. From 1st May 1918 To 31st May 1918. Volume 31		
War Diary	Chateau at 27/P.2.c.5.3	01/05/1918	20/05/1918
War Diary	Thil	21/05/1918	25/05/1918
War Diary	St. Vast	26/05/1918	31/05/1918
Miscellaneous	Handing Over Notes of Work on The Watou Line. Appendix A	12/05/1918	12/05/1918
Diagram etc	Appendix A		
Miscellaneous	Appendix B Locations etc of Units		
Miscellaneous	Locations etc of Units. Appendix B		
Miscellaneous	Locations etc of Units. Appendix C		
Miscellaneous	30th Division G. /250/708 Appendix B	04/05/1916	04/05/1916
Miscellaneous	30th Division No. A/8031. C.R.E. No. 147	26/05/1918	26/05/1918
Miscellaneous	Appendix F	28/05/1918	28/05/1918
Map	Appendix G.		
Miscellaneous	List of Awards During The Month of May Appendix H		
Map	Appendix		
Heading	War Diary of Headquarters, 30th Divisional Engineers. From 1st June 1918 To 30th June 1918 Volume 32		
War Diary	St Vast En Chaussee	01/06/1918	15/06/1918
War Diary	Eu.	16/06/1918	19/06/1918
War Diary	Rue.	20/06/1918	27/06/1918
War Diary	Eperlecques	28/03/1918	30/03/1918
Miscellaneous	33rd American Division. Appendix A.	12/06/1918	12/06/1918
Miscellaneous	30th Division "G" Appendix B.	13/06/1918	13/06/1918
Miscellaneous	A Form. Messages And Signals.		
Miscellaneous	A Form. Messages And Signals. Appendix D.		
Miscellaneous	Handing Over Notes on Work In The Eu Area. Appendix E	20/06/1916	20/06/1916
Miscellaneous	King's Birthday List of Honours and Awards Appendix F		
Heading	War Diary of Headquarters, 30th Divisional Engineers. From 1st July 1918 to 31st July 1918. Volume 33		
War Diary	Eperlecques	03/07/1918	07/07/1918
War Diary	Cassel	09/07/1918	30/07/1918
Miscellaneous	C.E. Xth Corps, 999/17 Appendix A	09/07/1918	09/07/1918
Map	Legend Demolitions		
Miscellaneous	Appendix. B		

Type	Description	Date From	Date To
Map	Appendix D		
Operation(al) Order(s)	30th Divisional Engineers Order No. 14 Appendix E	17/07/1918	17/07/1918
Map	Appendix F. Test Orders.		
Miscellaneous	Progress Report-Army Line, From 15-7-18 To 18-7-18 Appendix 4	15/07/1918	15/07/1918
Miscellaneous	C.E. Xth Corps. Progress Report.	25/07/1918	25/07/1918
Miscellaneous	Chief Engineer Xth Corps.	31/07/1918	31/07/1918
Miscellaneous	C.E., Xth Corps. Report On Demolitions. Appendix H	19/07/1918	19/07/1918
Miscellaneous	Progress Report For Week Ending 25.7.18	25/07/1918	25/07/1918
Miscellaneous	Progress Report.	31/07/1918	31/07/1918
Miscellaneous	Mentions London Gazette 20th May 1918 Appendix 1	20/05/1918	20/05/1918
Heading	War Diary Of Headquarters. 30th Divisional Engineers. From 1st August 1918 To 31st August 1918 (Volume)		
War Diary	Cassel	01/08/1918	09/08/1918
War Diary	Terdeghem	10/08/1918	30/08/1918
War Diary	La. Montagne	31/08/1918	31/08/1918
Miscellaneous	Handing Over Notes 2nd Position. Appendix A		
Miscellaneous	30th Divisional Engineers Order No. 15. Appendix. B	07/08/1918	07/08/1918
Miscellaneous	Handing Over Report Appendix C	09/08/1918	09/08/1918
Miscellaneous	Narrative Report On R.E. Work Appendix D	16/08/1918	16/08/1918
Miscellaneous	Progress Report Appendix E	16/08/1918	16/08/1918
Miscellaneous	Narrative Report On R.E. Work. Appendix F	24/08/1918	24/08/1918
Miscellaneous	Report On Work Carried Out By The R.E. During The Attack On The Dranoutre Ridge On 21-8-18 Appendix G	21/08/1918	21/08/1918
Miscellaneous	Appendix H. R.E. Dump And Workshops. August 1918	00/08/1918	00/08/1918
Miscellaneous	Appendix I. 30th Divisional Engineers.		
Heading	War Diary Of 30th Divisional Engineers From September 1st 1918. To September 30th 1918 Volume 35		
War Diary	La Montagne	01/09/1918	01/09/1918
War Diary	M.20.d.9.8	03/09/1918	06/09/1918
War Diary	M.21.a.1.1	07/09/1918	20/09/1918
War Diary	27/R.24.c. 6.3	21/09/1918	30/09/1918
Miscellaneous	Narrative Report On Work Carried Out By The Royal Engineers During Operation Between 30.8.18 & 5-9-18. Appendix A.	30/08/1918	30/08/1918
Map	State Of Forward Roads. 5.9.18		
Miscellaneous	Appendix. B. C.R.E., 30th Division.	21/09/1918	21/09/1918
Operation(al) Order(s)	30th (British) Divisional Engineers Order No. 16. Appendix C	24/09/1918	24/09/1918
Miscellaneous	Appendix A. Locations And Zones Of Work For Field Companies After Move On 25-9-18. Appendix E		
Operation(al) Order(s)	30th British Divisional Engineers Order No 17 Appendix D	26/09/1918	26/09/1918
Miscellaneous	Appendix E.		
Miscellaneous	Appendix. F. 30th Divisional Engineers.		
Heading	War Diary. H.Q. 30th Divisional Engineers From 1st October To 31st October. 1918		
War Diary	Mont Noir Chateau.	00/10/1918	00/10/1918
War Diary	28/P.14.a.2.0. 28/O.26.a.3.5	01/10/1918	01/10/1918
War Diary	28/O.19.c Central	02/10/1918	15/10/1918
War Diary	Tralee Farm	16/10/1918	17/10/1918
War Diary	Q.13.d.8.7	17/10/1918	18/10/1918
War Diary	Bousbecque Chateau	19/10/1918	19/10/1918

War Diary	Sterhoek	20/10/1918	21/10/1918
War Diary	Coyghem	22/10/1918	30/10/1918
War Diary	Rolleghem	31/10/1918	31/10/1918
Operation(al) Order(s)	30th Divisional Engineers Order No, 18. Appendix A.	12/10/1918	12/10/1918
Map	Map X Issued With 30th Divl Engrs. Order No. 18		
Operation(al) Order(s)	Amendment No 1 To 30th Divisional Engineers Order No. 18	13/10/1918	13/10/1918
Miscellaneous	Appendix. A.		
Map	Map To Accompany Amendment No 1 To 30th Divl. Engineers Order No. 18		
Miscellaneous	30th Division G./129/32. Appendix B	24/10/1918	24/10/1918
Miscellaneous	C.R.E., 30th Division.	24/10/1918	24/10/1918
Diagram etc	Infantry Footbridge Placed Across Scheldt Gap 80 Feet.		
Miscellaneous	C.E., Xth Corps. Appendix. C.	25/10/1918	25/10/1918
Miscellaneous	Narrative Report. Appendix D.	26/10/1918	26/10/1918
Heading	War Diary. 30th Divisional Engineers From 1st November. 1918 To 30th November. 1918. Volume 37		
War Diary	Rolleghem. 29/T.1.b.95.95	01/11/1918	03/11/1918
War Diary	Belleghem 29/N.27.a.o.I	04/11/1918	09/11/1918
War Diary	Heestert	10/11/1918	10/11/1918
War Diary	Watripont	10/11/1918	10/11/1918
War Diary	Ellezelles	11/11/1918	14/11/1918
War Diary	Renaix	15/11/1918	16/11/1918
War Diary	Heestert	17/11/1918	17/11/1918
War Diary	Mouscron	18/11/1918	30/11/1918
Miscellaneous	O.C. 200th Field Coy. R.E. Appendix "A"	08/11/1918	08/11/1918
Diagram etc	Appendix D		
Miscellaneous	Appendix "B" Transport & Working Parties For November 9th 1918	09/11/1918	09/11/1918
Miscellaneous	Appendix "C" O.C. 200th Field Coy. R.E.	15/11/1918	15/11/1918
Miscellaneous	Appendix "C" O.C. 200th Field Coy. R.E.	14/11/1918	14/11/1918
Miscellaneous	Appendix "D" O.C. 200th Field Coy. R.E.	16/11/1918	16/11/1918
Miscellaneous	Appendix "D" O.C. 202nd Field Coy. R.E.	16/11/1918	16/11/1918
Miscellaneous	30th Division R.E. Education Scheme. Appendix "E"	30/11/1918	30/11/1918
Miscellaneous	Summary Of Courses		
Miscellaneous	Appendix "F" Warning Order.	25/11/1918	25/11/1918
Miscellaneous	Appendix "F" O.C. 200th Field Coy. R.E.	27/11/1918	27/11/1918
Miscellaneous	Appendix "G" Honours & Awards For November 1918		
Heading	War Diary. Of 30th Divisional Engineers. From 1st December 1918 To 31st December 1918 Volume 38		
War Diary	Mouscron	01/12/1918	01/12/1918
War Diary	Renescure	02/12/1918	31/12/1918
Miscellaneous	Appendix A. O.C. 200th Field Coy. R.E.	27/12/1918	27/12/1918
Miscellaneous	Appendix. B.		
Miscellaneous	Appendix. C. The Adjutant. R.E. 30th (B) Division.	28/12/1918	28/12/1918
Miscellaneous	Appendix. D. Recreation 30th Division R.E. for Month Of December 1918	28/12/1918	28/12/1918
Miscellaneous	Appendix. E. Honours & Awards For Month Of December 1918		
Heading	War Diary Of 30th Div. R.E. H.Q.R.S For Month Of Jan 19		
War Diary	Renescure	01/01/1919	10/01/1919
War Diary	La Capelle	12/01/1919	28/01/1919
Miscellaneous	Appendix. "A" Honours & Awards		
Heading	War Diary For February, 1919 R.E. Headquarters, 30th Division. Volume 40		

War Diary	La Capelle	01/02/1919	28/02/1919
Heading	War Diary. Of the 30th Divisional Engineers. For the month of March. 1919 Volume No. 41		
War Diary	Condette Near Boulogne	01/03/1919	31/03/1919
Heading	War Diary of C.R.E. For March 1919		
War Diary	Condette	01/03/1919	24/03/1919
Heading	War Diary of C.R.E. For April 1919		

COMMANDER

ROYAL

ENGINEERS

30TH DIVISION
DIVL ENGINEERS

C. R. E.

NOV 1915 - APR 1919

Nov 15

Army Form C. 2118.

WAR DIARY of Headquarters
30th Divl. Engineers
INTELLIGENCE SUMMARY.

(Erase heading not required.)

Instructions regarding War Diaries and Intelligence Summaries are contained in F. S. Regs., Part II. and the Staff Manual respectively. Title pages will be prepared in manuscript.

Place	Date 1915 Novr.	Hour	Summary of Events and Information	Remarks and references to Appendices
LARKHILL.	7th.		Headquarters, Royal Engineers left AMESBURY STATION by troop train at 1-0pm, embarked at SOUTHAMPTON and arrived at HAVRE about 1-30am on 8th November 1915.	
HAVRE.	8th		Disembarked at HAVRE 7-0am and proceeded to No.5 Rest Camp. Entrained at 11-30pm at Point 4 GARE DES MARCHANDISES.	
PONT REMY.	9th		Arrived PONT REMY at 9-0am. Detrained and marched to AILLY LE HAUT CLOCHER, in which village Divisional Headquarters were situated. Went into billets. All arrangements for the move from England appeared to work very well.	
AILLY LE HAUT CLOCHER	9th to 17th		Remained at this place till 17th November. No events occurred worthy of record.	
FLESSELLES.	17th to 28th		Left AILLY at 8-30am on 17th November and proceeded to new billets at FLESSELLES accompanying Divisional Headquarters. Billeting arrangements at first not satisfactory owing to the fact that certain portions of 56th Division had not yet left. Remained at FLESSELLES till 28th November. During this period the Field Companies carried on training and assisted Infantry in certain small ways such as construction of Field ovens &c.	

P.T.O.

Army Form C. 2118.

WAR DIARY
~~Intelligence~~ SUMMARY.
(Erase heading not required.)

Instructions regarding War Diaries and Intelligence
Summaries are contained in F. S. Regs., Part II.
and the Staff Manual respectively. Title pages
will be prepared in manuscript.

Place	Date	Hour	Summary of Events and Information	Remarks and references to Appendices
			For billeting, and parading each Field Coy. was attached to an Executive Brigade and received Routine Orders from respective Brigade Headquarters.	
			Under orders of the C.R.E. each Field Coy. carried out reconnaissance of the sections of its Brigade area with a view to providing the next Division to occupy them with data respecting stores likely to be required such as timber, nails, tools &c.	
			On 27th November the 101st Field Coy. left the Quarries at a few minutes notice and to the 37th Division for instructions.	
			The 56th Field Coy. was also detailed to the Division to assist to similar fashion.	
			The 99th Field Coy. and Signal Company were attached to the 2nd Division.	
FIENVILLERS	28th to 30th		On the 28th the Division moved into the new billeting area. Headquarters Royal Engineers was at FIENVILLERS and Divisional Headquarters at LE MEILLARD a village about 7 miles away. This was only a temporary arrangement.	
			A scheme for improving existing billeting accommodation was got out by C.R.E. and approved by Headquarters on 30th instant. On 30th, Captain Walker, a Field Engineer from XIII Corps, was attached to Headquarters Royal Engineers to assist with the scheme of winter accommodation for the Division.	
			P.T.O.	

Army Form C. 2118.

No. 3 Sheet.
WAR DIARY
or
INTELLIGENCE SUMMARY.
(Erase heading not required.)

Place	Date	Hour	Summary of Events and Information	Remarks and references to Appendices
FIENVILLIERS. (Cont.)			No.5 R.E.Park was visited on this day by C.R.E. with a view to ascertaining what stores were available.	

Lieut-Col. R.E.
C.R.E. 30th Divisional Engineers.

1-12-15.

HISTORICAL RECORD OF THE 30TH DIVISIONAL (COUNTY PALATINE) ENGINEERS.

Shortly after the outbreak of the great European War in August 1914, a Committee was formed in Manchester to assist the War Office in recruiting for the New Armies which were being raised in the United Kingdom.

This committee working in cooperation with the Right Hon. the Earl of Derby, K.G., G.C.V.O., C.B., were eventually asked to raise locally a number of service battalions for the Manchester and Liverpool Regiments, which they very successfully accomplished.

On 14th January, 1915, Lord Derby and the Manchester Committee, which was then composed as under:-

>   Mr. A. Herbert Dixon (Chairman)
>   The Lord Mayor of Manchester
>   Mr. E. Tootal Broadhurst
>   Mr. E.N. Philips.
>   Mr. Arthur Taylor
>   Mr. Vernon Bellhouse.
>   Mr. Kenneth Lee.

were asked to consider the question of raising Royal Artillery and Royal Engineer units to make up a complete Division with the Service Battalions of the Manchester and Liverpool Regiments which they had raised locally.

After further negotiations this proposal was agreed to, the conditions under which the units were to be raised being as noted in War Office letter No. 20/Gen. No./367B (A.G.1) dated 11th January, 1915, copy of which is attached as appendix 1.

P.T.O.

On the Committee's application for the services of a Senior Royal Engineer Officer to assist in this work, Major A.E.Panet, R.E., was directed to report to Lord Derby on the 8th February, from which date he was appointed Commanding Royal Engineer of the Divisional Engineers to be raised.

At a meeting of Lord Derby and the Manchester Committee held in Manchester on February 9th., 1915., which Major Panet attended, it was definitely decided that Lord Derby should deal with the R.A. units, and that the Manchester Committee should be responsible for raising the R.E. units, viz., Headquarters of Divisional Engineers, three Field Companies and a Divisional Signal Company.

The Committee then obtained the Co-operation of the Mayors of all towns in Lancashire with a view to inaugurating a special recruiting campaign for the units which were to be known as the "County Palatine Royal Engineers" - (Appendix II.)

Another feature of this recruiting campaign was the erection of a large poster at the Town Hall in Albert Square, Manchester, on which the outline figures representing the various tradesmen required for the Royal Engineer units of a Division were blackened daily, according to the numbers recruited - (a copy of this poster on a small scale is attached as appendix III. Copies of this poster were distributed throughout Lancashire through the agency of the mayors.

Recruiting commenced on February 19th., Colonel F.R. Mc.Conell agreeing to take command of the men at Morecambe, where the units were to be billeted, until Major Panet completed the preliminary work.

Major Panet arrived at Morecambe on February 27th when he took over command of the men assembled there, who then numbered 263.

The units to be raised were to be the 200th, 201st and 202nd Field Companies (Manchester) R.E., and the 37th Divisional Signal Company (Manchester) R.E., which with the Headquarters establishment would form the 37th Divisional (Manchester) Engineers.

On March 1st the men already recruited were posted to Companies. The following statement shows the strength of the units, on the dates noted:-

Date.	Strength of Units.				Total Strength.
	200th Fd.Co.	201st Fd.Co.	202nd Fd.Co.	Signal Company.	
1st March	79	82	73	29	263
8th "	116	113	110	52	391
15th "	170	166	156	93	585
22nd "	203	201	195	116	715
29th "	257	254	248	166	925
5th April	271	271	264	188	994
12th "	297	294	291	201	1083
19th "	306	302	299	206	1113
26th "	313	308	306	217	1144
1st May.	317	312	311	233	1173
1st Sept.	303	303	305	273	1183

In addition the Headquarters, numbering 10 N.C.O's and men, were at full strength on September 1st. The strength shown for Companies includes the men recruited for the reserve for each Company.

The total number of men enlisted for the C.P.R.E. up to the 1st August 1915 was 1593, of which 210 had been discharged (a few transferred to other units). The cause for discharge in nearly all cases was either on account of physical defects, or much over the age limit.

The following Officers were provisionally appointed as shown, all appointments being subsequently confirmed by the Army Council, and the Officers gazetted to temporary Commissions in the Corps of Royal Engineers in the ranks noted:-

4.

UNIT.	NAME.	RANK.	Date of Temporary Commission in R.E.	Subsequent Promotion.		REMARKS.
				RANK.	DATE.	
Hdqrs.	Panet, A.E.	Major	28.7.1888	Lt-Col	9.2.15	✴ Held permanent Commission in R.E.
	Hebden, R.C.	Lieut	6.10.15.	Capt.	11.7.15.	
200th Field Co.	Bishope-Lunn A.	Capt.	27.2.15.	Major	2.9.15	※ Already held Temporary Commissions & Services were offered by War Office.
	Irwin, G.H.	Lieut	4.3.15.	Capt.	6.8.15.	
	Forbes L.J.B.	2ndLt.	14.12.14.	Lieut.	9.10.15	
	Hill L.A.	2ndLt.	27.2.15.	Lieut.	9.10.15	
	Billington E.E.	"	31.3.15.			
	Richmond F.A.D.	"	27.4.15.			
	Gibbins G.G.	"	28.5.15			
201st Field Co.	Swettenham J.P.	Capt.	24.2.15.	Major	2.9.15	⌀ Joined 24th June. Temporary commission anti-dated to Feby. for seniority but without pay. ✴ Transferred to other employment on 10.8.15.
	Liddell G.	Capt.	25.2.15.			
	Hulton A.R.	Lieut	20.3.15	Capt.	9.10.15	
	Tanner D.G.	"	17.5.15			
	Houston J.A.	2ndLt.	6.3.15.	Lieut.	9.10.15	
	Gervers R.J.W.	"	19.4.15.			
	Day M.S.D.	"	10.5.15.			
202nd Field Co.	Wraith H.O.	Lieut.	1.10.14.	Capt.	11.7.15	⌀ Transferred to 202nd Fd. Co. 9th Oct. 1915. // Transferred to 201st Fd. Co. 9th Oct. 1915.
	Williamson A.	Lieut.	20.3.15.	Major	9.10.15	
	Kirby W.H. //	2ndLt.	13.2.15.	Lieut.	9.10.15	
	Ellis N.T.	"	1.3.15.	Lieut.	6.8.15.	
	Rayner G.	"	17.3.15.	Lieut.	9.10.15	
	Buckley P.R.	"	31.3.15			
	Staniar H.D.	"	20.4.15.			
30th Div'l Signal Co.	Molesworth J.D.M.	Lieut	14.12.14.	Capt.	21.6.15.	✎ Already held temporary commission and posted to this unit by War Office. +-+ Transferred to R.A. (a) on sick leave and transferred to other unit - 1.10.15.
	Hindle E.	2ndLt	1.10.14.	Lieut	11.7.15.	
	Allen W.R.	"	18.12.14	Lieut.	9.10.15	
	Colley M.H.	"	18.3.15.			
	Creese H.R (a)	"	1.10.14.	Lieut.	6.8.15	
	Simpson B.R.	Lieut	16.3.15.			
	Vonburg W.R.(a)	2ndLt.	10.5.15			
	Hughes H.C.	Lieut.	26.8.15			
	Baker N.E.	2ndLt.	17.1.15			
	Hook, V.T.K.	Lieut.	11.7.15.			

Temporary Captain W.F.Trydell, R.E., was posted to the Division on April 23rd to assist the C.R.E. with the Instructional work, and remained with the Division till September 1915, when he was transferred to the 68th Divl. (Welsh Army) Engineers.

During their stay at Morecambe, the Divisional Engineers were under the medical charge of Dr. J.C.Ashton, M.B.

Lieut. G.F.P.Heathcote, R.A.M.C., joined the Headquarters of the Divisional Engineers on the 18th August, 1915, as their permanent Medical Officer.

A photograph of the officers of the Headquarters and the three Field Companies taken on August 31st., 1915, is attached as appendix IV.

It is interesting to note that a great number of applications for commissions were received.

The proportion of tradesmen enlisted for each unit was in accordance with the authorised number as laid down in R.E. Corps memo. No. 633 part II, and this proportion was well maintained throughout. Special inducements had to be offered by the War Office to obtain men of certain trades, viz., shoeing smiths, saddlers & wheelwrights, who were paid 5/- a day in addition to any other concessions, such as separation allowance, granted to men enlisted for the duration of the War, otherwise rates of pay, &c. were normal.

The men enlisted were of a good class, and their physique was good on the whole, notwithstanding the fact that the standard for recruits for locally raised R.E. Units was lower than that for recruits for the Regular Army R.E. Units.

These units were fortunate in obtaining a few ex-sappers who re-enlisted for the duration of the War. The services of a number of ex-R.E. Warrant & N.C.O's who had re-enlisted for Home Service, were also obtained through the Officer i/c., R.E. Records, Chatham, to assist in the training work.

A photograph of the Officers of the Headquarters, Ex.-R.E., W. & N.C.O's., and re-enlisted sappers with the 50th Divisional (County Palatine) Engineers on August 31st., is attached as appendix V.

Training in technical work commenced on March 30th 1915, when the first consignment of tools (Pickaxes and shovels) was issued to Field Companies.

It was decided in April that all mobilization equipment (excepting clothing and necessaries) should be obtained from the Army Ordnance Dept., the Committee providing all training and instructional stores. The result was that all units were very well equipped for training.

As regards the provision of mobilization equipment by the Army Ordnance Dept. and other Army Services, the following shows roughly how matters stood on the dates noted:-

8th April, 1915.	Pontoon wagons and cable carts received.
3rd June, 1915.	50 old rifles for drill purposes issued to each Company.
4th June, 1915.	Web equipment received
9th June, 1915.	Toolcarts & G.S. wagons, R.E., received.
1st July, 1915.	About one-third total equipment received.
1st August, 1915.	About half total equipment received.
31st July, 1915.	Full establishment of Riding horses and draught mules received.
1st Sept., 1915.	About three-quarters total equipment received.
27th Sept., 1915.	Service rifles issued to all Companies.

Under authority of War Office telegram dated 13th March, 1915, the designation of the units was changed to the following which was the designation originally proposed by the Committee:-

200th Field Co. (County Palatine) Royal Engineers.
201st   do.   do.   do.
202nd   do.   do.   do.

37th Divisional Signal Co., (County Palatine) Royal Engineers, the whole to form, with the Headquarters, the 37th Divisional (County Palatine) Engineers.

The number of the Division was subsequently changed to 30th, thus becoming part of the first division of the 4th New Army.

The units were inspected on the dates noted, by the undermentioned officers:-

12th March, 1915, at Morecambe.

By General Sir W.H.Mackinnon, K.C.B., K.C.V.O., General Officer Commanding in Chief, Western Command.

21st March, 1915.

A Party of two officers and 8 N.C.O's. and men represented the County Palatine Royal Engineers at an inspection by Lord Kitchener, K.G., K.P., Col.Comdt. R.E. &c. &c. at Manchester, of all the units raised locally by the Committee.

9th June, 1915, at Morecambe.

Major General W. Fry, C.V.O., C.B., Commanding 30th Division, inspected the men on works.

11th June, 1915, at Morecambe.

By Colonel H. Mullect, C.E., Western Command. - (Copy of report to G.O.C. 30th Division, attached as appendix VI.

On June 19th the Signal Company was moved to billets at Grantham, where the 30th Division was being concentrated. This unit was practically completely equipped by the 1st September.

A band of 29 instruments was formed on June 24th from the three Field Companies, under the direction of Capt. A. Bishope Lunn, all instruments being presented by the Manchester Committee.

The Manchester Committee, represented by Mr. A. Herbert Dixon, Chairman, and Mr. E. Tootal Broadhurst, inspected the three Field Companies at Morecambe on June 30th.

The Headquarters and three Field Companies were moved into Camp at Boultham Park, Lincoln, on July 29th.

From Boultham Park Camp the Field Companies went to Fiskerton for a fortnight's pontooning course on the following dates:-

200th Field Co.)
201st do. do.) - 1st August to 15th August.
202nd do. do. - 8th August to 22nd August.

On August 26th a day's Sports was held in camp under the patronage of Major General W. Fry, C.V.O., C.B. and the Manchester Committee. A copy of the Sports programme is attached as appendix VII.

The 30th Divisional (County Palatine) Engineers were finally taken over by the War Office on August 27th 1915.

The Inspecting Officer R.E. Northern Command, Colonel Foley, inspected the Signal Company at Grantham on 17th August 1915, and the three Field Companies at Boultham Park on 31st August. A Copy of his report is attached as appendix VIII.

The 30th Division moved to Larkhill Hutted Camp, Salisbury Plain, early in September, the 30th Divisional Signal Company (C.P.) R.E. arriving there on September 7th., and the Headquarters and three Field Companies on September 12th.

The Inspector General R.E., Major General A.E. Sanbach, C.B., D.S.O., inspected the four units on the 14th September. On the 16th September the 30th Divisional (C.P.) R.E. paraded with the 30th Division when the Division was inspected by the G.O.C. Salisbury Training Centre, General The Right Hon. Sir A.H.Paget, G.C.B., K.C.V.O.

Lieut. R.C.H.W. Stone, R.E., joined on the 29th September, 1915, as the permanent Adjutant. Temporary Capt. R.C.Hebden, R.E. was then posted to the 201st Field Co.

The strength and detail by trades of the units were slightly altered in October 1915, vide extract of War Office letter No. 20/Engineers/5037 (A.G.7) dated 4th October 1915, attached as appendix VIII.

The undermentioned officers were nominated to take command of the details and reserves of units as noted, and did not accompany their unit abroad:-

2nd Lt. F.A.D. Richmond 200th Field Co. (C.P.) R.E
  do.   R.J.W. Gervers, 201st Field Co. - do. -
Lieut. A. Williamson, 202nd Field Co. - do. -
  do.   H.C.Hughes, 30th Divisional Signal Co.
                                           (C.P.) R.E.

10.

The Manchester Committee represented by Mr. A.H. Dixon, The Lord Mayor of Manchester, Mr. E. Tootal Broadhurst and Mr. Vernon Bellhouse, inspected the Units at Larkhill Camp, on the 29th October, 1915, to bid them good-bye on the eve of their departure for active service.

On Sunday, October 31st. 1915, the 30th Divisional (County Palatine) Engineers were warned to be prepared to proceed overseas during the week ending November 6th. 1915.

The Headquarters, 200th, 201st and 202nd Field Companies and the 30th Divisional Signal Company (County Palatine) Royal Engineers left Larkhill Camp with the 30th Division for duty overseas on the 4th November, 1915.

The Historical Record will be kept separately for each unit from November 1st., 1915.

C.R.E. 30TH DIVISIONAL
(COUNTY PALATINE) ENGINEERS

20/Gen.No/3670 (A.G.)   WAR OFFICE,
                                         LONDON, S.W.

                                         11th January, 1915.

Sir,

I am commanded by the Army Council to inform you that the following decisions have been arrived at regarding the appointment of officers, warrant officers and non-commissioned officers in the local Royal Artillery and Royal Engineer Units which the Council have authorized communities or individuals to raise:-

1. OFFICERS - APPOINTMENT OF.

(i) The appointment of all officers must be approved by the Army Council.

(ii) Bodies or persons authorised to raise Royal Artillery and Royal Engineer units will put forward, for approval by the Army Council, through the General Officer Commanding-in-Chief, the names of any individuals whom they may wish to be appointed as officers.

(iii) The appointment of the Commanding Officer will be carried into effect as soon as possible after the unit has been authorised.

(iv) Pending the appointment of officers by the Army Council, the raiser of the unit is empowered to make temporary appointments as in (v) with the sanction of the General Officer Commanding-in-Chief the Command.

(v) Officers up to the numbers authorized for a unit in War Establishments, Part 1, may accordingly be provisionally appointed to each unit as soon as its formation is undertaken.

11. OFFICERS - PAY AND ALLOWANCES.

(i) The pay of officers will be as laid down in the Royal Warrant for Pay, &c. 1913 as amended by Army Order 493 of 1914. The allowances of officers will follow Army Rules as amplified in Army Order 337 of 1914 (paragraph 4 of that Order refers to serving officers on full pay only.) If they are living at their own homes they should draw lodging allowance.

(ii) The holders of temporary appointments will receive during the period of employment the emoluments of the rank in which they are employed, not those of any rank they may hold by virtue of previous service, e.g., a retired Major temporarily employed as a Captain will draw pay as Captain.

(iii) Officers holding temporary appointments will not be required to wear uniform, and will not therefore be eligible for any outfit allowance.

(iv) Pay and allowances will be issued in the manner laid down in paragraph 9 of the printed Financial Instructions relating to the raising of these units.

111. WARRANT OFFICERS AND NON-COMMISSIONED OFFICERS - APPOINTMENT OF.

The raiser of the unit, or the Commanding Officer when appointed, is empowered to appoint warrant officers and non-commissioned officers under the following regulations:-

(i) All appointments will be temporary and will carry acting rank. The appointment shall be made permanent if after two months' probation the holder is found satisfactory; otherwise he will be reverted.

(ii) The ranks, other than officers, in the headquarters, as laid down in War Establishments, part 1, will be appointed by the raiser of the unit, or the Commanding Officer when appointed, as soon as the unit is authorized.

(iii) As soon as possible after the formation of a unit is undertaken the battery or company sergeant-major and battery or company quartermaster-sergeant will be appointed. Other non-commissioned officers will be similarly appointed in the proportion of one sergeant to every 26 gunners, sappers, pioneers or drivers on the strength of the unit, and one corporal to every 20 gunners, sappers, pioneers or drivers, until the War Establishment is complete.

IV. — WARRANT OFFICERS AND NON-COMMISSIONED OFFICERS
PAY AND ALLOWANCES.

Soldiers given acting ranks or appointments will receive the Army pay and allowances thereof, except that until further instructions all unmarried men living and messed at their own homes will get a consolidated allowance of 2s. a day in addition to pay. Married soldiers separated from their wives will get separation allowance as usual. Further instructions on these allowances will be found in Army Order 428 of 1914, covering all cases of specially raised units.

Non-commissioned officers and men of Royal Engineer units will receive Engineer pay in accordance with the instructions prescribed for the Royal Engineers generally.

V. — CIVILIAN INSTRUCTORS — APPOINTMENT OF.

Ex-non-commissioned officers not under 45 years of age may be engaged temporarily, as civilian Instructors pending the appointment, and in lieu, of non-commissioned officers. These temporary instructors will be engaged for whole day employment on a civilian basis for not more than three months, which period shall not be extended.

They may be allowed to sleep at their own homes should this be convenient to them, and uniform will not be required. Applicants for these posts will be required to satisfy Commanding Officers that they are fully qualified for these duties.

VI. — CIVILIAN INSTRUCTORS PAY.

Instructors appointed under Section V. above will receive pay at 4s. a day or 28s. a week inclusive.

I am, Sir,
Your obedient Servant,

To General Officer Commanding-in-Chief,
Command.

20/General Number/3670.

Conditions to be fulfilled in the case of offers to raise new units of Royal Artillery or Royal Engineers.

----------oOOo---------

1. The Brigades, Batteries or Ammunition Columns of Royal Artillery and Field Companies or Divisional Signal Companies, Royal Engineers, must be raised on a regular basis.

2. Enlistment must be for three years or the duration of the War, and must be carried out at a regular recruiting office. The age for enlistment is between 19 and 38 years.

3. No special privileges or consideration can be given to any unit so raised.

4. The numbers offering to enlist must be sufficient, after a medical examination has been held, to produce a unit of Royal Artillery or Royal Engineers, of the strength given in one of the attached tables B and C.

5. The individual or community responsible for raising a unit of Royal Artillery or Royal Engineers must be willing and able to clothe, house (housing must be carried out by the hire of buildings or billeting only) and feed it at rates approved by, and to be paid by the War Office, as given in War Office letter Number 20/Infantry 3631 (Q.M.G.7.) of the 24th December 1914, and on the pamphlet regarding Financial Instructions (20/General Number/3670) 11th January 1915, forwarded herewith, and to arrange for its local training.

6. The Conditions as to the appointment and pay of officers Warrant Officers and non-commissioned officers are laid down in War Office letter Number 20/General Number/3670 (A.G.L.) of the 11th January 1915, forwarded herewith.

7. The Battery or Company will be designated as follows:-

e.g. if raised in Birmingham:-

1000th Field Artillery Battery (1st Birmingham) 250th Brigade

or

1000th Field Company Royal Engineers (1st Birmingham).

20/Gen. No./3424
(A.G.1.)

WAR OFFICE

LONDON. S.W.

29th September, 1914.

Sir,

    With reference to the local battalions which have been raised by individuals, committees, &c. I am commanded by the Army Council to state that these units have been sanctioned only on the clear understanding of all concerned that they shall be organized, administered and trained by the raiser or raisers (under the supervision of General Officers Commanding in Chief) until such time as they are taken over by the War Office; this probably will not be for some months. Arrangements for their accommodation and training during this winter therefore must be made by those to whom their formation has been entrusted in communication with General Officers Commanding-in-Chief.

                I am,

                    Sir,

                        Your obedient Servant,

                          (Sd.) B.B.Cubitt.

The General Officer,
    Commanding-in-Chief,
        Command.

ROYAL ENGINEERS.

Divisional Engineers.

Ranks.	Field Co.	Divl. Signal Co.	Hdqrs. Divl. Engrs.	Total for each Divn. Divl. Hd.Qrs. 3 Field Companies. 1 Divl. Signal Co.
Lieut. Colonel	-	-	1	1
Majors	1	1x	-	4
Adjutant	-	-	1	1
Captains	1	-	-	3
Subalterns	4	5	-	17
Total Officers	6	6	2	26
Co. Sergt. Majors	1	1	-	4
Co. Q.M. Sgts.	1	1	-	4
Engineer Clerks	-	-	1	1
Sergeants	6	10	-	28
Farrier Sergts.	1	-	-	3
Total Sergts.	9	12	1	40
Trumpeters & Buglers	2	1	-	7
Shoeing & Carr. Smiths	1	2	-	5
Corporals	8	16	-	} 61
2nd corporals	7	-	-	
Sappers including Pioneers	153‡	119‡‡	2	580
Drivers	42	37	2	165
Batmen	8	14	5	43
Total Rank & File	219	188	9	854
Motor Cyclists.				
Sergeants	-	1	-	1
Corporal Artificer	-	1	-	1
Corporals	-	16	-	16
Total MotorCyclists	-	18	-	18
Total All Ranks	236	225	12	945
Required in addition for Reserve.				
Motor-cyclist.				
Corporal Artificer.	-	1	-	1
Motor-cyclist. } Corporals. }	-	4	-	4
Sappers	50	40	-	190
Drivers	25	15	-	90
				1230
To include -				
Sergeants	1	1		
Corporals	1	1		
2nd Corporals	2	1		
Lance Corporals	3	2		

    x Major or Captain
    ‡ Field Cos. may include 50% of men of the pioneer class.
    ‡‡ Include 65 men of the pioneer class (Signalmen).

NOTE.

    A pioneer is an educated or handy man who has not the necessary trade qualification for a Sapper and only gets 6d. a day Engineer pay.

RECRUITS - ROYAL ENGINEERS..

	Age.	Minimum Height.	Expanded Chest Measurement.
Sappers (except as specified below)	19-38	5'4"	35ᵡ
Engine Drivers	19-38	5'4"	35ᵡ
Pioneers	19-38	5'7"	35ᵡ
Pioneers (Army Signal Service)	19-38	5'5"	35ᵡ
Drivers	19-38	5'3" to 5'7"	35ᵡ

Recruiting Officers may at their discretion accept recruits for the Royal Engineers if within 1 inch of the Standards of height and chest measurements shewn above.

ᵡ Range of expansion not less than 2 inches.

ROYAL ENGINEERS.

Proportion of Establishment of Trades of a Field Company.

(Approximate Excludes Sergts. and higher ranks, Trumpeters and Buglers.

Trades.	No.
Shoeing & Carriage Smiths	1
Drivers and Batmen	50
Blacksmiths	17
Bricklayers	22
Plasterers	2
Slaters	2
Carpenters (Including Joiners)	44
Clerks	6
Coopers	2
Draughtsmen (Architectural)	2
Electricians (Field)	2
Engine Drivers (Field)	4
Fitters and Turners	9
Harness Makers	3
Masons	13
Painters	7
Plumbers (Including Gasfitters)	9
Shoemakers	1
Surveyors	2
Tailors	4
Wheelwrights	6
Miscellaneous	8
Corporal Storeman	1
Corporals (Mounted)	1
2nd Corporals (Mounted)	1
Total	219

A pioneer is a handy man who has not the necessary trade qualification for a Sapper and only gets 6d. a day Engineer Pay.

ROYAL ENGINEERS.

Proportion of Establishment of Trades of a Divisional Signal Co. (Approximate - Excludes Sergeants and higher ranks and Trumpeters.)

Trades.	No.
Drivers and Batmen	51
Harness makers	2
Instrument repairers (telegraphs)	2

Motor Cyclists:-

Corporal Artificers.	1
Corporals	16
Pioneers (x) (Signalmen)	65
Shoeing & Carriage Smiths	2

Telegraphists.

Line	26
Office	34
Wheelwrights & Carpenters	2
Miscellaneous	3
Corporal - Storeman	1
Total	205

(x) A pioneer is an educated man who has not the necessary trade qualification for a Sapper and only gets 6D. a day Engineer pay.

10.

Copies of this letter have been sent direct to General Officer Commanding Aldershot Training Centre, General Officers Commanding Divisions of the New Armies, and Officers in Charge of Records concerned.

    I am,

        Sir,

            Your obedient Servant,

                B. B. Cubitt.

(Appendix II.)

Extract from letter dated 10th May, 1915,
from Chairman, Manchester City Battalions.

———————————————

"County Palatine" in England was formerly a county distinguished by particular privileges, so called because the owner or the holder has royal powers, or the same powers in the administration of justice as the king had in his palace, but all such powers are now vested in the Crown.

The counties Palatine in England are Lancaster, Chester and Durham, which were no doubt made separate Royalties on account of their respective proximity to Wales and to that turbulent Northumbrian province which could be accounted a portion neither of England nor of Scotland.

The most brilliant period in the history of Lancaster was in the days of the ancient earls of Lancaster, and during the early years of Henry V, who caused the gateway tower to be erected.

The town which had previously received a Charter from King John was favored with additional privileges in the reign of Edward III, who conferred the Duchy of Lancaster upon his Son John of Gaunt then Earl of Richmond in 1342 and in whose favor the county was also made a County Palatine.

----------oOo----------

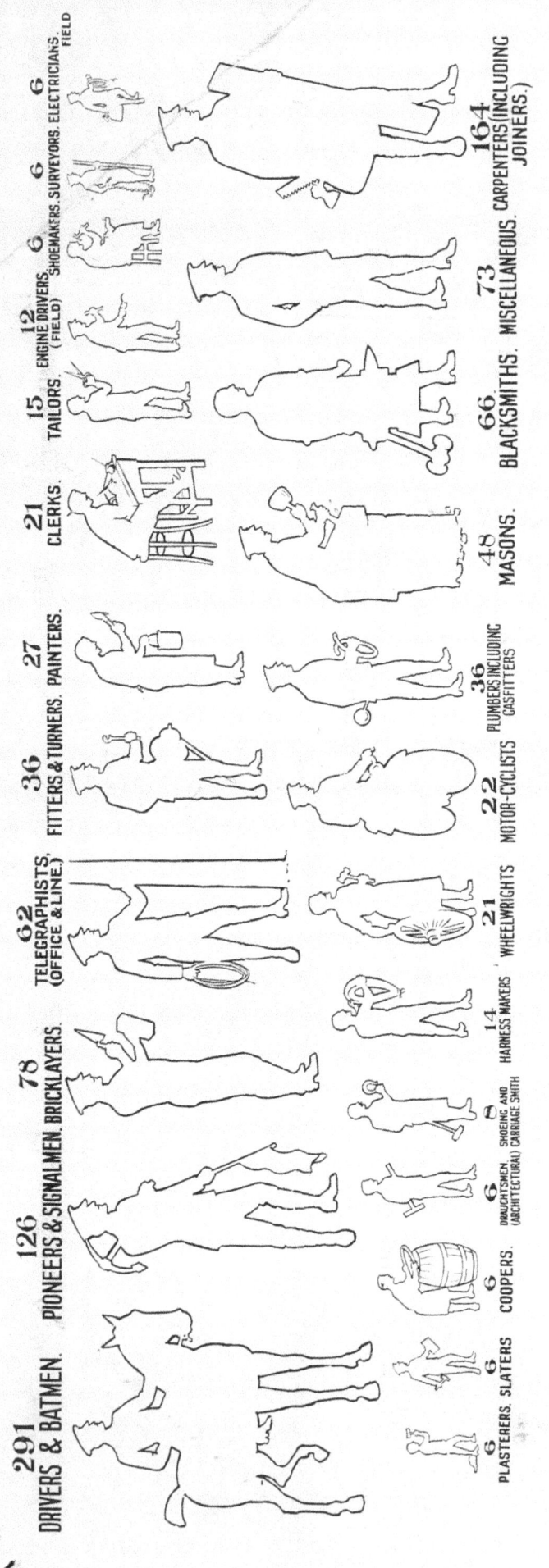

(Appendix IV.)

Officers
of
Headquarters & Field Companies
30th Divisional
(County Palatine) Royal Engineers.

STANDING FROM LEFT TO RIGHT:-

2nd Lieut. E.E.Billington, 200th Co.; 2nd Lieut. P.B.Buckley, 202nd Co.; 2nd Lieut. R.J.W.Gervers, 201st Co.; Capt. R.C.Hobden (Adjutant); 2nd Lieut. G.Rayner, 202nd Co.; 2nd Lieut. W.H.Kirby, 202nd Co.; 2nd Lieut. L.A.Hill, 200th Co.; 2nd Lieut. H.D.Standar, 202nd Co.; 2nd Lieut. G.G. Gibbins, 200th Co.; 2nd Lieut. L.J.B.Forbes, 200th Co.; 2nd Lieut. F.A.D.Richmond, 200th Co.; Lieut. D.G.Tanner, 201st Co.; 2nd Lieut. J.A.Houston, 201st Co.

SITTING FROM LEFT TO RIGHT:-

Lieut. A.Williamson, 202nd Co.; Rev. E.G.Cocks, T.C.F.; Lieut. N.T.Ellis, 202nd Co.; Capt. G.H.Irwin, 200th Co.; Major J.P.Swettenham, 201st Co.; Lieut.-Col. A.E.Panet, C.R.E.; Major A.Bishope Lunn, 200th Co.; 2nd Lieut. M.S.D. Day, 201st Co.; Capt. H.O.Wraith, 202nd Co.; Lieut. A.R. Hulton, 201st Co.; Capt. W.F.Trydell (Attached Headquarters.).

------------oOo------------

Appendix V

Officers of Headquarters, Ex.-R.E. Warrant and
N.C.O's, and re-enlisted Sappers.

Standing from left to right:-

No. 81905 Sgt. Tobin, re-enlisted. No. 99786 C.S.M. Rundle, re-enlisted. No. 12756 Sgt. Smith - serving. No. 19216 Sgt. Tucker, serving. No. 57045 C.S.M. Gould, Ex.-R.E. No. 14391 C.S.M. Harris, serving. No. 97716 Cpl. Chivers Ex.-R.E. No. 83434 Cpl. McLean, re-enlisted. No. 52867 C.S.M. Meaded Ex.-R.E. No. 83436 Cpl. Summers re-enlisted. No. 83163 L/Cpl. Arkwright, re-enlisted. No. 57401 C.S.M. Bell, Ex.-R.E.

Sitting from left to right:-

No. 28308 Sgt. Muttycombe, serving. No. 52976 Q.M.S. MacKay, Ex.-R.E. No. 404 Q.M.S. Merrick, serving (C.R.E's Clerk). No. 61755 R.S.M. Legg, ex.-R.E. (R.S.M. of Divisional Engineers). Lt.-Col. A.E.Panet, C.R.E. Capt. R.C.Hebden, adjutant. No. 89209 R.S.M. Hughes, ex.-R.E. No. 47963 Q.M.S. Davis, ex.-R.E. No. 95445 Q.M.S. Nolan ex.-R.E. No. 52941 Q.M.S. Fensom Ex.-R.E.

----------oOo----------

Appendix VI.

General Officer
    Commanding-in-Chief.

I have to report that I inspected the County Palatine Royal Engineers at Morecambe on Friday last, and was very well satisfied with what I saw. The Officer Commanding has shown great zeal and tact, and the result is most satisfactory, both to him and to the Committee of Raisers responsible for the units.

The Officers are all men of really good professional attainments and experience in civil life. Their physique and keeness are both excellent. As soon as they have acquired the necessary familiarity with military conditions, they will form a valuable acquisition to the Service.

The men have been very carefully selected, are of suitable trades, and on the whole are of finer physique than any other unit that has come under my notice since the beginning of the War. The steady drill without arms was particularly good and smart, but they have as yet no knowledge of how to handle their rifles. The field works were very well executed, and all ranks appear to take the greatest possible interest both in the earth work and the bridging.

Complete technical equipment is urgently required, as the units are quite sufficiently advanced to be able to take full advantage of it.

There are no mounted N.C.O. instructors, and the want of them will be much felt as soon as horses and harness are available, but the drivers in nearly every case are men used to the care and management of horses.

The Signal Company is also doing very well.

(Sd.) H. Hulcatt, Colonel.
Chief Engineer, Western Command.

Chester,
13.6.15.

Appendix VII.

30th Divisional (County Palatine) Engineers.

S P O R T S.

Under the patronage of Major-General W. Fry, C.V.O., C.B., Commanding 30th Division, and The Chairman and Members of the Manchester Committee. Thursday, August 26th, 1915, at 2 p.m. Boultham Park, Lincoln.

President........Lt.-Col. A.E.Panet, C.R.E.

COMMITTEE:-

Capt. G.H.Irwin, Lieut. J.W.Ellis, 2nd Lieut. W.S.D.Day, R.S.M. Hughes, S.M.Legge, Q.M.S.Davies, Sergt. Tobin, C.S.M.Rundle.

JUDGES:-

Capt. G.H.Irwin, Lieut. J.W.Ellis, C.S.M. Harris, Sergt. Tobin.

STARTERS:-

Capt. R.C.Hebden, S.M.Legge, Capt. H.O.Wraith, C.S.M. Rundle.

TIMEKEEPER..........Capt. A.Bishope Lunn.

REFEREE............Capt. J.P.Swettenham.

STEWARDS..All Officers & Senior N.C.O's.

PROGRAMME OF MUSIC.

1. March......"The National Fencibles"..............J.P.Sousa
2. Selection.."The Merry Widow"....................Franz Sehar
3. Valse......"Songe D'Automne"....................A. Joyce
4. ...."Les Contes D'Hoffman"...............Offenbach
5. Selection.."Memories of the Past"..............W.Rimmer
6. March......"Right - Left"......................J.P.Sousa.
7. Valse......"Oh! Oh! Delphine"..................Ivan Cargll
8. Descriptive
   Piece.."Uncle Rastus Scating Party".........J.Ord Hume
9. ...."Pomp and Circumstance".............Elgar
10. March..............Selected...............................
11. ...."The National Anthem"........................

BANDMASTER.......F.E.Cartwright.

-----------------oOo-------------

GOD SAVE THE KING. -

(2)

PROGRAMME OF SPORTS.

Heats will be run off for the following Events, starting at 11-a.m.

> Throwing the Cricket Ball.
> High Jump.
> Long Jump.
> 100 Yards Race.
> 200 Yards Race.
> Tilting the Bucket
> Bayonet Fighting
> Inter-section Tug-of-War.
> Sack Race.

The decision of the Referee shall be final in all cases of dispute arising in any of the events.   POST ENTRIES FOR ALL EVENTS. -

EVENTS

1. Throwing the cricket Ball. 2 p.m. First Prize. Second Prize.

2. High Jump. 2 p.m. First Prize. Second Prize. Third Prize.

3. Long Jump. 2-15 p.m. 1st Prize. 2nd Prize. 3rd Prize.

4. 100 yds. Flat Race. 2-30 p.m. 1st Prize. 2nd Prize. 3rd Prize.

5. Tug of War. Open to Garrison 10 men aside
   (Catch Weights) 2-45 p.m. First Prize.

6. 200 yds. Flat Race. 3-15 p.m. 1st Prize. 2nd Prize. 3rd Prize.
   Given by Capt. G.H.Irwin.

7. Three-legged Flat Race. 3-25 p.m. 1st Prize. 2nd Prize. Double Prizes.

8. 440 yards Flat Race. 3-35 p.m. 1st Prize. 2nd Prize. 3rd Prize.
   Given by Capt. J.P.Swettenham.

9. Tilting the Bucket (3 runs each) 3-35 p.m. 1st prize. 2nd Prize. 3rd prize. Prizes given by the Manchester Committee.

10. 100 yds. Flat Race. (officers) 3-40 p.m. 1st prize. 2nd prize.

11. 100 yds. Flat Race. (N.C.O's Mess) 3-50 p.m. 1st Prize. 2nd prize.
    Given by Lt.-Col. A.E.Panet, C.R.E.

12. 30 yds Boot Race. 4-p.m. 1st prize. 2nd prize. 3rd prize.

13. 100 yds Veterans Race. (Over 12 years service) 4 yds. start for every year over 12 years. 4-15 p.m. 1st prize. 2nd prize. Prizes given by the Manchester Committee.

14. 1-mile flat race. (Open to garrison) 4-30 p.m. 1st prize. 2nd prize. 3rd prize. Given by Capt. R. C. Hebden.

15. Wheelbarrow Race. (60 yds.) 4-45 p.m. 1st prize. 2nd Prize. Double /Prizes.
    Prizes given by the Manchester Committee.

16. Half-mile Flat Race. 5-p.m. 1st prize. 2nd prize. 3rd prize.
    Given by Capt. H.O.Wraith.

17. Obstacle race. 5-15 p.m. 1st prize. 2nd prize. 3rd prize. 4th prize.
    Given by Lt.-Col. A.E.Panet, C.R.E.

18. Band Race (With instruments) 100 yards 5-30 p.m. 1st prize. 2nd prize. 3rd prize. Prizes given by the Manchester Committee.

19. Sack race. 5-45 p.m. 1st prize. 2nd prize. 3rd prize.

20. Tug of War Final (Teams of ten) 6-p.m. 1st prize. 2nd prize. 3rd prize.

Appendix VIII.

(COPY.)

20/Engineers/5037 (A.G.7).

4th October, 1915.

Sir,

In continuation of the letter from this office dated 26th June, 1915, No. 20/General Number/3899 (Q.M.G.7), I am commanded by the Army Council to forward herewith the attached schedules showing the detail by trades of Royal Engineer Units.

I am, Sir,

Your obedient Servant,

(Signed) R.H.BRADE.

The General Officer,
    Commanding-in-Chief,
        Command.

FIELD COMPANY.

Exclusive of Sergeants and Higher Ranks.

Trades.	Establishment of Company	Plus 10 per cent	Reserves	Total
Bricklayers	21	2	4	27
Slaters	2	-	-	2
Plasterers	2	-	-	2
Carpenters & Joiners	41	4	10	55
Clerks	6	1	1	8
Draughtsmen (Arch)	2	-	-	2
Coopers	2	-	-	2
Electricians (Field)	2	-	-	2
Engine Drivers (Field)	4	-	-	4
Fitters & Turners	12	2	3	17
Harness Makers	3	-	1	4
Masons	13	1	3	17
Painters	6	1	2	9
Plumbers & Gasfitters	12	1	3	16
Shoemakers	1	-	1	2
Surveyors	2	-	-	2
Tailors	4	-	1	5
Blacksmiths	17	-	5	22
Wheelwrights	5	1	1	7
Miscellaneous & Pioneers	6	3	14	23
Drivers	47	5	23	75
Shoeing & Carriage Smiths	1	-	1	2
Corporals (Mounted)	1	-	-	1
2nd Corporals (Mounted)	1	-	1	2
TOTAL	213	21	74	308

DIVISIONAL SIGNAL COMPANY.

(Exclusive of Sergeants and Higher Ranks)

Trades.	Establishment of Company	Plus 10 per cent	Reserves	Total
Telegraphists Office	28	3	4	35
Cable Men	12	2	6	20
Brigade Section Pioneers	36	3	13	52
General Duty Pioneers	37	4	13	54
Shoeing & Carriage Smith (Corporals)	1	-	-	1
Shoeing & Carriage Smiths	1	-	1	2
Drivers & Batmen	47	5	14	66
Wheelwrights	2	-	1	3
Harness Makers	2	-	1	3
Instrument Makers	2	-	1	3
Miscellaneous	2	-	-	2
Motor Cyclists.				
Corporal Artificer	1	-	1	2
Corporals	14	1	4	19
TOTAL	185	18	59	262

DIVISIONAL ENGINEERS.

RANKS.	Field Company	Divisional Signal Co.	Headquarters Divisional Engineers.	Total each Division. Divisional Headquarters 3 Field Cos. 1 Divisional Signal Co.
Lieutenant Colonel	-	-	1	1
Majors	1	1	-	4
Adjutant	-	-	1	1
Captains	1	-	-	3
Subalterns	4	5	-	17
Total Officers	6	6	2	26
Sergeant Major	-	-	1	1
Company Sergeant Major W.O. Class II.	1	1	-	4
Total Warrant Officers	1	1	1	5
Company Quartermaster Sergeant	1	1	-	4
Engineer Clerks	-	-	1	1
Sergeants	6	10	-	28
Farrier Sergeants	1	-	-	3
Total Sergeants	8	11	1	36
Shoeing & Carriage Smith Corporal	-	1	-	1
Shoeing & Carriage Smith	1	1	-	4
Corporals	9	8	-	35
2nd Corporals	9	7	-	34
Sappers including Pioneers	147	106	3	550
Drivers	39	35	-	152
Batmen	8	12	5	41
Total Rank & File	213	170	8	817
Plus 10 per cent	21	17	-	80
	234	187	8	897

2.

Motorcyclists.				
Sergeants	-	1	-	1
Corporal Artificer	-	1	-	1
Corporals	-	14	-	14
	-	16	-	16
Plus 10 per cent	-	1	-	1
	-	17	-	17
Total all ranks	249	222	12	981

Required in addition for reserve.

Motor Cyclist Corporal Artificer	-	1	-	1
Motor Cyclist Corporals	-	4	-	4
Sappers	50	40	-	190
Drivers	24	14	-	86
Shoeing & Carriage Smith	1	1	-	4
	324	282	-	1,266

To include:-

Sergeants	1	1	-	-
Corporals	1	1	-	-
2nd Corporals	2	1	-	-
Lance-Corporals	3	2	-	-

Apl. 30th Stephen
Vol 2
131
1798

Army Form C. 2118.

HEADQUARTERS 30TH DIVL. ENGINEERS.   WAR DIARY.   VOL.2. DECEMBER, 1915.

INTELLIGENCE/SUMMARY.

(Erase heading not required.)

Instructions regarding War Diaries and Intelligence Summaries are contained in F. S. Regs., Part II. and the Staff Manual respectively. Title pages will be prepared in manuscript.

Place	Date	Hour	Summary of Events and Information	Remarks and references to Appendices
FIENVILLERS	1st Dec.		Instructions were made out by C.R.E. for improving billeting accommodation in the Divisional area and providing accessory buildings, horse standings etc. It was explained that the Field Coys.R.E. would usually not be available to carry out any of this work as they would each be away for a fortnight training with one of the Divisions in the line. In the instructions the order of urgency of the various works was laid down, and it was proposed that each Brigade should start a Brigade workshop. Tools and materials were to be provided by the C.R.E.	
	2nd Dec.		Capt. Walker, R.E., a Field Engineer from the 13th Corps, was attached to the Division in order to assist the various units by advice as regards the work they were to do, and also to carry out purchase of materials available locally.	
			A conference was held at FIENVILLERS at which were present Commanding Officers of all units in the Divisional area, and Staff Captains of Brigades. The above scheme was explained, and copies of it, together with rough sketches of suggested types of accessory buildings etc., were distributed.	
	5th Dec.		C.R.E. held a conference as above to explain scheme to Divisional Artillery. Headquarters R.E. moved to LE MEILLARD.	
LE MEILLARD,	7th Dec.		C.R.E. held a conference to explain scheme to 91st Brigade who had returned to Divisional area after instructional attachment to a Division in the line.	
	8th to 20th Dec.		During this period and the rest of the month large quantities of material were drawn from No. 5 R.E.Park and Corps Timber Store CANDAS and issued to units. Other materials such as brick and clinker were purchased locally and issued. Tools were distributed to each Brigade and R.A. in sufficient quantity to allow for each Brigade to set up a small workshop and to lend to all units a proportion of assorted tools. These tools were obtained partly from No. 5 R.E.Park and partly by purchase.	
	21st Dec.		Instructions received from XIII Corps to start a Hutting Scheme for doubling the accommodation in the Divisional area, which was to be divided into 2 areas each capable of taking a Division. Owing to a complete stoppage of the timber supply there was no immediate prospect of actually erecting the huts required. R.E.Officers	

2353 Wt. W2544/1454 700,000 5/15 D. D. & L.   A.D.S.S./Forms/C. 2118.

Army Form C.

HEADQUARTERS 30TH DIVL. ENGINEERS   WAR DIARY   VOL.2   DEC.1915   Sheet 2.

Instructions regarding War Diaries and Intelligence
Summaries are contained in F. S. Regs., Part II.
and the Staff Manual respectively. Title pages
will be prepared in manuscript.

INTELLIGENCE/SUMMARY

(Erase heading not required.)

Place	Date	Hour	Summary of Events and Information	Remarks and references to Appendices
LE MEILLARD	22nd to 27th DEC.		R.E. Officers were appointed to be i/c of each area and reconnaissances were carried out to settle sites and find all materials available locally.	
ACHEUX.			C.R.E. and Adjutant visited 4th Division to see R.E. work going on on this front. Capt. Walker R.E. remained at LE MEILLARD to continue work on Hutting Scheme.	
LE MEILLARD	27th to 30th Dec.		C.R.E. and Adjutant returned to 30th Division Headquarters. Instructions had been received that 30th Division was to take over the portion of the line then held by 5th Division.	
CHIPILLY.	30th Dec.		C.R.E. and Adjutant with the Captain of each Field Co. went to 5th Division area to commence taking over R.E. work.	
	31st Dec,		C.R.E. commenced going over 5th Division area with C.R.E. 5th Division.	

Lieut. Col, R.E.
C.R.E. 30th Divisional Engineers.
1st January, 1916.

30th Divisional Engineers

WAR DIARY

C. R. E.

30th DIVISION

JANUARY 1916.

HEADQUARTERS, 30th. DIVL. ENGINEERS WAR DIARY. VOL.3. JANUARY, 1916.

INTELLIGENCE SUMMARY
(Erase heading not required).

Place	Date 1916.	Hour	Summary of Events and Information	Remarks and references to Appendices
CHIPILLY.	Jan. 1st.		C.R.E. and Adjutant attached to Headquarters, R.E., 5th. Division for the purpose of taking over R.E. work in the Divisional area.	
			A section of the front or locality in which R.E. work was taking place was visited each day.	
	5th.		201st. Field Company, R.E. arrived at SUZANNE and took over R.E. work in "A" Sector.	
			202nd. Field Company, R.E. arrived at BRAY and took over R.E. work in "B" Sector.	
	6th.		200th. Field Company, R.E. arrived at BRAY and took over R.E. work in "C" Sector.	
	9th.		C.R.E. and Headquarters, R.E., 5th. Division left after handing over to C.R.E., 30th. Division. At this time practically the whole of each Field Company was employed in front line work on its own Sector. This was necessary on account of the large amount of work required to improve the trenches which had suffered considerably from the weather.	
	12th.		Headquarters, 30th. Division took over from Headquarters, 5th. Division.	
	16th.		Work commenced on light railway BRONFAY FARM - Point 104 by 11th. South Lancs (Pioneer) Battalion.	
			2 Platoons 11th. South Lancs commenced road repairs on main BRAY-CORBIE road.	
			2½ Platoons commenced repairs and clearing in CARNOY AVENUE.	

No.2 Sheet.

HEADQUARTERS, 30TH. DIVL. ENGINEERS   WAR DIARY   VOL. 3, JANUARY, 1916.

INTELLIGENCE SUMMARY

(Erase heading not required.)

Army Form C. 2118.

Place	Date 1916	Hour	Summary of Events and Information	Remarks and references to Appendices
CHIPILLY (cont)	Jany 19th		202nd Field Coy. R.E. started work on Scheme for supplying water to the Left Sector of the Front. This had been started by 5th Division and was now continued under C.R.E's direction. In connection with this scheme the pumping station at SUZANNE was handed over to the 202nd Field Coy. R.E.	
			100 men of the 7th Entrenching Bn. lent by 10th Corps, started work on road repairs on BRAY-CORBIE road under C.R.E's direction.	
	22nd		2 Platoons of 11th Bn. South Lancs: Regt. commenced work in improving and clearing SHEFFIELD AVENUE.	
	25th		Work on new survey post for 3rd Army was started by 202nd Field Coy. Materials for this had previously been collected.	
	28th		Work on scheme for installing a steam laundry in an existing building at CERISY was commenced under C.R.E's direction.	
	29th		Owing to a change in the situation new defences at CAPPY and FROISSY bridges were put in hand in accordance with a scheme drawn up by C.R.E.	
			Communication trench to provide covered communication between SUZANNE and BRAY was started by a detachment of 11th Bn. South Lancs: Regt.	

No.3 Sheet.

Army Form C. 2118.

HEADQUARTERS, 30TH. DIVL. ENGINEERS WAR DIARY VOL. 3. JANUARY, 1916.

INTELLIGENCE SUMMARY.

(Erase heading not required.)

Instructions regarding War Diaries and Intelligence Summaries are contained in F. S. Regs., Part II. and the Staff Manual respectively. Title pages will be prepared in manuscript.

Place	Date 1916 Jany	Hour	Summary of Events and Information	Remarks and references to Appendices
CHIPILLY (cont)	29th		During the month C.R.E. inspected daily some part of the front line system of trenches.	

6-2-16.

[signature]

Lieut-Col. R.E.
C.R.E., 30th Division.

30th Divisional Engineers

WAR DIARY

C. R. E.

30th DIVISION.

FEBRUARY 1916.

Army Form C. 2118.

HEADQUARTERS, 30TH.DIVL.ENGINEERS WAR DIARY VOL. 4. FEBRUARY, 1916.

~~INTELLIGENCE SUMMARY.~~

(Erase heading not required)

Place	Date 1916.	Hour	Summary of Events and Information	Remarks and references to Appendices
CHIPILLY.	Feb. 4th.		200th Field Coy. completed handing over of work in "C" Sector which had been taken over by 7th Division.	
	8th.		A first consignment of roadmetal arrived at CHIPILLY by barge.	
	9th.		C.R.E. attended a Road Conference at Headquarters, 13th Corps. At this Conference the responsibility of each Division for road repair and maintenance was defined. Previously the 10th Corps had undertaken to be responsible for the repair of a considerable portion of the roads in the rearmost part of the Divisional area, but this portion was now to be taken over again by the Division, thus involving a considerable amount of extra work on roads. Good progress was made on repairs, the ETINEHEM - ECLUSE de MERICOURT road being practically remetalled.	
	11th.		"A" Company, 2nd Labour Battalion arrived in the Division area. They were allotted to C.R.E. for roadwork. A certain number of wagons from No.9 Reserve Park were provided for carriage of roadmetal.	
	22nd.		A new communication trench between BRONFAY FARM and BILLON WOOD was laid out and work started under C.R.E's direction.	
	25th.		Barge-load of roadmetal arrived at CHIPILLY	
	26th.		First consignment of road metal by train arrived at BRAY.	

HEADQUARTERS, 30TH.DIVISIONAL ENGINEERS WAR DIARY VOL.4. FEBRUARY, 1916. (Sheet 2.) Army Form C. 2118.

INTELLIGENCE SUMMARY

(Erase heading not required.)

Place	Date 1916.	Hour	Summary of Events and Information	Remarks and references to Appendices
CHIPILLY. (contd.)	Feb. 26th.		During the month the C.R.E. visited daily some portion of the Front line or Intermediate line system. Work proceeding under his direction in the Front line system was principally the opening up and reconstruction of main communication avenues which were more or less derelict. Considerable progress was made during the month. In the intermediate line, the defences at CAPPY Bridge were practically completed and 1000 yards of new communication trench from the BRAY-CAPPY road towards SUZANNE was completed. The work on the Division Steam Laundry at CERISY which was being carried out by a Section of the 200th Field Coy. R.E., made good progress. Fair progress was made on the construction of the BRONFAY FARM - PERONNE Road Railway. Bad weather and enemy's fire delayed the work.	

Lieut.Col.R.E.
C.R.E., 30th. Division.

4/3/1916.

30th Divisional Engineers

WAR DIARY

C. R. E.

30th DIVISION.

MARCH 1916.

Army Form C. 2118.

HEADQUARTERS, 30TH DIVISIONAL ENGINEERS WAR DIARY VOL.5. MARCH, 1916.

INTELLIGENCE SUMMARY

Instructions regarding War Diaries and Intelligence
Summaries are contained in F. S. Regs., Part II.
and the Staff Manual respectively. Title pages
will be prepared in manuscript.

(Erase heading not required.)

Place	Date	Hour	Summary of Events and Information	Remarks and references to Appendices
CHIPILLY.	1916 March 1st to 20th		During this period very bad weather was experienced and trenches and roads suffered severely in consequence. The enemy artillery was also active and compelled most of the work on trenches in intermediate line to be done at night. The chief work done under C.R.E's direction during this period was as follows: (a) Repair, reflooring and improvement of several long support and communication trenches, the principal ones being SHEFFIELD AVENUE and BILLON AVENUE. (b) Two new avenues were about $\frac{3}{4}$ completed. (c) Work on a supporting point (U work) was continued. (d) In the intermediate line the CAPPY bridge defences were practically completed and a length of wiring North of SUZANNE was completed to half required depth. (e) The BRONFAY FARM water supply scheme and BRONFAY FARM railway were practically completed. (f) Good progress was made in constructing shelters at various places. (g) The Division steam laundry at CERISY was completed as regards the essential parts and was taken into use. The C.R.E. visited some portion of the front line system or locality in which R.E. work was going on, daily during the period under review.	
	17th		200th Field Company, R.E. left BRAY for FRECHENCOURT and QUERRIEUX to work under XIII Corps.	

Army Form C. 2118.

HEADQUARTERS, 30TH DIVISIONAL ENGINEERS WAR DIARY VOL.5. MARCH, 1916. (Sheet 2).

~~INTELLIGENCE SUMMARY~~

(Erase heading not required.)

Place	Date	Hour	Summary of Events and Information	Remarks and references to Appendices
CHIPILLY (Cont).	1916 March 20th		201st Field Company, R.E. left SUZANNE en route for LA NEUVILLE. H.Q. R.E., moved with Division H.Q. to MONTIGNY having been relieved by 18th Division. The 202nd Field Company, R.E. remained at BRAY for work under 13th Corps.	
MONTIGNY	24th		H.Q. R.E., moved with Division H.Q. to DAOURS.	
DAOURS	28th		H.Q. R.E., moved with Division H.Q. to AILLY-SUR-SOMME. The first course for Infantry Officers and N.C.O's commenced at Division R.E. School at LA NEUVILLE in charge of O.C. 201st. Field Company, R.E.	
AILLY-SUR-SOMME	31st		201st Field Company, R.E. with Division R.E. School moved from LA NEUVILLE to PICQUIGNY.	

4/4/1916.

[signature]

Lieut.Col.R.E.
C.R.E., 30th Divisional
(County Palatine) Engineers.

30th Divisional Engineers

WAR DIARY

C. R. E.

30th DIVISION.

APRIL 1916.

Army Form C. 2118.

HEADQUARTERS, 30TH. DIVISIONAL ENGINEERS WAR DIARY VOL. 6. APRIL. 1916.

~~INTELLIGENCE~~ SUMMARY.

(Erase heading not required.)

Instructions regarding War Diaries and Intelligence Summaries are contained in F. S. Regs., Part II. and the Staff Manual respectively. Title pages will be prepared in manuscript.

Place	Date	Hour	Summary of Events and Information	Remarks and references to Appendices
AILLY SUR SOMME.	1916 April 1st. to April 30th.		During this period the Division was in rest and there are no events to record. The majority of the R.E.Labour in the Field Coys.was employed on works under 13th.Corps. Those portions of Field Coys. not so employed were engaged in training and increasing accomodation in billets by the erection of bunks. A considerable amount of work of this nature was carried out. A Divisional R.E.School was established at PICQUIGNY in which classes of Officers and N.C.O's from the Infantry Battalions of the Division were given instructions in elementary work necessary in the trenches. 5/ 5/ 16.	

Lieut-Col.R.E.
C.R.E.30th.Divisional.
(County Palatine) Engineers.

30th Divisional Engineers

C. R. E.

30th DIVISION.

MAY 1916.

Army Form C. 2118.

R2 300

HEADQUARTERS, 30TH DIVISIONAL ENGINEERS WAR DIARY VOL. 7. MAY, 1916.

Instructions regarding War Diaries and Intelligence
Summaries are contained in F. S. Regs., Part II.
and the Staff Manual respectively. Title Pages
will be prepared in manuscript.

~~INTELLIGENCE~~ SUMMARY.

(Erase heading not required.)

Place	Date	Hour	Summary of Events and Information	Remarks and references to Appendices
ETINEHEM.	1916. May 1st. to May 31st.		Headquarters, R.E. were at ETINEHEM throughout the month (with Division Headquarters). During this period a considerable amount of work was carried out by Field Companies and the Pioneer Battalion under the C.R.E's direction. It consisted almost entirely of preparing the Division front for active operations by the construction of additional communication trenches, shelters, assembly places, battle Headquarters, etc., Progress was hampered by lack of sufficient labour. A noteworthy piece of work was undertaken by the 21st Infantry Brigade assisted by the 202nd Field Company, R.E., on the night of the 28th/29th May. A new trench 660 yards long was dug in advance of our existing front line and successfully completed including wiring and communication trenches. Casualties very slight.	

5-6-1916.

Lieut.Col.R.E.
C.R.E., 30th Divisional
(County Palatine) Engineers.

2353 Wt. W₌544/4454 700,000 5/15 D. D. & L. A.D.S.S./Forms/C 2118.

30th Divisional Engineers

WAR DIARY

C. R. E.

30th DIVISION.

JUNE 1916.

For Engineer preparations & Instructions for the attack see Appendix "A" to July diary.

Army Form C. 2118.

WAR DIARY

~~INTELLIGENCE~~ SUMMARY

Vol. 8. June 1916.

(Erase heading not required.)

HEADQUARTERS 30TH DIVISIONAL ENGINEERS.

Instructions regarding War Diaries and Intelligence
Summaries are contained in F. S. Regs., Part II.
and the Staff Manual respectively. Title pages
will be prepared in manuscript.

C.R.E 30 D.D

Vol 8 June

Place	Date	Hour	Summary of Events and Information	Remarks and references to Appendices
ETINEHEM.	June 1st to 22nd 1916.		H.Q.R.E. were at ETINEHEM with Divisional H.Q. During this period a considerable amount of work was carried out by Field Companies and the Pioneer Battalion under C.R.E's direction. It consisted almost entirely of preparing the Divisional Front for active operations by the construction of additional communication trenches, shelters, assembly places, dressing stations, Battle H.Q. &c. During the last week of this period assistance was given by 1½ Field Companies and Pioneers of the 9th Division. By the 23rd the Division's Battle Front was complete in all essentials.	
DUGOUTS 1 MILE EAST BRAY.	23rd to 30th		On 23rd June 23rd H.Q.R.E. moved with Divisional H.Q. to Battle H.Q. in dugouts close to BRAY. During this week the preliminary bombardment of the German lines took place. The Field Companies, who had been working very long hours during the period of preparation, were withdrawn to Camps in the neighbourhood of BRAY where they rested, only having to work on a few small jobs which it was necessary to carry out. On the evening of the 30th all Field Cos and the Pioneer Btn. moved into their places of assembly.	

2353 Wt. W2544/4454 700,000 5/15 D. D. & L. A.D.S.S./Forms/C 2118.

Sheet 2.

Army Form C. 2118.

WAR DIARY
~~INTELLIGENCE~~ SUMMARY.
(Erase heading not required.)

Instructions regarding War Diaries and Intelligence Summaries are contained in F. S. Regs., Part II. and the Staff Manual respectively. Title pages will be prepared in manuscript.

Place	Date	Hour	Summary of Events and Information	Remarks and references to Appendices
DUGOUTS ½ MILE EAST BRAY	June 1916. 23rd to 30th.		Copies of instructions issued in connection with the operations will be attached to the War Diary for July which deals with the course of the operations in so far as they affected the R.E. 8th July 1916. [signature] Lieut-Col. R.E. C.R.E., 30th Divl. (C.F.) Engineers.	

30th Divisional Engineers

WARN DIARY

C. R. E.

30th DIVISION.

J U L Y 1916.

Appendices :-

Orders & Instructions for Operations commencing
1st July 1916.

Reports on Engineer Operations :-
         1st & 2nd July 1916.
         8th - 13th   "   "
         26th-29th   "   "

Army Form C. 2118.

WAR DIARY

HEADQUARTERS 30TH DIVISIONAL ENGINEERS.

VOL. 9. July 1916.

Instructions regarding War Diaries and Intelligence
Summaries are contained in F. S. Regs., Part II.
and the Staff Manual respectively. Title pages
will be prepared in manuscript.

INTELLIGENCE SUMMARY.

(Erase heading not required.)

Place	Date 1916	Hour	Summary of Events and Information	Remarks and references to Appendices
Dugouts near BRAY.	July 1st		Attached are copies of instructions issued to Technical Troops and for general information prior to the commencement of operations (Appendix A). The distribution of the Technical Troops before the attack is shewn. The extract from Division Operation Orders which was sent out to Technical Troops is also attached. It will be observed that besides the 11th S.Lancs. Pioneers there were under C.R.E's orders 2 sections of 258th Army Troops Co. R.E. for roadwork.	
	July 2nd		The account of the R.E. operations which took place during the first phase of the battle from 7-30am 1st July to 12 noon 2nd July is attached (Appendix B). During the night the 9th Division relieved the parties of 11th S. Lancs. on two of the main communication trench extensions. Work on the other two and also on the MARICOURT-MONTAUBON road was continued. O.C. 11th S.Lancs. reported at 9-20pm that all four main communication trenches were usable for 500 yards beyond old German front line. 90th Infantry Brigade was relieved during the night by a Brigade of 9th Division. The 202nd Field Coy. was ordered to withdraw, on relief, to Divisional Reserve. They bivouacked near TALUS BOISE.	
	July 3rd. July 4th.		Work on strong points and MARICOURT-MONTAUBON road was continued, but was much hampered in places by shelling. 200th and 202nd Field Coys were relieved during the evening by 9th Division units and moved to bivouacs near BRAY. 11th S.Lancs. moved Headquarters to GROVETOWN and on following morning to BOIS DE TAILLES.	
ETINEHEM.	July 5th.		H.Q.R.E. moved with Div. H.Q. to ETINEHEM after handing over to 9th Division. At 6-10pm orders were received placing 202nd Field Coy. and 2 Coys 11th S.Lancs. at dispossal of 21st Infantry Brigade. These units were ordered to move during the night to assembly trenches between OXFORD and CAMBRIDGE Copse.	
	July 6th.		Subsequently permission was obtained for only 2 Sections 202nd Field Coy. to move that night and for the other 2 Sections to follow the next morning. Orders were amended accordingly.	

Army Form C. 2118.

Sheet 2.
WAR DIARY
of
INTELLIGENCE SUMMARY.
(Erase heading not required.)

Instructions regarding War Diaries and Intelligence Summaries are contained in F. S. Regs., Part II. and the Staff Manual respectively. Title pages will be prepared in manuscript.

Place	Date 1916	Hour	Summary of Events and Information	Remarks and references to Appendices
ETINEHEM (Cont).	July 7th.		At 6-20pm on 7th July orders were sent to 200th Field Co. R.E. to be prepared to move at half an hours notice from 7-0am the following day. 200th and 201st Field Coys were warned to be prepared to carry out some extensive wiring. It was thought that this would probably be necessary in connection with the consolidation of TRONES WOOD after its capture on the 8th July. Orders were also sent to 11th S. Lancs. at 7-40pm to move their 2 remaining Coys to TAIUS BOISE by 5-0pm on 8th July.	
ETINEHEM and COPSE VALLEY.	July 8th to 13th		An account of R.E. operations during this period is attached (Appendix C). On 10th July H.Q.R.E. moved up to COPSE VALLEY which became Div. H.Q. Work on the MARICOURT-BRIQUETERIE road was proceeded with, assistance being given by the Royal Sussex Pioneers of the 18th Division. On 13th July Div. H.Q. moved back to ETINEHEM on relief by 18th Division. H.Q.R.E. moved to a point near BRAY.	
CORBIE.	July 14th		H.Q.R.E. with Div. H.Q. moved back to CORBIE. The Field Coys. moved back to rest under orders of Infantry Brigades into area round CORBIE.	

Army Form C. 2118.

Sheet 3.
WAR DIARY
or
INTELLIGENCE SUMMARY.
(Erase heading not required.)

Instructions regarding War Diaries and Intelligence Summaries are contained in F. S. Regs., Part II. and the Staff Manual respectively. Title pages will be prepared in manuscript.

Place	Date 1916.	Hour	Summary of Events and Information	Remarks and references to Appendices
CORBIE (Cont)	July 14th to 19th.		H.Q.R.E. remained at CORBIE with Div. H.Q.	
BILLON COPSE	July 20th to 30th.		H.Q.R.E. moved with Div. H.Q. to BILLON COPSE. An account of the work done by Technical Troops during period 20/29th July and during operations on 30th July is attached (Appendix D).	
CITADEL.	July 31st.		H.Q.R.E. moved to the CITADEL with Div. H.Q. on relief by 55th Division.	

6-8-16.

Lieut-Col. R.E.
C.R.E., 30th Divisional (County Palatine) Engineers.

Appendix A

SECRET

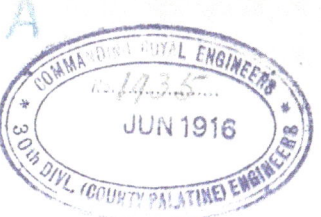

O.C. 200th Field Coy. R.E.
O.C. 201st Field Coy. R.E.
O.C. 202nd Field Coy. R.E.
O.C. 238th Army Troops Co. R.E.
O.C. 11th Bn. South Lancs. Reg.
H.Q. 30th Division "G"
H.Q. 30th Division "Q"

H.Q. 89th Infantry Brigade.
H.Q. 90th Infantry Brigade.
H.Q. 21st Infantry Brigade.
C.R.A.
C.R.E. 9th Division.
C.R.E. 18th Division.
C.E. XIII Corps.

Herewith the following in connection with the forthcoming operations :-

Arrangements for Provision of R.E. Stores during operations.

List "B" - Stores at the Advanced R.E. Dump North of MARICOURT Chateau.

List "C" - Stores at the Advanced R.E. Dump in TALUS BOISE.

List "D" - Stores at Divisional R.E. Dump BRAY at commencement of operations.

List "F" - Pontoon Wagon Loads.

Instructions in connection with ROADS.

Instructions in connection with WATER SUPPLY.

20th June 1916.

Lieut-Col. R.E.
C.R.E., 30th Divisional
(County Palatine) Engineers.

SECRET.

Arrangements for Provision of R.E. Stores during Operations.

1. R.E. Stores will be available at the following R.E. Dumps as under:-

Advanced R.E. Dump 'B.' Avenue of trees just N. of MARICOURT CHATEAU (in charge of 200th Fd.Co.R.E.) Stores as per list "B".

Advanced R.E. Dump 'C.' TALUS BOISE (in charge of 202nd Fd.Co.R.E)

Divl. R.E. Dump 'D.' Divisional R.E. Dump, BRAY, (in charge of Captain Fraser).

Stores can be drawn from these Dumps by any unit sending for them.

2. Every endeavour will be made to keep Dumps 'B.' & 'C.' supplied with stores. To effect this 9 pontoon wagons and 3 G.S. wagons will be sent up every night during operations with stores from the Divisional Dump, BRAY.
   These wagons will take their stores as far forward as possible and Field Companies will arrange to have guides on the MARICOURT-MONTAUBAN Road opposite Dump 'B.' to wait for the wagons and conduct them to where the stores are required. If the situation admits, the entire convoy will go up to 201st Field Coy at MONTAUBAN on the first night. On subsequent nights the N.C.O. i/c Convoy will receive orders from the C.R.E. as regards number of wagons to go to each Field Coy. As soon as wagons are offloaded they will return to Divisional R.E. Dump, BRAY. Should it be found impossible for the wagons to go beyond MARICOURT they will offload at Dump 'B.' and return.

3. The convoy of wagons will be parked loaded on the day prior to the Assault at Divisional Dump, BRAY. On the night following the Assault the teams will take the wagons up as noted above. On this night the convoy will be taken up by Lieut. Ellis, R.E., and on subsequent nights by a N.C.O. of the 202nd Field Coy.R.E., who will have accompanied Lieut. Ellis on the first night.

4. The loading of the wagons each day at Divisional R.E.Dump will be carried out under orders of Captain Fraser.
   Unless Field Companies send word to the contrary the wagons will carry up approximately the same selection of stores nightly, starting from Divisional Dump, BRAY.

[signature]

Lieut.Col.R.E.
C.R.E. 30th Divisional
(County Palatine) Engineers.

SECRET

In Avenue just North of MARICOURT CH. on MARICOURT-MONTAUBAN Road.

North of MARICOURT CH.

(200th Field Company, R.E.)

LIST "B".

Sandbags	17,000
Barbed Wire coils	300
Plain Wire coils	12
French Wire coils (5 in bundle)	15
Pickets	1,500
Shovels	300
Picks	200
Mauls	12
Crowbars	10
Billhooks	20
Hand Axes	20
Tracing tapes	10
Spunyarn	3
Safety Fuze tins	4
Rubber Solution tins	2
Rubber Tape tins	2
Pitprops	30
Loophole Plates	10
Corr. Iron sheets	200
~~Wirecutters Mark 5.~~	~~100~~
~~Wirecutters Long~~	~~50~~
Hedging Gloves	—
Knife Rests	100
Hurdles	—
Nails, 3", 4", 6". Cwts.	2
Hammers Boring	4
Chisels Brick	4
Hammers, Masons	4
✻ Blocks, double 2½"	3
✻ " snatch 2½"	3
Iron spikes	50
✻ Cordage 2". Fms.	60
Screw posts Long	250
✻ Girders	50
✻ Timber 12', 9" x 9"	25
Hammers Hand	6
Saws Hand	10

✻ Road Party Dump.

18th June, 1916.

Lieut.Col.R.E.
C.R.E., 30th Divisional
(County Palatine) Engineers.

TALUS BOISE. (Square A.15.a.2.8.).

(202nd Field Company, R.E.)

LIST "C".

Sandbags	34,000
Barbed wire coils	400
Plain " "	24
French " "	30
Pickets	3,000
Shovels	500
Picks	400
Mauls	20
Crowbars	25
Billhooks	40
Hand axes	40
Tracing tapes	20
Spunyarn	5
Safety Fuze tins	8
Rubber solution tins	4
Rubber tape tins	4
Pitprops	100
Loophole Plates	20
Corr. Iron sheets	400
Hand saws	20
Hand Hammers	12
~~Wirecutters, Mark 5.~~	~~300~~
~~Wirecutters, Long~~	~~150~~
Hedging Gloves	—
Knife Rests	100
Hurdles	—
Nails, 3", 4", & 6". Cwts.	3
Bars, Boring	8
Hammers, Boring	6
Chisels, Brick	6
Hammers, Masons	6
Cordage 2". Fms	40
Screw posts. Long	150
Girders	20

18th June, 1916.

Lieut.Col.R.E.
C.R.E., 30th Divisional
(County Palatine) Engineers.

SECRET

List of Stores at Divisional R.E. Dump, BRAY, at commencement of active operations. Square L.15.b. (BRAY-ALBERT Road).

LIST "D".

Sandbags	60,000
Barbed wire	800
Plain wire	35
French wire (with staples) Coils	50
Pickets	2,200
Screw posts	500
Shovels	500
Picks	800
Mauls	17
Crowbars	23
Billhooks	120
Hand axes	120
Hammers Hand	6
Tracing tapes	15
Spunyarn	2
Saws Hand	10
Safety Fuze tins	3
Pitprops	250
Dogs sawyers	600
Corr. Iron sheets	300
Girders	30
Wire rope $\frac{3}{4}$" fms.	250
Knife Rests	100
Hurdles	—
Nails, 3", 4" & 6". cwts.	3
Cordage 2" fms.	100
Canvas rolls.	5
Wirecutters Mark 5.	174
Hedging Gloves	50

As much of these materials as transport and time available permit will be conveyed to the Advanced Dump in MARICOURT before "U" day.

20th June, 1916.

Lieut.Col.R.E.
C.R.E., 30th Divisional
(County Palatine) Engineers.

LIST "F".

Pontoon Wagon Loads

6 Wagons each	1,500 Sandbags (in bundles of 30).
	20 coils Barbed wire.
	25 shovels.
	10 picks.
	100 5' pickets.
	50 3'6" pickets.
	2 mauls.
	2 bundles (5 coils) French wire (with 50 staples).
	1 coil plain wire.
	2 hand hammers.
	1 crowbar.
3 Wagons each	10 pitprops.
	10 9" x 3" planks.
	50 dogs sawyers.
1 G.S. Wagon	20 coils Barbed wire.
	60 screw posts.
2 G.S. Wagons each	40 portable wire entanglements.

20th June, 1916.

Lieut.Col.R.E.
C.R.E., 30th Divisional
(County Palatine) Engineers.

R O A D S.

SECRET

A.

1. The 30th Division is responsible for the preparation of the following roads :-

   (a) From A.20.a.1.1 to A.21.a.1.9.

   (b) PERONNE Road from East of LAPREE WOOD to HIGH STREET in MARICOURT.

   (c) MARICOURT-MONTAUBAN Road from PERONNE Road to our front line trench.

This work is in hand as also the distribution, as available, of roadmetal along the roadside for maintenance during operations.

2. On the commencement of operations the Chief Engineer will be responsible for the maintenance of roads South of the PERONNE Road inclusive.

3. The O.C. 200th Field Coy. will be responsible for opening the MARICOURT-MONTAUBAN road for traffic by the night Y/Z.

He will also detail road-party of a Section Field Coy. R.E. (1 Platoon Infantry to be attached) for opening this road through the enemy's lines (front line trench inclusive) up to MONTAUBAN as circumstances admit.

4. Two Sections of 238th Army Troops Coy. R.E. will be attached to the 30th Division on the commencement of operations, for roadwork North of PERONNE Road.

The O.C. will be responsible for opening and maintaining the following roads and tracks North of PERONNE Road as soon after the assault as the situation permits :-

   (a) Road from A.21.b.2.9 to A.15.c.40.85, and the track (and bridges over trenches) marked out to OXFORD COPSE.

   (b) A 6' footpath across our trenches with trench bridges, from the Water Point by the 4 willow trees to our front line trench.

   (c) A 6' footpath across our trenches to the West of the FLECHE back to the Water Point in TALUS BOISE. Trench bridges to be used.

   (d) Maintenance of the MARICOURT-MONTAUBAN road from PERONNE road to enemy's front line trench (exclusive).

20th June, 1916.

Lieut.Col.R.E.
C.R.E., 30th Divisional
(County Palatine) Engineers.

WATER SUPPLY.
----------oOo----------

Chief Engineer, XIIIth Corps, will be responsible for the maintenance of the Water Supply up to the two forward "Water Points" fixed for this Division, i.e: (a) at TALUS BOISE, and (b) by the four willow trees S.E. of MACHINE GUN WOOD.

2. The 200th Field Company will be responsible for the Water point near the four willows S.E. of MACHINE GUN WOOD. An Infantry party of 4 men for work at this point will be found under Divisional Orders, the 200th Field Company providing one fitter only.

3. The 202nd Field Company are to draw four Metre gauge Railway trucks from 280th Army Troops Coy. R.E., and fit them with water tanks. These water trucks will be used on the metre gauge line forward of TALUS BOISE as soon as the line has been repaired by Corps troops.

4. The 202nd Field Company will be responsible for fixing and maintaining two hand pumps at the TALUS BOISE Water Point. The Infantry (4 men) for working the pumps will be found under Divisional Orders. One fitter should be left for the maintenance of the pumps.

5. Field Companies are responsible for placing water tanks in Assembly trenches, Keeps, Collecting Stations and Brigade Battle Headquarters they are constructing. The responsibility for water storage receptacles in all other places rests with Infantry Brigades concerned.

6. Infantry Brigades will be responsible for filling all water tanks, etc., which are not connected to a piped system, except those in Collecting and Dressing Stations which are to be filled by the R.A.M.C. unit concerned.

Lieut.Col.R.E.
C.R.E., 30th Divisional
(County Palatine) Engineers.

20th June, 1916.

Copy No..........

Copy of the undermentioned instructions to technical troops supplementary to 30th Division Operation Order No.19, forwarded for information :-

(i) Table of Dispositions of R.E's and Pioneers.

(ii) Instructions to the O.C. 200th Field Company, R.E.

(iii) Instructions to the O.C. 201st Field Company, R.E.

(iv) Instructions to the O.C. 202nd Field Company, R.E.

(v) Instructions to the O.C. 238th Army Troops Coy. R.E.

(vi) Instructions to the O.C. Section detailed to command party to form "Strong Points" with 21st Infantry Bde.

(vii) Instructions to the O.C. Section detailed to command party to form "Strong Points" with 89th Infantry Bde.

(viii) Instructions for O.C. Section 200th Field Coy detailed for road-making party.

(ix) Instructions for forward communication trench parties.

(x) Instructions for Communication Trench Maintenance parties

(xi) List "A". Stores to be handed over to Infantry Brigades.

(xii) List "P". Equipment for Strong Point party: 21st Infy. Bde.

(xiii) List "PP". Equipment for Strong Point party: 89th Infy. Bde.

(xiv) List "Q". Equipment for 201st Field Coy. R.E. and Infantry Party.

(xv) List "R". Equipment for road-party (a).

(xvi) List "S". Equipment for road-party (b).

2. Lists "B", "C", "D" & "F" were forwarded to all concerned on 20th June, 1916.

21st June, 1916.

Lieut.Col.R.E.
C.R.E., 30th Divisional
(County Palatine) Engineers.

```
Copy No.1. to O.C. 200th Field Coy. R.E.    No.8. to H.Q. 89th Infantry Bde.
  "    " 2. "  O.C. 201st Field Coy. R.E.    " 9. "  H.Q. 90th Infantry Bde.
  "    " 3. "  O.C. 202nd Field Coy. R.E.    "10. "  H.Q. 21st Infantry Bde.
  "    " 4. "  O.C. 238 Army Troops Co.R.E.  "11. "  C.R.A.
  "    " 5. "  O.C. 11th Bn. South Lancs.
  "    " 6. "  H.Q. 30th Division "G".
  "    " 7. "  H.Q. 30th Division "Q"        "14. "  C.E. XIIIth Corps.
```

SECRET

DISPOSITION OF R.E's AND PIONEERS.

Affiliation	Strength, etc., of Parties	Place of Assembly	Objective	Remarks
	1. STRONG POINTS PARTIES.			
89th Infantry Brigade.	(a) 1 Section 200th Field Co. R.E., 1 Platoon Pioneers, 2 Platoons Infantry.	Trenches in MARICOURT (N) (East Face and part of South Face of CHAPEAU KEEP - 1403 of trench).	To prepare "Strong Points" at A.10.a.3.6 and A.10.a.4.6.	(i) To move under Brigade Orders. (ii) To be equipped as per list "PP".
21st Infantry Brigade.	(b) 1 Section 202nd Field Co. R.E., 1 Platoon Pioneers, 1 Platoon Infantry.	Assembly Trench x x	To prepare "Strong Points" at A.3.d.6.2	(i) To move under Brigade Orders. (ii) To be equipped as per list "P".
90th Infantry Brigade.	(c) 201st Field Co.R.E. 1 Company Infantry.	Copse Valley	Defence of MONTAUBAN Village.	(i) To move under Brigade Orders. (ii) To be equipped as per list "Q".
Division.	2. COMMUNICATION TRENCH PARTIES. (a) ½ Coy. Pioneers.	Trenches in MARICOURT (S). (East Face of NAPIER KEEP - 300X of trench).	To open Communication Trench from Sap A.P.3 to GERMAN WOOD (STANLEY AVENUE).	To move as detailed in separate instructions.
	(b) 1 Coy. Pioneers.	-ditto-	To open Communication Trench from Sap A.P.4 to enemy's trenches and onwards. (MARICOURT AVENUE).	
	(c) ½ Coy. Pioneers.	"U" Works North of PERONNE Road	To open Communication Trench from Sap No.6 (A/9/3)(SUPPORT AVENUE) to enemy's trenches and onwards.	

SECRET

Affiliation	Strength, etc., of parties	Place of Assembly	Objective	Remarks
	(d) ½ Coy. Pioneers.	"U" Works North of PERONNE Road.	To open Communication Trench from Sap No.5 (A/9/4) (WEST AVENUE) to enemy's trenches and onwards.	To move as detailed in separate instructions.
	3. ROAD PARTIES.			
Division.	(a) 1 Section 200th Field Coy.R.E.	MARICOURT Trenches. (South Face of NAPIER KEEP - 200X of trench).	Roads and bridges North of PERONNE Road.	(1) Equipped as per list "R".
	1 Platoon Infantry.			
	(b) 2 Sections 238th A.T.Coy. R.E.			(1) Equipped as per list "S".
	4. TRENCH MAINTENANCE PARTIES.			
	(a) 1 Platoon Pioneers.	STANLEY & MARICOURT AVENUES.	Maintenance STANLEY and MARICOURT AVENUES.	
	(b) 1 Platoon Pioneers.	SUPPORT & WEST AVENUES.	Maintenance SUPPORT and WEST AVENUES.	
	5. DIVISIONAL RESERVES.			
	× 200th Field Coy.(less 2 secs)	Copse Valley.	Divisional Reserve.	
	202nd Field Coy.(less 1 sec.)	Trigger Valley.		
	2 Platoons Pioneers.	Copse Valley.		

× 1 sect & move up to
MERSEY ST at 2 hrs
from hr under orders
of 89X Bde.

17th June, 1916.

Lieut.Col.R.E.
C.R.E., 30th Divisional
(County Palatine) Engineers.

SECRET

Copy No............

Instructions to the O.C. 200th Field Company, R.E.

(Supplementary to 30th Division O.O. No.19.)

1. You will be responsible for detailing the following parties and seeing that they are in their places of assembly at 8 pm on "Y" day, with tools and stores as noted opposite each :-

(a) Strong Point Party;   1 Section 200th Field Co.R.E. Equipped as per
                              (1 Platoon Pioneers.)   List "PP".
                              (2 Platoons Infantry.)

(b) Road Party;   1 Section 200th Field Co.R.E. Equipped as per
                 (1 Platoon Infantry).   List "R".

(c) Water Point Party;   1 Sapper - Fitter.
                         (4 Infantry - to work pump.)

(d) Advanced R.E. Dump Party;   1 R.E. N.C.O.
                              3 Infantry (to be found from H.Q.R.E.)
                              i/c Dump 'B'.

(Separate instructions for each Party are attached).

2. You will see that your Company (less 2 Sections) is at its place of assembly at 8 pm on "Y" day with tools and stores.

3. Further instructions will be issued as regards equipment to be carried by all ranks.

4. All first line transport (less pontoon and trestle wagons) is to be parked complete at your present wagon lines and kept ready to move.

5. Pontoon and trestle wagons with teams of your Company will be attached to 202nd Field Company, R.E. and will be at Divisional R.E. Dump, BRAY, at 9 am on "X" day.
They will work under C.R.E's orders.

6. All pontoon equipment and surplus kit is to be stored at Divisional R.E. Dump, BRAY, by 12 noon on "Y" day.
A guard for this will be provided from H.Q.R.E.

7. You will satisfy yourself that all stores as per List "B" are collected at the Advanced R.E. Dump North of MARICOURT CHATEAU by 8 am on "U" day.

8. You will see that the stores as per List "A", also trench ladders and bridges according to instructions already issued are drawn and issued to 89th Infantry Brigade by "U" day.

                                                     Lieut.Col.R.E.
                                    C.R.E., 30th Divisional
                                    (County Palatine) Engineers.

21st June, 1916.

SECRET

Copy No............

Instructions to the O.C. 201st Field Company, R.E.

(Supplementary to 30th Division O.O. No.19.)

1. (a) You will see that your Company with 2 Platoons Infantry is at its place of assembly at 8 pm on "Y" day with tools and stores as per List "Q".

   (b) You will move your party under the orders of the Brigadier 90th Infantry Brigade.

   (c) Your objective will be MONTAUBAN Village which is to be prepared for defence in accordance with scheme prepared by the 90th Infantry Brigade.

2. Further instructions will be issued as regards the equipment to be carried by all ranks.

3. All first line transport (less pontoon and trestle wagons) is to be parked complete at your present wagon lines and kept ready to move.

4. Pontoon and trestle wagons with teams of your Company will be attached to 202nd Field Company, R.E. and will be at Divisional R.E. Dump, BRAY, by 9 am on "X" day.
   They will work under C.R.E's orders.

5. All pontoon equipment and surplus kit is to be stored at Divisional R.E. Dump, BRAY, by 12 noon on "Y" day.
   A guard for this will be provided from H.Q.R.E.

6. You will see that the stores as per List "A", also trench ladders and bridges according to instructions already issued, are drawn and issued to 90th Infantry Brigade by "X" day.

                                                Lieut.Col.R.E.
                                           C.R.E., 30th Divisional
21st June, 1916.   (County Palatine) Engineers.

SECRET Copy No............

Instructions to the O.C. 202nd Field Company, R.E.

(Supplementary to 30th Division O.O. No.19).

1. You will be responsible for detailing the following parties and seeing that they are in their places of assembly at 8 pm on "Y" day with tools and stores as noted opposite each:-

(a) Strong Point Party; 1 Section 202nd Field Co.R.E.   Equipped as
    (1 Platoon Pioneers.)   per List "P".
    (1 Platoon Infantry.)

(b) Water Point Party;   1 Sapper - Fitter.
    4 Infantry to work pump.
    1 R.E. N.C.O.) For working
    10 Infantry.) trollies.

[margin note: Cancelled ride instead for Water Truck Party. Issued on 26-6-16]

(c) Advanced R.E. Dump   1 R.E. N.C.O.
    Party;   3 Infantry,(to be found from H.Q.R.E.)
    i/c Dump 'C'.

(d) "U" Works Pump   2 Infantry for working pump in "U" Works.
    Party;

2. You will see that your Company (less 1 Section) is at its place of assembly at 8 pm on "Y" day, with tools and stores.

3. Further instructions will be issued as regards equipment to be carried by all ranks.

4. All first line transport (less pontoon and trestle wagons) is to be parked complete at your present wagon lines and kept ready to move.

5. Pontoon and trestle wagons with teams of your Company will remain at your wagon lines and will work under C.R.E's orders.

6. All pontoon equipment and surplus kit is to be stored at Divisional R.E. Dump, BRAY, by 12 noon on "Y" day.
    A guard for this will be provided from H.Q.R.E.

7. You will satisfy yourself that all stores as per List "C" are collected at the Advanced R.E. Dump in TALUS BOISE by 8 am on "U" day.

8. You will see that the stores as per List "A", also trench ladders and bridges according to instructions already issued, are drawn and issued to 21st Infantry Brigade by "U" day.

[signature]
Lieut.Col.R.E.
C.R.E., 30th Divisional
(County Palatine) Engineers.

21st June, 1916.

SECRET   Copy No..........

Instructions for the O.C. 238th Army Troops Coy.R.E.

(Supplementary to 30th Division O.O. No.19).

You will see that your party is in its place of assembly at 8 pm on "Y" day, equipped as per List "S".

2. You will tell off parties for the maintenance of the following road and tracks:-

  (a) Road from A.21.b.2/8 to A.15.c.40.85 and the track (and bridges over the trenches) marked out to OXFORD Copse.

  (b) A 6' footpath to be made across our trenches with trench bridges from the 4 Willows water point to our front line trench.

  (c) A 6' footpath across our trenches to the West of the FLECHE back to the water point in TALUS BOISE. Trench bridges to be used.

  (d) Maintenance of the MARICOURT-MONTAUBAN road from PERONNE road to enemy's front line trench (exclusive).

These to be open for traffic as soon as the situation permits. The MARICOURT (HIGH ST.) - MONTAUBAN Road as far as our front line trench, inclusive, to be open for wheel traffic, a report regarding this road to be submitted to C.R.E. by 10 pm on "Z" day.

3. You will see that tracks over our own trenches are clearly marked with <u>signboards painted white.</u>

4. Officers who are to be in charge of these parties should be given every opportunity of studying the ground over which they will work, before operations begin.

                                             Lieut.Col.R.E.
                              C.R.E., 30th Divisional
21st June, 1916.   (County Palatine) Engineers.

SECRET.

Instructions for O.C. Section detailed to command party to form "Strong Points" with 21st Infantry Brigade.

----

1. You will move your party under the orders of the Brigadier.

×
A.3.d.6/2.
+
A.4.c.5/5.
o
A.4.c.1/9½.

2. Your first objective will be 1/21 × (vide:attached map), and your second if the circumstances admit 2/21 + and 3/21 o.

3. Strong point No. 1 is to be made for a garrison of 1 Platoon and 2 Machine Guns.

2/
17-6-1916.

for R. G. Stone
Capt R.E.
Lieut. Col. R.E.
C.R.E. 30th Divisional
(County Palatine) Engineers.

SECRET

Instructions for O.C. Section detailed to command party to form "Strong Points" with 89th Infantry Brigade.

A.10.d.1/6.
A.10.a.4/6.

A.10.b.8/7.

1. You will move your party under the orders of the Brigadier.

2. Your first objectives will be 1/89 and 2/89 (vide; attached map), and your second if the circumstances admit 3/89.

3. The Strong points at 1/89 and 2/89 are to be made for a garrison of 1 Platoon and 2 machine guns.

17-6-1916.

G. Stone
Captain
for Lieut. Col. R.E.
C.R.E. 30th Divisional
(County Palatine) Engineers.

Instructions for O.C. Section 200th Field Company
detailed for road-making party.
----

1. You will move out from your place of assembly as soon as the situation admits and make a 9' track through all parapets and trenches in the enemy's lines along the MARICOURT-MONTAUBAN road, your first objective being the junction of the MARICOURT-MONTAUBAN road with the enemy's first line of trenches.

                                                                                [signed] Capt R.E.
                                                                   for Lieut.Col.R.E.

21st June, 1916.   C.R.E., 30th Divisional
                                    (County Palatine) Engineers.

SECRET   Copy No.........

Instructions for the Forward Communication

Trench Parties.

※ Each man to) carry pick &) shovel and) 8 sandbags.)

The O.C. 11th South Lancs will be responsible for seeing that the following parties required for this work are detailed and equipped as per margin ※ , and that they are at their places of assembly at 8 pm on "Y" day.

(a) ½ Coy to open communication trench from Sap A.P.3 to GERMAN WOOD (STANLEY AVENUE).
(b) 1 Coy to open communication trench from Sap A.P.4 to enemy's trenches and onwards (MARICOURT AVENUE).
(c) ½ Coy to open communication trench from Sap No.6 (A.9/3) (SUPPORT AVENUE) to enemy's trenches and onwards.
(d) ½ Coy to open communication trench from Sap No.5 (A.9/4) (WEST AVENUE) to enemy's trenches and onwards.

2. He will also see that the following instructions are communicated to the O.C. of each party.

(i) All parties to move as follows:-
(a) and (b) parties, the latter leading, to move up to our own front line trench via STANLEY AVENUE as soon as the supporting Battalion of 89th Infantry Brigade has left its Assembly trenches, the leading man to wheel to the left on arrival at our own front line trench. Both parties should then be opposite the Sap they are to deal with.   They should move out to their objectives as soon as the Supporting Battalion has crossed the enemy's Support Line trench.

(c) and (d) parties, the latter leading, to move up to our front line trench via SUPPORT AVENUE as soon as the Supporting Battalion of 21st Infantry Brigade has left its Assembly trenches, the leading man wheeling to the left on arrival at our front line trench. Both parties should move along the front line until opposite the Saps they are to deal with. They should move out to their objectives as soon as the Supporting Battalion 21st Infantry Brigade, has crossed enemy's support line.

(ii) Work on the communication trench to be made between the head of the Russian Saps and the enemy's first line to be commenced at both ends.

(iii) On completion of these trenches each party is to prolong its trench into the enemy's lines along existing trenches as shewn on the attached map. The Officer in charge each party should reconnoitre the enemy's trench he is to deal with before his party complete their first task.

[signature]

Lieut-Col. R.E.
C.R.E., 30th Divisional
(County Palatine) Engineers.

21st June 1916.

SECRET

Copy No..........

Instructions for the Communication Trench Maintenance Parties.

Each man a shovel, every 4th man a pick. Each Platoon to have 500 sandbags dumped at suitable points outside the Avenues.

1. The O.C. 11th South Lancs will detail the following parties equipped as per margin ✱, and see that they are properly distributed in their respective trenches on the commencement of operations; i.e. 8 am "U" day.

   (a) 1 Platoon for maintenance of STANLEY and MARICOURT AVENUES.

   (b) 1 Platoon for maintenance of SUPPORT and WEST AVENUES.

2. He will also be responsible for the collection of the following stores by "T" day at the places noted, these to be at the disposal and in charge of the parties noted in Para.1.

   (a) <u>In NAPIER KEEP</u>

   - 1,000 sandbags.
   - 10 rolls wire netting.
   - 50 sheets expanded metal.
   - 50 7' pickets.
   - 100 long angle iron posts (if available).
   - 2 coils plain wire.

   (b) <u>In "U" Works</u>

   - 1,000 sandbags
   - 10 rolls wire netting
   - 50 sheets expanded metal
   - 50 7' pickets
   - 100 long angle iron posts (if available).
   - 2 coils plain wire
   - 30 pitprops
   - 20 planks 9" x 3".

   These stores are to be provided from current issues from the Divisional Dump.

3. He will be responsible for explaining to all ranks of these parties that on no account are they to move along the trenches for which they are responsible, in the opposite direction to which the trenches are marked to be used. Should they have to move in the opposite direction, they must leave the trench and go across country.

21st June, 1916.

Lieut.Col.R.E.
C.R.E., 30th Divisional
(County Palatine) Engineers.

LIST "A".

Issued by	202nd Field Co.R.E.	200th Field Co.R.E.	201st Field Co.R.E.
Issued to	21st Inf.Brigade.	89th Inf.Brigade.	90th Inf. Brigade.
Tools & Stores.			
Sandbags	17,000	19,500	22,000
*Picks	465	350	400
*Shovels	1,700	1,600	1,600
Barbed wire	400	300	300
Pickets	300	300	300
Mauls	10	8	8
Screw Posts	1,000	1,000	1,000
Wirecutters No.V.	~~250~~ 200+50	~~240~~ 190+50	~~240~~ 190+50
" Long.	126	120	120
" Decimal.	~~400~~ 300	~~500~~ 300	~~500~~ 400
" Breakers.	~~400~~ 300+100	~~500~~ 300+100	~~500~~ 400+100
Hedging Gloves.	66	66	68

* N.B. The following transfers and drawals of picks and shovels will take place on the 19th June, 1916:-

　　202nd Field Co. will draw 100 shovels from Divisional R.E. Dump.
　　200th Field Co. will draw 150 shovels from 201st Field Co.
　　201st Field Co. will issue 150 shovels to 200th Field Co.

　　　　　　　　　　　　　　　　　　　　　Lieut.Col.R.E.
　　　　　　　　　　　　　　C.R.E., 30th Divisional
17th June, 1916.　　　　　　　　(County Palatine) Engineers.

SECRET

Copy No................

LIST "P".

STRONG POINT - PARTY; 21st Infantry Brigade.

Party   1 Section 202nd Field Co. R.E.   32 men)
            1 Platoon Pioneers.   40 men) R.E. Officer
            1 Platoon Infantry (Carriers)   40 men) in charge.

Stores   Carried by
         (20 coils barbed wire   20 Infy;
         (50 short pickets   10   "
         (300 sandbags   10   "
         (448   "   (4 each Sapper
         ((and Pioneer and
         ((40 Infantry.
         (Guncotton   10-lb. 2 charges.

Tools.   Sappers (6 hand axes or billhooks.
                     (2 saws.
                     (2 crowbars.
                     (6 prs. wirecutters.
                     (2 hammers and 5" nails.
                     (2 mauls.
                     (remainder pick and shovel.

        Pioneers - Each man pick and shovel.

                                                             Lieut.Col.R.E.
                                         C.R.E.,   30th Divisional
21st June, 1916.   (County Palatine) Engineers.

 Copy No............

LIST "PP".

Strong Point Party - 89th Infantry Brigade.

Party;   1 Section 200th Field Co. R.E.   32 men)
         1 Platoon Pioneers.   40 ") R.E. Officer
         2 Platoons Infantry.   80 ") in charge.

Stores; 20 coils barbed wire   Carried by
                                      20 Infantry.
         50 short pickets   10   "
         300 sandbags   10   "
         448   "   (4 each Sapper
                                      (and Pioneer
                                      (and 40 Infy:

         Guncotton 10-lb. 2 charges.   2 Sappers.

Tools;   Sappers (6 hand axes or billhooks.
                  (
                  (2 saws.
                  (
                  (2 crowbars.
                  (
                  (6 prs. wirecutters.
                  (
                  (2 hammers and 5" nails.
                  (
                  (2 mauls.

                  remainder pick and shovel.

         Pioneers: Each man pick and shovel.

         Infantry: 40 men - each man pick and shovel.

                                        Lieut.Col.R.E.
                                        C.R.E., 30th Divisional
21st June, 1916.   (County Palatine) Engineers.

SECRET

LIST "Q".

Copy No..........

20lst Field Company, R.E.,

For each Section.

Carrying Party;

    1 Section R.E.   32 men
    1 Platoon Infantry   40 "

   20 Infantry carry   :   20 coils barbed wire.
   20   "   "   :   600 sandbags.

   32 R.E. carry   :   10 bricklayers chisels.
                            :   10 masons hammers.
                            :   5 felling axes.
                            :   10 billhooks.
                            :   1 X cut saw.
                            :   2 hand saws.
                            :   4 crowbars.
                            :   6 wirecutters.
                            :   20 lbs. 5" nails.
                            :   2 mauls.
                            :   20 picks.
                            :   20 shovels.
                            : 192 sandbags.
                            :   1 10-lb. charge Guncotton.

[signature]

Lieut.Col.R.E.
C.R.E., 30th Divisional
(County Palatine) Engineers.

21st June, 1916.

LIST "R".

ROAD PARTY (a).

Organisation: 1 Section 200th Field Coy. R.E.
                1 Platoon Infantry.

Stores: **Carried by**

    Sandbags   300 (bundles of 30)   10 Infantry
    Short pickets 40 (bundles of 5)   8   "
    Coils Plain wire 1   1   "
    Iron Spikes 25 in bag.   1   "
    Charge made up 10-lbs. 1   1 Sapper.
    Blocks double 2½" 1   )
      "   snatch 2½" 1   ) 1 Sapper.
    Cordage 2" Fms. 30   )
    1 bundle Spunyarn   ) 1 Sapper.

Tools:

    Infantry   (1 Shovel per man.
              (1 Pick every 4th man.

    Sappers   (2 saws hand.
              (2 axes hand.
              (4 prs. wirecutters longhandled.
              (2 hammers hand and 5" nails.
              (1 maul
              (4 axes felling.
              (1 Pick and 1 shovel per man of remainder.

N.B.   Above stores to be drawn from current issues as far
as possible and completed from stores on List "B".

                                                Lieut.Col.R.E.
                              C.R.E., 30th Divisional
17th June, 1916.   (County Palatine) Engineers.

SECRET

LIST "S".

Road Party (b).

Organisation: Headquarters and 1 Section 238th Army Troops
Company, R.E.,

Stores: Blocks double 1)
     " single 1)
Iron spikes 25 in bag) 2 Sappers.
Cordage 2" Fms. 30)
1 bundle Spunyarn)

Tools: 2 saws hand
2 axes hand
4 prs. wirecutters longhandled
2 hammers hand and 5" nails
1 maul
4 axes felling
1 pick and 1 shovel per man
Sign boards

N.B. Above stores to be drawn from current issues as far as possible and completed from stores on list "B" at the Advanced R.E. Dump in Avenue North of MARICOURT CHATEAU.

R.E. Stone
Capt R.E.
for. Lieut.Col.R.E.
C.R.E., 30th Divisional
(County Palatine) Engineers.

218th
17th June, 1916.

C.R.E's No. 1944.

S E C R E T.

Copy No. 13.

With reference to this office No.1944 of 21st June 1916, herewith for information "Instructions for Water Truck Party". Para. 3 of "Instructions in connection with Water Supply" forwarded with this office No.1935 on 20th June is cancelled, as also is para. 1 (b) of "Instructions to the O.C. 202nd Field Co. R.E." regarding Water Point Party as far as detailing party of 1 R.E. and 10 Infantry is concerned.

2. With regard to para. 4 (a) and (b) of "Instructions in connection with Roads", the Road from A.21.2.9. to A.15.c.40.85 and the track via OXFORD COPSE then to water point at 4 willow trees on to our front line trench has been bridged and will take Field Artillery.

This road and track will be maintained by party of O.C. 253th Army Troops Co. R.E.

(Sd) R.C.Stone, Capt. R.E.
for Lieut-Col. R.E.
26.6.16.
C.R.E., 30th Divl. (C.P.) Engrs.

```
Copy No.1 to O.C.200th Field Co.R.E.    No.8 to H.Q. 89th Infy. Bde.
  "   " 2 "  O.C.201st       do          " 9 "  H.Q. 90th      do
  "   " 3 "  O.C.202nd       do          "10 "  H.Q. 21st      do
  "   " 4 "  O.C.253th A.T. Co.R.E.      "11 "  C.R.A.
  "   " 5 "  O.C.11th S. Lancs.          "12 "  C.E. XIII Corps.
  "   " 6 "  H.Q. 30th Division "Q".    "13 "  File.
  "   " 7 "  H.Q. 30th Division "Q".    "14 "  C.E. Fourth Army.
```

SECRET.

WATER TRUCK PARTY.

The O.C.11th South Lancs. will be responsible for detailing the following party for working the water trucks from CARNOY and TALUS BOISE forward:-

X
Lieut. CULSHAW
   11th S.Lancs.

1 Officer ˣ
6 men
(10 men already detailed by 21st Infantry Brigade for duty with 202nd Field Co.R.E.)

ˣ each carrying a 400-gallon tank.

2. The Officer i/c Party will take over 4 water trucks from the 202nd Field Co.R.E. on the 26th June and arrange at once in direct communication with Lieut. Beattie R.E. 92nd Field Co.R.E. (18th Division) for filling all tanks at TALUS BOISE as well as the tanks on the trucks by night Y/Z.

3. The party under O.C.202nd Field Co.R.E. (1 sapper fitter and 4 Infantry) will be at the disposal of the Officer i/c water trucks for this purpose.

4. Arrangements have been made with the 18th Division for the construction of a siding at TALUS BOISE sufficient to take the water trucks of both Divisions.

                                  Sd. R.G.Stone Capt.R.E.
                                       for Lieut.Col.,R.E.
26.6.16.   C.R.E.30th Divisional
                                  (County Palatine) Engineers.

Extracts from Operation Order No.19, dated 21st June, 1916.

By Major General J.S.M. Shea, C.B. D.S.O. Commdg. 30th Division.

Reference : 1/10,000 Trench Map, Sheets.

1. (i) On 'Z' day, hour zero, (time of zero to be notified later) the 30th Division will assault the enemy's trenches.

   (ii) On our right will be the 39th Division of the French XX Corps, on our left the 18th Division.

   (iii) Boundaries between this and neighbouring Divns. and between brigades of this Division, are shewn on attached plan. The MARICOURT - BRIQUETERIE road is inclusive to the French and as far as A.10.d.2/6.
   The boundary between 30th and 18th Divisions is the TALUS BOISE tram line as far as A.3.c.8/6, thence the road due N. to MONTAUBAN, thence Northwards to the trench running from S.27.c.8/6 to S.27.a.7/2 (inclusive to 30th Division).

3. (i) <u>First objective will be consolidated.</u>

   (a) by the formation of Strong points in order given:-

	21st Bde:		89th Bde:
At once.	(1) A.3.d.6/2 (2) A.4.c.5/5 (3) A.4.c.1/9 (4) A.3.d.5/8	At once	(1) A.10.a.4/6. (2) About A.10.d.15/60. (3) A.10.b.8/7.
		Later	(4) About A.4.d.0/2) ends of a (5) About A.10.b.0/7) new C.T. (6) A.10.a.58.24.

   Garrisons 21 (1), 89 (1) and (2) 1 platoon and 2 machine guns; remainder 2 sections and 1 M.G. each, to be enlarged when opportunity admits.

   (b) by connecting these points by a continuous line of trenches.

   (ii) The system under which this consolidation is to be accomplished was laid down in Appendix 'A' G.304 9th June, published to all concerned.

   (iii) <u>Second objective will be consolidated</u> on a scheme to be made out by G.O.C. 90th Infantry Bde; who will keep strong reserves in hand to meet expected counter-attack.
   The consolidation of the second objective will be accompanied by the 21st Bde: constructing 3 more strong points at
   (5) A.4.a.4/7 as soon as possible.
   (6) A.4.a.4/3) later.
   (7) A.4.a.0/6)
   and in due course by the preparation of the German C.T. running from A.4.c.29.90 to the S.E. corner of MONTAUBAN for use as a fire trench.

Ammunition. 12. Each man will carry on his person 170^X rounds S.A.A. and 2 grenades.
^{X}4 battalions 220, see App: E. Technical troops will also carry 2 grenades.
Other arrangements as shewn in Appendix 'E'.

Rations and water supply. 13.(i) Every man will carry on his person :-
The unexpended portion of the ration for 'Z' day.
His iron ration.

(ii) Every man starts with a full water bottle.
Great importance is attached to supervision by
regimental/

regimental officers and N.C.O's of the use of water bottles.
(iii) For system of supply see Appendix "F".

Messages. 20. Messages intended for <u>Battle Headquarters</u> will be addressed :-
30th Div.
21st Bde.
89th "
90th "

Other messages will be addressed :-
30th Div: "Q" (at ETINEHEM CHATEAU).
Staff Captain 21st Bde: (in Brigade Office, BRAY).
   "   "   89th " (in Brigade Office, BRAY).
   "   "   90th " (at ETINEHEM CHATEAU).

Great care is to be taken as regards the address of messages, so as to prevent routine work reaching Battle Headquarters.
The whole Divl. Artillery and Divl. Engineer Staffs will be found at Divl. Battle Headquarters.
The A.D.M.S. will be found at "Q" Office.

Battle Headquarters. 21. Battle Headquarters :-
XIII Corps ... ... CHIPILLY.
XIII Corps Heavy Arty: ... ... L.14.b.2/2.
31st Heavy Arty: Group ... ... L.12.a.25.75.
30th Divn: ... ... L.16.b.5/2.
89th Infy: Bde: ... ... A.21.b.3/2 (later CHATEAU Redoubt, MARICOURT.)

21st " ") ... ... Copse B, A.21.a.3/5,
90th " ")   (later A.15.a.4/7.)

XX French Corps ... ... L.18.a.5/5.
39me.French Divn: ... ... BREWERY Redoubt, MARICOURT, A.22.a.9/5.
77th French Brigade ... ... A.16.b.7/8.
18th Divn: ... ... L.16.b.3/7.
55th Infy: Bde: ... ... A.25.d.6/5.
9th Divn: ... ... GROVETOWN.
"A" Infy: Bde: ... ... BILLON WOOD VALLEY.
"B" " " ... ... GROVETOWN.

<u>System of Liaison and Intercommunication.</u>

Communication (i) with aeroplanes and Kite balloons.
Flares will be carried by officers, N.C.O's and selected men at the rate of 220 per battalion in first instance. Each Brigade will be issued with 1,500.
They will only be used by order of a company or platoon commander and only from the front line.
When used they will mean "We are here and so far as we know we are the leading infantry or within 50 yards of the leading infantry".
Like flags they will be used only:

(a) on reaching "Infantry line 0.20" by 21st & 89th Bdes:
"Infantry line 1.00" by 21st & 89th Bdes:
"MONTAUBAN Village" by 90th Bde:

Co-operation
with artillery./

Co-operation with artillery.	(i) Every infantryman in the Division will wear a yellow patch on his back and a tin disc, shiny side outwards. Observers must be cautioned that these patches and discs are worn by all infantry; they therefore do not mark (like flags, flares, and mirrors) the front line.

(ii) Every company and every platoon will carry one coloured flag to help show its position to the artillery, <u>if in the front line</u>. These flags will mean nothing unless waved, and they are only to be waved by the front line. Waving means "We are here and so far as we know we are the leading infantry or within 50 yards of the leading infantry"
   30th Div: flags are blue & yellow, halved diagonally.
   18th "   "   "   "   red & yellow,   "   "
   9th   "   "   "   "   red & yellow, quartered diagonally.

They will be used in the same way as flares, see sub-para. (i) of the previous paragraph - i.e.

  (a) on reaching "Infantry line 0.20" by 21st and 89th Bdes:
              "Infantry line 1.00" by 21st and 89th Bdes:
              "MONTAUBAN Village" by 90th Bde:

  (b) <u>if checked</u> before reaching the line given. |

Appendix 'E' to O.O. 19.

System of supply of Ammunition.

S.A.A. and Grenades.	From front to rear the echelon of supply is as follows:-

(i) On the man 170 or 220 rounds (see App: 'J').

(ii) Forward Dumps near our front line at
    89th Bde: A.16.b.1/7, A.16.a.5/7, A.15.b.3/3
    21st and 90th Bdes: A.9.c.9/8.

(iii) Bde: Reserve Dumps at
    89th Bde: MARICOURT CHATEAU, to be refilled from
                                    NAPIER'S Redoubt.
    21st and 90th Bdes: A.15.a.4/9, to be refilled from
                                        CAMBRIDGE COPSE.

    to be refilled under Bde: arrangements from (iv).

(iv) Advanced Divl. Dumps at
  (a) NAPIER'S Redoubt and CAMBRIDGE COPSE, to be
       refilled under Divl: arrangements.
  (b) "U" Works which keeps CAMBRIDGE COPSE filled.

(v) Advanced Divl. Dumps are to be refilled at night by D.A.C. from Ammunition Refilling Point.

(vi) Grenades are stored and detonated at BRAY (Divl: Grenade Store) and ETINEHEM, and forwarded thence detonated to Advanced Divl. Dumps. |

                                                                       Appendix "F".

Ration & Water Supply.

Rations	(i) Every man will carry his iron ration on his person, in addition to the unexpended portion of rations "Z" day.
The 21st and 90th Bdes: will carry rations for the next day as well.
(ii) About 20,000 rations are dumped at :-
NAPIER'S Redoubt, MARICOURT for 21st Brigade.
CHATEAU REDOUBT/

CHATEAU REDOUBT, MARICOURT for 89th Bde:
A.21.b.9/5   "   for 90th Bde:

Troops N. of PERONNE road will be fed from NAPIER'S Redoubt. These Dumps will be under a Supply Officer and troops will be rationed nightly from them, using sacks. The Dumps will be refilled by 1st Line Transport from BRAY at night.

(iii) 1st Line Transport will get rations daily from the Divl Train in the usual way.

(iv) Units S. of PERONNE road will be fed as at present.

Water.

(v) Every man starts with a full water bottle.
Great importance is attached to supervision by regimental officers and N.C.O's of the use of water bottles.

(vI) It is hoped that there will be Water Points ready at:-
TALUS BOISE (A.9.c.2/1).
WILLOW TREES near MACHINE GUN WOOD(A.15.b.5/4.)
COPSE VALLEY (A.20.d.3/5).

There are tanks in CHATEAU REDOUBT, MARICOURT, and four 400-gallon tanks on trucks on METRE GAUGE railway at CARNOY.
Tanks are also being placed in assembly trenches.

(vii) Carriage from Water Points by petrol tins on mules.
8 Mules per battalion carrying 12 gallons each (6 petrol tins).
400 petrol tins per Bde: for hand carriage and storage in addition to the 48 carried on mules. The tanks now in the trenches can be carried forward under Bde: arrangements.

(viii) If supply fails owing to damage of pipes by shell fire, supply will be by water carts as far as MARICOURT and "U" Works, thence forward by hand.

Appendix 'H'.

Working Parties etc. to be found by Brigades
for Operation purposes.

21st.

1 Platoon to 202nd Field Coy. R.E. for 'Strong Points'
see App: 'C'.
4 men to C.R.E. to work pumps at Water Point) 21st Bde: to
10 men   "   "   "   trollies.   ) arrange assembly
2 men   "   "   "   pump in 'U' Works) with C.R.E.

1 platoon to join 4" Stokes battery in DONE'S
REDOUBT (W. of MARICOURT AVENUE)
by 7 pm. 'Y' day.

89th.

2 platoons to 200th Field Co. R.E. for 'Strong Point' party -
see App: 'C'.
1 Platoon to 200th Field Coy. R.E. for Road party - see App:'C'

4 men to C.R.E. for working pump - 89th Bde: to arrange
assembly with C.R.E.

90th.

2 Platoons to 201st Field Co.R.E. Defence of MONTAUBAN, see
Appendix 'C'.

Appendix 'J'/

Appendix 'J'.

Appendix 'J' to O.O. 19.

Extra stores to be carried in accordance with these Orders.

Every man   Rations (a) unconsumed portion "Z" day ration and
                                                iron ration.

           Ammunition (b) 170 rounds.
           Grenades   2
           Sandbags   4
           Pick or Shovel or entrenching tool.
           Yellow patch.
           Shiny disc.
           1 Gas helmet.
           Water bottle.

By bombers. 10 grenades, but only 50 rounds of ammunition.
Throwers not to carry rifles.

2 leading battalions 89th and right-hand leading battalion 21st - 1 smoke candle per man with box of lighters.

Strong Point Parties - R.E. material.

Lamps, Screens and ground sheets, by Battalion Headquarters
        as available, for signalling to aeroplanes.

Flares - 220 per battalion - every Officer and N.C.O. one.

Vigilance mirrors - 80 per Battalion.

Light Morse discs - 24 per Battalion.

A few electric torches.

Wirecutters)
) as many as are issued.
Knobkerries)

Every company and every platoon - 1 flag.

Notes:-   (a) 21st and 90th Bdes: to carry 1 extra day's rations.

        (b) 2 battalions (of each of 21st & 90th Bdes:) to
            carry 50 rounds extra.

SECRET   Appendix B.
No 64.   3.7.16

Account of R.E. operations from morning 1st July to

Mid-day 2nd July, 1916.

1.   200th Field Company R.E. (89th Infy. Bde.)

Two Sections were at disposal of Brigadier, one party for Strong Points and one for work at the BRIQUETERIE.

The Strong Point party was moved from its Assembly place at 9.42 a.m. and commenced work on Strong Point 1/89 (A.10.d.1.6.) at 10.15 a.m., a party going on to Strong Point 2/89 (A.10.a.4.6.)

At 6 p.m. 1.7.16 O.C.200th Field Co.R.E. reported that site originally selected for Strong Point 1/89 (A.10.d.1.6.) was too churned up to make any work possible and that it was then being made 50 yards West of that site. Work was much hampered by shell fire at this site and no work was possible above ground.

A considerable amount of work had been done on Strong Point 2/89 (A.10.a.4.6.) and some wire put up.

Both works suffered from want of stores, the carrying party being unable to cope with the demand.

The party detailed for the BRIQUETERIE was ordered to move up about 11 a.m. on 1.7.16. It came under heavy shell fire on the way and most of the stores were lost; half the carrying party became casualties. The subaltern in charge went to report to O.C. 20th King's Liverpool Regt. and during his absence the Sergeant in charge, who had been wounded and was considerably shaken, through some misunderstanding withdrew the party to MARICOURT. Practically no work was done.

This party was replaced next morning by another under a more experienced R.E. subaltern.

One Section of this Company was employed on the MARICOURT → MONTAUBAN road. By 6 p.m. the road was opened to 200 yards beyond the German front line, a track having to be made through the German trenches where no trace of the road could be found.

This party was relieved at about 10 p.m. on 1.7.16 by a Section of the Company and 1 Platoon Pioneers in Divisional Reserve.

By 11 a.m. 2.7.16 the road was open to MONTAUBAN.

14 tons of road metal were sent up on night 1st/2nd 7.16 in order to improve tracks through German trenches.

The road is being improved and widened.

2.   201st Field Company R.E. (90th Infy. Bde.)

The whole Company was at disposal of Brigadier. 2 Sections were in Assembly trenches and 2 Sections in COPSE VALLEY.

The 2 Sections in COPSE VALLEY moved forward at 7.55 a.m. and at 12 noon the whole Company was reported to be entering MONTAUBAN.

The

2.

The Company at this stage was under the command of Lieut Day, the Company Commander (Capt. Hall) having been retained at the Headquarters of the Brigade.

No further reports were received from the Company until 12.3 a.m. on 2.7.16 when the Company Commander reported (dispatched 9.20 p.m. 1.7.16) that he had just returned from MONTAUBAN. He stated that MONTAUBAN no longer existed as a village, and that scheme of defence had had to be modified in consequence. He found his Company very much disorganised, only 70 men being accounted for up to the time of his visit.

In accordance with G.O.C's instructions two Sections of the 202nd Field Co.R.E. in Divisional Reserve were placed at disposal of Brigadier for employment in MONTAUBAN, the first at 9.55 p.m. and the second at 11.30 p.m.

At 12.25 a.m. on 2.7.16 a third Section of this Company was also placed at his disposal.

At 9.15 a.m. on 2.7.16 the O.C.201st Field Co.R.E. reported 2 Officers and 50 other ranks of his Company had been withdrawn from MONTAUBAN to TALUS BOISE area, and that the third Officer left with the Company was following with the remainder, the fourth Officer, 2nd Lieut. Murphy, having been killed.

He also reported the arrival at MONTAUBAN of 2 Sections of the 202nd Field Co.R.E., the third Section of this Company having been stopped at Southern end of TALUS BOISE.

At 10.10 a.m. 2.7.16 the O.C. was asked to report what work had actually been done in MONTAUBAN. He reported that very little except improvements to trenches and erection of a little plain wire and German collapsible wire had been possible. The Officer i/c party of 202nd Field Co.R.E. in MONTAUBAN reported at same time that no other work but improvements to trenches possible.

The 201st Field Co.R.E. appears to have come under heavy shell fire which prevented any work being done.

Up to mid-day on 2.7.16 the Company had had the following casualties.-
                1 Officer killed.
                3 O.R. killed.
                2 O.R. missing, believed killed.
                28 O.R. wounded.

3.   202nd Field Company, R.E. (21st Infy. Bde.)

One Section was under Brigadier's orders for making Strong Point 1/21 and three Sections in Divisional Reserve.

The Strong Point party was ordered to move at 9 a.m. and arrived at site of Strong Point 1/21 at 11 a.m. This party came under heavy shell fire on the way up, losing one Officer and 17 men of the Pioneers. The Infantry carrying party were scattered and parted with their stores the loss of which greatly hampered the work subsequently.

Work continued intermittently, enemy's artillery fire making it impossible to work at times.

3.

The remaining Sections of this Company were placed at the disposal of the 90th Infantry Brigade for work at MONTAUBAN, vide para.2.

4. 11th Bn. South Lancs. Rgt. (Pioneers)

At the commencement of operations 1 Platoon was attached to 200th Field Co.R.E. Strong Point party, and 1 Platoon to 202nd Field Co.R.E. Strong Point party. Two and a half Companies divided into four parties were in readiness to make 4 forward communication trenches in continuation of our existing ones. Two Platoons were engaged in maintenance of our 4 main communication trenches and two Platoons were in Divisional Reserve in COPSE VALLEY.

The four parties detailed for forward communication trenches started work about 8.30 a.m. (exact time not reported). At 2.48 p.m. the continuations of MARICOURT and WEST AVENUES by Nos. 2 and 4 parties had been completed to a depth of 4 ft. up to German front line, and at 3.23 p.m. it was reported that the continuation of STANLEY AVENUE by No.1 party had been completed to a depth of 5 ft up to German front line. Work on the continuation of SUPPORT AVENUE by No.3 party had been held up by heavy shelling and the party had suffered heavy casualties. At 6.18 p.m. No.1 party reported trench completed up to Strong Point 1/89 and were starting work on the continuation to CASEMENT TRENCH. At 9.22 p.m. No.4 party reported that they had practically finished trench up to German front line and at 9.31 p.m. a similar report was received from No.2 party.

At 8.45 p.m. instructions were sent to O.C.11th South Lancs to send up 1 Platoon in Divisional Reserve to assist in work on the MARICOURT - MONTAUBAN road.

At 9.20 p.m. instructions were sent for the remaining Platoon in Divisional Reserve to commence opening Russian Saps continuing STANLEY and MARICOURT AVENUES.

O.C.11th South Lancs reported at 10.42 p.m. that he had already arranged for his original trench maintenance parties to carry out this work, and that it was in progress. He was consequently directed to employ the reserve Platoon to open the Russian Saps continuing WEST and SUPPORT AVENUES.

At 11.20 p.m. the O.C.11th South Lancs was directed to withdraw his communication trench parties for rest and to continue work the following morning.

5. Water Supply.

A party under an Officer has kept the tanks at TALUS BOISE full. The Corps piped supply failed after delivering a small supply on the 30th June. The right Brigade have continued to draw their supply from MARICOURT.

Lt.Col.,R.E.
3.7.16. C.R.E.30th Divl.(C.P.)Engrs.

ACCOUNT OF OPERATIONS (TECHNICAL TROOPS)
8th to 13th July, 1916.

7th July.   The 202nd Field Co.R.E. and 2 Coys. 11th South Lancs. were moved to the TALUS BOISE area and placed at the disposal of the 21st Infy. Bde. for operations against TRONES WOOD.

8th July.   Nos 2 and 4 Sections R.E. were attached (by order of the Brigadier) to the 2nd Yorks and 2nd Wilts respectively, the two battalions detailed for the assault of the Wood.

Both these Sections were moved forward to CHIMNEY TRENCH by 7.15 a.m.; The remainder of the Field Coy. and the two Coys. 11th South Lancs being left in the TALUS BOISE area.

At 11 a.m. No.4 Section was ordered by O.C. 2nd Wilts to follow his supports in the advance. The party proceeded as far as A.5.a.2.8, where it remained till noon. The Section was then ordered to return to CHIMNEY TRENCH.

While in CHIMNEY TRENCH these two Sections came under heavy shell fire. This applied to practically the whole advanced area and no work could be done.

At 1 p.m. a party was sent to the BRIQUETERIE to reconnoitre for and clear the well.

On account of casualties, the Sections in CHIMNEY TRENCH were moved to NORD ALLEY and subsequently to GLATZ REDOUBT.

About 9.30 p.m. the whole Company was concentrated near GLATZ REDOUBT but did not go forward.

During the day the Company had the following casualties:- 5 killed and 14 wounded, all O.R.

The remainder of the Technical Troops were moved to COPSE VALLEY on the evening of the 8th July.

9th July.   During the night 8th/9th July, the 21st Infy. Bde. was relieved by the 90th Infy. Bde.

Situation remained the same as regards Technical Troops and except for repairs to bridges on the MARICOURT - MONTAUBAN road, no work was done during the day.

Two Sections 201st Field Co.R.E. and another Coy. 11th South Lancs were ordered to move up to reinforce the Technical Troops with the Brigade.

At 9p.m. 3 Sections 202nd Field Co.R.E. and 2 Sections 201st Field Co.R.E. with the 3 Coys. 11th South Lancs proceeded to dig and wire a trench from the S.E.corner of BERNAFAY WOOD and to fire-step and wire the SUNKEN ROAD (BRIQUETERIE - HARDICOURT) i.e. from S.29.c.3.2. to A.5.d.3.5.

10th July.   This work was successfully carried out and at 2.30. a.m. on July 10th the whole party marched back to the TALUS BOISE area.

At 2 p.m. the 202nd Field Co.R.E. was relieved by the 200th Field Co.R.E.

One Section 200th Field Co.R.E. was detailed by the Brigadier 89th Infy. Bde. for operations to take place on the 11th.
This

2.

10th July. This Section assembled at the BRIQUETERIE.

In the evening 3 Sections 200th Field Co.R.E., 2 Sections 201st Field Co.R.E. and 3 Coys. 11th South Lancs went up for work under arrangements made with the 90th Infy. Bde., who were relieved during the night 10th/11th by 89th Infy. Bde.

Work done during the night.-
Trench from BERNAFAY WOOD to SUNKEN LANE completed and wired.
Wire erected along SUNKEN LANE as far as CHIMPANEZEE Trench by 201st Field Co.R.E.
Support trench S. of TRONES WOOD, 130 yards traversed trench at Southern end dug to a depth of 3 feet.
Trench to MALTZ HORN FARM, 120 yards at N. end deepened 1'6". About 100 yards wire fence erected in front.
All work rather interrupted by shelling.

On completion of night's work all returned to COPSE VALLEY.

11th July. The 202nd Field Co.R.E. returned to BRAY.

During the day the Section of 200th Field Co.R.E. detailed for special work seems to have gone astray and failed to carry out any work.

In the evening 2 Sections 200th Field Co.R.E., 2 Sections 201st Field Co.R.E. and 3 Coys. 11th South Lancs went up for work under 89th Infy. Bde.

During the night there was a heavy counter attack on TRONES WOOD and all troops (including Technical units) were standing to. No R.E. work was possible.

12th July. On the morning of 12th the Section 200th Field Co.R.E. with 89th Infy. Bde. was relieved by another Section.

The relieving Section was ordered to wire the S. end of TRONES WOOD. Unfortunately owing to the guide provided taking the Section to the wrong place the Section Commander became a casualty and the Section could not be collected by the Officer sent up to replace him, in time to do any work.

During the afternoon the 201st Field Co.R.E. was sent back to BRAY.

13th July. 200th Field Co.R.E. marched back to BRAY.

The Division was relieved at 10 a.m. by the 13th Division, the 38th Infy. Bde. having taken over from the 89th Infy. Bde. during the night 12th/13th.

The casualties during the period 9th to 13th July were:-
200th Field Co.R.E. Wounded 4 (includes two slightly at duty)
202nd Field Co.R.E. Killed 6, Wounded 18 (includes 1 slightly at duty).

Lieut.Col.,R.E.
16.7.16. C.R.E.30th Divl. (C.P.)Engineers.

NOTE re WORK DONE BY TECHNICAL UNITS DURING THE PERIOD
20th - 29th JULY AND DURING THE OPERATIONS
29th 30th JULY.

200th Field Co.R.E.

A collecting station for 50 lying cases was completed at the junction of the BRIQUETERIE road and CASTLE'S trench. Splinter proof cover only was made.

Four Battalion Headquarters were made in trenches to be used by the 89th Infy. Bde. in operations.

The Coy. supervised the digging of a 6' cable trench from BRICK POINT to the BRIQUETERIE with a branch to TRAIN ALLEY.

201st Field Co.R.E.

Huts were erected at the CITADEL and near BILLON FARM for Divisional Headquarters.

A track was opened from TALUS BOISE water point through the North road in HARDECOURT to join with the MARICOURT - BRIGHT ROW road. This was made to enable water carts being taken up from the water point direct to the BRIQUETERIE and forward area.

Tapes were laid to the East of TRONES WOOD for two Coys. to form up on for the advance on GUILLEMONT.

Two "Dugouts" for use as an Advanced Brigade Headquarters were commenced at A.5.a.0.3. These were about half completed by the evening of 30th July and all frames and other materials to complete them were left at site ready for erection.

Two visual Signal stations were made, one at the BRIQUETERIE and the other at the HAIRPIN.

The Company also supervised the digging of Assembly trenches East and West of TRONES WOOD and the preparation of rides or passages through TRONES WOOD.

202nd Field Co.R.E.

A well at F.10.b.8.4. was repaired and fitted with appliances for drawing water.

Brigade Headquarters dug outs in TRAIN ALLEY were strengthened and improved.

Ten "Dugouts" were completed at Divisional Headquarters near BILLON FARM.

11th South Lancs:

Cable trenches 5' deep were made from the BRIQUETERIE to TRONES WOOD and to the West of Matz Horn Farm trench.

COBHAM trench was completed and the trench leading to the Dug Outs in the BRIQUETERIE was also completed in order to provide communication to the Dugouts.

Four Assembly trenches each 120 yards long were dug to a depth of 3'9" (average) on the East side of TRONES WOOD.

An assembly trench between TRONES and BERNAFAY WOODS was extended South for 450 yards and dug to a depth of 3'9" (average).

Four Rides were cleared through TRONES WOOD and marked with strips of calico.

One platoon worked with the 202nd Field Co. R.E. on Divisional Headquarters Dug Outs near BILLON FARM.

OPERATIONS - 29th-30th July.

The 200th and 201st Field Cos. R.E. worked with their affiliated Brigades, i.e., 89th and 90th Infantry Brigades respectively.

Both Companies were assembled in the TALUS BOISE Area on July 29th.

Beyond sending forward reconnoitring parties under officers no R.E. work was possible.

The 202nd Field Co.R.E. and 11th South Lancs. were kept in Divisional Reserve at TALUS BOISE.

All Technical Troops were withdrawn on the night 30/31st July.

1st August 1916.

Lt-Col.R.E.
C.R.E., 30th Division.

30th Divisional Engineers

C. R. E.

30th DIVISION

AUGUST 1 9 1 6

Army Form C. 2118.

SECRET

30TH DIVISIONAL ENGINEERS   WAR DIARY VOL. 10.   AUGUST, 1916.

INTELLIGENCE SUMMARY.

(Erase heading not required.)

Instructions regarding War Diaries and Intelligence Summaries are contained in F. S. Regs., Part II. and the Staff Manual respectively. Title pages will be prepared in manuscript.

Place	Date	Hour	Summary of Events and Information	Remarks and references to Appendices
	1916.			
CITADEL.	Aug. 1st.		H.Q.R.E. with Division H.Q. were at the CITADEL near BRAY the 30th Division having been withdrawn from the line the previous day.	
HALLENCOURT.	Aug. 2nd & 3rd.		The following day H.Q.R.E. moved to HALLENCOURT with Division H.Q. where they remained the following day.	
BUSNES	Aug. 4th.		On 4th H.Q.R.E. proceeded by train to BERGUETTE and thence by road to BUSNES in the First Army area.	
	5th to 11th.		Remained at BUSNES resting. During this period C.R.E. and Adjutant R.E. visited H.Q.R.E. 39th Division from whom we were to take over the FESTUBERT - GIVENCHY sector at an early date. The trenches in this sector were also visited as well as store dumps, etc.,	
BETHUNE.	12th.		H.Q.R.E. moved with Division H.Q. to BETHUNE taking over on the same day the above mentioned sector from 39th Division.	
	12th to 31st		Remained at BETHUNE which was Division H.Q. for the FESTUBERT - GIVENCHY sector. Field Companies were stationed as follows :- 200th Field Co. R.E. - GORRE - Working in FESTUBERT sector. 201st " " " - LE TOURET - Back area and VILLAGE LINE. 202nd " " " - GORRE - GIVENCHY sector.	

Army Form C. 2118.

Sheet 2.

WAR DIARY.
INTELLIGENCE SUMMARY.
(Erase heading not required.)

Instructions regarding War Diaries and Intelligence Summaries are contained in F. S. Regs., Part II. and the Staff Manual respectively. Title pages will be prepared in manuscript.

Place	Date	Hour	Summary of Events and Information	Remarks and references to Appendices
BETHUNE. (contd.)	1916. Aug. 12th to 31st.		During the month normal maintenance work was carried out in the line and calls for no special comment. To each Field Company was attached 1 Company 11th South Lancs (Pioneers) for work. The fourth Company 11th South Lancs was employed on drainage. The Divisional R.E. Dump was established at GORRE BREWERY, this site being more convenient than LE TOURET where that of the 39th Division had been situated.

5-9-1916. | |

Rylend Capt RE
for
Major. R.E.
Actg. C.R.E. 30th Division.

30th Divisional Engineers

WAR DIARY

C. R. E.

30th DIVISION.

SEPTEMBER 1916.

Army Form C. 2118.

30TH DIVISIONAL ENGINEERS WAR DIARY VOL. 11. SEPTEMBER, 1916.

INTELLIGENCE SUMMARY.

(Erase heading not required.)

Instructions regarding War Diaries and Intelligence Summaries are contained in F. S. Regs., Part II. and the Staff Manual respectively. Title pages will be prepared in manuscript.

Place	Date	Hour	Summary of Events and Information	Remarks and references to Appendices
BETHUNE.	1916. 1st to 19th		H.Q.R.E. remained at BETHUNE with Divisional H.Q. during this period. Preparations for an offensive in the GIVENCHY Section were continued but were given second place in order of priority to work on upkeep of the front line. On 10th instant the 11th South Lancs (Pioneer Battalion) received orders to leave the Division for work under 17th Corps, and on the 12th instant the 200th Field Co. R.E. received similar orders. This necessitated a change in the distribution of the 2 remaining Field Companies. The 201st Field Company, R.E. took over the FESTUBERT Section; The 202nd Field Company, R.E. continued work in the GIVENCHY Section. The Drainage work which had been under the 11th South Lancs was continued by a party of 50 R.A.M.C. and 6 Sappers and remained in charge of the same officer of the 11th South Lancs who was retained for the purpose. The Division was relieved of back work in connection with repairs to and improvements of billets by a strong Army Troops Company working under C.E. XIth Corps.	
DOULLENS	19th		H.Q.R.E. left BETHUNE for DOULLENS by train on the same day as Divisional H.Q. after handing over to the 31st Division.	
DOULLENS	20th		Remained at DOULLENS.	
VIGNACOURT	21st to 30th		Moved by road to VIGNACOURT where Divisional H.Q. was established. The Division was engaged in a short course of training during this period. The Field Companies unfortunately, were not given the opportunity to benefit much by this as they were ordered, together with 11th South Lancs, to join the 15th Corps on the 27th instant, They were employed under 15th Corps on road repairs between MONTAUBAN and BAZENTIN.	

Lieut-Col.R.E.
C.R.E.,30th Divisional
(County Palatine) Engineers.

3-10-1916.

30th Divisional Engineers

WAR DIARY

C. R. E.

30th DIVISION.

OCTOBER 1916.

Original [handwritten]
SECRET [handwritten]

Army Form C. 2118.

30TH DIVISIONAL ENGINEERS WAR DIARY VOL. 12. OCTOBER, 1916.

INTELLIGENCE SUMMARY.

(Erase heading not required.)

Instructions regarding War Diaries and Intelligence Summaries are contained in F.S. Regs., Part II and the Staff Manual respectively. Title pages will be prepared in manuscript.

Place	Date	Hour	Summary of Events and Information	Remarks and references to Appendices
VIGNACOURT	1916. 1st to 4th		Headquarters, R.E. remained at VIGNACOURT with Division H.Q.	
BUIRE	4th to 11th		Headquarters, R.E. moved on 4th October with Division H.Q. to a camp near BUIRE, this being the Reserve Area of XVth Corps which the 30th Division had now joined.	
FRICOURT CHATEAU	11th to 17th		On the 11th October Headquarters R.E. moved with Division H.Q. to FRICOURT CHATEAU on taking over from the 41st Division a portion of the front between EAUCOURT L'ABBAYE and GUEUDECOURT. The Field Companies and 11th South Lancs (Pioneers) were all camped near MONTAUBAN. Subsequently the Field Companies moved forward to camps between BAZENTIN and MONTAUBAN, this bringing them nearer their work.	
	12th		The 30th Division was ordered to attack on 12th October (two Brigade front). Table shewing the distribution of the Technical Troops for this attack is attached. Appendix 'A'. This appendix formed part of Division Operation Orders. Attached also (Appendix 'B') is a copy of an Extract from Division Operation Orders which was issued to Field Companies. Owing to failure of the attack the Technical Troops were not able to carry out the work which it was proposed that they should undertake. All Field Companies assembled according to orders. The O.C. 200th and 201st Field Companies after consultation with G.O.C's Brigades moved their Companies forward to do any work that was required. Owing to the situation and great congestion in the communication trenches very little work was possible. The 201st Field Coy was able to carry out some repairs to our front line trench and communication trenches. Both Companies returned to camp in the early morning of the 13th Oct. The 11th South Lancs (Pioneer Battalion) was retained in its place of assembly till late in the evening, it was then sent forward and was able to dig a continuation to FISH ALLEY (one of our main communication trenches Right Brigade) behind our original front line and also to dig a communication trench 140 yards long from the end of GOOSE ALLEY (a main communication trench Left Brigade) to a strong point which had been formed slightly in advance of our original front line.	

SHEET '2.

Army Form C. 2118.

30TH DIVISIONAL ENGINEERS WAR DIARY VOL. 12. OCTOBER, 1916.

INTELLIGENCE SUMMARY.

(Erase heading not required.)

Instructions regarding War Diaries and Intelligence Summaries are contained in F.S. Regs. Part II. and the Staff Manual respectively. Title pages will be prepared in manuscript.

Place	Date	Hour	Summary of Events and Information	Remarks and references to Appendices
FRICOURT CHATEAU	13th to 17th		From the 13th October the distribution of the Technical Troops was as follows :-	
			200th Field Co. R.E. in Reserve Brigade Area employed on (a) repairs to the LONGUEVAL - HIGH WOOD road with a daily working party of a weak battalion of infantry. (b) Advanced Div. H.Q. in CARLTON TRENCH near LONGUEVAL.	
			201st Field Co. R.E. in Right Brigade sector of the front employed on work in this sector as decided on in consultation between G.O.C. Right Brigade and C.R.E.	
			202nd Field Co. R.E. in Left Brigade sector of the front employed on work in this sector as decided on in consultation between G.O.C. Left Brigade and C.R.E.	
			11th South Lancs (Pioneers), working in both sectors on extending and improving communication trenches under C.R.E's direction.	
			On 17th October Headquarters, R.E. with Division H.Q. moved to dug-outs in CARLTON TRENCH.	
	18th		The 30th Division was ordered to attack on the 18th October against an objective on the Left Brigade front. Attached is Appendix 'C' shewing disposition of Technical Troops for this attack also extract from Division Operation Orders which was issued to Field Companies (Appendix 'D'). O.C. 202nd Field Co. R.E. was at Left Brigade H.Q. Owing to the failure of the attack the consolidation work which was to have been carried out was abandoned. One Section of the 202nd Field Co. R.E. which was under the orders of the Left Brigade was ordered at 2 p.m. to go forward to assist the 2nd Wilts Regt. in constructing a strong point near what was then the front line. The site for the work was very exposed, work was rendered impossible by the continual shelling and the Section was withdrawn. In the afternoon it was decided to dig a new trench to connect with the 9th Division (next Division on left of 30th Division). The line for this trench was traced by 2 Officers of the 202nd Field Coy and the trench was dug during the night by 11th South Lancs (Pioneers) under C.R.E's orders. The 2 Sections of the 202nd Field Coy were employed in extending TURK LANE (main communication trench) to join up with the above mentioned new trench. The remaining 2 Sections of the 202nd Field Coy together with the 2 Sections 200th Field Coy attached were employed during the afternoon under C.R.E's orders in carrying up wiring stores	

Army Form C. 2118.

30TH DIVISIONAL ENGINEERS

SHEET 3.

WAR DIARY VOL. 12.

OF

INTELLIGENCE SUMMARY.

OCTOBER, 1916.

(Erase heading not required.)

Instructions regarding War Diaries and Intelligence Summaries are contained in F. S. Regs., Part II. and the Staff Manual respectively. Title pages will be prepared in manuscript.

Place	Date	Hour	Summary of Events and Information	Remarks and references to Appendices
FRICOURT CHATEAU	18th (contd.) 19th.		and sandbags to the end of TURK LANE, no infantry being available. The 2 Sections 202nd Field Coy which had been at disposal of Left Brigade returned to camp at 2 pm.	
	19th to 21st		The 30th Division remained in the line during this period. The Field Companies and Pioneer Battalion worked daily under C.R.E's orders. 2 Sections of the 200th Field Coy. with a working party of 1 Battalion were employed daily on repairs to the LONGUEVAL - HIGH WOOD Road. The remainder of the technical labour was concentrated on improving and extending the main communication trenches which were getting into a bad state, chiefly owing to the weather. On 21st and 22nd October the 201st Field Coy was employed in erecting as many huts as possible in the neighbourhood of MONTAUBAN for accommodation of the incoming 5th Australian Division. During the period that the 30th Division was in the line two main R.E. Dumps were used. One at MAMETZ and an advanced one at LONGUEVAL. Both these Dumps were replenished by lorry and no difficulty was experienced in keeping them well filled. It was, however, a matter of great difficulty to get stores forward from LONGUEVAL. The state of the road permitted wagons to reach FLERS and stores were, when possible, sent up by this means. FLERS was, however, heavily shelled with considerable regularity and wagons were usually unable to get there. This meant that nearly all stores had to be carried forward by hand over a very considerable distance. Trenches were frequently congested and walking on the top was very bad owing to shell holes and subsequently mud. Casualties during the period 11th to 22nd October were as follows:- 202nd Field Co.R.E. Killed O.R. 5; Wounded O.R. 10, of which 1 slightly woundedremained at duty.	
RIBEMONT	22nd to 25th.		On the 22nd October Headquarters, R.E. moved with Division H.Q. to RIBEMONT on relief by the 5th Australian Division.	
PAS	26th to 30th.		On the 26th October the 30th Division was transferred to 3rd Army and Headquarters, R.E. with Division H.Q. moved to PAS.	
BAVINCOURT	31st.		On the 31st October the 30th Division took over the portion of the line held by 46th Division. Headquarters, R.E. was established with Division H.Q. at BAVINCOURT.	

[signature] Lieut-Col.R.E.
C.R.E., 30th Divisional
(County Palatine) Engineers.

A.D.S.S./Forms/C.2118. 5-11-1916.

Appendix 'C'.

DISPOSITION OF R.E. AND PIONEERS.

Affiliation.	Strength &c. of Parties	Place and Time of Assembly 12th Instant.	Objective.	Remarks.
	1. CONSOLIDATION PARTIES.			
90th Inf.Bde.	(a) 1 Section 201st Field Co. R.E.	Under Brigade orders.		These Parties to move under Brigade orders.
89th Inf.Bde.	(b) 1 Section 200th Field Co. R.E.	" " "		
Division	(c) 201st Field Co.R.E. (less 1 Section). 2 Platoons Infantry. X (from 90th Bde.)	FLAG TRENCH (Portion East of FISH ALLEY). 2-30 pm. X	Consolidation of Green line on 90th Inf.Bde.front. Strong points to be made as shewn on attached map. Sites are provisional, O.C. Coy being responsible for actual siting after necessary R.E. reconnaissance.	To move forward in time to commence work on GREEN line by 6 pm.
	(d) 200th Field Co.R.E. (less 1 Section). 2 Platoons Infantry. X (from 89th Bde.)	FIG TRENCH (near FERRET TR.) 3-0 am. X	ditto on 89th Inf. Bde. front.	
	2. COMMUNICATION TRENCH PARTIES.			
	(a) 2 Coys 11th S.Lancs	CREST TRENCH 2-30 pm. X	Continuation of FISH ALLEY to Front line as shewn on attached map.	To move forward in time to commence work (from both ends of trench) by 6pm
	(b) 2 Coys 11th S.Lancs	CREST TRENCH 2-30 pm. X	Continuation of GOOSE ALLEY to Front line as shewn on attached map.	
	3. DIVISIONAL RESERVE.			
	202nd Field Co. R.E.	BAZENTIN-LE-GRAND.	In Divisional Reserve.	To be in readiness to move at 15 minutes notice

X Orders for Assembly will be sent later. X Subject to arrangements between C.R.E. and G.O.C. 21st Inf. Bde.

Appendix 'B'

S E C R E T.

30th Division Operation Order No.40.

11th October, 1916.

Reference attached plan 1/10,000.

1. The Fourth British and Sixth French Armies will continue the attack tomorrow, 12th October, at an hour Zero to be notified later.
    The whole XVth Corps is attacking. The 30th Division will have on its right 12th Division, on its left the 9th Division of the IIIrd Corps. Boundaries are shewn on the attached plan.
    The troops believed to be opposite us are 6th Bavarian Reserve Division and the 6th Active (Brandenburg) Division.

2. The 30th Division will capture and consolidate the objective indicated by the brown line on the attached plan.
    The operation is to be conducted in three stages :-
    (i) At Zero the Artillery barrage will begin and the Infantry will advance to the attack and establish itself on the green line.
    (ii) At Zero 20 the Infantry will advance to the brown line which will be consolidated.
    (iii) After the capture of the brown line, every effort will be made to establish posts on the approximate line marked red: —O—O—O—O , so as to obtain observation to the North.
    It is intended later to join up these posts so as to form a trench of departure for subsequent operations.

3. The 90th Infantry Brigade will be on the right, the 89th Infantry Brigade on the left and the 21st Infantry Brigade in Divl. Reserve.
    Boundary between Brigades is shown on the attached plan.

Consolidation 4. The first objective will be consolidated by the R.E. by a series of strong points, approximate position shewn on attached plan.
    The second objective will be consolidated, by the Infantry in the first instance, by the conversion of the Northern portion of GIRD SUPPORT and LIME TRENCH and the construction of a series of posts across the interval between.

Exploiting a success. 5. Every effort is to be made to establish posts on the red line to which detachments of Infantry and Lewis Guns will be pushed out.
    Approximate positions to be occupied :-
        M.18.a.8.3. (To command trough running through M.12.c).
        M.18.b.8.5. (Observation over S. edge of LE BARQUE).
        M.13.b.4.4.

Method of attack. 6. The Brigades will be assembled by dawn 12th October in accordanec with instructions and plan issued under this Office G.159 of 10th October.
    Each Brigade will have two Battalions in the front line, one in Support, and one in Reserve.

    x   x   x   x
(c) Artillery Bombardment. Lift arrangements are as follows:
    (i) The barrage will commence without previous warning at Zero and will be on, and some distance in front of the enemy first line trench. The Infantry must get in as close as possible to it.
    (ii) From 0.2. it will gradually creep back until it is on the enemy front line trench only (between 0.4 and 0.6).
    (iii) At 0.6 it will lift off the green line altogether to a general line about 150 yards to 200 yards North of it

6. (iv) At 0.20 it will again begin to creep back at the rate of 50 yards a minute until it reaches the final barrage beyond the brown line.

7.　　　x　　　　x　　　　x　　　　x

Artillery

8. The attack of the 30th Division will be supported by 21st and New Zealand Divl. Artilleries.

Communications.

9. Contact aeroplanes will be in the air from Zero until dark on 12th and from 6-30 am. till 8-0 am. on 13th.
Flares will be lit :-
(a) On reaching the green line.
(b) On reaching the brown line.
(c) At certain stated times on 12th instant to be notified later.
(d) At 7-0 am. on 13th October.
No.3 Kite Balloon will be prepared to receive messages during the night 12/13th.

Technical Troops.

10. One Section, 201st Field Co. R.E., will be attached to 90th Infantry Brigade, and one Section, 200th Field Co. R.E., to 89th Infantry Brigade.

The remainder of the Technical Troops will be kept in Divl. Reserve under C.R.E.

They will be assembled in 21st (Reserve) Brigade area under arrangements to be arrived at between C.R.E. and 21st Infantry Brigade, and will be employed for consolidation purposes and for cutting new C.T's as opportunity occurs.

Further details as to Technical Troops and working parties required from the Infantry will be contained in Appendix C.

　　　x　　　　x　　　　x　　　　x

(sd). W.F.WEBER, Lieut-Col.
General Staff.

30th Division.

Appendix 'C' to War Diary.

Appendix 'C' to O.O.

SECRET.

DISPOSITION OF R.E. & PIONEERS.

Affiliation.	Strength &c. of Parties.	Place & time of assembly 18th Oct.16.	Objective.	Remarks.
21st Inf.Bde.			Under Brigade arrangements.	To move under Brigade orders.
Division.	1. CONSOLIDATION PARTIES. (a) XXX 2 Sections 202nd Fd.Co. R.E.			To move under orders of O.C.Coy. as soon as situation admits
	(b) 202nd Fd.Co.R.E. (less 2 Sections) and 2 Sections 200th Fd.Co. attached. 2 Platoons Infantry. (To be detailed by 90th Inf. Bde.)	SWITCH TRENCH 4 p.m.	Construction of Strong Points as shown on attached map in following order of priority:- 1.2.3.4 & 6. Sites shown are provisional only. O.C.Coy is responsible for actual siting after necessary R.E. reconnaissance has been made.	of work being commenced.
	(c) 2 Platoons 11th South Lancs.	CREST TRENCH 4 p.m.	Trench on right flank to join up Infantry Posts along line N.19.a.5.8. to N.13.c.3.3.	To move under orders of the 21st Inf.Bde. as soon as situation admits of work being commenced. O.C.Party to report at 21st Inf.Bde.H.Q. at 4.pm.
Division.	2. COMMUNICATION TRENCH PARTIES. (a) 1 Coy. 11th South Lancs.	CREST TRENCH 4.30 p.m.	Continuation of C.T. from M.24.b.9.8. due North to front line. Existing trench South of M.24.b.9.8. to be cleared.	To move under orders of O.C.11th South Lancs as soon as the situation admits of work being commenced. Officers from each party to make necessary reconnaissance.
	(b) 2½ Coys.11th South Lancs.	CREST TRENCH 4 p.m.	Continuation of TURK LANE from M.24.a.1.7. to front line at M.18.d.3.7. as shown on map.	
Division.	3. DIVISIONAL RESERVE. 200th Fd.Co. (less 2 Sections) 201st Fd.Co.	Camp at S.21.a.8.9.	In Divisional Reserve.	To be ready to move at short notice.

S E C R E T.

Extract from 30th Division Operation Order No.42, dated 17th October, 1916.

Reference attached Sketch Map.

1. The attack will be continued on October 18th.
The 12th Division on our right will be co-operating with XIV Corps.
30th Division in conjunction with 9th Division is to capture and consolidate the German trenches from about N.13.c.4/2 through N.18.c. 2/4 to the West.
The hour of Zero will be communicated later.
Boundaries are shown on the map.
The troops opposite us come from the 40th Division of XIX (Saxon) Corps, which has already been engaged on the SOMME and suffered heavily.

2. Objective is as marked on the map. The operation comprises two phases :-
  (i) The capture of the blue line.
  (ii) The capture and consolidation of the green line..

3. The attack will be carried out by 21st Infantry Brigade supported by one Battalion 90th Infantry Brigade.
89th Infantry Brigade (less 1 Battalion) will hold the right of the line between the Eastern limit of operations and the FLERS - THILLOY road. It will assist the 21st Infantry Brigade by rifle and machine gun fire.
90th Infantry Brigade (less 1 Battalion) and one Battalion 89th Bde. will be in Divl. Reserve in the area South (and exclusive of) SWITCH TRENCH.

PRELIMINARY REDISTRIBUTION. 4. As a preliminary to the operation the front has been redistributed, the new dividing line being shewn on the map.

CONSOLIDATION. 5. The G.O.C. 21st Infantry Brigade will make special arrangements to form defensive flanks (a) to join up with our original line through N.13.c.5/0. (b) Along the EAUCOURT L'ABBAYE - LE BARQUE Road to join up with the right of the 9th Division for which special instructions have been issued to him.
The C.R.E. will give the necessary instruction in consultation with the G.O.C. 21st Infantry Brigade to dig or improve C.T's to the new line. Rough trace shewn on map.
Strong points will be constructed approximately on the points shewn on the map.

6.   x   x   x
7.
8.
9.   x   x   x

TECHNICAL TROOPS. 10. Two Sections 202nd Field Co. R.E. will be attached to 21st Infantry Brigade. The remainder of the Technical Troops will be assembled in Divl. Reserve in accordance with arrangements to be made by C.R.E. in consultation with 21st Infantry Brigade. Details in connection with the employment of Technical Troops will be forwarded under Appendix C.
Lewis Guns of 11th South Lancs will remain with their Unit.

COMMUNICATIONS. 11. Details as to communications are contained in Appendix B. to O.O. 40, which will not be changed except that no flags will be taken into action.

12.
13.   x   x   x
14.

APPENDICES. 15.   Appendix 'A' Artillery   ) will be issued
                           'C' Technical Troops) separately to those
) concerned.
                   Appendices 'B' (Communications), 'D' (Intelligence),
                   'E' (Ammunition), 'F' (Rations & Water), 'G' (Stragglers
                   & Prisoners of War), 'H' (Medical arrangements),
                   'J' (Position of 2nd Echelons), will remain as before
                   except :-
              (a) Every man of the 21st Brigade will carry one days'
              rations in addition to his iron ration.
              (b) Medical (i) Wounded will be carried to Adv. Dressing
                               Station at THISTLE DUMP.
                          (ii) There will be no Collecting Station.
                          (iii) Main Dressing Station at BECORDEL.
                          (iv) Lightly wounded collecting station at
                               F.7.b.5/2.
                          (v) Walking wounded will be collected at FLAT
                               IRON COPSE, S.14.c.4/2.

HEADQUARTERS. 16. 30th Division -   FRICOURT CHATEAU with an Adv. H.Q.
                                     in CARLTON TRENCH. S.16.b.2/3.
                   21st Inf. Bde.-   M.30.c.3/1.
                   89th Inf. Bde.-   S.6.a.5/9 (FERRET TRENCH).
                   90th Inf. Bde.-   M.26.d. (as at present).
                   35th Bde. of 12th Div. - S.12.d.8/8.
                   26th Bde. of 9th Div. - BAZENTIN-LE-GRAND.
                   Others as before.

                                           (sd). W. F. WEBER, Lt-Col.
                                                  General Staff.

30th Divisional Engineers

WAR DIARY

C. R. E.

30th DIVISION.

NOVEMBER 1916.

30th. DIVISIONAL ENGINEERS

WAR DIARY.

VOLUME 13.

NOVEMBER, 1916.

-----------oOo-----------

Army Form C. 2118.

30TH DIVISIONAL ENGINEERS WAR DIARY VOL. 13. NOVEMBER, 1916.

Instructions regarding War Diaries and Intelligence Summaries are contained in F. S. Regs., Part II. and the Staff Manual respectively. Title pages will be prepared in manuscript.

(Erase heading not required.)

Place	Date	Hour	Summary of Events and Information	Remarks and references to Appendices
BAVINCOURT	1st to 30th		Headquarters remained at BAVINCOURT with Division Headquarters. During the month Field Coys. worked in Sectors as under: 200th Field Co. R.E. Southern (B); 201st Field Co. R.E. Northern (D); 202nd Field Co. R.E. Centre (C). The 11th Bn. South Lancs (Pioneers) were employed mainly on work on Division Line, Village Dug-outs, and Roads, the latter under VIIth Corps. The following work was carried out or commenced during the month; Front Line System: Revetting and improving trenches continued and a great deal of work done. Owing to the bad weather each Field Company had to employ 3 Sections in the trenches. Reserve Line: Construction of new Battalion H.Q. Dug-outs off FARNBOROUGH ROAD commenced. Existing dug-outs improved and strengthened. 5 New dug-outs commenced. Division Line: (1) BERLES Defences - Be. 1 to Be. 12: Clearing, draining, revetting and repairing fire-bays continued and good progress made. Be. 7 and Be. 11: Mined dug-outs in each place in hand. (2) Strong Points A.D.H: Cleared and revetted. Completion of dug-outs in hand. (3) GASTINEAU: Clearing, revetting, and flooring trenches. Deep dug-out in hand. (4) ALOUETTE: Clearing, revetting and flooring trenches. Kitchen constructed. Deep dug-out in hand. (5) BOUNDARY POST: Old dug-outs being enlarged and strengthened. (6) BURNT FARM, STARFISH, ORCHARD POSTS: Maintenance work carried out. (7) Work on a new Strong Point at Junction of BLAIRVILLE STREET and CHANCERY LANE in hand. BERLES. 14 Dug-outs West of Village completed. BRETENCOURT Water Supply in progress. Dug-out for engine and pump completed and engine and pump installed. 400 yards of pipe connected up. A System of trench tramways is being laid, about 1,800 yards completed.	

Army Form C. 2118.

30TH DIVISIONAL ENGINEERS WAR DIARY VOL. 13. NOVEMBER, 1916.

SHEET 2.

Instructions regarding War Diaries and Intelligence Summaries are contained in F. S. Regs., Part II. and the Staff Manual respectively. Title pages will be prepared in manuscript.

(Erase heading not required.)

Place	Date	Hour	Summary of Events and Information	Remarks and references to Appendices
BAVINCOURT. (continued).	1st to 30th		Billets in the Area occupied by the Division were improved and about 600 bunks added. The Divisional R.E. Dump was at LARBRET. The C.R.E. inspected works in progress daily during the month.	

3rd December, 1916.

(signature), Captain,
for C.R.E., 30th Divisional
(County Palatine) Engineers.

30th DIVISIONAL ENGINEERS
))))))))))))))))

W A R   D I A R Y

30th DIVISION:: C. R. E.

DECEMBER 1916.

Vol 14

HEADQUARTERS, 30TH DIVISIONAL ENGINEERS

WAR DIARY

FOR THE MONTH OF

DECEMBER, 1916.

VOLUME 14.

Army Form C. 2118.

30TH DIVISIONAL ENGINEERS WAR DIARY VOL.14. DECEMBER, 1916.

Instructions regarding War Diaries and Intelligence Summaries are contained in F.S. Regs., Part II. and the Staff Manual respectively. Title pages will be prepared in manuscript.

INTELLIGENCE SUMMARY

(Erase heading not required.)

Place	Date	Hour	Summary of Events and Information	Remarks and references to Appendices
BAVINCOURT	1st to 31st.		Throughout the month H.Q.R.E. remained at BAVINCOURT with Division Headquarters. Field Companies worked in Sectors of the Division front as follows:- 200th Field Co.R.E. Southern Sector (B) 89th Infantry Brigade; 202nd Field Co.R.E. Centre Sector (C) 21st Infantry Brigade; 201st Field Co.R.E. Northern Sector (D) 90th Infantry Brigade. The 11th South Lancs (Pioneer) Battn: was employed mainly on work in Division Line and Roadwork under VIIth Corps. Work in the Division Line consisted in improving the state of existing defences and the construction of dug-outs. A new work to link up our Division Line with the Division Line of the Division on our Left was put in hand and practically completed during the month. The Pioneer Battalion also provided, under C.R.E's orders, parties for work on certain main communication trenches, a portion of front line trenches and a new Battalion H.Q. in B.2 Sub-sector. During the last few days of the month work was concentrated on assisting Brigades in the opening up of main communication trenches which had suffered severely from the bad weather. The Field Companies normally employed 3 Sections on work in the front line system which was arranged by Field Company Commanders in consultation with the Brigadiers concerned. The fourth Section of each Field Coy. was employed under the direction of the C.R.E. as follows :- 1 Section, 201st Field Co. RIDGE ROAD Scheme for Piped Water Supply; The engine and pump were installed at BRETENCOURT and the pipe line was practically complete up to RENFREW ROAD by the end of the month. 1 Section, 202nd Field Co. BERLES Tramline Scheme; By the end of the month the track was complete from BERLES along RIDGE ROAD to LLANDAFF STREET, and from BERLES along the RAVINE as far as Battn: H.Q., B.2 Sub-sector, with two branches to Heavy Trench Mortar Emplacements. 1 Section, 200th Field Co. which was billeted at H.Q.R.E. on back work in the Division Area. This included repair of screens, minor water supply work, construction of Divisional Baths and Laundry and construction of huts to accommodate 1 Field Ambulance in BAVINCOURT. This latter work was rather more than half completed by the end of the month.	

Army Form C. 2118.

30TH DIVISIONAL ENGINEERS. **WAR DIARY** VOL.14. DECEMBER, 1916.

SHEET 2.

INTELLIGENCE SUMMARY

(Erase heading not required.)

Instructions regarding War Diaries and Intelligence Summaries are contained in F. S. Regs., Part II. and the Staff Manual respectively. Title pages will be prepared in manuscript.

Place	Date	Hour	Summary of Events and Information	Remarks and references to Appendices
BAVINCOURT (continued)	1st to 31st.		Work was carried on continuously at the Division R.E. Workshops, BAVINCOURT. The principal articles manufactured being 'A' Frames, trench gratings, bodies for trucks for light railway, oil drum stoves, wire gates for blocking trenches, etc., The output shewed a satisfactory increase during the month. The supply of stores to the Division R.E. Dump, LARBRET, was generally satisfactory. At times during the month there was a shortage of corrugated iron and scantling owing to the supply of these stores from the Base being inadequate.	

5-1-1917.

Lieut-Col.R.E.
C.R.E. 30th Divisional
(County Palatine) Engineers.

30TH DIVISIONAL ENGINEERS.

WAR DIARY
VOLUME 15,
JANUARY, 1917.

SECRET

original.

Army Form C. 2118.

30TH DIVISIONAL ENGINEERS WAR DIARY VOL. 15. JANUARY, 1917.

INTELLIGENCE SUMMARY.

(Erase heading not required.)

Instructions regarding War Diaries and Intelligence Summaries are contained in F. S. Regs., Part II., and the Staff Manual respectively. Title pages will be prepared in manuscript.

Place	Date 1917.	Hour	Summary of Events and Information	Remarks and references to Appendices
BAVINCOURT.	Jan 1st to 7th.		During the month Headquarters, R.E. moved twice. Up to the 7th work continued in the Forward area as already described in last month's War Diary, but on the 7th the 30th Division moved out of the Line and went back for training to the LUCHEUX and LE CAUROY areas, Divisional and R.E. Headquarters being situated at LUCHEUX. The Field Companies each sent out an advanced Section to the back area to take over from a Section of the Field Companies of the 49th (West Riding) Division on the 5th, the remainder of the Companies moving on the 8th.	
LUCHEUX.	7th to 28th.		The Companies were employed on a large Hutting and Bunking Scheme, the Scheme being to increase the accommodation in each area to hold one Division, the Companies were widely scattered; each Section living in a village and providing the necessary accommodation in that village before moving on elsewhere. The work was considerably held up by lack of transport and material, for instance, although several thousand sheets of Corrugated Iron were required, the first large supply was only obtained on the 18th. To keep pace with the work 27 lorries were required, but, although on the 17th 40 were obtained and on the 18th 23, only an average of 10 daily were forthcoming.

On the 14th, Captain R.G.W.H.STONE vacated the appointment of Adjutant R.E., 30th Division, on being appointed G.S.O. 3., 46th Division. On the 23rd, Lieutenant Colonel A.E.PANET, C.M.G., R.E., C.R.E. 30th Division, was appointed Chief Engineer, IInd ANZAC Corps. The vacancies thus caused were filled by Lieutenant O.D.ATKINSON, R.E., 201st Field Co. R.E., and Major G.W.DENISON, D.S.O., R.E., 68th Field Co. R.E., respectively.

On the 22nd the 201st Field Co. R.E. left the back area and moved up to ACHICOURT to start new work for the 30th Division who were about to take over half the line held by the 14th Division. Their work was taken over by 1 Section of the 200th Field Co. R.E. On the 28th the 200th Field Co. R.E. and 1 Section 202nd Field Co. R.E. attached came up into the new area to start work on Trench Mortar Emplacements. The whole of the work in the back area formerly done by all three Companies was then done by 3 Sections of 202nd Field Co. R.E. | |
| BERNEVILLE | 28th to 31st. | | Headquarters, R.E. moved to BERNEVILLE in the new area, in advance of Divisional Headquarters, on the 28th, the accommodation scheme then being handed over to Captain THORNLEY, Field Engineer VIIth Corps, under whose charge the 3 Sections of the 202nd Field Co. R.E. were left till the end of the month | |

Army Form C. 2118.

SHEET 2.

30TH DIVISIONAL ENGINEERS WAR DIARY VOL. 15. JANUARY, 1917.

INTELLIGENCE SUMMARY.

(Erase heading not required.)

Instructions regarding War Diaries and Intelligence Summaries are contained in F. S. Regs., Part II. and the Staff Manual respectively. Title pages will be prepared in manuscript.

Place	Date	Hour	Summary of Events and Information	Remarks and references to Appendices
BERNEVILLE	28th to 31st.		Work was carried on continuously from the 8th till the end of the month at the Divisional R.E. Workshops, LUCHEUX. The principle articles manufactured were horse troughs, and the saw was employed in cutting up timber into 3" x 2" for bunking, as the saw had only a 13" blade, and the timber was mostly 3", the output was limited to 6,000 ft. run a day, with the result that the Companies were held up by lack of 3" x 2" timber.	

4-2-1917.

[signature]

Lieut-Col.R.E.,
C.R.E., 30th Division.

SECRET

Original
Vol 16

Army Form C. 2118.

30TH DIVISIONAL ENGINEERS WAR DIARY VOL. 16. FEBRUARY, 1917.

Instructions regarding War Diaries and Intelligence
Summaries are contained in F. S. Regs., Part II.
and the Staff Manual respectively. Title pages
will be prepared in manuscript.

INTELLIGENCE SUMMARY.

(Erase heading not required.)

Place	Date	Hour	Summary of Events and Information	Remarks and references to Appendices

BERNEVILLE	1917. Feb. 1st to 28th.		Throughout the month Headquarters, R.E. remained at BERNEVILLE with Divisional Headquarters. Field Companies worked in Sectors of the Division front as follows:-
			     200th Field Company, R.E. : Southern Sector : 89th Infantry Bde. front;
			     202nd Field Company, R.E. : Northern Sector : 21st Infantry Bde. front.
			 The 201st Field Company was taken away from the Division to work under Chief Engineer, VIIth Corps on the 1st. Their work consisted entirely of repairing and extending a system of trench tramways (Decauville track).
			 The Officers Commanding the 200th and 202nd Field Companies were not arranging their work in consultation with the Brigadiers concerned, as had formerly been the custom, but the principle employed was that all technical troops were concentrated under the C.R.E. who was responsible for all work on the Divisional front. These technical troops comprised, in addition to the 200th and 202nd Field Companies, the 11th South Lancs (Pioneers), the 181st Tunnelling Company, R.E., 2 of whose Sections were for a short time removed from the Division, and "P" Company, No.4 Special Brigade, R.E.
			 The work was briefly as follows:-
			     200th Field Company was constructing : A Grenade Store;
			                                       A Brigade Dump;
			                                         A Row of Dug-outs for Orderlies;
			                                         A Divisional Bomb Store;
			                                         A Brigade Headquarters.
			     202nd Field Company " " " : Three Battalion Headquarters;
			                                         Three Aid Posts;
			                                         A Battalion Bomb Store;
			                                         A Brigade Bomb Store.
			 In addition to which these two Companies were between them constructing 50 Medium Trench Mortar Emplacements and 19 Heavy Trench Mortar Emplacements.
			 The 11th South Lancs were constructing:-
			 4 Dug-outs to serve as Advanced Dressing Stations, Collecting Station, and Aid Posts;
			 2 Battalion Headquarters.
			 They were also keeping the roads in repair and doing various other small works.
			 The 181st Tunnelling Company were constructing:-
			 4 Brigade Headquarters;
			 2 Battalion Headquarters;
			 2 Artillery Group Headquarters.	

Army Form C. 2118.

SHEET 2.

30TH DIVISIONAL ENGINEERS **WAR DIARY** VOL. 16. FEBRUARY, 1917.

INTELLIGENCE SUMMARY.

(Erase heading not required.)

Instructions regarding War Diaries and Intelligence Summaries are contained in F.S. Regs., Part II. and the Staff Manual respectively. Title pages will be prepared in manuscript.

Place	Date	Hour	Summary of Events and Information	Remarks and references to Appendices
continued:	1917.		"P" Company, No.4 Special Brigade, R.E., supplied working parties for the other Companies. The average working parties employed daily were about 1,000 men consisting of Infantry and Trench Mortar personnel.	
BERNEVILLE	Feb. 1st to 28th.		The work was somewhat held up at times owing to lack of transport particularly when the roads were closed owing to the thaw, but the supply of R.E. material throughout the month was good. Work was carried on continuously at the Divisional Workshops at LARBRET. The principle articles manufactured were Mining Frames and Trenchboards; a large number of Notice Boards, Stokes Mortar Bomb Carriers, and Pack Mule Water Carriers were also made up for the use of the Infantry.	

4th March, 1917.

[signature]

Lieut-Col. R.E.
C.R.E., 30th Division.

30TH DIVISIONAL ENGINEERS.

WAR DIARY.

VOLUME 17. MARCH, 1917.

SECRET

Army Form C. 2118.

30TH DIVISIONAL ENGINEERS WAR DIARY VOL.17. MARCH, 1917.

Instructions regarding War Diaries and Intelligence Summaries are contained in F. S. Regs., Part II. and the Staff Manual respectively. Title pages will be prepared in manuscript.

INTELLIGENCE-SUMMARY.

(Erase heading not required.)

Place	Date 1917.	Hour	Summary of Events and Information	Remarks and references to Appendices
BERNEVILLE	Mar. 1st to 24th.		The month of March was divided into two distinct parts. Up to and including the 17th, work continued as during last month, and preparations for an offensive from the AGNY Sectors were nearing completion. Further details of this work appear in Field Company diaries. Throughout this time, and a few days longer, Headquarters R.E. remained at BERNEVILLE with Divisional Headquarters. On the morning of the 18th, the enemy retired from our front, our troops occupying MERCATEL with posts that evening. During the day all work was stopped on preparations and Technical Troops were employed as follows:- 200th Field Co. and 202nd Field Co. at the disposal of G.O.C. 89th Infantry Bde., who employed them in making 4 Strong Points in the German front line system; 201st Field Co. and 11th South Lancs (Pioneers) on the opening up of the ARRAS-BUCQUOY and AGNY-BUCQUOY roads. On the 19th a small party of the 201st Field Co. went out to open up the Water Supply of MERCATEL. On the 21st and 22nd all Divisional Technical Troops (less Water party) were employed on the roads. The ARRAS-BUCQUOY road was open to wheel traffic on the evening of the 20th, and the road to MERCATEL on the evening of the 22nd. Throughout this time the 181st Tunnelling Company was employed on opening up old German dug-outs in the front and support lines. Several German "booby-traps", usually consisting of hand grenades connected to Helmets, Shovels, Trenchboards, etc., were found, but no casualties were caused by them, except for two men of the 181st Tunnelling Co. who were slightly wounded and returned to duty.	
BRETENCOURT.	24th to 31st.		On the 23rd. Field Coys. and 11th South Lancs moved to BLAIRVILLE, and on the 24th. H.Q.R.E. moved with Divisional Headquarters to BRETENCOURT. The work of preparation was started anew, as time was limited. Details of this work, and instructions issued from this Office will be forwarded with next month's War Diary. A great deal of work was entailed by the state of the roads. The Germans had blown large mines at all important cross-roads, and owing to the amount of heavy transport, and the previous hard and continuous frost followed by the thaw - the state of the roads was very bad indeed. The C.R.E. had under his charge for a considerable period 38 miles of road, most of this being a lorry route, and had only a limited amount of labour to put on it. No lorries for roadmetal were available but 8 G.S. wagons were. This did not go far, when the state of the roads is taken into consideration.	

Army Form C. 2118.

SHEET 2.

30TH DIVISIONAL ENGINEERS   WAR DIARY VOL.17. MARCH, 1917.

~~INTELLIGENCE~~ SUMMARY.

(Erase heading not required.)

Place	Date	Hour	Summary of Events and Information	Remarks and references to Appendices
BRETENCOURT. (contd:)	24th to 31st.		A good part of these roads was due to be taken over by the Transportation Department, but as the latter were short of labour, the C.R.E. had to continue to work on the whole of the former Divisional Road area till the end of the month. The supply of material throughout the first part of the month was satisfactory, but by the 18th the supply of timber was running low. When the new area was reached, timber was not needed in anything like such quantities, as very little mining was done, and large dumps of mining frames were found behind the old German front lines. The task of getting sufficient R.E. Stores forward to form forward battle dumps was rendered very difficult by the shortage of transport; on some days no lorries were available and generally only 3. Stores such as Sandbags, Screw pickets, etc., had to be brought from as far back as MONDICOURT, and on some occasions lorries had to be sent to SAVY. The help of 10 G.S. wagons from the D.A.C. was obtained for this purpose, and of 3 G.S. and 2 Limbered G.S. wagons from the 96th Field Ambulance. This eased the situation, but very careful organisation was needed to ensure that stores arrived by the required time. The Divisional workshops at LARBRET continued to turn out made up R.E. Stores throughout the month.	

5-4-1917.

Lieut-Col.R.E.
C.R.E., 30th Division.

HEADQUARTERS 30th DIVISIONAL ENGINEERS.

WAR DIARY

VOLUME 18   APRIL 1917.

SECRET   Original

Army Form C. 2118.

Instructions regarding War Diaries and Intelligence   **WAR DIARY**
Summaries are contained in F.S. Regs., Part II.   30TH DIVISIONAL ENGINEERS.   VOL. 18.   APRIL 1917.
and the Staff Manual respectively. Title pages   INTELLIGENCE SUMMARY.
will be prepared in manuscript.   (Erase heading not required.)

Ref. Map. 51.b.s.w.

Place	Date 1917.	Hour	Summary of Events and Information	Remarks and references to Appendices
BRETEN-COURT.	April. 8th.		On 1.4.17. the C.R.E's Headquarters was still with Divisional Headquarters at BRETENCOURT, the work of preparation was continued, and instructions had been received that the work had to be completed by the 6th of April. The C.R.E. held a Conference of Field Company Commanders and issued verbal instructions as to the work of preparation to be undertaken by each Company, giving each Company Commander a copy of the assembly map for this purpose. The chief points of interest were; Headquarters for 3 Brigades and 4 Artillery Groups in the Railway cutting at S.3.a. and d. which were constructed by 200th Field Co. and a new communication trench from S.4.d.5.5. to S.5.c.10.5. which was constructed by 201st Field Coy. Each Company had its proportion of the remaining work which consisted of the construction of Battalion Headquarters, Grenade Dumps, R.E. Stores Dumps and Medical Collecting Stations. On the 2nd of April an amendment (Appendix A.1.) was issued to the "Arrangements for R.E. Stores" (Appendix A.) which had been issued on the 11th March. This amendment was necessitated by the enemy retirement. On the 4th instructions for work on "Z" day were issued to all technical troops. See attached Appendix B. On the 8th C.R.E's Headquarters moved with Advanced Divisional Headquarters to BLAIRVILLE QUARRY. An account of the work carried out by the technical troops from the 8th to 12th April is attached (Appendix C.).	
BLAIRVILLE	8th.			
POMMIER.	12th.		On the 12th the 30th Division was taken out of the line, and the C.R.E's Headquarters moved with Divisional Headquarters to POMMIER.	
ACHICOURT.	19th.		Technical troops were all employed at training until the 19th, when the 30th Division again went into the line, Headquarters being at ACHICOURT. On the 21st instructions for work of technical troops on the 23rd were issued (Appendix D). An account of the operations of technical troops between the 19th and 29th is attached (Appendix E.).	
NEUVILLE VITASSE.	25th.		On the 25th the C.R.E's Headquarters moved with Advanced Divisional Headquarters to M.18.d.central near NEUVILLE VITASSE. These Headquarters had been constructed by 1 section of 202nd Field Co. with 1 section 200th Field Co. and 1 Platoon 11th South Lancs. helping.	

P.T.O.

Army Form C. 2118.

WAR DIARY

SHEET 2.

INTELLIGENCE SUMMARY

(Erase heading not required.)

Instructions regarding War Diaries and Intelligence Summaries are contained in F. S. Regs., Part II. and the Staff Manual respectively. Title pages will be prepared in manuscript.

Place	Date	Hour	Summary of Events and Information	Remarks and references to Appendices
ROELLE-COURT.	April 1917 30th.		On the 30th the Division was again relieved, and Headquarters moved to ROELLECOURT. After the 19th April, the Divisional R.E. Park at LARBRET was too far away from the line to be of any great value, but a dump had been started at NEUVILLE VITASSE by the 56th Division, and was of sufficient size to meet the demand for stores. It was supplied by lorries working from the VII Corps Advanced R.E. Depot at DAINVILLE. On the 28th an Advanced Divisional Dump was started at HENINEL. Men were still kept at the Divisional Workshops at LARBRET and were chiefly employed in making petrol tin carriers for mule transport. A short account of the employment of R.E. and Pioneers during the German Retirement from the 18th to the 22nd of March, is attached (Appendix F.).	
	5-5-17.			

C.R.E., 30th Division.
Lieut-Col. R.E.

Appendix A.

SECRET

ARRANGEMENTS FOR R.E. STORES.

The following arrangements are suggested for the provision of R.E. Stores in an Offensive.

1. Stores will be required in the following categories:
    (i) Stores to be carried by the Infantry in the attack;
    (ii) Battalion Dumps;
    (iii) Field Company (Brigade) Dumps;
    (iv) The stores that will be required by specially detailed working parties within the first 24 hours.

As regards (i); The stores required will be 3 Sandbags, and either a Pick or Shovel for each man.

The proportion of Picks to Shovels that will be required will be in accordance with the wishes of the Brigadiers.

These will be issued as follows, a short time before the attack, on receipt of orders from 30th Division:

    21st Infantry Bde. issued by 202nd Field Coy. R.E.
    89th Infantry Bde.   "   " 200th Field Coy. R.E.
    90th Infantry Bde.   "   " 30th Divl. R.E. Park, LABERET.

Allowing an average of 650 men per Battalion in the attack, the following will be set aside at once for each Brigade, and issued when orders are received as above:-
    8,000 Sandbags;
    2,600 Picks or Shovels G.S.

As regards (ii); It is proposed to issue the following stores to each of the Battalion Dumps in the 21st and 89th Inf. Bdes.

    Sandbags   6,000   (These are most conveniently done up in bundles of 30).
    Screw Pickets - Medium 300
       "   "   - Short 300   (Each Btn. will have about 300x of front, allowing 4 Btns. in line).
    French Wire   30 coils.
    Shovels G.S.   150
    Picks   150
    Barbed Wire   150 rolls.

These Stores will be set aside and issued as in (i).

As regards (iii); It is not proposed to have an advanced Divisional Dump, but the 200th, 201st and 202nd Field Companies will each have large Dumps in AGNY, situated at M.8.b.6.3, M.8.b.4.0, and M.8.b.8.1, respectively.

The Forward Corps Dump is at AGNY CHATEAU. Any of these Company Dumps will issue stores to any Brigade or Battery on indent after Zero. The stores held at these three Dumps are shewn on Table "A" attached for 200th Field Coy, and Table "B" for 201st and 202nd Field Coys.

Owing to the closing of the roads, it will not be possible to send convoys of wagons to improvised Dumps, as far forward as possible, as was done last year. It remains to be decided as to how the stores will be carried forward from these Dumps.

Field Companies will have separate Dumps at the same spots, containing stores such as Explosives, Timber, etc., that they will require for their own use.

As to (iv); It is not yet possible to give exact figures.

2./

2. Parapet Ladders and Trench Bridges will be issued to Brigades from R.E. Park, LARBRET. Hedging Gloves and Wire Cutters that will be required to be carried on the men attacking will also be issued from R.E. Park, LARBRET. The number that will be required for each Brigade will be :-

    300 prs. Hedging Gloves
    500 " Wire Cutters, Mark V.
    200 " Long-handled Wire Cutters (a G.S. supply).

3. The Tools and Stores for the 11th Bn. South Lancs will be dealt with in the same way as for Field Companies.

4. In order to bring up the complement of Picks, Shovels and Wire Cutters to the numbers above, it is presumed that Trench Stores will be used, but not Mobilization Store Equipment.

5. In order to facilitate the delivery of the Tools at the Forward Dumps, it would be a great help if Brigades and Field Companies would let me know how many of each they have on their charge.

6. Field Companies and Officer i/c. R.E. Park will report, as soon as the Stores above are ready for issue.

                                                    Lieut-Col.R.E.
11-3-1917.   C.R.E., 30th Division.

Copies to:)

    Headquarters, 30th Division "G".
    Headquarters, 30th Division "Q".
    C.R.A.
    Headquarters, 89th Infantry Brigade.
    Headquarters, 90th Infantry Brigade.
    Headquarters, 21st Infantry Brigade.
    Chief Engineer, VIIth Corps.
    O.C. 200th Field Co. R.E.
    O.C. 201st Field Co. R.E.
    O.C. 202nd Field Co. R.E.
    O.C. 30th Divl. Signal Co. R.E.
    O.C. 11th Bn. South Lancs Regt.
    Officer i/c. 30th Divl. R.E. Park.

TABLE "A".

Sandbags	50,000
Barbed Wire, rolls	500
Plain Wire, rolls	25
French Wire, rolls	200
Screw Pickets, medium	2,500
" " short	2,500
Picks	1,000
Shovels	1,000
Hedging Gloves) Wire Cutters)	as available.

....

TABLE "B".

Sandbags	25,000
Barbed Wire, rolls	250
Plain Wire, rolls	13
French Wire, rolls	100
Screw Pickets, medium	1,500
" " short	1,500
Picks	500
Shovels	500
Hedging Gloves) Wire Cutters)	as available.

....

O.C. 200th Field Co. R.E.
O.C. 201st Field Co. R.E.
O.C. 202nd Field Co. R.E.
Lieut. LINDSAY, R.E.
----

1. In addition to the forward Battle dumps of R.E. Stores that are in process of formation, there will be an advanced Divisional dump of R.E. Stores at BLAIRVILLE.

2. It will be located at the site at present held by the 202nd Field Company, R.E. dump, and will be managed by Corporal LAWSON, 202nd Field Company, R.E., and 8 men (as loaders) from the Divisional dump, LARBRET.

3. Its primary purpose will be to refill the advanced dumps, and stores for this purpose can be drawn without indenting on this Office, but it will also contain a small amount of timber, nails, etc., for use by Field Companies, which can be drawn on indent to the C.R.E. at Advanced Divisional Headquarters.

4. The method of refilling the advanced dumps cannot as yet be decided, but for the first few days, at any rate, the onus of keeping the advanced dumps full will fall on the Companies, under whose charge the advanced dumps are.
This may be altered, either

(i) when other transport is available;
or (ii) when the roads are open to lorries.

5. It cannot be definitely said what Stores will be available at the Advanced Divisional dump, but generally speaking it will contain all the Stores that there will be sufficient transport to carry up to BLAIRVILLE after the Field Company dumps have been filled.

6. All spare Stores - particularly tools - that are surplus to requirements, or are salved, should be dumped at this spot by Companies.

7. Corporal LAWSON and the 8 men will arrive at BLAIRVILLE on the evening of the 4th, and will start to form the dump. He will be rationed from Headquarters, R.E.,

8. A Stock Sheet of materials that it has been possible to collect at Advanced Divl. R.E. Dump, will be issued to Companies before Z day.

202 only { Will you kindly arrange with Town Major, BLAIRVILLE, for the billeting of these men on the site of the dump.

2-4-1917.

Captain. R.E.
Adjt. R.E., 30th Division.

SECRET.

Appendix. B.

COPY NO: 13

4th April, 1917.

Copy of the undermentioned instructions to Technical Troops forwarded for information.

1. Table of Disposition of R.E. and Pioneers.
2. Instructions to O.C. 200th Field Co. R.E.
3. do. do. 201st do. do.
4. do. do. 202nd do. do.
5. do. do. 11th South Lancs (Pioneers).
6. do. as to Issue of R.E. Stores.
7. do. in reference to Roads.
8. do. do. Water Supply.

G. W. Davison
Lieut-Col. R.E.
C.R.E., 30th Division.

Copy No. 1 O.C. 200th Field Coy. R.E.
" " 2 O.C. 201st Field Coy. R.E.
" " 3 O.C. 202nd Field Coy. R.E.
" " 4 O.C. 11th Bn. South Lancs.
" " 5 Headquarters, 30th Division G.
" " 6 Headquarters, 30th Division Q.
" " 7 Headquarters, 89th Infantry Bde.
" " 8 Headquarters, 90th Infantry Bde.
" " 9 Headquarters, 21st Infantry Bde.
" " 10 C.R.A.
" " 11 Chief Engineer, VIIth Corps.
" " 12 War Diary.
" " 13
" " 14 File.

Appendix 'A'.

Distribution of R.E. and Pioneers.

Affiliation.	Strength of Parties.	Place of Assembly.	Objective.	Remarks.
	1. STRONG POINT PARTIES:			
88th Brigade:	(a) 1 Section 2OOth Field Co. R.E. 2 Platoons Infantry.	In trenches in M.6.d. and M.7.b	To clear Strong Points at M.29.b.4.6. and M.24.c.6.5.	
	(b) 1 Section 2OOth Field Co. R.E. 1 Platoon Infantry.	In trenches in M.6.d. and M.7.b.	Defence of north and east face of station.	
31st Brigade:	(c) 1 Section 9Ord Field Co. R.E. 2 Platoons Infantry.	In trenches in M.20.a and c.	To clear Strong Points at M.24.b.2.1 and M.18.d.4.1.	
	(d) 1 Section 9Ord Field Co. R.E. 1 Platoon Infantry.	In trenches in M.20.a and c.	Defence of north and east face of JACQUET.	
	2. WATER SUPPLY PARTY:			
31st Brigade	(a) 1 Section 9Ord Field Co. R.E.	In trenches in M.20.a and c.	To clear up water supply in JACQUET.	
	3. BRIDGE PARTY:			
88th Brigade:	(a) 1 Section 2OOth Field Co. R.E.	In trenches in M.6.d. and M.7.b.	To bridge the River OURCQ III at points A and B.	Primarily at bridge.
	4. ROADS PARTIES:			
Division:	(a) 1 Company 11th Railway Pioneers.	To make it M.6.d. and M.7.b.	To repair roads leading to the HILL-JACQUET ROAD, and which are used for wheel traffic.	
	(b) 1 Company 11th Railway Pioneers.	In trenches in M.6.d. and c.	To repair roads leading to the MAMELON-OURCQ ROAD and for wheel traffic.	

Appendix 'D'.

DISPOSITION OF R.E. AND PIONEERS.

Affiliation.	Strength of parties.	Place of Assembly.	Objective.	Remarks.
continued:				
	4. DIVISIONAL RESERVE:			
	H.Q. and 1 Section 200th Fd.Co.R.E.	In trenches in S.1.d. and S.7.b.		
	" " 4 " 201st " "	In trenches in M.20.a and d.		
	" " 4 " 202nd " "	In trenches in M.20.a and d.		
	" " 2 Companies 11th S.Lancs.	In trenches in M.26.a and c.		
NOTE:	All parties will move under orders from C.R.E., 30th Division.			

4-4-1917.

G.W. Dawson
Lieut-Col. R.E.
C.R.E., 30th Division.

INSTRUCTIONS TO O.C. 200th FIELD COY.R.E.

1. You will be responsible for detailing the following parties and seeing that they are in their places of assembly by midnight Z - 1/2.

2. You will also be responsible for making the necessary arrangement for the tools and stores required by following parties in order to carry out work detailed in Appendix 'B' attached.

(a) STRONG POINT PARTIES: 2 Sections 200th Field Co. R.E.
(3 Platoons Infantry).

(b) BRIDGING PARTY: 1 Section 200th Field Co. R.E.

(c) ADVANCED R.E. DUMP PARTY:
1 R.E. N.C.O.
2 Infantry (to be found by E........)
1/c your advanced dump.

3. You will have your trestle wagon packed, with one Weldon trestle and sufficient superstructure for 30' bridge, and have it moved up to HABLE on the right of Z - 2/Z - 1 day ready to move on to HABLEN when ordered.

4. You will be responsible for the filling of your advanced R.E. Dump at S.12.a./.7 by 6 a.m. Z - 2 day, and the replenishing of it afterwards from Advanced Divisional Dump, HABLEN. Transport is not to use the roads without reference to this Office.

5. You will receive direct orders from me when to move parties out.

G. W. Davidson
Lieut-Col.R.E.
C.R.E., 30th Division.

4/4/1917.

INSTRUCTIONS TO O.C. 201st FIELD COY. R.E.

1. You will see that your Company is at its place of assembly by midnight 2 - 1/2.

2. You will not move without my orders.

G. W. Denison
Lieut-Col. R.E.
C.R.E., 30th Division.

4/4/1917.

INSTRUCTIONS TO O.C. 202nd FIELD COY. R.E.

1. You will be responsible for detailing the following parties and seeing that they are in their places of assembly by midnight Z - 1/2.

2. You will also be responsible for making the necessary arrangement for the tools and stores required by the following parties in order to carry out work detailed in Appendix 'B' attached.

   (a) STRONG POINT PARTIES: 2 Sections 202nd Field Co. R.E.
                                       (3 Platoons Infantry).

   (b) WATER PARTY: 1 Section 202nd Field Co. R.E.

   (c) ADVANCED R.E. DUMP PARTY:
                              1 R.E. N.C.O.,
                              2 Infantry (to be found by H.Q.R.E.) i/c your advanced dump.

3. You will be responsible for the filling of your Advanced R.E. Dump at M.35.d.3.6, by 8 am. on Z - 2 day, and the replenishing of it afterwards from Advanced Divisional Dump, BLAIREVILLE. Transport is not to use the roads without reference to this Office.

4. You will receive direct orders from me when to move parties out.

                                                       G. W. Denison
                                                          Lieut-Col. R.E.
4/4/1917.   C.R.E., 30th Division.

INSTRUCTIONS TO THE O.C. 11TH SOUTH LANCS
PIONEERS.

1. You will assemble your Battalion as follows;

   H.Q. and 3 Coys in trenches at M.20.a.and b. 1 Coy. in trenches at B.1.d. and B.7.b.

   The whole to be at their places of assembly by midnight Z - 1/2.

2. You will detail the following parties;

   (a) One Company on preparing MERCATEL - NEUVILLE VITASSE - WANCOURT road for wheel traffic.

   (b) One Company on preparing HENIN - ST.MARTIN - HENINEL - WANCOURT road and HENIN - N.27.b. - N.22.c. - WANCOURT road for wheel traffic.

3. You will receive direct orders from me when to move parties out.

G. W. Davison
Lieut-Col. R.E.
C.R.E., 50th Division.

4/4/1917.

ARRANGEMENTS FOR PROVISION OF R.E. STORES DURING ACTIVE OPERATIONS.

The following are the arrangements for R.E. Stores during the offensive in continuation of, and in amendment to, the "Arrangements for R.E. Stores" issued from this Office on the 11th of March.

1. Tools will be issued to Brigades for the purpose of being carried by the Infantry in the attack as follows :-

Issued to	21st Inf. Bde.	89th Inf. Bde.	90th Inf. Bde.
Issued by	200nd Field Co. R.E.	206th Field Co. R.E.	30th Div. …
at	MARICHEL	MARICHEL	…
Shovels G.S.	1250	1250	1250
Picks	650	650	650
Sandbags	6000	6000	6000

2. There will be no Battalion dumps, but there will be 2 advanced Field Company dumps as follows :-

  200th Field Co.R.E. will have an advanced dump at S.12.d.4.7.
  92nd Field Co. R.E. will have an advanced dump at M.35.t.d.6.

A table of the Stores held at these dumps is subjoined.
Stores will be issued from them, on receipt, to any unit.

3. Wirecutters and Hedging Gloves are now a General Staff supply, and will be issued under a separate arrangement (see 30th Divn: S/601 of 31-3-17).

4. There will be an advanced Divisional dump at MARICHEL whose purpose will be to refill the advanced Field Company dumps.

5. The Divisional Artillery are being issued Sandbags at the rate of 500 per gun from 30th Divl. R.E. Park, L——.

Table of Stores held at R.E. Dump at M.35.t.d.6. and S.12.d.4.7.

    Sandbags   : 50,000
    Barbed wire rolls   :   500
    Plain Wire   "   :   25
    French Wire   "   :   200 (or as available).
    Screw pickets   :   3,000 (in proportion of long, medium
                                     and short that are available).
    Picks   :   1,000
    Shovels   :   1,000

J.H.Dawson
Lieut-Col. R.E.
C.R.E., 30th Division.

4-/4/1917.

R O A D S

The following roads will be prepared for wheel traffic:-

(a) From MERCATEL through NEUVILLE-VITASSE to WANCOURT;

(b) From HENIN through ST.MARTIN through HENINEL to WANCOURT;

(c) From HENIN through N.27.b. through N.28.a. to WANCOURT.

Two Companies of 11th South Lancs Pioneers will be employed on this work, one Company on (a), one Company on (b) and (c).

4/4/1917.

                        Lieut-Col, R.E.
                    C.R.E., 30th Division.

WATER SUPPLY.

One Section from 202nd Field Company, R.E. will open up wells in WANCOURT.

The COJEUL River will give a plentiful supply of water and flows from our lines towards the enemy.

4/4/17.

                      Lieut-Col, R.E.
                    C.R.E. 30th Division.

S E C R E T

2124/1.

In reference to Table of Disposition of R.E. and Pioneers forwarded under this Office No.2124 dated 4th April, 1917, the Assembly place for all Technical Troops and attached 6 Platoons Infantry will now be BLAIREVILLE and not in trenches at M.1 d. and M.20 a & c.

[signature]

Lieut.Col., R.E.
6th April, 1917.　　　　　　　　　　C.R.E.30th Division.

Copy to recipients of C.R.E. No. 2124 d/- 4.4.17.

Appendix C.

REPORT ON WORK CARRIED OUT BY THE TECHNICAL TROOPS DURING
OPERATIONS FROM 8TH TO 12th APRIL 1917.

8.4.17.   During the afternoon of 8th April the three Field Coys. were employed on training in making Strong Points, rapid wiring and bridge building. The 11th South Lancs. (Pioneers) were repairing roads East of FICHEUX. Six platoons of the 17th Manchesters joined the Field Coys. on this date, three to the 200th Field Co. and three to the 202nd Field Co. to assist the Field Coys. in making Strong Points.

The Headquarters, 30th Division R.E. moved from RIVIERE to BLAIRVILLE QUARRY.

9.4.17.   At 10.30 a.m. on 9th April one company of 11th South Lancs Pioneers was sent out to clear the MERCATEL – NEUVILLE VITASSE road. They worked on this road all the afternoon and nearly all night and by 3 a.m. 10.4.17 this road was clear for horse transport as far as NEUVILLE VITASSE.

9.4.17.   At 12.30 p.m. a party of 1 N.C.O. and 6 Sappers from 200th Field Co. was sent to repair bridge over trench at S.4.d.1.5; this was done and party returned to their billets same night.

At 12.45 p.m. two officers of the 11th South Lancs were sent to reconnoitre the ARRAS – BAPAUME road inside our Divisional area. This was done and copies of report sent to Headquarters 30th Division and to C.E. VII Corps.

At 2.50 p.m. one company of 11th South Lancs was sent out to clear the HENIN – ST MARTIN road for horse transport. They worked on this road all night, being relieved on the morning of 10.4.17 by another company of the same battalion.

At 2.50 p.m. two sections of 200th Field Co.R.E. and three platoons of 17th Manchesters were sent out to construct Strong Points at N.29.b.4.6. and N.24.c.6.3.and to consolidate the East face of HENINEL, also one section of 200th Field Co.R.E. to construct bridges over the COJUEL River S.W. HENINEL and S.W. of WANCOURT. Two Sections of 202nd Field Co.R.E. and three platoons of 17th Manchesters were sent out to construct Strong Points at N.24.b.2.1. and N.18.d.4.1. and to consolidate the East face of WANCOURT, also one section of 202nd Field Co.R.E. to open up water supply in WANCOURT.

As the above objectives were still in the hands of the enemy orders were sent at 9.5 p.m. for above parties to assist Infantry in the firing line to consolidate the positions they were then holding in front of HINDENBURG Line; 200th Field Co. to assist the 89th Infantry Brigade and 202nd Field Co. the 90th Infantry Brigade. As 200th Field Coy's assistance was not required by 89th Infantry Brigade it was used to help the 90th Infantry Brigade as well as 202nd Field Co. in consolidating a line from N.20.c.6.1. through N.26.c.7.1. to N.27.c.1.5. This work was completed about dawn on the 10.4.17 when the above parties returned to their billets.

10.4.17.

2.

10.4.17. Two companies of 11th South Lancs Pioneers were employed all day on opening up the MERCATEL - NEUVILLE VITASSE and the HENIN - ST MARTIN Roads being relieved in the evening by two other companies of the same battalion who worked on these roads all night. The MERCATEL - NEUVILLE VITASSE Road was open and used by motor lorries on night of 10th/11th. The HENIN - ST MARTIN Road was open for horse transport by morning of 11th.

As 2.30 p.m. the whole of 201st Field Co.R.E. and one section of 200th Field Co.R.E. were sent out to consolidate the East face of HAEN HENINEL and to make a Strong Point at N.29.c.6.6. Arrangements were made for three platoons of Infantry from 90th Infantry Brigade to meet above parties at S.12.a.0.5 to assist in above work. At 9.30 p.m.(as the attack on HENINEL was postponed until the morning of the 11th) the O.C.201st Field Co.R.E. sent the attached three platoons back to their own battalion and employed his company and the one section of 200th Field Co.R.E. on repair of the roads in HENIN and ST.MARTIN.

11.4.17 Two companies of the 11th South Lancs Pioneers were employed all day on repair of the FICHEUX - MERCATEL - NEUVILLE VITASSE and FICHEUX - BOILLEUX AU MONT - BOIRY BECQUERELLE - HENIN - ST MARTIN Roads which owing to the very bad weather and very heavy traffic were in a bad condition. These two companies were relieved by two other companies of the same battalion who worked on the above roads all night of 11th/12th.

At 3.15 p.m. the whole of 202nd Field Co.R.E. and three sections of 200th Field Co. R.E. were sent out to work on roads in and to east of HENIN. They worked all night returning to their billets about dawn of morning of 12th.

At 6. p.m. orders were sent to O.C.201st Field Co.R.E. to move his Company to the BAILLEULMONT-BASSEUX area. This Company moved out from BLAIRVILLE about midnight.

Two Field Coys. of the 33rd Division were met on evening of 11th at BLAIRVILLE and guided to their billets.

12.4.17 Two Companies of 11th South Lancs Pioneers (less two platoons) were employed in the morning on repair of roads in Divisional area East of FICHEUX.

At 9 a.m. one section of 200th Field Co.R.E. and two platoons of 11th South Lancs Pioneers went out to construct three Strong Points in the Support line of the HINDENBURG Line. Strong Points were constructed by above parties at N.27.b.95.45 - N.28.c.45.65 - and N.28.d.25.40.

At 9.50 a.m. orders were sent to O.C.202nd Field Co.R.E. to move to the BAILLEULMONT-BASSEUX area.

At 4.p.m. Headquarters 30th Divisional R.E. handed over to Headquarters 33rd Divisional R.E. and left BLAIRVILLE QUARRY for POMMIER.

Lieut.Col., R.E.
C.R.E.30th Division.

13.4.17.

SECRET

Appendix D.

ORDERS BY C.R.E., 30TH DIVISION.   Copy No. 10

(On 30th Divn. Operation Order No.79. para.4.)

1. Two Sections of 202nd Field Co. R.E. will assist the 90th Infantry Brigade to consolidate German front system. They will be attached to and take their orders from G.O.C. 90th Brigade. O.C. 202nd Field Co. will arrange place of assembly of these sections with 90th Brigade H.Q.

2. The whole of 201st Field Co. R.E. and four platoons Infantry from 21st Brigade will construct strong points at:-
   O.31.a.2.5.
   O.31.a.9.9.
   O.25.d.4.5.
   O.25.b.8.0.

3. 201st Field Co. and attached four platoons infantry will assemble in the HINDENBURG LINE North of River COJEUL in N.28.c.

4. O.C. 201st Field Co. R.E. will keep in close touch with 90th Brigade H.Q. and will send officers forward to reconnoitre the position as soon as the situation admits but will not commence work until dusk.

5. C.R.E's Headquarters will remain at ACHICOURT.

21-4-17.

Lieut-Col. R.E.
C.R.E., 30th Division.

Copy No. 1. to 30th Divn G.
"   "   2. " O.C.200th Field Co. R.E.
"   "   3. " O.C.201st Field Co. R.E.
"   "   4. " O.C.202nd Field Co. R.E.
"   "   5. " Headquarters 21st Infy. Bde.
"   "   6. " Headquarters 89th Infy. Bde.
"   "   7. " Headquarters 90th Infy. Bde.
"   "   8. " File.
"   "   9. " War Diary.
"   " 10. " War Diary.

Appendix. E.

Report on Operations of Technical Troops
from 19-4-1917 to 29-4-1917.

Technical Troops of 30th Division moved from rest area to forward area and were located as follows :-

Headquarters, 30th Divl. R.E.	: ACHICOURT;
200th Field Coy. R.E.	: BEAURAINS;
201st Field Coy. R.E.	: NEUVILLE VITASSE;
202nd Field Coy. R.E.	: BEAURAINS;
11th South Lancs (Pioneers)	: NEUVILLE VITASSE.

20-4-17.   Field Companies and Pioneers were employed on repair of roads between NEUVILLE VITASSE and HENINEL.

21-4-17.   Dressing Station in NEUVILLE VITASSE and shelters for Brigade Headquarters at N.29.c.6.4. were taken in hand by 201st Field Coy. R.E.
    200th Field Coy, 202nd Field Coy and Pioneers were employed on roads.
    On morning of 21-4-17 a reconnaissance was made for a line of posts and Machine Gun emplacements to West and North-West of HENINEL and report was submitted to Headquarters, 30th Division on evening of 21-4-1917, (this line was called the Corps Defence Line).

22-4-1917.   202nd Field Coy. R.E. commenced work on Corps Defence Line of five posts and three Machine Gun emplacements, and on Advanced Divl. H.Q.
    201st Field Coy. R.E. was employed on Dressing Station, shelters for Brigade Headquarters and the construction of two bridges over the River COJEUL, one at HENINEL and the other East of HENINEL.
    200th Field Coy. R.E. and Pioneers were employed on roads and crossings of River COJEUL at HENINEL.

23-4-17.   At 4.00am. two Sections from 202nd Field Coy. R.E. were assembled at N.28.b.5.6 with orders to assist 90th Brigade to consolidate the German front system. Shortly after the Infantry advanced Lieutenants SEARLE and CAMPBELL went forward to reconnoitre, but unfortunately Lieut. SEARLE, R.E. was killed and Lieut. CAMPBELL, R.E. was severely wounded. As the attack was only partially successfull these two Sections were not employed, and at 7-30pm.(at the request of OC. 202nd Field Coy. R.E.) I relieved these two Sections with two Sections from 200th Field Coy.R.E.
    The whole of 201st Field Coy. R.E. and 4 Platoons of Infantry from 21st Infantry Bde: were ordered to assemble in HINDENBURG LINE just North of River COJEUL ready to move out and construct four Strong points on the Blue line at 0.31.a.2.5, 0.31.a.9.9, 0.25.d.4.5, 0.25.b.8.0.,
    As the Blue line was not captured on this day 201st Field Company and the two Sections of 200th Field Company returned to NEUVILLE VITASSE and the 4 Platoons Infantry rejoined their own Battalions in the early morning of 24-4-1917.
    One Section of 202nd Field Coy. R.E. was employed on Corps Defence Line and one Section of 202nd Field Coy. on Divl. H.Q.

About/

About 8-30pm. on 23-4-17 I was instructed by G.S.O.1 to send troops out and occupy the Corps Defence Line, this I did with six Platoons of the 11th South Lancs (Pioneers) who remained there until relieved by Infantry next day.

The Pioneers were employed on roads except two Platoons on Divisional H.Q.

24-4-17.

One Section of 202nd Field Coy. R.E. was employed on Corps Defence Line, and one Section on Divisional H.Q.

One Section of 200th Field Coy. R.E. was employed on Divisional H.Q., and one Section on Brigade H.Q., and two Sections on helping Infantry to consolidate the German front line system which was carried out successfully.

The whole of 201st Field Coy. R.E. and four Platoons Infantry were sent out on afternoon of 24-4-17 to construct the four Strong Points on the Blue line. They worked the whole night of 24th/25th and completed the works, and they were garrisoned on the early morning of the 25th by the Infantry holding the line.

The Pioneers were employed on roads especially those East and South of the River COJEUL between HENINEL and CHERISY. The Corps Defence Line was completed on morning of 24-4-1917.

25-4-17.
to
28-4-17.

The Field Companies were employed on Roads, Dressing Stations, Shelters and Divisional H.Q.
The Pioneers on Roads.

29-4-17.

Handed over to the C.R.E. 18th Division.

200th Field Coy.R.E. carried out the consolidation of the German front system very successfully, they also did good work on the roads and crossings of the River COJEUL at HENINEL.

201st Field Coy.R.E. carried out the construction of the Strong Points on the Blue line very successfully.

202nd Field Coy.R.E. completed the Corps Defence Line and the construction of Divisional H.Q. very quickly and very satisfactorily.

The 11th South Lancs (Pioneers) did very important work on the roads under heavy shell-fire. The Officers of this Battalion also carried out some very useful road reconnaissance. The six Platoons which went out to occupy the Corps Defence Line on the night of 23-4-17 had already worked all day on roads but went out when called upon to defend the line with cheerfulness and without a murmur and worked on this line all night.

Lieut-Col.R.E.
C.R.E. 30th Division.

30-4-1917.

SHORT ACCOUNT OF EMPLOYMENT OF R.E. AND PIONEERS DURING PAST OPERATIONS 18TH MARCH to 22ND MARCH, 1917.

18th March, 1917.

On the morning of the 18th March I received word that the Germans had retired from our front South-East of AGNY, I at once withdrew all R.E. and Pioneers from work on Dug-outs, etc., and distributed them as follows:-
200th Field Co. and 202nd Field Co. at the disposal of G.O.C. 89th Infantry Brigade;
201st Field Co. and 11th South Lancs (Pioneers) on opening up the ARRAS-BUCQUOY and AGNY-BUCQUOY roads for wheel traffic.

19th March, 1917.

200th Field Co. and 202nd Field Co. were employed under orders of G.O.C. 89th Infantry Brigade on making four Strong Points in German front line system about M.15.c and d. and M.16.a I sent a small party from 201st Field Co. to look for and open out water supply in MERCATEL. The remainder of 201st Field Co. and the whole of the 11th Bn. South Lancs (Pioneers) were employed on opening up roads. In the evening the 200th Field Co.R.E. and 202nd Field Co. R.E. were again put under my orders

20th March, 1917.

Whole of the Technical Troops (except water party) employed on roads as follows:-
200th Field Co. and 11th South Lancs (Pioneers) on ARRAS-BUCQUOY, AGNY-BUCQUOY, CHAT MAIGRE-MERCATEL roads;
201st Field Co. (less water party) on ARRAS-BUCQUOY road in M.27.a and c.
Small party from 201st Field Co. on opening up water supply in MERCATEL.
202nd Field Co. on clearing road at broken railway bridge at M.21.c.7.3.

21st and 22nd March, 1917.

Field Companies and Pioneers employed on roads, except small water party and a small party helping infantry to build shelter for Battalion Headquarters.
From the 18th to 22nd March the one Section, 181st Tunnelling Company, R.E., was employed on opening out old German dug-outs in old front and support lines.

The ARRAS-BUCQUOY road was open for wheel traffic on the evening of the 20th March, and road to MERCATEL on the evening of the 22nd.
All wells in MERCATEL had been destroyed, also ponds. Three ponds were opened out and made available for watering horses. We were unsuccessful in getting any good water for drinking purposes and the attempt was abandoned. Good water was obtainable from the River COJEUL.

4-4-1917.

Lieut-Col. R.E.
C.R.E., 30th Division.

HEADQUARTERS, 30TH DIVISIONAL ENGINEERS.

WAR DIARY.

VOLUME 19.   MAY 1917.

SECRET

Original

Army Form C. 2118.

HEADQUARTERS, WAR DIARY VOL. 19. MAY 1917.
30TH DIVISIONAL ENGINEERS.
INTELLIGENCE SUMMARY.

(Erase heading not required.)

Instructions regarding War Diaries and Intelligence Summaries are contained in F. S. Regs., Part II. and the Staff Manual respectively. Title pages will be prepared in manuscript.

Place	Date	Hour	Summary of Events and Information	Remarks and references to Appendices
ROELLECOURT	1-5-17.		Throughout the month, up to the 22nd May, the Division was training in a back area, the Field Companies training under their own arrangements, which appear in the Field Company War Diaries.	
			On the 21st the Division started marching northwards with a view to occupying the HOOGE Sector. Headquarters R.E. moved with Divisional Headquarters as follows:-	
			3-5-17, ROELLECOURT to OEUF. 15-5-17, OEUF to WILLEMAN. 21-5-17, WILLEMAN to PERNES. 22-5-17, PERNES to NORRENT FONTES. 24-5-17, NORRENT FONTES to STEENBECQUE. 25-5-17, STEENBECQUE to CAESTRE. 26-5-17, CAESTRE to WATOU. 30-5-17, WATOU to BRANDHOEK.	
			The Divisional Workshops remained at LARBRET throughout the month, the number of men employed being considerably reduced. On the 1st, 20 attached Infantry were returned to their units, leaving the R.S.M. and 46 men at the dump.	
			This party was employed in making Pack Mule Water Carriers, and in doing work for the 18th Division, which had taken over the 30th Division's line.	
	4-6-17.			

Lieut-Col. R.E.
C.R.E., 30th Division.

HEADQUARTERS
30TH DIVISIONAL ENGINEERS.

WAR DIARY.

VOLUME 20.   JUNE 1917.

SECRET.

Army Form C. 2118.

HEADQUARTERS, WAR DIARY
30TH DIVISIONAL ENGINEERS.
INTELLIGENCE SUMMARY.
VOLUME 20. JUNE 1917.

(Erase heading not required.)

Instructions regarding War Diaries and Intelligence Summaries are contained in F. S. Regs. Part II. and the Staff Manual respectively. Title pages will be prepared in manuscript.

Place	Date 1917.	Hour	Summary of Events and Information	Remarks and references to Appendices

BRANDHOEK. RENINGHELST.	1-6-17. 15-6-17.		During the month of JUNE, the Division occupied the HOOGE-OBSERVATORY RIDGE Sector, the C.R.E's Headquarters being with Divisional Headquarters up to the 14th at BRANDHOEK, after the 14th at RENINGHELST.
			Field Companies were located as follows :-
			
			200th Field Coy. R.E. Post Office YPRES From 1-6-17 to 11-6-17.
			                             BRANDHOEK. " 12-6-17 " 13-6-17.
			                             Sheet 28. A.26.b.1.9. " 14-6-17 " 21-6-17.
			                             ZILLEBEKE BUND. " 22-6-17 " 30-6-17.
			
			201st Field Coy. R.E. BRANDHOEK. From 1-6-17 to 11-6-17.
			                             Post Office YPRES. " 12-6-17 " 13-6-17.
			                             ZILLEBEKE BUND. " 13-6-17 " 30-6-17.
			
			202nd Field Coy. R.E. Infantry Barracks YPRES. From 1-6-17 " 12-6-17.
			                             ZILLEBEKE BUND. " 13-6-17 " 21-6-17.
			                             Sheet 28. H.26.b.1.9. " 22-6-17 " 30-6-17.
			
			The principle being that 2 Field Companies were located in the forward area, doing work in the forward area, and 1 Field Company was located in the back area, doing work in back area, any Field Company being relieved out of the forward area after staying there 20 days. Of the 2 Field Companies working in the forward area, one was employed in front, that is to say, it provided any technical labour required by the Brigade in the line, and otherwise worked in an area between the front line, and a North and South line through the West end of MAPLE COPSE.
			The other worked in the intermediate area, that is to say, an area bounded on the West by the LILLE Road and on the East by a North and South line through the West end of MAPLE COPSE. It was found necessary to diverge slightly from this principle, in order to distribute the work equally.
			The work actually undertaken, which is given in greater detail in Field Company War Diaries, was generally as follows :-
			
			P.T.O.	

SECRET.

Sheet 2.

Army Form C. 2118.

WAR DIARY

HEADQUARTERS, VOLUME 20. JUNE 1917.
30TH DIVISIONAL ENGINEERS
INTELLIGENCE SUMMARY.

(Erase heading not required.)

Place	Date 1917.	Hour	Summary of Events and Information	Remarks and references to Appendices

(a) Field Company in the front area.

1. General repair of trenches, and supervision of construction of new trenches.
2. The construction of a Battalion Headquarters in MAPLE COPSE I.23.d.7.9.
3. The construction of 2 Heavy Trench Mortar Emplacements on OBSERVATORY RIDGE I.24.d.5.1.
4. The construction of 2 Battalion Headquarters in MAPLE TRENCH I.24.a.2.5.

In addition to which this Company controlled the Advanced Divisional R.E. Dump, which throughout the month was located at the GAS WORKS YPRES.

(b) Field Company in the intermediate area.

1. The construction of a Dressing Station in MAPLE TRENCH I.24.a.2.4.
2. The construction of a Dressing Station in RITZ STREET I.23.a.5.6.
3. The construction of a Dressing Station in the embankment at the North side of ZILLEBEKE LAKE I.22.a.9.3. The Dressing Station

These three were all on the "cut and cover principle", by the side of the LAKE was subsequently abandoned, as it was noticed by the enemy, and was frequently heavily shelled.

4. The construction of a Regimental Aid Post in VINCE STREET I.24.a.5.4. This was a mined dugout.
5. The strengthening of a Dressing Station in ZILLEBEKE BUND I.21.b.1.5.
6. The strengthening of a Dressing Station in WOODCOTE HOUSE.
7. The construction of a Battalion Headquarters in WELLINGTON CRESCENT I.17.d.4.2.

(c) The Field Company in the back area.

1. The construction of a miniature relief picture ground under II Corps arrangement.
2. The construction of a Divisional picture ground at TOURNEHEM.
3. Various work at the Divisional workshops.
4. Training.

P.T.O.

SECRET

Army Form C. 2118.

Sheet 3.

HEADQUARTERS, WAR DIARY
30TH DIVISIONAL ENGINEERS. & VOLUME 20. JUNE 1917.

INTELLIGENCE SUMMARY.

(Erase heading not required.)

Instructions regarding War Diaries and Intelligence Summaries are contained in F.S. Regs., Part II. and the Staff Manual respectively. Title pages will be prepared in manuscript.

Place	Date 1917.	Hour	Summary of Events and Information	Remarks and references to Appendices
			The 11th Btn. South Lancs. Regt. (Pioneers) were employed throughout the month in digging assembly trenches, and in maintaining the roads in the Divisional Area. The latter entailed considerable labour as they were very frequently damaged by shell fire.	
			The 2nd Canadian Tunnelling Company was attached to the Division for work, less one section which was employed under the Controller of Mines, Fifth Army on the maintenance of TORR TOP TUNNELS. They were employed as follows :-	
			One Infantry Brigade Headquarters at I.17.d.10.25. One Infantry Brigade Headquarters at I.17.c.7.0. One Battalion Headquarters at I.23.b.1.8. Four Artillery Headquarters in RAILWAY EMBANKMENT in vicinity of point I.21.c.5.7. each to accommodate 3 Officers, 15 Other Ranks and Signal Office. Two Artillery Headquarters at I.17.d.1.2. each to accommodate 3 officers, 15 Other Ranks and Signal Office. Three Observation Posts (Artillery) at I.17.d.4.4. One Observation Post (Artillery) at I.30.b.6.8.	
			From the 21st, the 80th Field Coy. 18th Division, was attached to the Division for work, and was employed on opening up the trench that runs along the embankment on the North Side of ZILLEBEKE LAKE for 300 yards from the North West corner. One Company, 8th Royal Sussex Regt. (Pioneers) was also attached to the Division for work, this company being employed on relieving one company of the 11th South Lancs. Regt. the latter Regiment having suffered heavy casualties. Throughout the month work was considerably held up by the enemy's shell fire. The difficulty of getting stores to the forward positions was considerable. Stores were run up to the Advanced Divisional R.E. Dump by Light Railway, and from there were taken to the forward works by Tramway. The Tramway however was cut in many places by the enemy's shell fire almost every night, which rendered the supply of stores somewhat precarious. The Divisional R.E. are indebted to the Officer-in-Charge of the Tramway, for the energetic manner in which he maintained his line, and repaired any damage done by the enemy.	
			P.T.O.	

SECRET.

Army Form C. 2118.

Sheet 4.

HEADQUARTERS, **WAR DIARY**
30TH DIVISIONAL ENGINEERS. **INTELLIGENCE SUMMARY.** VOLUME 20. JUNE 1917.

Instructions regarding War Diaries and Intelligence Summaries are contained in F. S. Regs., Part II. and the Staff Manual respectively. Title pages will be prepared in manuscript.

(Erase heading not required.)

Place	Date	Hour	Summary of Events and Information	Remarks and references to Appendices
	1917.			

The supply of R.E. stores was on the whole good, except that the supply of sawn timber was very low, and work was frequently held up by the lack of it.

During the first part of the month, the Divisional R.E. Park was located at H.14.b.4.7. but on the 18th a new Park at H.27.d.0.4. was taken over from the X Corps the former Park being subsequently handed over to C.R.E. 8th Division.

The R.S.M. and 46 O.R. remained at the Divisional Parks throughout the month, where they were employed at loading and offloading duties, and the making of water carriers, notice boards, infantry track boards, the making up of collapsible trench boards, and sundry other small jobs.

4-7-17.

[signature]
Lieut-Colonel R.E.
C.R.E., 30th Division.

S E C R E T.

HEADQUARTERS 30TH DIVISIONAL
ENGINEERS.

WAR DIARY.

VOLUME 61.   JULY 1917.

SECRET.

Army Form C. 2118.

HEADQUARTERS 30TH DIVISIONAL ENGINEERS.

WAR DIARY
or
INTELLIGENCE SUMMARY.

VOLUME 21. JULY 1917.

(Erase heading not required.)

Instructions regarding War Diaries and Intelligence Summaries are contained in F. S. Regs., Part II. and the Staff Manual respectively. Title pages will be prepared in manuscript.

Place	Date 1917.	Hour	Summary of Events and Information	Remarks and references to Appendices
RENINGHELST.	1-7-17.		From the 1st to the 7th July, Headquarters R.E. remained with Divisional Headquarters at RENINGHELST, the Field Companies being employed in carrying on the work described in last month's War Diary, which was in preparation for the coming offensive. They were located as follows :-	
NORDAUQUES.	7-7-17.		200th Field Coy. R.E. ZILLEBEKE BUND. 201st Field Coy. R.E. ZILLEBEKE BUND. 202nd Field Coy. R.E. Sheet 28. H.26.b.6.8.	
STEENVOORDE.	19-7-17.		On the night of the 6th/7th, the 30th Division was relieved by the 18th Division, Headquarters moving back to NORDAUQUES on the 7th. The Field Companies and Pioneers remained in the forward area, being employed as follows :-	
H.27.b.65.70.	24-7-17.		200th Field Coy. R.E. working under the orders of C.R.E. 18th Division. 201st Field Coy. R.E. working under the orders of C.E. II Corps. 202nd Field Coy. R.E. working under the orders of C.R.E. 8th Division. One Company, 11th South Lancs. (Pioneers) working under C.R.E. 18th Division. Three Coys, 11th South Lancs. (Pioneers) working under C.R.E. 8th Division. On the 13th one Company of the 11th South Lancs. were taken away, to be employed on Light Railway work under the A.D.L.R. Fifth Army. On the 19th Headquarters R.E. moved with Divisional Headquarters to STEENVOORDE, and on the 24th they moved from STEENVOORDE to the Advanced Divisional Headquarters at H.27.b.65.70. The defence of the line having been taken over by the G.O.C. 30th Division, the completion of the work of preparation was taken over on this date by the 202nd Field Coy. R.E. from the 18th Divisional R.E. and the former moved into the CHATEAU SEGARD Area No.7. (Sheet 28. H.23.d.3.5.) on the night 23rd/24th in order to be nearer to their work. The work was completed on the night of the 29th. The 200th Field Coy. R.E. returned to the Division as soon as the command of the Sector passed to the G.O.C. 30th Division, and was employed on the construction of dry weather tracks from the KRUISTRAATHOEK - SHRAPNEL CORNER Road forwards. The 201st Field Coy. R.E. returned to the Division on the 24th, and were employed P.T.O.	

SECRET.

Army Form C. 2118.

Sheet 2.
WAR DIARY
or
INTELLIGENCE SUMMARY.

HEADQUARTERS 30TH DIVISIONAL ENGINEERS.   VOLUME 21. JULY 1917.

Summary of Events and Information

employed, under the G.O.C. 90th Infantry Brigade, on effecting repairs to the trenches which had been considerably damaged by the enemy's shell fire and on the construction of two Battalion Headquarters in STANLEY TRENCH to replace two in LOVER'S WALK that had been demolished by enemy shell fire. The 11th Btn. South Lancs. Regt., less one Company working under the A.D.L.R. Fifth Army, were as usual employed on the maintenance of roads and tracks.
On the night 29th/30th 200th Field Coy. R.E. moved to CHATEAU SEGARD Area No.9 (Sheet 28. H.22.d.10.1.) and on the night 30th/31st the 201st Field Coy. R.E. moved to CHATEAU SEGARD Area No.10 (Sheet 28. H.22.d.5.3.).
ZERO for the Fifth Army Offensive was 3-50am 31st.
An account of the operations of Technical troops during the offensive will be attached を to next month's War Diary.
The Operation Orders for the technical troops are attached as Appendix A., and the "Arrangements for R.E. Stores" as Appendix B.
Throughout the month the R.S.M. 30th Divisional Engineers and 46 other ranks remained at the Divisional R.E. Park, H.27.d.0.4., working, during the time the Division was out of the line, under the orders of the C.R.E. 18th Division.
The supply of R.E. Stores was on the whole good, but sawn timber was still scarce.

3rd August 1917.

Lieut-Colonel R.E.
C.R.E., 30th Division.

Appendix A   Copy No 11   C.R.E. No.3041/2

OPERATION ORDER No.1.

By Lt. Col. G.W.DENISON, D.S.O., R.E.,

C.R.E. 30th Division.

1. The 30th Division will assault the enemy's position on our front on "Z" day, which will be notified later. The 8th Division will be on our Left and the 24th Division on our Right.

2. The Technical Troops will be assembled by "Y/Z" night in CHATEAU SEGARD Areas as follows :-

   200th Field Coy. R.E., in Area No.9.
   201st   "   "   "   "   No.10.
   202nd   "   "   "   "   No.7.
   11th South Lancs.   "   No.8.

3. The Technical Troops will carry out the work as detailed in Appendix A attached.

4. The arrangements for R.E.Stores will be in accordance with instructions issued under my No.2991 and No.2991/6.

5. (a) O.C. 200th Field Coy.R.E. will arrange direct with O.C. 11th South Lancs. as to where and when the 3 Platoons Pioneers joins his party for construction of strong points.
   (b) He will also arrange direct with 89th Infantry Brigade Head Quarters as to where and when the 3 Platoons Infantry will join his party.
   (c) He will leave his Assembly Area at Zero plus 2 hours and move forward by Track No.1.
   (d) He will keep in close touch with the 89th Infantry Brigade, ascertaining from them the situation, and will move his party on to the site of his work as soon as the Military situation permits.

6. (a) O.C. 202nd Field Coy.R.E. will leave his Assembly area at Zero plus one hour and move forward to the site of his work by Track No.1.
   (b) He will detail one N.C.O., to take charge of R.E.Dump at BORDER LANE.
   (c) He will detail one Officer (Lt. McCALLUM) to take command of the Party detailed in Appendix A for marking captured Trenches.

7. (a) O.C. 11th South Lancs.Pioneers will detail 4 Platoons for work on Road forward from OBSERVATORY RIDGE. This party will leave Assembly Area at Zero plus 1 hour and will move forward to site of work by Track No.1.
   (b) He will detail one Platoon for work on Artillery Track from ZILLEBEKE to I.24.a.8.8. and back to ZILLEBEKE. This party will leave Assembly Area at Zero minus 2 hours and will move to site of Work by Track No.1., commencing work as early as possible.
   (c) He will detail 3 Platoons for work on strong points under Major N.W.NAPIER-CLAVERING,D.S.O., R.E., in accordance with para 5 (a)above and Appendix A.
   (d) He will detail 2 Officers and 6 Pioneers for work under Lt. McNALLUM,R.E., in accordance with para.8. and Appexdix A.
   (e) He will detail one Officer to supervise an Infantry working party of one Platoon Infantry on repair of SHRAPNEL CORNER - TRANSPORT FARM - ZILLEBEKE Road. This party will leave Assembly area at CHATEAU SEGARD at Zero plus 3 hours and will keep the above road in repair.

8. Lieut.McCALLUM,R.E., will be in command of the party for marking captured Trenches. He will assemble his party at 11th South Lancs. Pioneers Head Quarters at CHATEAU SEGARD at Zero plus 1 hour and move forward by Track No.1. to the site of his work.

9. O.C. 201st Field Coy.R.E., and one Company of 11th South Lancs Pioneers will remain at CHATEAU SEGARD in Divisional Reserve.

10.   O.C. 200th Field Coy. R.E. will detail one N.C.O., to take charge of R.E. Dump at VALLEY COTTAGES.

11.   30th Divisional R.E. Head Quarters will be at Advanced Divisional Head Quarters H.27.b, 6,7.

                                                Atkinson

                                                     Capt. R.E.

7.17.   Adjt. 30th Divisional Engineers.

```
Copy No. 1.  O.C. 200th Field Coy. R.E.
    "    2.  O.C. 201st    "    "    "
    "    3.  O.C. 202nd    "    "    "
    "    4.  O.C. 11th South Lancs. Pioneers.
    "    5.  Head Quarters 30th Division "G".
    "    6.       "           "      "   "Q".
    "    7.       "         21st Infantry Brigade.
    "    8.       "         89th    "        "
    "    9.       "         90th    "        "
    "   10.  Chief Engineer, II Corps.
    "   11.)
    "   12.) War Diary.
    "   13.  File.
    "   14   LT. McCALLUM.
    "   15.  CRE 24° DIVN
    "   16.  CRE 18° DIVN.
    "   17   CRA 30° DIVN.
```

Copy to A.

DISPOSITION OF R.E. AND PIONEERS ON "Z" DAY.

WORK.	Strength of Party.	Place of Assembly.	OBJECTIVE.	Remarks.
Consolidation.	200th Field Coy.R.E. 3 Platoons Pioneers.	CHATEAU SEGARD.	Construction of 3 Strong Points (each for a garrison of 2 Platoons) at J.15.a.40.15, J.15.c.40.95, J.21.a.05.95.	42 Mules.
Roads.	2 Platoons Pioneers. 1 Platoon Pioneers.	CHATEAU SEGARD.	Preparing track for Artillery from OBSERVATORY RIDGE Road at I.24.d.4.3. through J.19.a.1.0, J.19.a.4.3, to J.19.b.1.5.	
		CHATEAU SEGARD.	Preparing track for Artillery from ZILLEBEKE, past YEOMANRY POST to about I.24.a.8.8. and back to ZILLEBEKE.	
Mule Track.	202nd Field Coy.R.E.	CHATEAU SEGARD.	Preparing track for pack animals from YEOMANRY POST to vicinity of FITZCLARENCE FARM via J.13.c.1.4, J.13.c.9.2, and J.13.d.9.8.	
Artillery Track.	2 Platoons Pioneers.	CHATEAU SEGARD.	Preparing track for Field Artillery under orders of C.R.A. 30th Division. Cancelled ReDennison	
Light Railways	One Company Pioneers.	--	For work on Light Rlys. under orders of A.D.L.R., Fifth Army.	
Loading Party.	1 R.E., N.C.O. 10 Infantry. 1 R.E., N.C.O. 6 Infantry.	CHATEAU SEGARD.	Loading Party at R.E.Dump at BORDER LANE I.24.a.8.3. Loading Party at R.E.Dump at VALLEY COTTAGES, I.23.d.1.6.	
Marking Trenches.	1 R.E.Officer. 2 Pioneer Officers. 6 Pioneers.	CHATEAU SEGARD.	Placing notice boards in German Trenches.	2 Mules.
Divisional Reserves.	201st Field Coy.R.E. One Company Pioneers.	CHATEAU SEGARD.		

14.7.17.

G. W. Dennison Lt. Col. R.E.
C.R.E. 30th Division.

Appendix B   C.R.E.No.2901.

The following are the arrangements for the Supply of R.E.Stores and Tools during the forthcoming operations :-

1. ARTILLERY.

This will be issued later to those concerned.

2. ROYAL ENGINEERS.

3 Support Line Posts, each to hold 2 platoons, are being constructed on the GREEN LINE, under the command of Major N.W.NAPIER CLAVERING, D.S.O., R.E.

Each of these Posts will need a convoy of 2 Groups of 7 Pack Mules each, i.e., the consolidation of this Support Line will need 6 Groups in all (R.E.Convoy No.1.). 5 of these Groups will be found under the arrangement mentioned in 30th Division letter A.9430 of 6th Inst. The remaining Group will be found by the Divisional R.E.

This convoy will draw the stores it requires on "X" day, and the convoy, complete with the Stores it will carry, will be parked at CHATEAU SEGARD on "Y/Z" night.

The constitution of the Convoy is given in Appendix 1.

3. INFANTRY.

(a) TOOLS. 50% of the Infantry attacking will carry a pick or a shovel in the proportion of 1 Pick to 4 Shovels. Brigades should inform me of their requirements, and of the day on which it will be suitable for them to draw, as early as possible.

Arrangements will be made for them to be issued from the 30th Divisional R.E.Park, DICKEBUSCH at H.27.d.0.4.

(b) STORES. The 89th Brigade are responsible for the construction of five posts along the GREEN LINE.

For the construction of these a convoy (R.E.Convoy No.2.) of 5 Groups of 7 Pack Mules each will be required. This has been arranged by 30th Division under 30th Divn.letter A.9430 of 6th Inst.

This convoy can be loaded up at DICKEBUSCH Park on any day that the 89th Brigade inform me is suitable to them.

When this convoy has taken up its load for the consolidation of the GREEN LINE, it will return to the Dump at BORDER LANE (see para. 4) and will reload with materials which it will take up to the 21st and 90th Brigades, for the consolidation of the BLACK LINE. The loading will be done by a permanent loading party at BORDER LANE Dump. See Appendix 1.

4. DUMPS.

(a) The main 30th Divl. R.E.Park will remain at H.27.d.0.4. throughout the operations.

(b) An advanced Divl.R.E.Park is located at KRUISTRAAT at H.18.d.4.2.

(c) The main "Battle Dump" (BORDER LANE Dump) will be located at I.24.a.9.3. This dump will be connected to a Pack Transport Track, that will be opened up shortly after Zero, which will run to CLAPHAM JUNCTION and then on to FITZCLARENCE FARM.

It will be under the charge of O.C. 202nd Field Coy.R.E. and will be manned by 1 N.C.O., detailed by O.C. 202nd Field Coy. and 10 attached Infantry, as a permanent loading party. The stores it will contain are shown on attached Table A.

(d) A small Battle Dump, Stores as on attached Table B will be located at VALLEY COTTAGES, I.23.d.1.2. This dump will be on the track which will be opened as soon after Zero as possible through I.24.d.2.2, I.19.a.4.3, I.13.d.0.4. to CLAPHAM JUNCTION. It will be under the charge of O.C.200th Field Coy.R.E. and will be manned by 1 N.C.O. detailed by O.C. 200th Field Coy. and 6 attached Infantry as a permanent loading party.

(e) Any of these dumps will issue on demand to any Battalion or Battery immediately after Zero.

(f) There will be a small supply of timber, explosives &c. at the BORDER LANE DUMP FOR USE by the technical troops only.

PLEASE ACKNOWLEDGE.

11.7.17.

G.W.Dawson
Lt.Col.R.E.
C.R.E. 30th Division.

APPENDIX 1.

Material.	One Mule load.	One Group load.	Total carried by R.E.Convoy No.1.	Carried by R.E.Convoy No.2.
Sandbags.	500	500	3000	2500
Barbed Wire.	6	12	72	60
Concertina Wire.	8 Coils	8 Coils	48 Coils	40 Coils
Long Screw Posts.	24	24	144	120
Short Screw Posts.	44	44	264	220
Picks)	6	6	36	30
Shovels.)	22	22	132	110

TABLE A.

BORDER LANE BATTLE DUMP.

Sandbags	50,000
Barbed Wire, Rolls	400
Plain Wire, Rolls.	10
French Wire, Coils.	250
Screw Pickets, Long.	750
Screw Pickets, Short.	1500
Picks.	500
Shovels.	1500

TABLE B.

Sandbags	25,000
Barbed Wire, Rolls.	200
Plain Wire, Rolls.	5
French Wire, Coils.	120
Screw Pickets, Long.	380
Screw Pickets, Short.	750
Picks.	100
Shovels.	500

Copies to :-
　Headquarters, 30th Division "G".　　Headquarters, 89th Infy.Brigade.
　Headquarters, 30th Division "Q".　　Headquarters, 90th Infy.Brigade.
　C.R.A.　　　　　　　　　　　　　　　Headquarters, 21st Infy.Brigade.
　O.C.200th Field Coy.R.E.　　　　　　O.C.11th South Lancs.Regt.
　O.C.201st Field Coy.R.E.　　　　　　C.E. II Corps.
　O.C.202nd Field Coy.R.E.　　　　　　C.R.E. 8th Division.
　O.C. 30th Divl.Signal Co.R.E.　　　C.R.E. 18th Division.
　　　　　　　　　　　　　　　　　　　　C.R.E. 24th Division.
　　　　　　　　　　　　　　　　　　　　R.S.M. i/c 30th Divl. R.E.Park.

S E C R E T.   C.R.E. No. 2991/6.

        In continuation of this office No.2991 of 11th instant, the following further arrangements for R.E. Stores are notified for information :-

1.   The attached Appendix shews the distribution of R.E. Stores

   (a) Columns A. B. & C. shew the stores that will be required to be carried by the infantry attacking.
   (b) Column D. shews the stores that will be required by the R.A. for the Brigades moving to forward positions.
       These will be drawn from the 30th Divl. R.E. Park DICKEBUSCH by the Artillery, who will take them forward, and dump them in equal parts at the BORDER LANE and VALLEY COTTAGES Dumps.
       When these Stores have been placed on the dumps, they will be in the charge of the O's C. Field Companies in charge of the Dumps, who will reserve them for use of the R.A.
       To facilitate this, the R.A. should notify the Officers Commanding the Field Companies concerned, as soon as any material has been dumped.
   (c) The Stores in Column G. will be drawn from the Divl. R.E. Park at DICKEBUSCH by O.C. 200th Field Coy. R.E., under his own arrangements.
   (d) The Stores in Column H., which will be substituted for the column "R.E. Convoy No.2" in my No.2991, are the stores required for consolidation by the 89th Infantry Brigade.
       They will be drawn from the Divl. R.E. Park and dumped at the Divisional Bomb Store under arrangements made by Headquarters 30th Division Q. Office.

2.   Any of the Stores on the attached Appendix may be drawn by the formation or unit concerned from the Divl. R.E. Park without further indent, on the signature of the Staff Captain concerned.

3.   The Advanced Divisional R.E. Dump at KRUISTRAAT has ceased to exist, owing to the explosion of an ammunition dump, and it is not intended to form a new one.

4.   It is considered advisable to distribute the Stores on the "Battle" Dumps as fas as is convenient, so as not to attract undue attention. For this reason the BORDER LANE Dump will stretch as far West as the abandoned trench running E. and W. along the NORTH EDGE of MAPLE COPSE, and the Stores at VALLEY COTTAGES will be distributed along the ditches on either side of the OBSERVATORY RIDGE ROAD.

5.   The BORDER LANE and VALLEY COTTAGES Dumps will be filled by the 23rd instant.

6.   Please acknowledge.

                                        G. W. Denison
                                        Lieut-Col. R.E.
18-7-17.   C.R.E., 30th Division.

Copies to :-

30th Division G.	21st Infantry Brigade.
30th Division Q.	89th Infantry Brigade.
C.R.A.	90th Infantry Brigade.
O.C. 200th Field Co. R.E.	C.E. II Corps.
O.C. 201st Field Coy. R.E.	R.S.M. i/c Divl. R.E. Park.
O.C. 202nd Field Coy. R.E.	

APPENDIX.

MATERIAL.	A. 21st Bde.	B. 89th Bde.	C. 90th Bde.	D. Artilly.	E. Table A.	F. Table B.	G. R.E.Convoy No.1.	H. R.E.Convoy No.2.	K. Total.
Sandbags.	5000	8000	6000	50000	50000	25000	3000		147000.
Barbed Wire.				400	400	200	72	144	816.
Plain Wire.					10	5			15.
French Wire, Coils.					250	120	48		418.
Screw Pickets, Long.					750	380	144	290	1564.
Screw Pickets, Short.					1500	750	264		2514.
Picks.	260	240	200	100	500	100	36		1436.
Shovels.	930	1830	800	400	1500	500	132		6192.
Corr: Iron.				400					400.
Curved Corr: Iron. (If available)				400					400.

SECRET.

HEADQUARTERS

30TH DIVISIONAL

ENGINEERS.

WAR DIARY.

AUGUST 1917 VOLUME 22.

SECRET.

Army Form C. 2118.

Instructions regarding War Diaries and Intelligence Summaries are contained in F. S. Regs., Part II. and the Staff Manual respectively. Title pages will be prepared in manuscript.

WAR DIARY

~~INTELLIGENCE SUMMARY~~

(Erase heading not required.)

HEADQUARTERS 30TH DIVISIONAL ENGINEERS.

VOLUME 22. AUGUST 1917.

Ref: Map Sheet 28. 1/40,000.

Place	Date	Hour	Summary of Events and Information	Remarks and references to Appendices
			From the 1st to the 4th, Headquarters R.E. remained with Advanced Divisional Headquarters at H.27.b.65.70. near DICKEBUSCH. An account of the work of 30th Divisional Technical Troops during offensive operations from 31st July to 3rd August is attached as Appendix A. The Division was then relieved by the 18th Division, Headquarters R.E. moving to RENINGHELST on the 4th, GODEWAERSVELDE on the 5th and to MERRIS on the 7th. Field Companies moved with Brigade Groups :- 200th Field Coy. R.E. with 21st Brigade Group. 201st Field Coy. R.E. with 89th Brigade Group. 202nd Field Coy. R.E. with 90th Brigade Group. On the move from the GODEWAERSVELDE to the MERRIS Area, a readjustment was carried out, Field Companies joining the following Brigade Groups :- 200th Field Coy. R.E. - 89th Brigade Group. 201st Field Coy. R.E. - 90th Brigade Group. 202nd Field Coy. R.E. - 21st Brigade Group. The Division moved into the ST.JANS CAPPEL - BERTHEN Area on the 11th, Field Companies moving with Brigade Groups and Headquarters R.E. being billeted at ST.JANS CAPPEL with Divisional Headquarters. The Field Companies were then employed at training, each Company training parties of Infantry from their Brigade in revetting and wiring. On the 16th the Divisional Engineers and 11th Bn. South Lancs. Regt. (Pioneers) marched to the VIERSTRAAT Area being placed at the disposal of C.E. IX Corps from the 17th for work on the Ridge Defences. Each Brigade attached 100 infantry to their affiliated Field Company as a working party for this work, and this arrangement was subsequently made permanent. On the 23rd the 30th Division took over the line from the 4th Australian Division, Field Companies moving to the new area on the 22nd, and Headquarters R.E. moving to DRANOUTRE on the 23rd. FIELD COMPANIES	

SECRET.   Sheet 2.   Army Form C. 2118.

HEADQUARTERS 30TH   WAR DIARY   VOLUME 22. AUGUST 1917.
DIVISIONAL   INTELLIGENCE SUMMARY.
ENGINEERS.   (Erase heading not required.)   Ref: Map Sheet 28. 1/40,000.

Place	Date	Hour	Summary of Events and Information	Remarks and references to Appendices
			Field Companies were employed as follows :-	
			200th Field Coy. R.E. — On BOB STREET & DORSET STREET Communication Trenches under orders of C.R.E.	
			201st Field Coy. R.E. — "Y" line under orders of C.R.E.	
			202nd Field Coy. R.E. — Front Line under orders of G.O.C. 21st Infantry Brigade.	
			11th South Lancs. Rgt. — MANCHESTER STREET Communication Trench, Roads and Screens.	
			Operation Order No.2 is attached as Appendix B. On the 30th the Divisional Front was extended as far South as the River DOUVE, and the 201st Field Coy. R.E. took over the work on the Front Line, Right Sector under orders of the G.O.C. 90th Infantry Brigade, the 200th Field Coy. R.E. taking over work on the "Y" Line from 201st Field Coy. R.E.	
			The R.S.M. 30th Divisional Engineers and 46 other ranks remained at the Divisional R.E. Park, H.27.d.0.4. from 1st to 16th, working under the orders of the C.R.E. 18th Division. On the 16th they moved to 202nd Field Coy. R.E. billet F.7.b.90.35, and on the 18th to N.17.c.1.1. near VIERSTRAAT, and on the 22nd this party took over the dump at LINDENHOEK, which then became the 30th Divisional R.E. Park.	
			On the 22nd, 1 N.C.O. and 8 men of this party took over a Forward Divisional R.E. Dump at 0.20.c.2.5. near WYSCHAETE.	
	3-9-17.			
			, Lieut-Colonel R.E.	
			C.R.E., 30th Division.	

Appendix A

WORK CARRIED OUT BY THE TECHNICAL
TROOPS 30TH DIVISION DURING ACTIVE
OPERATIONS FROM 31-7-17 TO 3-8-17.

200th Field Coy. R.E.

On the night of 31st/1st the 200th Field Coy. R.E. with 3 platoons of the 11th South Lancs. Pioneers constructed three Strong Points (each for one platoon) at

J.19.b.25.80.
J.13.d.45.65.
J.13.d.6.8.

these were not wired in as the mule convoy carrying wiring material was unable owing to heavy shelling and bad country to get to the site of the work.

On the night of 2nd/3rd the 200th Field Coy. R.E. with two sections of 201st Field Coy. R.E. and 2 platoons of the 11th South Lancs. Pioneers constructed a wire entanglement along 900 yards of our front line. This work was carried out very successfully under very difficult circumstances.

201st Field Coy. R.E.

On the 1st August the 201st Field Coy. R.E. worked all day on mule track from YEOMANRY POST through SANCTUARY WOOD towards CLAPHAM JUNCTION. They also had two sections out wiring on night of 2nd/3rd as stated above.

202nd Field Coy. R.E.

On 31st July and again on 2nd August the 202nd Field Coy. R.E. worked on the mule tracks from YEOMANRY POST through SANCTUARY WOOD to CLAPHAM JUNCTION and in spite of heavy shelling and M.G. fire which caused heavy casualties (about 15%) this track was made passable for Pack Transport by night of 31st July, but owing to very heavy rain on night of 31st/1st and following days this track has only been kept open for traffic with great difficulty.

11th South Lancs. (Pioneers).

One Company of the 11th South Lancs. was taken away for work on Light Railways under the A.D.L.R. Fifth Army, thus only leaving 3 Coys. for Divisional work. In addition to the work already given above, this Battalion did exceptional good work on upkeep of old, and construction of new roads.

A road for Artillery from ZILLEBEKE to just West of SANCTUARY WOOD (I.24.a.8.7.) was opened out and used by our Artillery a few hours after Zero, one platoon was employed on this work and on keeping this road in repair.

The OBSERVATORY RIDGE ROAD was opened for traffic from RODKIN HOUSE to our old front line about I.24.d.8.3. by night of 31st and to German front line about J.19.c.1.4. by the morning of 1st August, and from there a mule track was pushed on another 500 yards in the direction of STIRLING CASTLE by morning of 3rd August. Work was very much delayed owing to very bad weather and to heavy shelling and M.G. fire which caused considerable casualties.

They also kept in repair the main road from SHRAPNEL CORNER to ZILLEBEKE and Tracks 10 and 11, work again being much delayed by bad weather, which turned all tracks into deep mud.

3-8-17.

Lieut-Colonel R.E.
C.R.E., 30th Division.

Copies to :-

30th Division "G".
C.E. II Corps.

Appendix B

SECRET.   Copy No. 7

OPERATION ORDER NO. 2.
BY
LIEUT-COL. C. H. DENISON, D.S.A.S.C.
C.R.E. 30TH DIVISION.

Ref: Map Sheet WYTSCHAETE - Edn 6A -   20th August 1917.
     1/10,000 & Sht.28, Scale 1/40,000.

1.   The front held by the IX Corps will be extended
     outwards as far as the BLAUWEPOORTBEEK.

2.   The 30th Division will relieve the 4th Australian
     Division (II ANZAC Corps) in the above sector, taking over
     the portion of the front at present held by the 12th
     Australian Infantry Brigade. The relief will be completed
     during the night 22nd/23rd August.

3. (a) On completion of the relief the Northern boundary of
       the 30th Division will be the present southern boundary
       of IX Corps, as given in map attached to 30th Division
       G/265/213 dated 16-8-17.

   (b) The Southern boundary of the 30th Division, which will
       also be the Southern boundary of the IX Corps, will be:-

       BLAUWEPOORTBEEK O.34.b.15.65 - along the BEEK to
       O.35.b.45.55. - cross roads O.35.a.50.55.- HINDLE Farm
       (inclusive to II ANZAC) - O.31.central - ODELL Farm
       (inclusive to IX Corps) - O.T.Farm N.35.d.8.7. (inclusive
       to IX Corps) - DIXON Farm N.35.c.6.5. (inclusive to IX
       Corps) - TOA Farm N.34.d.1.6. (inclusive to IX Corps) -
       N.34.c.5.6. - T.3.b.5.8.- road junction N.33.c.70.15. -
       along North of road to road junction N.31.d.7.5. -
       N.6.b.70.05.- along South of road to N.5.a.3.2. -
       N.34.d.9.3.

   (c) The 63rd Infantry Brigade of the 37th Division will
       be on the left of the 30th Division, and the 4th
       Australian Infantry Brigade of the 4th Australian
       Division will be on its right.

4. (a) Movements will be carried out in accordance with the
       attached march table, all details being arranged between
       unit commanders concerned.

   (b) Movements East of a line drawn N.& S. through the
       centre of Squares N.23, 29, 35. will be by companies at
       100 yards interval.

   (c) Movements East of the dividing line between Squares
       N. & O. will be carried out after dark.

5.   The 202nd Field Coy. R.E. will take over the work in
     the front system from the 12th Australian Field Coy.
     The 201st Field Coy. R.E. will take over the work in
     the reserve line from the 13th Australian Field Coy.
     The 11th South Lancs. Pioneers will take over work on
     C.T's and roads from the 4th Australian Pioneer Battalion.

6.   Move of the 200th Field Coy. R.E. will be notified
     later.

7.   Completion of all reliefs will be reported to this
     office.

Sheet 2. of OPERATION ORDER No.2.

8. The Headquarters, Divisional R.E. will close at ST. JANS CAPPEL at 10-0am on the 23rd August, re-opening at ULSTER CAMP, DRANOUTRE (N.35.d.0.2). at the same hour.

                                            Captain R.E.
                             Adjt., 30th Divisional Engineers.

Copy No.1 to O.C.200th Field Coy.R.E.
  "   " 2 " O.C.201st Field Coy.R.E.
  "   " 3 " O.C.202nd Field Coy.R.E.
  "   " 4 " O.C.11th Bn. South Lancs. Regt.
  "   " 5 " 30th Division "G".
  "   " 6 " 30th Division "Q".
  "   " 7 " File.

MARCH TABLE OF TECHNICAL TROOPS.

Serial No.	Date.	Unit.	From.	To.	Relieving.	Remarks.
1.	22-8-17.	201st Field Coy. R.E.	N.16.d.5.6.	SPY FARM N.28.c.8.6.	13th Australian Field Coy.	Relief to be completed by 10-0am, 23-8-17
2.	22-8-17.	202nd Field Coy. R.E.	N.17.c.1.1.	VROILANDHOEK. N.28.a.6.3.	12th Australian Field Coy.	-do-
3.	22-8-17.	11th South Lancs. (Pioneers)	N.10.d.5.2.	SPY FARM N.28.c.cent.	4th Australian Pioneer Batt.	-do-

20-8-17.

Captain R.E.
Adjt., 30th Divl. Engineers.

SECRET.

HEADQUARTERS
30TH
DIVISIONAL ENGINEERS.

W A R   D I A R Y.

VOLUME 23.
SEPTEMBER 1917.

S E C R E T.

WAR DIARY

HEADQUARTERS 30TH DIVISIONAL ENGINEERS.

INTELLIGENCE SUMMARY.

VOLUME 23.   SEPTEMBER 1917.

Reference Map Sheet 28. 1/40,000.

Army Form C. 2118.

Instructions regarding War Diaries and Intelligence Summaries are contained in F.S. Regs., Part II. and the Staff Manual respectively. Title pages will be prepared in manuscript.

(Erase heading not required.)

Place	Date	Hour	Summary of Events and Information	Remarks and references to Appendices
DRANOUTRE.	Sept.1917.		Throughout the month of September Headquarters R.E. remained at DRANOUTRE with Divisional Headquarters. On the 4th, Lieut-Col. G.W.DENISON, D.S.O.,R.E., C.R.E. 30th Division was granted six weeks leave of absence to CANADA, and on the 7th, Major J.E.CHIPPINDALL, M.C. R.E., returning from leave of absence to ENGLAND, assumed the duties of C.R.E. temporarily. On the 20th, Major N.W.NAPIER CLAVERING, D.S.O., R.E., rejoining from Hospital assumed the duties of C.R.E. temporarily, Major J.E.CHIPPINDALL rejoining the 202nd Field Coy. R.E. On the night 2nd/3rd the 30th Division handed over the Sector South of the BLAUWEPOORTBEEK CANAL from the 37th Division to the 14th (Light) Division and took over the Sector from the YPRES-COMINES CANAL from the 37th Division. The relief of Technical Troops is given in O.O. No.3, attached at Appendix "A", the table attached to this Order shewing the distribution of Technical Troops for work. Details of work are given in Field Company War Diaries. Starting on the 8th a winter hutting scheme was taken in hand, which consisted as follows :-	

Description.	Location.	Work being done by
A hutted camp for 1 Battalion less transport.	N.27.c.9.2. N.33.a.7.5.	202nd Field Coy. (mens' quarters) 11th South Lancs.(offrs. ")
A hutted camp for 1 Inf: Bde. Transport & Fd.Amb.	N.33.c.9.7.	200th Field Coy.
A hutted camp for 1 battery R.F.A.	T.3.b.3.9.	Started by 202nd Field Coy. & carried on by 200th Field Coy.
A hutted camp for 3 batteries R.F.A. This was subsequently altered to 1 battery, another battery camp being started at	N.33.c.9.7. N.21.c.2.0.	11th Bn. South Lancs. Regt.
A hutted camp for 1 Field Company.	N.21.b.0.2.	11th Bn. South Lancs. Regt.
A hutted camp for 2 Machine Gun Companies.	N.21.b.0.2.	ditto
A hutted camp for 1 A.F.A., B.A.C.	N.32.b.0.0.	201st Field Coy. R.E.
A hutted camp		

SECRET.

Sheet 2.
Army Form C. 2118.

WAR DIARY

Instructions regarding War Diaries and Intelligence Summaries are contained in F. S. Regs., Part II. and the Staff Manual respectively. Title pages will be prepared in manuscript.

HEADQUARTERS 30TH DIVISIONAL ~~INTELLIGENCE SUMMARY~~ ENGINEERS.

VOLUME 23. SEPTEMBER 1917.

Reference Map Sheet 28. 1/40,000.

(Erase heading not required.)

Place	Date	Hour	Summary of Events and Information			Remarks and references to Appendices
			Description.	Location.	Work being done by.	(Con)
			A hutted camp for 4 Batteries, A.F.A. This last was approved during September but work was not started till 1st October.	N.32.c.5.8.	201st Field Coy. R.E.	
			A hutted camp for 1 Infantry Battalion.	N.27.b.1.8.	C.E. IX Corps.	
			A hutted camp for 1 Inf: Bde. Group Transport Lines) 1 Pnr. Battalion Transport Lines)	N.32.b.6.6.	C.E. IX Corps.	
			The work proceeded satisfactorily, but was held up at times by shortage of parts of Nissen Huts which were demanded from the Base. On the nights 20th/21st and 21st/22nd, an Inter-Brigade relief occurred, the distribution of work being shewn in Order No.4, attached as Appendix "B". Owing to the frequent reliefs and consequent disorganization of the work, it was decided on the 30th to reorganize the work, each Field Company being given an area in which it was intended it should work as long as the Division remained in the line. This reorganization is shewn in the attached letter, Appendix "C". The R.S.M. and 36 other ranks remained at the Divisional R.E. Park at LINDENHOEK throughout the month; two advanced dumps were in use, each manned by 1 N.C.O. and 4 men. One dump was at WYTSCHAETE O.20.c.2.3. and the other at PARMA, N.12.c.5.0. The supply of stores throughout the month was fairly good, sawn timber and corrugated iron being scarce at times.			
	3-10-17.					

Major R.E.
A/C.R.E., 30th Division.

Appendix 'A'

SECRET.   Copy No. 13

OPERATION ORDER NO.3
BY
LIEUT-COL. G.W. DENISON, D.S.O. R.E.
C.R.E., 30TH DIVISION.

Ref: Map, Sheet 28. 1/40,000.   1st September 1917.

1. On the night of 2nd/3rd September the 30th Division will be handing over the present Right Sector to the 14th Division, and will take over the Right Sector of the 37th Division.

2. The Technical Troops will be employed as shown in the attached Table. Details of reliefs to be arranged between O's C. Units concerned.

3. 37th Divisional Technical Troops are located as follows :-

    Hdqrs. 152nd Field Coy.,   R.E.FARM. N.15.c.7.5.
    Hdqrs. 153rd Field Coy.,   N.10.c.5.9.
    Hdqrs. 154th Field Coy.,   N.16.b.6.7.
    Hdqrs. Pioneer Battn.,   N.10.d.2.5.

4. All reliefs are to be completed by 10-0am, 3rd September, and to be reported to this Office.

5. The two sections of 201st Field Coy. R.E., with attached Infantry, will return to SPY FARM.

6. Two sections of 200th Field Coy. R.E. and 50 attached Infantry will move to GRAND BOIS and take over the billets of 153rd Field Coy. R.E. Transport lines and the remaining two sections will remain in their present camp.

7. The 201st Field Coy. R.E. will hand over the work in the Right Sector to Field Company of the 14th Division.

8. The 11th South Lancs. Pioneers will hand over the work in the Right Sector to Pioneer Battalion of the 14th Division.

9. The Advanced Divisional R.E. Dump will be at WYSCHAETE, O.20.c.2.3.

                                                  Captain R.E.
                                   Adjutant, 30th Divisional Engineers.

Copy No. 1 to   O.C. 200th Field Coy. R.E.
  "   " 2 " O.C. 201st Field Coy. R.E.
  "   " 3 " O.C. 202nd Field Coy. R.E.
  "   " 4 " O.C. 11th South Lancs. Pioneers.
  "   " 5 " 30th Division "G".
  "   " 6 " 30th Division "Q".
  "   " 7 " 21st Infantry Brigade.
  "   " 8 " 89th Infantry Brigade.
  "   " 9 " 90th Infantry Brigade.
  "   " 10 " C.R.E. 14th Division.
  "   " 11 " C.R.E. 37th Division.
  "   " 12 & 13 War Diary.
  "   " 14   File.

TABLE TO ACCOMPANY C.R.E. OPERATION ORDER NO.3.

Serial No.	Unit.	Where now employed.	Nature of work to be taken over.	Work to be taken over from.	Remarks.
1.	2 Sec: 200th Fd.Co.	BOB STREET & DORSET STREET.	Front Line, Left Sector.	153 Fd. Co. R.E. 37th Divn.	Under orders of G.O.C., 89th Inf.Bde.
2.	2 Sec: 200th Fd.Co.	Reserve Line.	Pioneer Lane. Olive Trench.	37th Div. Pioneers & 153rd Fd. Co. R.E.	
3.	2 Sec: 201st Fd.Co.	Right Sector Front Line.	Reserve Line. Right Sector.	200th Fd. Co. R.E.	
4.	2 Sec: 201st Fd.Co.	FANNY C.T. & CROSS Trench.	Reserve Line. Left Sector.	153rd & 154th Fd. Coys. R.E.	
5.	2 Sec: 202nd Fd.Co.	Left Sector Front Line.	Right Sector. Front Line.	No change.	Under orders of G.O.C. 21st Inf: Bde.
6.	2 Sec: 202nd Fd.Co.	Left Sector Front Line.	BOB ST. & DORSET ST. C.T's.	200th Fd. Co. R.E.	Under orders of C.R.E.
7.	1 Coy. 11th S.Lancs.	MANCHESTER STREET.	MANCHESTER ST.	No change.	
8.	1 Coy. 11th S.Lancs.	MANCHESTER STREET.	Screens.	152nd Fd.Co.R.E. 37th Divn.	
9.	1 Coy. 11th S.Lancs.	Roads, Left Sector.	Roads, Right Sector.	No change.	
10.	1 Coy. 11th S.Lancs.	Roads, Tramlines & Screens, Right Sector.	Roads, Left Sector.	37th Divn. Pioneers.	

Appendix B

SECRET.   Copy No. 9.

30TH DIVISIONAL ENGINEERS
ORDER NO. 4.

Reference Map Sheet 28 S.W. Scale 1/20,000
and Sheet WYTSCHAETE, Scale 1/10,000.

1. The following inter-brigade reliefs will take place, to be completed by 4-0am, 22nd September :-

   (a) 21st Infantry Brigade will take over the Right Sector of the front line.

   (b) 90th Infantry Brigade will take over the Left Sector of the front line.

   (c) 89th Infantry Brigade will move into Divisional Reserve.

2. Up to and including the night of the 19th/20th, work will continue as at present.

3. On the 20th, two sections 202nd Field Coy. R.E. will relieve two sections 200th Field Coy. R.E. in GRAND BOIS, the latter returning to the 200th Field Coy. camp at N.28.b.8.4.

4. On the night 20th/21st 202nd Field Coy. R.E. will take over the work on the front line Left Sector and on OAK AVENUE and OLIVE TRENCH from 200th Field Coy. R.E., and 200th Field Coy. R.E. will take over work on "X" and "Y" LINES from 202nd Field Coy. R.E.

5. No working parties will be available for work on the nights 20th/21st and 21st/22nd.

6. Work in the back area will be carried on by the same Companies as before the relief.

7. Further instructions on working parties on and after the 22nd will be issued to all concerned.

8. ACKNOWLEDGE.

                                                Captain R.E.
18-9-17.   Adjt., 30th Divl. Engineers.

Copy No. 1   to   30th Division "G".
 "   "   2   "   30th Division "Q".
 "   "   3   "   21st Infantry Brigade.
 "   "   4   "   89th Infantry Brigade.
 "   "   5   "   90th Infantry Brigade.
 "   "   6   "   200th Field Coy. R.E.
 "   "   7   "   201st Field Coy. R.E.
 "   "   8   "   202nd Field Coy. R.E.
 "   "   9   "   War Diary.
 "   " 10   "   War Diary.
 "   " 11   File.

Appendix "C"

SECRET. C.R.E's No. 4119/84.

O.C. 200th Field Coy. R.E.
O.C. 201st Field Coy. R.E.
O.C. 202nd Field Coy. R.E.
O.C. 11th Bn. South Lancs. Regt.

With a view to avoiding the disorganisation of work consequent upon frequent reliefs and in order to gain the advantages of a consistent policy of work in the forward area, the undermentioned arrangements will come into force on 2nd October 1917.

1.   The forward Divisional Area will be divided into three R.E. Areas. As far as can be foreseen the Field Companies will work in these areas until the Division is relieved, irrespective of Brigade reliefs. This arrangement may be modified in the event of three Brigades being in the line at the same time.

2.   The 201st Field Coy. R.E. is allotted the southern area between the southern boundary of the Divisional Area and a line following the course of the WAMBEKE from the front line to O.21.c.8.9. thence along VERNE ROAD to TORREKEN CORNER thence to O.20.c.2.2. This does not coincide with the inter-battalion boundary which is at present a line drawn from O.23.c.7.0. to ULSTER HOUSE O.27.a.1.1.
    The 200th Field Coy. R.E. is allotted the centre area which is bounded on the north by the inter-brigade boundary, that is, the line of the ROOZEBEEK from the front line to O.15.b.8.3.- O.15.b.2.5.- along road to ESTAMINET CORNER.
    The 202nd Field Coy. R.E. is allotted the northern area - that held by the Left Brigade.

3.   Each Company will place one section at the disposal of the Brigade concerned for work on the support line and machine gun emplacements in the front system, working parties found by Brigades being additional to those shewn in Appendix A.

4.   With reference to this office letter No.4119/80 of 27-9-17, working parties are allotted as shewn in Appendix A. These parties are intended for work other than that on the front system.

5.   The 11th South Lancs. Regt. (Pioneers) will, as heretofore, be allotted work direct from this office. Working parties are shewn in Appendix A.

6.   The work in the back area, that is to say, the Divisional Area west of the ST.ELOI - MESSINES Road, will be distributed to Companies as the circumstances at the moment may direct. The Companies will continue to work upon the schemes which they now have in hand.

P.T.O.

7. As regards the work for the Royal Artillery the Companies will arrange to assist Brigades as under :-

    200th Field Coy. R.E. - 149th Brigade R.F.A.
    201st Field Coy. R.E. - 148th Brigade R.F.A.
    202nd Field Coy. R.E. - 104th A.F.A. Brigade.

Locations will be circulated on a separate paper.

8. ACKNOWLEDGE.

30-9-17.

Captain R.E.
Adjt., 30th Divl. Engineers.

Copies to :-

30th Division "G".
C.R.A.
21st Infantry Brigade.
89th Infantry Brigade.
90th Infantry Brigade.

APPENDIX "A".

WORKING PARTY TABLE.

Serial No.	Nature of Work.	W.P. required.	Battalion finding W.P.	Unit under which working.	Location of Battalions.	Remarks.
1.	Work in Right Sector.	100.	"D" Bn. Right Brigade.	201st Field Coy. R.E.	"D" Bn. Right Bde. IRISH HOUSE.	Field Company Commanders and O.C. 11th South Lancs. will arrange all details of work direct with Battalion Commanders concerned.
2.	MANCHESTER STREET.	50.	"D" Bn. Right Brigade.	11th South Lancs. Rgt.	"B" Bn. Left Bde. DENYS WOOD.	
3.	Work in Centre Sector.	150.	"D" Bn. Left Brigade.	200th Field Coy. R.E.	"C" Bn. Left Bde. CHINESE WALL.	
4.	Work in Left Sector.	100.	"C" Bn. Left Brigade.	202nd Field Coy. R.E.	"D" Bn. Left Bde. W. of IRISH HOUSE.	
5.	All roads in forward area.	50.	"C" Bn. Left Brigade.	11th South Lancs. Rgt.		

SECRET.

HEADQUARTERS

30TH

DIVISIONAL ENGINEERS.

WAR DIARY.

VOLUME 24.   OCTOBER 1917.

SECRET.

Army Form C. 2118.

WAR DIARY

HEADQUARTERS 30TH DIVISIONAL ENGINEERS.

~~INTELLIGENCE SUMMARY~~

VOLUME 24. OCTOBER 1917.

Reference Map Sheet 28. 1/40,000.

(Erase heading not required.)

Instructions regarding War Diaries and Intelligence Summaries are contained in F. S. Regs., Part II. and the Staff Manual respectively. Title pages will be prepared in manuscript.

Place	Date	Hour	Summary of Events and Information	Remarks and references to Appendices
	1917.			
DRANOUTRE.	October.		Throughout the month of October Headquarters R.E. remained at DRANOUTRE with Divisional Headquarters.	
			On the 26th Lieut-Colonel G.W.DENISON, D.S.O., R.E. returned from leave of absence, and took over the duties of C.R.E. from Major N.W.NAPIER CLAVERING, D.S.O., R.E.	
			The work on the hutting scheme continued as in the last month, no new hutted camps being started. Work proceeded satisfactorily. During the early part of the month it was considerably held up by lack of Stores, but later the situation improved.	
			On the 16th, the C.R.E. became no longer responsible for work in the Reserve Line, Brigadiers becoming responsible for work in their Sectors back to and including that line. O.C. 11th South Lancs. Pioneers placed 1 officer and 50 men at the disposal of Brigadiers for each Battalion in the line, one section of each Field Company being employed in the forward area.	
			The personnel at the R.E. Dumps remained the same throughout the month.	
	4-11-17.			

Lieut-Colonel R.E.
C.R.E., 30th Division.

SECRET.

HEADQUARTERS 30TH
DIVISIONAL ENGINEERS.

WAR DIARY.

VOLUME 25.   NOVEMBER 1917.

SECRET.

HEADQUARTERS 30TH
DIVISIONAL
ENGINEERS.

WAR DIARY

VOLUME 25. NOVEMBER 1917.

Reference Map Sheet 28. 1/40,000.

Army Form C. 2118.

(Erase heading not required.)

Place	Date 1917.	Hour	Summary of Events and Information	Remarks and references to Appendices
DRANOUTRE.	1st Novr.		From the 1st to the 14th November, Headquarters R.E. remained with Divl. Hdqrs at DRANOUTRE. Work continued normally both in the forward area, and on the hutting scheme in rear. The situation as regards R.E. Stores was good. This work calls for no comment.	
GOLDFISH CHATEAU, H.11.a.8.1.	14th Novr.		On the 14th, Headquarters R.E., the 3 Field Coys. and 11th South Lancs. Pioneers were detached from the 30th Division and were temporarily attached to the CANADIAN CORPS in the PASSCHENDAELE Sector. When the VIII Corps took over this sector from the CANADIAN CORPS, the technical troops of the 30th Division remained at the same work, and were returned to the VIII Corps. The work was carried out under the orders of the Chief Engineer of the Corps concerned. The C.R.E. was given charge of the "SOUTH ROAD" from FREZENBURG past DEVIL'S CROSSING to SEINE, the labour available being as follows :- 201st Field Coy. R.E. 202nd Field Coy. R.E. 171 Tunnelling Coy. R.E. 254 Tunnelling Coy. R.E. 187 Labour Coy. R.E. 2 Companies, 9th Bn. K.R.R. The labour was employed as follows :- FREZENBURG to FROST HOUSE - 254 Tunnelling Coy. R.E. 187 Labour Coy. R.E. FROST HOUSE to DEVIL'S CROSSING - 171 Tunnelling Coy. R.E. Work from SEINE towards ZONNEBEKE STATION - 201st Field Coy. R.E. 202nd Field Coy. R.E. The latter Companies worked in reliefs, the first relief being taken from 6-0am to 11-0am by the 202nd Field Coy. R.E. and 1 Coy. 9th K.R.R. each morning, the second relief from 11-0am onwards was taken by the 201st Field Coy. and 1 Coy. 9th K.R.R. On several occasions the work on the later relief was stopped by shell fire. During this period the 200th Field Coy. R.E. was employed under the orders of C.R.E. 14th Divn. From midnight 18th/19th November there was a redistribution of work, which is shewn in the letter attached as Appendix A. Work continued in accordance with this distribution until the night 22nd/23rd when 2 companies previously employed on the SOUTH ROAD were put onto the road between GRAVENSTAFEL and BELLEVUE, in order to make it passable for Field Guns manhandled. These two companies also worked on this road on the nights 23/24th and 24/25th. ON THE	

S E C R E T.　　HEADQUARTERS 30TH　　VOLUME 25.　NOVEMBER 1917.
　　　　　　　　　DIVISIONAL INTELLIGENCE SUMMARY.
　　　　　　　　　ENGINEERS.　　　　Reference Map Sheet 28. 1/40,000.

Sheet 2.

WAR DIARY

(Erase heading not required.)

Army Form C. 2118.

Place	Date 1917.	Hour	Summary of Events and Information	Remarks and references to Appendices
BESTOUTRE.	24th Novr.		On the 24th, the 30th Divisional Technical Troops (less 2 companies 11th South Lancs.) moved to the 39th Divisional Area (See Appendix B.) and came under the orders of G.O.C. 39th Division until this area was taken over from the 39th Division by G.O.C. 30th Division. The order to Field Coys. and 11th South Lancs. Pioneers is shewn as Appendix B. Field Coys. continued the work of the Field Coys. 39th Division whom they relieved, till the 27th. After the 27th the distribution of work was as follows :-	
			200th Field Coy. R.E. : 1 section working on SUSSEX AVENUE.	
			2 sections working on Reserve Line.	
			1 section reclaiming German "Pillboxes" South of A Track.	
			201st Field Coy. R.E. : 2 sections working under the orders of G.O.C. Brigade in the line.	
			1 section working on Cookhouses in the forward area under the orders of the C.R.E.	
			1 section working on reclaiming German "Pillboxes" North of A Track.	
			202nd Field Coy. R.E. : Working on hutted camps in the back area.	
			11th Bn. South Lancs. : 1 Company working under the orders of G.O.C. Brigade in the line.	
			1 Company working under the orders of O.C. 200th Field Coy. R.E.	
			1 Company on Roads and Tracks.	
			1 Company working on PERTH AVENUE.	
			All details of this work will be given in the War Diary of the unit concerned.	
			The R.S.M. and Divisional Dump Party of attached Infantry remained at LINDENHOEK Dump till the 18th of the month when it moved to the VIII Corps R.E. Park at CAESTREGAT working under the orders of the Officer in charge VIII Corps R.E. Park.	
			On the 24th the Party moved to the 39th Divl. R.E. Park and named the Dump at CAFE BELGE, H.29.b.1.1, a party of 1 N.C.O. and 3 men being sent forward to man a forward Dump (MANOR Dump) at I.28.a.6.5.	
	4-12-17.			

Lieut-Colonel R.E.
C.R.E. 30th Division.

O.C. 200th Field Coy. R.E.
O.C. 201st Field Coy. R.E.
O.C. 202nd Field Coy. R.E.
O.C. 11th Bn. South Lancs.

1.   The 201st Field Coy. R.E. will take over the control, maintenance and extension of the HARDAS CROSS - SHINE Tramway from the 5th A.T. Company, Canadian Engineers (located at H.13.a.6.7) at midnight of 18th/19th and also that work which is being done on the tramline by the 61st Field Coy. R.E., from that Company, as early as can be arranged.

        The 4th Canadian Labour Battalion (located at SALVATION CORNER, I.1.c.9.7) will work on above tramline under the orders of O.C. 201st Field Coy. R.E.

2.   The 202nd Field Coy. R.E. will take over the work now being done by the 201st Field Coy. R.E. on the SOUTH ROAD between BOESINGHE STATION and SHINE at midnight 18th/19th.

3.   The 200th Field Coy. R.E. will hold themselves in readiness to proceed to the HUSTHULST Area.

4.   Two companies of the 11th South Lancs. Pioneers will take over the work of the 9th K.R.R. on the SOUTH ROAD from midnight 18th/19th and will work under the orders of O.C. 202nd Field Coy. R.E.

5.   One company of the 11th South Lancs. Pioneers will work on the NORTH ROAD under the orders of C.R.E. 14th Division.

        One company of the 11th South Lancs. Pioneers will hold themselves in readiness to proceed to the HUSTHULST Area.

6.   The 171 Tunnelling Coy. R.E., the 254 Tunnelling Coy. R.E. and the 157 Labour Coy. R.E. will continue work as at present on the SOUTH ROAD.

7.   The 9th Bn. K.R.R. will come under the orders of C.R.E. 14th Division at midnight 18th/19th.

8.   Field Companies and 11th South Lancs. will acknowledge receipt.

                                        Captain R.E.
17-11-17.   Adjt., 30th Divl. Engineers.

Copies to 38th Division "G".
         30th Division "Q".
         C.R.E. VIII Corps Troops.
         C.R.E. 14th Division.
         5th A.T. Coy. C.E.
         4th Canadian Labour Btn.
         9th Bn. K.R.R.
         171 Tunnelling Coy. R.E.
         254 Tunnelling Coy. R.E.
         157 Labour Coy. R.E.
         War Diary.
         File.

39th DIV. ENGINEERS ORDER No. [?]   B   Copy No. 9

1. The 39th Divl. R.E. will move to the 39th Division area
to-morrow, 24th instant, and will take over the work of the
39th Divl. R.E. as follows :-
    227th Field Coy. R.E.   117th Field Coy. R.E.
    201st Field Coy. R.E.   77th Field Coy. R.E.
    222nd Field Coy. R.E.   234th Field Coy. R.E.
Units will be billeted as follows :-
    227th Field Coy. R.E. at I.20.c.5.5.
                Transport at I.19.c.3.5.
    201st Field Coy. R.E. at two sections I.15.c.0.5.
                           two sections I.9.a.5.5.
                Transport at C.1.a.5.5.
    222nd Field Coy. R.E. at I.21.a.5.5.
                Transport at C.5.d.5.5.

2. The 39th Divl. R.E. are located as follows :-
    117th Field Coy. R.E. at [?] TUNNEL, I.15.c.2.5.
                Transport at [?] FARM, C.1.a.3.5.
    77th Field Coy. R.E. at in [?], I.20.a.5.5.
                Transport at C.15.c.5.5.
    234th Field Coy. R.E. at [?] FARM, I.21.a.5.5.
                Transport at C.5.d.5.5.

3. Each Field Coy. will send an advanced party ahead to take
over billets as early to-morrow morning as possible.

4. Each Field Coy. will leave a rear party of 1 officer and
10 men to hand over to incoming Field Coys. their billets and
work. These parties will be rationed by incoming Field Coys.
for the 25th and 26th and will rejoin their units on the 26th.

5. The 11th South Lancs. Pioneers will move to the 39th Divl.
area as follows :-
    Headquarters and 2 companies on 24th.
    2 companies on 25th.
    They will take over work and billets from the 13th
Gloucestershire Regt. (Pioneers) who will also move in two
parties on 24th and 25th.
    Work will therefore not stop on the BULLECOURT Road.
    The 13th Gloucesters are located at [?] at
I.21.d.5.5. with Transport at C.16.b.5.5.
    Advanced parties will be sent ahead to take over work and
billets early to-morrow morning. A rear party of 1 officer
and 10 men will remain behind to show incoming Battalion work
and billets.

6. The main Divisional R.E. Dump will be at FARM Road,
B.29.b.7.5. The Advanced Divisional R.E. Dump will be at
I.28.a.3.9.

7. Headquarters 39th Divisional Engineers will move to
BATTOURS on the 24th.

8. ACKNOWLEDGE.

                                    [signature]
                                    Captain R.E.
23-11-17.   Adjt., 39th Divl. Engineers.

Copy No.1 to O.C. 227th Field Coy. R.E. A
    "   2 " O.C. 201st Field Coy. R.E. A
    "   3 " O.C. 222nd Field Coy. R.E. A
    "   4 " O.C. 11th S. Lancs. [?]
    "   5 " 39th Division G.S. A
    "   6 " 39th Division [?]
    "   7 " C.R.E. 39th Division.
    "   8 " [?] Corps. A
    "   9 " War Diary.
    "   10 " File.

S E C R E T.

H E A D Q U A R T E R S

30TH

DIVISIONAL ENGINEERS.

W A R   D I A R Y.

VOLUME 26.   DECEMBER 1917.

SECRET.

HEADQUARTERS 30TH DIVISIONAL ENGINEERS.

WAR DIARY ~~INTELLIGENCE SUMMARY~~

(Erase heading not required.)

Army Form C. 2118.

VOLUME 26. DECEMBER 1917.

Reference Maps, Sheet 28, Scale 1/40,000.
Sheet ZILLEBEKE, Scale 1/10,000.

Place	Date 1917.	Hour	Summary of Events and Information	Remarks and references to Appendices
WESTOUTRE.	1st Dec.		From the 1st to the 31st December 1917, H.Q.R.E. remained with Divisional Headquarters at WESTOUTRE. Work continued normally in the Sector, both in the forward area and on the hutting schemes in the rear. On the night of the 5/6th the Divisional front was extended North from the SCHEERIABEEK to the REUTELBEEK, relieving the 2nd New Zealand Infantry Brigade. The Field Companies were located as follows :- Left Sector. 201st Field Coy. R.E. JASPER TUNNELS, J.19.a.8.9. Right Sector. 200th Field Coy. R.E. CANADA TUNNELS, I.30.a.5.0. Back Area. 202nd Field Coy. R.E. VOORMEZEELE, I.31.a.3.1. Transport Lines, KRUISSTRAATHOEK, H.30.c. Inter-Company reliefs were carried out every 9 days, each Company being 18 days in the line and 9 days in reserve. (See Appendix 1.) The distribution of work was as follows :- In the Line. Reserve Line - (a) Construction of 7 Strong Points with shelters for accommodation of the garrison. (b) Wiring. Maintenance of Duckboard Tracks. Reclaiming German Pill-boxes. Gum Boot Drying Sheds in JASPER and CANADA TUNNELS. Fitting gas doors - TORR TOP & HEDGE STREET TUNNELS. Back Areas. Hutted Camps & Horse Standings - WARBURG CAMP, H.30.d.1.3., H.36.b.5.7., H.30.c., H.32.d.3.1. A.R.P.; HORNBY SIDINGS. Y.M.C.A., BEDFORD HOUSE. Gum Boot Drying Shed, H.36.b.5.7. Artillery. Each Field Coy. had a detachment attached to the Artillery for work as follows :- 200th Field Coy. R.E. attached to 149th Brigade R.F.A. 201st Field Coy. R.E. attached to 88th Brigade R.F.A. 202nd Field Coy. R.E. attached to 87th Brigade R.F.A. Sheet 2.	

Army Form C. 2118.

Sheet 2.

WAR DIARY

~~INTELLIGENCE SUMMARY~~

(Erase heading not required.)

Place	Date	Hour	Summary of Events and Information	Remarks and references to Appendices
	3-1-18.		PIONEERS (11TH SOUTH LANCS.)	

One Company in the line under orders of G.O.C. Left Brigade.
One Company under the Field Coy. working on Reserve Line.
One Company on tracks West of Brigade Hdqrs. including a new track from J.19.a.5.4. to J.20.a.3.3.
One Platoon attached to No.8 Tramway Coy.
Three Platoons on PLUMER'S DRIVE (Plank Road) & GLOUCESTER DRIVE (Mule Track).

All details of this work will be given in the War Diary of the unit concerned.

The supply of R.E. Stores for existing Camps in the back areas was in the hands of the D.O.R.E. He had a small party attached to him and took charge of :-

(1) The erection of a Divisional Theatre.
(2) The erection of huts for Battalion Messes & Recreation Rooms in CHIPPEWA CAMP.
(3) The erection of new huts in existing camps.

The R.S.M. and the Divisional Dump party of attached Infantry remained throughout the month at the 30th Divisional R.E. Dump, CAFE BELGE, H.29.b.1.1. A party of 1 N.C.O. and 3 men manning the Forward Dump (MANOR DUMP) at I.28.a.6.5.

The situation as regards R.E. Stores was good; latterly sawn timber was scarce.

Lieut-Colonel R.E.
C.R.E. 30th Division.

SECRET.   Appendix 1.   Copy No. 10

30TH DIVISIONAL ENGINEERS ORDER NO.6.

Reference Map Sheet 28, 1/40,000.   1st December 1917.

1.   No.1 Group (89th Brigade Hdqrs.) will relieve No.2 Group (90th Bde Hdqrs.) in the line on 3rd/4th and 4th/5th December: relief to be completed by 8-0am on 5th.

2.   G.O.C. 89th Infantry Brigade will assume command of the front at 11-0am on 4th December.

3.   2 sections 202nd Field Coy. R.E. will relieve 2 sections 201st Field Coy. R.E. at J.19.a.9.9. on the 3rd December, the 2 sections 201st Field Coy. R.E. returning to the 202nd Field Coy. R.E. Camp, I.31.a.3.2.
      Headquarters and 2 sections 202nd Field Coy. R.E. will relieve Headquarters and 2 sections 201st Field Coy. R.E. on the 4th December.
      The relief will be completed by 6-0pm, 4th.

4.   All work in hand or proposed will be handed over to the incoming unit and every effort must be made to ensure continuity.

5.   ACKNOWLEDGE.

                                                         Captain R.E.
                                                 Adjt., 30th Divl. Engineers.

Copy No.1 to 200th Field Coy.   Copy No.7 to 21st Infantry Brigade.
  "   " 2 " 201st Field Coy.   "   " 8 " 89th Infantry Brigade.
  "   " 3 " 202nd Field Coy.   "   " 9 " 90th Infantry Brigade.
  "   " 4 " 11th Bn. South Lancs.   "   " 10 " War Diary.
  "   " 5 " 30th Division "G".   "   " 11 " War Diary.
  "   " 6 " 30th Division "Q".   "   " 12 " File.

S E C R E T.   Appendix 1   Copy No. 10

30TH DIVISIONAL ENGINEERS ORDER NO. 7.

Reference Map Sheet 28, 1/40,000.   9th December 1917.

1. No.2 Group (21st Brigade Hdqrs.) are relieving No.1 Group (89th Bde. Hdqrs.) in the line on 11th/12th and 12th/13th December: relief to be completed by 10-0am on 13th.

2. G.O.C. 21st Infantry Brigade will assume command of the front at 10-0am on the 12th December.

3. 2 sections 201st Field Coy. R.E. will relieve 2 sections 200th Field Coy. R.E. at I.30.a.5.0. on the 12th December, the 2 sections 200th Field Coy. R.E. returning to the 201st Field Coy. R.E. Camp I.31.a.3.2.
   Headquarters and 2 sections 201st Field Coy. R.E. will relieve Headquarters and 2 sections 200th Field Coy. R.E. on the 13th December.
   The relief will be completed by 12 noon 13th.

4. All details to be arranged between Os C. Field Coys. concerned.

5. All work in hand or proposed will be handed over to the incoming unit and every effort must be made to ensure continuity.

6. ACKNOWLEDGE.

                                                    Lieut. R.E.
                                            Adjt., 30th Divl. Engineers.

Copy No. 1 to 200th Field Coy.   Copy No. 7 to 21st Infantry Brigade.
  "   " 2 " 201st Field Coy.   "   " 8 " 89th Infantry Brigade.
  "   " 3 " 202nd Field Coy.   "   " 9 " 90th Infantry Brigade.
  "   " 4 " 11th Bn. South Lancs.   "   " 10 " War Diary.
  "   " 5 " 30th Division "G".   "   " 11 " War Diary.
  "   " 6 " 30th Division "Q".   "   " 12 " File.

SECRET.   Copy No. 11

30TH DIVISIONAL ENGINEERS ORDER NO.8.

Reference Map Sheet 28 Scale 1/40,000.
          Sheet ZILLEBEKE, Scale 1/10,000.   17th Decr. 1917.

---

1.   In consequence of operations 1 Battalion of No.1 Group moved on the 14th instant from SCOTTISH WOOD to TORR TOP TUNNELS, in relief of 1 Battalion of No.2 Group, which moved forward.

2.   No.1 Group (90th Inf: Bde. Hdqrs), under command of Brigadier General G.D. GOODMAN, C.M.G., will relieve No.2 Group in the line on the 17th/18th and 18th/19th December: relief to be completed by 10-0am on the 19th December.

3.   No.1 Group Commander will assume command of the front at 10-0am on 19th December.

4.   G.O.C. 89th Infantry Brigade (Hdqrs. at ZEVECOTEN CAMP) will assume command of No.2 Group from 6-0am on 19th December: and will detail working parties required from it for the 19th and subsequent dates.

5.   2 sections 200th Field Coy. R.E. will relieve 2 sections 202nd Field Coy. R.E. at JASPER TUNNELS, J.19.a.8.9. on the 21st December, the 2 sections 202nd Field Coy. R.E. returning to the 200th Field Coy. R.E. Camp I.31.a.3.2.
        Headquarters and 2 sections 200th Field Coy. R.E. will relieve Headquarters and 2 sections 202nd Field Coy. R.E. on the 22nd December: relief to be completed by 12 noon 22nd.

6.   All details to be arranged between Os.C. Field Coys. concerned.

7.   All work in hand or proposed will be handed over to the incoming unit and every effort must be made to ensure continuity.

8.   ACKNOWLEDGE.

                                                        Lieut. R.E.
                                            Adjt., 30th Divl. Engineers.

Copy No.1 to 200th Field Coy.   Copy No.8 to 21st Infantry Brigade.
  "   " 2 " 201st Field Coy.   "   " 9 " 89th Infantry Brigade.
  "   " 3 " 202nd Field Coy.   "   "10 " 90th Infantry Brigade.
  "   " 4 " 30th Divl. Signal Coy.   "   "11 " War Diary.
  "   " 5 " 11th Bn. South Lancs.   "   "12 " War Diary.
  "   " 6 " 30th Division "G".   "   "13 " File.
  "   " 7 " 30th Division "Q".

Appendix 1

S E C R E T. Copy No. 11.

30TH DIVISIONAL ENGINEERS ORDER NO. 9.

Reference Maps, Sheet 28, Scale 1/40,000.
Sheet ZILLEBEKE, Scale 1/10,000.
---

1. The 89th Infantry Brigade are relieving the 90th Infantry Brigade in the left sector of the line on the 29th/30th and 30th/31st December 1917, the relief to be completed by 10-0am on the 31st December 1917.

2. Units of 89th Infantry Brigade on arriving in the forward area will come under orders of G.O.C. 90th Infantry Brigade till 10-0am on the 31st December.

3. G.O.C. 89th Infantry Brigade will assume command of the left sector at 10-0am on the 31st December.

4. Two sections 202nd Field Coy. R.E. will relieve two sections 201st Field Coy. R.E. at I.30.a.5.0. on the 29th December, the two sections 201st Field Coy. R.E. returning to the 202nd Field Coy. R.E. Camp, I.31.a.3.2.
   Headquarters and two sections 202nd Field Coy. R.E. will relieve Headquarters and two sections 201st Field Coy. R.E. on the 30th December. Relief to be completed by 12 noon 30th.

5. All details to be arranged between Os.C. Field Companies concerned.

6. All work in hand or proposed will be handed over to the incoming unit and every effort must be made to ensure continuity.

7. ACKNOWLEDGE.

27-12-17.

W. Davison
Lieut-Colonel R.E.
C.R.E. 30th Division.

```
Copy No. 1 to 200th Field Coy. R.E.
 "    "  2  "  201st Field Coy. R.E.
 "    "  3  "  202nd Field Coy. R.E.
 "    "  4  "  30th Divl. Signal Coy. R.E.
 "    "  5  "  11th Bn. South Lancs. Regt.
 "    "  6  "  30th Division "G".
 "    "  7  "  30th Division "Q".
 "    "  8  "  21st Infantry Brigade.
 "    "  9  "  89th Infantry Brigade.
 "    " 10  "  90th Infantry Brigade.
 "    " 11  "  War Diary.
 "    " 12  "  War Diary.
 "    " 13  "  File.
```

APPENDIX 2.

Army Form C. 2118.

WAR DIARY
or
INTELLIGENCE SUMMARY.
(Erase heading not required.)

Place	Date	Hour	Summary of Events and Information	Remarks and references to Appendices
	1917.		**MOVEMENT OF OFFICERS.**	
	2nd December.		T/Lieut. C.J.BARKER, R.E., 200th Field Coy. R.E. took over duties of D.O.R.E. in accordance with 30th Divisional Administrative Notes No. A/7966 dated 23-1-17.	
	7th December.		Captain (A/Major) N.W. NAPIER CLAVERING, D.S.O., R.E. 200th Field Coy. R.E. left to take up appointment of Instructor, R.E. School of Instruction, BLENDECQUES.	
	8th December.		Captain (A/Major) O.D.ATKINSON, M.C. R.E., Adjutant 30th Divisional Engineers, assumed command of 200th Field Coy. R.E.	
			T/Lieut. C.C.LINDSAY R.E., 202nd Field Coy. R.E. took over duties of Adjutant vice Captain O.D.ATKINSON, M.C. R.E.	
	24th December.		T/Captain N.T.ELLIS R.E. 202nd Field Coy. R.E. assumed command of 201st Field Coy. R.E. vice Captain (A/Major) J.MIDDLETON, R.E.	
			T/Lieut. C.C.LINDSAY R.E., Adjutant 30th Divisional Engineers, appointed Second in Command 202nd Field Coy. R.E., vice T/Captain N.T. ELLIS R.E.	
			T/Lieut. C.J.BARKER R.E., 200th Field Coy. R.E. appointed Adjutant vice T/Lieut. C.C.LINDSAY R.E.	
			T/Lieut. G.V.SCOTT, R.E., 200th Field Coy. R.E. took over duties of D.O.R.E. vice T/Lieut. C.J.BARKER R.E.	

SECRET.

HEADQUARTERS 30TH DIVISIONAL ENGINEERS.

WAR DIARY.

VOLUME 27.   JANUARY 1918.

SECRET.

WAR DIARY

HEADQUARTERS 30TH DIVISIONAL ENGINEERS.

VOLUME 27. JANUARY 1918. Army Form C.2118.

Reference Maps Sheet 28, 1/40,000.
Sheet ZILLEBEKE, 1/10,000.
AMIENS, 1/100,000.
ST. QUENTIN, 1/100,000.

Place	Date 1918.	Hour	Summary of Events and Information	Remarks and references to Appendices
WESTOUTRE.	1st Jany.		Work continued normally in the Sector, both in the forward area and on hutting schemes in the rear. The Field Companies were located as follows :-	
			Left Sector, 200th Field Coy. R.E., JASPER TUNNELS, J.19.a.8.9. Right Sector, 202nd Field Coy. R.E., CANADA TUNNELS, I.30.a.5.0. Back area, 201st Field Coy. R.E., VOORMEZEELE, I.31.a.3.1. Transport Lines, KRUISTRAATHOEK, H.30.c. 11th South Lancs. (Pioneers) - Location and employment as in Volume 26.	
			On January 5th and 6th the 30th Division was relieved by the 20th Division. The relief of the technical troops is given in Order No.10 attached as Appendix "A". On January 7th the Division started to move Southwards to the ST. QUENTIN Area, H.Q.R.E. moving with Divisional Headquarters as follows :-	
			January 7th - From WESTOUTRE to BLARINGHEM. January 8th - From BLARINGHEM to STEENBECQUE. LONGEAU (AMIENS) at 8-0pm, detrained and marched to CORBIE. " 14th - By train from CORBIE to NESLE (transport by road). " 19th - From NESLE to HAM. Here the unit entrained at 11-58am, arrived at	
HAM.	19th Jany.		From 19th to 31st January, Headquarters R.E. and the Technical Troops were detached from the 30th Division for work as follows :-	
			(a) H.Q.R.E., two Field Coys. and 2 Coys. Pioneers under C.E. XVIII Corps. (b) One Field Coy., Hdqrs. and 2 Coys. Pioneers under C.E. Fifth Army.	
			The C.R.E. was given charge of the Second Line of Defences on the whole of the Corps front from MEISSEMY on the North to ESSIGNY on the South. This line was known as the Corps line or Battle Zone. It was divided into 2 Divisional fronts, which were sub-divided into seven Battalion subsectors. Work on the defences had been commenced by the French.	
				A Field Coy.

1st January 1918 H.Q.R.E. remained with Divisional Headquarters at WESTOUTRE.

Army Form C. 2118.

Sheet 2.
WAR DIARY
INTELLIGENCE SUMMARY

(Erase heading not required.)

Instructions regarding War Diaries and Intelligence Summaries are contained in F. S. Regs., Part II. and the Staff Manual respectively. Title pages will be prepared in manuscript.

Place	Date	Hour	Summary of Events and Information	Remarks and references to Appendices
HAM. (Continued).	Jan. 1918		A Field Company was given charge of a Divisional Front as follows :-	
			200th Field Coy. R.E. Northern Division (4 Battalion Subsectors) located at ATILLY. 201st Field Coy. R.E. Southern Division (3 Battalion Subsectors) located at HAMEL. The Transport Lines at VAUX and HAMEL respectively. One Company of Pioneers was attached to each Field Company.	
			A R.E. Subaltern was put in charge of each Battalion Subsector and had one Battalion available as working party, the Battalion working on the Sector it would occupy in case of alarm. Details of this work will be given in the War Diaries of the Units concerned.	
			The 202nd Field Coy. R.E. and H.Q. and 2 Coys. Pioneers were located at NESLE. They were employed under the C.E. Fifth Army on the provision of Army Headquarters at NESLE. Details will be given in the War Diaries of the Units.	
			On the detachment of the Technical Troops from the Division, the supply of R.E. Stores was in the hands of the D.O.R.E, Lieut. H.RAINE, 202nd Field Coy. R.E., from 19-1-18.	
	1-2-18.		The R.S.M. and the Divisional Dump Party of attached Infantry remained at the 30th Divisional R.E.Dump, CAFE BELGE, H.29.b.1.1. until January 4th when they were relieved by the 20th Division. They were attached to the 201st Field Coy. R.E. for the move. In the new area half the party was attached to each of the Field Coys. employed on the Battle Zone and were used for offloading Battle Zone Stores at the Forward Divisional Dumps of the Division in the line.	

[signature]
Lieut-Colonel R.E.
C.R.E. 30th Division.

Appendix A

S E C R E T.   Copy No.

30TH DIVISIONAL ENGINEERS ORDER NO. 10.

Reference Maps, Sheet 28, Scale 1/40,000.
               Sheet ZILLEBEKE, Scale 1/10,000.
----

1. The 30th Divisional R.E. and Pioneers will be relieved by the 20th Divisional R.E. and Pioneers in the line on January 5th and 6th as follows :-

   JANUARY 5TH.

   201st Field Coy. R.E. located at VOORMEZEELE (I.3d.a.3.1.) will be relieved by the 96th Field Coy. R.E.
   202nd Field Coy. R.E. located at CANADA TUNNELS (I.30.a.5.0.) will be relieved by the 84th Field Coy. R.E.
   11th South Lancs. (Pioneers), located at ZILLEBEKE BUND (I.15.d.2.2.) will be relieved by the 11th D.L.I. Pioneers.

   JANUARY 6TH.

   200th Field Coy. R.E. located at JASPER TUNNELS (J.19.a.8.9.) will be relieved by the 83rd Field Coy. R.E.

2. The Advance Party of the 96th Field Coy. R.E. will arrive on the 3rd and will be accommodated by the 201st Field Coy. R.E.

3. All details of reliefs will be arranged between Os.C. units concerned.

4. The Field Coys. of the 30th Division will move under orders of their affiliated Brigade.

5. Headquarters, 30th Divisional R.E. will close at WESTOUTRE at 10-0am on 7th January and will re-open at BLARINGHEM same day.

6. ACKNOWLEDGE.

                                        G.W. Denison
                                        Lieut-Colonel R.E.
2-1-18.   C.R.E. 30th Division.

```
Copy No. 1 to 200th Field Coy. R.E.
     "   " 2 "  201st Field Coy. R.E.
     "   " 3 "  202nd Field Coy. R.E.
     "   " 4 "  30th Divl. Signal Coy. R.E.
     "   " 5 "  11th Bn. South Lancs.
     "   " 6 "  30th Division "G".
     "   " 7 "  30th Division "Q".
     "   " 8 "  21st Infantry Brigade.
     "   " 9 "  89th Infantry Brigade.
     "   " 10 " 90th Infantry Brigade.
     "   " 11 " C.R.E. 20th Division.
     "   " 12 " C.E. IX Corps.
     "   " 13 " War Diary.
     "   " 14 " War Diary.
     "   " 15 " File.
```

HEADQUARTERS 30TH DIVISIONAL ENGINEERS.

WAR DIARY.

VOLUME 28.   FEBRUARY 1918.

S E C R E T.

HEADQUARTERS 30TH DIVISIONAL ENGINEERS.

WAR DIARY ~~INTELLIGENCE SUMMARY~~

(Erase heading not required.)

VOLUME 28. FEBRUARY 1918. Army Form C. 2118.

Reference Maps Sheets 62c S.E.)
62c S.W.) Scale
66d N.E.) 1/20,000.
66a N.W.)

Instructions regarding War Diaries and Intelligence Summaries are contained in F.S. Regs., Part II. and the Staff Manual respectively. Title pages will be prepared in manuscript.

Place	Date Hour 1918.	Summary of Events and Information	Remarks and references to Appendices
HAM.		From 1st to 23rd February 1918 Headquarters R.E. and the Technical Troops remained detached from the 30th Division for work as follows :-	
		(a) H.Q.R.E., two Field Coys. and 2 Coys. 11th South Lancs. Pioneers continued work on the Battle Zone under C.E. XVIII Corps.	
		(b) One Field Coy., H.Q. and 2 Coys. Pioneers continued work on Fifth Army Headquarters NESLE under C.E. Fifth Army.	
	Feby.4th.	The C.R.E. left for BLENDECQUES to attend a Conference of C.R.Es at the R.E. School of Instruction, returning on the 7th.	
	Feby.14th.	The Commander-in-Chief inspected B. and C. sub-sectors of the Battle Zone.	
	Feby.19th.	202nd Field Coy. R.E., H.Q. and 2 Coys. Pioneers moved from NESLE to the XVIII Corps Area. A redistribution of the work was made as follows :-	
		200th Field Coy. R.E. - Battle Zone - (3 Battalion subsectors) located at ATILLY. 201st Field Coy. R.E. - Battle Zone - (2 Battalion subsectors) located at HAMEL. 202nd Field Coy. R.E. - Battle Zone - (2 Battalion subsectors) located at ROUPY. 1 Coy. Pioneers was attached to each Field Company. H.Q. and 1 Coy. Pioneers with one section 201st Field Coy. R.E. were employed on the construction of a new Divisional Headquarters at DURY.	
	Feby.23rd.	The 30th Division took over the centre of the XVIII Corps front, taking over the Northern portion from the 61st Division and the Southern portion from the 36th Division. Divisional Headquarters at HAM. Each Division became responsible for the Battle Zone in its own front. 202nd Field Coy. R.E. took over the whole of the Battle Zone on the 30th Divisional Front. The other Field Coys. took over the work in the line as follows :-	
		200th Field Coy. R.E. - Left Brigade Subsector - located at DOUCHY. 201st Field Coy. R.E. - Right Brigade Subsector - located at VAUX. Distribution:- Two sections in the line; one section with the Artillery; one section /back areas. H.Q. 1 Coy. & Transport Pioneers moved to FLUQUIERES. Distribution:- 1 Coy. attached to each Field Coy. H.Q. Coy. employed on Divisional Headquarters and hutting.	DURY.

Sheet 2.

WAR DIARY

~~INTELLIGENCE/SUMMARY~~

(Erase heading not required.)

Army Form C. 2118.

Place	Date 1918.	Hour	Summary of Events and Information	Remarks and references to Appendices
DURY.	Feb. 26th		H.Q.R.E. moved with Divisional Headquarters to DURY. **R.S.M. and Divisional Dump Party of attached Infantry.** A third of the party was attached to each Field Company and were used for offloading Battle Zone Stores at the Forward Divisional Dumps.	
	Feb.23rd.		The 30th Divl. R.E. Dump was established at ETREILLERS, the R.S.M. and the Dump party assembled here and took over the Dump from the 61st Division. **Stores.** The supply of wiring material was very short throughout the month. Very little stock was handed over by the 61st Division at ETREILLERS. For a time the utmost difficulty was experienced in meeting the demands for R.E. Stores. The situation eased somewhat towards the end of the month. 4-3-18. [signature] Lieut-Colonel R.E. C.R.E. 30th Division.	

Headquarters,

ROYAL ENGINEERS, 30th Division.

M A R C H

1 9 1 8

Attached:-

Appendices "A" & "B".

S E C R E T.

HEADQUARTERS 30TH
DIVISIONAL ENGINEERS.

W A R   D I A R Y.

VOLUME 29 - MARCH 1918.

SECRET.

WAR DIARY

Instructions regarding War Diaries and Intelligence Summaries are contained in F.S. Regs., Part II. and the Staff Manual respectively. Title pages will be prepared in manuscript.

HEADQUARTERS 30TH DIVISIONAL ENGINEERS.

VOLUME 29. MARCH 1918.

Reference Maps Sheets (62c S.E.
Scale   (62c S.W.
1/20,000.   (66d N.E.
               (66d N.W.

Army Form C. 2118.) Scale
ST.QUENTIN 18.) 1/100
AMIENS 17.   000
ABBEVILLE 14.

(Erase heading not required.)

Place	Date	Hour	Summary of Events and Information	Remarks and references to Appendices
DURY.	1st		On 1st March H.Q.R.E. was still with Divisional H.Q. at DURY. Work continued normally in the Sector. The Field Coys. and Pioneers were located as follows :- Left Brigade Subsector - 200th Field Coy. R.E. - located at DOUCHY. Right Brigade Subsector - 201st Field Coy. R.E. - located at VAUX. Battle Zone. - 202nd Field Coy. R.E. - located at ROUPY. Pioneers, 11th Bn. South Lancs. Regt. - located at FLUQUIERES. Distribution and work as last month. On March 1st the 201st Field Coy. R.E. was attached to the 61st Division (the Division on the left) for work on a redoubt in this Divisional area. H.Q. and transport remained at VAUX. A redistribution of work was made as follows :- The 200th Field Coy. R.E. took over the work in the line on the whole Divisional front. Distribution - two sections in the line, two sections with the Artillery. Pioneers :- 2 Coys. attached to 200th Field Coy. R.E. 1 Coy. attached to 202nd Field Coy. R.E. and hutting. 1 Coy. employed on Divisional H.Q. and hutting.	
	6th		Army Commander visited Battle Zone with C.R.E.	
	19th		201st Field Coy. R.E. rejoined from attachment to 61st Division. See Operation Order No.11 attached as Appendix "A". A redistribution of work was again made as follows :- 200th Field Coy. R.E. - Left Brigade Subsector - 2 sections in line, 2 sections with Artillery. 201st " " " - Right " " " " " " " " " " Throughout the subsequent operations H.Q.R.E. remained with Advanced Divisional H.Q.	
	21st	5-5am.	Received order "Man Battle Stations".	
		5-15am.	Sent out the order "Man Battle Stations". The Field Coys. and Pioneers assembled at FLUQUIERES, the pre-arranged Battle Station, upon receipt of the order. The Transport moved to Battle Stations as follows :- 200th Field Coy. R.E. - DURY. 201st Field Coy. R.E. - VILLERS ST. CHRISTOPHE. 202nd Field Coy. R.E. - VILLERS ST. CHRISTOPHE. Pioneers (11th South Lancs). - DURY.	
		1-10pm.	Received orders to move the Field Coys. and Pioneers to the Quarry behind AVIATION WOOD.	
		1-30pm.	Sent out above orders to Field Coys. and Pioneers.	
		3-0pm.	Received orders to move the Field Coys. to AUBIGNY. The Pioneers remained at AVIATION WOOD and during the subsequent operations were under the orders of the G.O.C. Division.	

Army Form C. 2118.

Sheet 2.

WAR DIARY
INTELLIGENCE SUMMARY

(Erase heading not required.)

Instructions regarding War Diaries and Intelligence Summaries are contained in F. S. Regs., Part II. and the Staff Manual respectively. Title pages will be prepared in manuscript.

Place	Date	Hour	Summary of Events and Information	Remarks and references to Appendices
DURY.	21st	8-20pm.	Sent out above orders to Field Coys.	
		9-45pm.	Received orders to move the transport of the Field Coys. and Pioneers to ESMERY HALLON. Transport not to move until midnight and to be clear by 2-0am.	
HAM.	22nd	10-15pm	Sent out above orders.	
		3-30am	Divisional H.Q. moved to HAM.	
		9-30am	Sent out orders to Field Coys. to assemble at HAM for work on the HAM Bridgehead defences.	
		10-0am	Received verbal orders from C.E. XVIII Corps to take over Corps R.E. Dump HAM. L/Cpl. TINSLEY from the Divisional Dump Party put in charge.	
		11-30am	C.R.E. Corps Troops called with an order from Corps to the effect that the Division became responsible for the issue of the orders for the firing of the charges on bridges which had been prepared for demolition as follows :- Bridges from SOMMETTE EAUCOURT exclusive to HAM inclusive, excluding the Railway bridge East of HAM. The 172nd Tunnelling Coy. were responsible for the bridges East of HAM, and No.1 Siege Coy. R.A.R.E. for the HAM bridges. Interviewed the Officers concerned. C.R.E. reconnoitred HAM Defences with G.O.C. 89th Brigade i/c HAM Defences.	
		6-30pm	One Officer from each of 200th and 201st Field Coys. R.E. ordered to report to 89th Brigade to await orders re demolition of HAM Bridges.	
		7-0pm	L/Cpl. TINSLEY withdrawn from HAM Dump and ordered to move with his party to ERCHEU.	
		7-30pm	Orders to Field Coys. to withdraw to ESMERY HALLON on the manning of the HAM Defences by 89th Brigade.	
		9-0pm	Above order cancelled. Field Coys. ordered to move into billets in HAM and to commence wiring the Canal defences in the morning.	
ERCHEU.	22nd	11-0pm	Divisional H.Q. ordered to move to ERCHEU.	
	23rd	9-0am	Orders sent to Field Coy's Transport to move to ROIGLISE. Wired to C.E. XVIII Corps for 1,000 shovels.	
		3-15pm	Orders sent to 202nd Field Coy. R.E. to take over the following bridges which had been prepared for demolition by the 96th Field Coy. R.E. :- 3 bridges over the canal on the ERCHEU - LIBERMONT Road. 2 bridges over the canal on the ERCHEU - ESMERY HALLON Road.	
		6-15pm	Field Coys. ordered to concentrate during the night on placing ESMERY HALLON in a state of defence.	
		7-0pm	2/Lieut. BURFORD, 202nd Field Coy. R.E. reported he had taken over the bridges from the 96th Field Coy. R.E.	
		8-0pm	Received request from Field Coys. for Tool Carts & extra shovels. Sent out necessary orders to Transport Lines.	

Sheet 3.

WAR DIARY

~~INTELLIGENCE~~ SUMMARY.

(Erase heading not required.)

Army Form C. 2118.

Instructions regarding War Diaries and Intelligence Summaries are contained in F. S. Regs. Part II. and the Staff Manual respectively. Title pages will be prepared in manuscript.

Place	Date	Hour	Summary of Events and Information	Remarks and references to Appendices
ERCHEU	23rd	9-20pm	Field Coys. placed under the orders of G.O.C. 21st Brigade.	
	24th	3-10am	1000 shovels arrived by lorry. These were sent to ESMERY HALLON.	
		9-30am	Field Coys. ordered to withdraw from ESMERY HALLON to West of the canal near RAMECOURT.	
		12 noon	Orders issued to the Field Coys. to assist the French in preparing positions West of the canal, French troops having arrived to assist the British in the defence of the canal.	
SOLENTE	24th	2-0pm	Divisional H.Q. moved to SOLENTE.	
		3-25pm	Field Coys. ordered to cease work on the canal defences and withdraw to SOLENTE. Concentration completed at 5-30pm. "G" informed 5-40pm.	
		6-0pm	C.R.E. held a conference with the Field Coy. Commanders and explained the work to be undertaken by the Field Coys. on the defences of SOLENTE and OMENCOURT on the 25th.	
		7-0pm	Lorry despatched to draw 1000 shovels from CHAULNE to be delivered at SOLENTE.	
	25th	6-0am	Field Coys. commenced work on the defences of SOLENTE and OMENCOURT. Wired to C.E. for barbed wire and pickets.	
ROIEGLISE		2-0pm	Divisional H.Q. moved to ROIEGLISE.	
		3-15pm	Orders sent to 201st Field Coy. to put a few men on the defences to the N.W. and N. side of SOLENTE. Above order cancelled. Field Coys. ordered to withdraw to ROIEGLISE.	
		3-45pm	Field Coy. R.E. ordered to prepare the bridges on the ROIEGLISE – VERPILLIERS Road for demolition. Capt. HILL, 200th Field Coy. R.E. ordered to prepare the bridges on the ROIEGLISE at ROIEGLISE completed.	
		5-0pm	Concentration of Field Coys. at ROIEGLISE completed.	
		5-30pm	Field Coys. ordered to move to ARVILLERS, PLESSIER & LA NOUVILLE at 5-0am the 26th, to be brigaded with their affiliated Brigades on arrival. Owing to the change in the situation the Companies moved during the night.	
HANGEST-EN-SANTERRE.		6-0pm	H.Q.R.E. moved to HANGEST-EN-SANTERRE.	
	26th	8-30am	The 30th Division took up a line from ROUVROY to LE QUESNOY, the 89th Brigade on the left, 90th Brigade on the right. The 200th and 201st Field Coys. R.E. were attached to their affiliated Brigades. 202nd Field Coy. R.E. in reserve at PLESSIER.	
		12-20pm	202nd Field Coy. R.E. moved from PLESSIER to HANGEST.	
		1-0pm	170 men of the 21st Entrenching Battalion sent by C.E. XVIII Corps to assist on defensive line of 30th Division.	
		3-15pm	201st Field Coy. R.E. Transport moved from ARVILLERS to PLESSIER.	
		3-30pm	400 shovels arrived. Handed over to 90th Brigade Transport Officer.	
		4-35pm	202nd Field Coy. R.E. moved from HANGEST to PLESSIER to commence work on the Army line in front of the latter village.	
		7-0pm	An officer from the 23rd Entrenching Battalion reported that he had some men available at PLESSIER. Ordered to report to the 202nd Field Coy. for work on the Army line.	

Army Form C. 2118.

Sheet 4.

WAR DIARY
~~INTELLIGENCE SUMMARY~~

(Erase heading not required.)

Instructions regarding War Diaries and Intelligence
Summaries are contained in F.S. Regs., Part II.
and the Staff Manual respectively. Title pages
will be prepared in manuscript.

Place	Date	Hour	Summary of Events and Information	Remarks and references to Appendices
HANGEST-EN-SANTERRE.	26th	8-40pm	Communication sent to each Brigade in the line to the effect that they should use their affiliated Field Coys. for blocking the roads against the passage of armoured cars.	
		9-15pm	One tool cart ordered to be sent up to each Field Coy. in the line.	
QUESNEL	27th	3-0am	Divisional H.Q. moved to QUESNEL.	
HANGEST-EN-SANTERRE.		6-0am	" " returned to HANGEST.	
BRACHES.		11-30am	" " moved to BRACHES.	
			C.R.E. reconnoitred line from PLESSIER South to the canal at CONTOIRE.	
		2-30pm	Field Coy's Transport ordered to move to MAILLY.	
		4-30pm	Orders sent to 202nd Field Coy. and 23rd Entrenching Battalion to man the defences in front of the wood South of PLESSIER from the right flank of the French to the ~~Rixxxxxxx~~ canal.	
		9-30pm	Orders sent to 200th and 202nd Field Coys. to withdraw to MOREUIL as the Division was being relieved by the 133rd French Division.	
		9-50pm	200th and 202nd Field Coys. ordered to move from MOREUIL to ROUVREL early on the 28th.	
ROUVREL.	28th	11-30pm	Divisional H.Q. moved to ROUVREL.	
ESTREE.	28th	5-0pm	Divisional H.Q. moved to ESTREE.	
	29th	10-30am	200th and 202nd Field Coys. ordered to dig the trenches on the West bank of the River AVRE defending the bridges at MOREUIL. Field Coy's transport moved to SAINS-EN-AMIENOIS.	
		8-10pm	201st Field Coy. R.E. placed under orders of G.O.C. 90th Brigade.	
		8-50pm	Above order cancelled.	
	30th	1-45am.	Field Coys. standing fast at ROUVREL. Warned to be prepared to move at short notice.	
		8-0am	Orders for the move of the Division to ST. VALERY-SUR-SOMME received.	
		8-15am	Orders issued to Field Coys. to march from ROUVREL to SALEUX starting at 10-0am. H.Q.R.E. and Field Coys. entrained at SALEUX detraining at ST. VALERY-SUR-SOMME. Transport proceeded by road.	
ST.VALERY-SUR-SOMME	31st		H.Q.R.E. with Divisional H.Q. at ST.VALERY-SUR-SOMME. Field Coys. located as follows:-	
			200th Field Coy. R.E. - VANDRICOURT.	
			201st Field Coy. R.E. - TILLOY.	
			202nd Field Coy. R.E. - WATHIEHURT.	

Army Form C. 2118.

Sheet 5.
WAR DIARY
INTELLIGENCE SUMMARY
(Erase heading not required.)

Place	Date	Hour	Summary of Events and Information	Remarks and references to Appendices
	21st.	9-0am.	R.S.M. and Divisional Dump Party of attached Infantry. From March 1st. to March 21st the R.S.M. and the Divisional Dump Party manned the 30th Divisional R.E. Dump at ETREILLERS. On receipt of the order "Man Battle Stations" the R.S.M. and his party were ordered to withdraw to the Transport lines of the 202nd Field Coy. R.E. at VILLERS ST. CHRISTOHPE and remained with them throughout the operations. Owing to the unprecedented amount of work being done in this Sector the supply of certain R.E. Stores at times was very short, particularly mining frames, lagging and wiring material. A report on the operations of the 30th Divisional R.E. from 21-3-18 to 31-3-18 is attached as Appendix "B". 3-4-18. Lieut-Colonel R.E. C.R.E. 30th Division.	

A P P E N D I C E S   "A" and "B".

SECRET. Appendix "A" Copy No. 14

30TH DIVISIONAL ENGINEERS ORDER NO. 11.

1. On the return of the 201st Field Coy. R.E. to the 30th Division on the 19th instant, the three Field Companies will be distributed for work as follows :-

   (a) 200th Field Coy. R.E.

   2 sections on work on Forward Zone in Right Brigade Area.
   2 sections on work on Battery positions in Right Brigade Area.

   (b) 201st Field Coy. R.E.

   2 sections on work on Forward Zone in Left Brigade Area.
   2 sections on work on Battery positions in Left Brigade Area.

   (c) 202nd Field Coy. R.E.

   Work on the Battle Zone on the whole Divisional front.

2. (a) One section of 200th Field Coy. R.E. will move from SAVY WOOD to DALLON.

   (b) One section of 200th Field Coy. R.E. now working with Artillery Brigade in Left Brigade Area will move to Right Brigade Area for work with Artillery Brigade in that area.

   (c) Two sections of 201st Field Coy. R.E. will move from 61st Division Area to SAVY WOOD.

   (d) Two sections of 201st Field Coy. R.E. will move from 61st Division Area to VAUX.

3. All necessary details will be arranged direct between Os.C. 200th and 201st Field Coys. R.E. and O.C. Artillery Brigades concerned.

4. Field Companies will ACKNOWLEDGE RECEIPT.

Captain R.E.
Adjt. 30th Divl. Engineers.

18-3-18.

Copy No. 1 to O.C. 200th Field Coy. R.E.
"   " 2 " O.C. 201st Field Coy. R.E.
"   " 3 " O.C. 202nd Field Coy. R.E.
"   " 4 " O.C. 30th Divl. Signal Coy. R.E.
"   " 5 " O.C. 11th Bn. South Lancs. Regt.
"   " 6 " 30th Division "G".
"   " 7 " 30th Division "Q".
"   " 8 " C.R.A. 30th Division.
"   " 9 " 21st Infantry Brigade.
"   " 10 " 89th Infantry Brigade.
"   " 11 " 90th Infantry Brigade.
"   " 12 " C.E. XVIII Corps.
"   " 13 " War Diary.
"   " 14 " War Diary.
"   " 15 " File.

Appendix "B"

REPORT ON OPERATIONS OF 30TH DIVISIONAL R.E. FROM 21-3-18 TO 31-3-18.

On the morning of March 21st the three Field Coys. and Pioneers were located as follows :-

200th Field Coy. R.E. - Headquarters at DOUCHY.
         2 sections with Artillery in Right Bde Front.
         2 sections at DALLON.
201st Field Coy. R.E. - Headquarters at VAUX.
         2 sections with Artillery in Left Bde. Front.
         2 sections in SAVY WOOD.
202nd Field Coy. R.E. - Headquarters & 3 sections at ROUPY.
         1 section at SAVY.
Pioneers.   - Headquarters at FLUQUIERES.
         1 Company in SAVY WOOD.
         1 Company at DALLON.
         1 Company at ROUPY.

  Field Coys. and Pioneers had orders to assemble at FLUQUIERES on the order "MAN BATTLE STATIONS". On the opening of the enemy's bombardment the Field Coys. and Pioneers started to move to FLUQUIERES and most of them had assembled there by 8-0am. The sections of the Field Coys. and Pioneers in SAVY WOOD and DALLON suffered heavy casualties in endeavouring to get back to their assembly position. In the afternoon the Field Coys. and Pioneers were moved from FLUQUIERES to QUARRY West of AVIATION WOOD and the same evening the Field Coys. were moved back to AUBIGNY, the Pioneers remaining in the Quarry. From this time on the Pioneers were used as Infantry under the direct orders of the Divisional Commander. During the morning of 22nd March the Field Coys. were moved from AUBIGNY to HAM and during the afternoon of the 22nd worked on the defences of HAM.:-

  200th Field Coy. on the N.E. side of HAM from the HAM - ST.QUENTIN Road Southward to the Canal.
  201st Field Coy. on the N.W. side of HAM from the HAM - ST.QUENTIN Road to the Canal.
  202nd Field Coy. on the South of HAM on both sides of the HAM - CHAUNY Road.

  During the night of 22nd/23rd the Field Coys. were withdrawn and went into billets in HAM. On the afternoon of 22nd the demolition of the 5 bridges in HAM were handed over to us. Officers of the Field Coys. were put in charge of this work and all five bridges were successfully destroyed during the night of 22nd/23rd, except the large iron bridges leading to HAM railway station. This bridge was only partially destroyed owing to the charge not being large enough. The charges were not prepared by us, being already charged when handed over to us to fire. In the early morning of 23rd March the Field Coys. moved from HAM to ESMERY - HALLON. 200th and 201st Field Coys. dug themselves in in front of the village and 202nd Field Coy. behind the village. About 9-0am 24th the Field Coys. were withdrawn from their positions at ESMERY - HALLON and moved to RAMECOURT behind the Canal and from 11-0am to 4-0pm assisted the French Infantry in digging trenches in front of ERCHEU, and in the evening the three Field Coys. moved into billets at SOLENTE. On the morning of 25th March the three Field Coys. were employed on digging trenches for the defence of the villages of SOLENTE and OMENCOURT, 202nd on the right in front and around the S.E. of SOLENTE, 201st between the two villages and 200th Field Coy. all round the outskirts of OMENCOURT. In the afternoon the Field Coys. were withdrawn from this work and marched back to ROIGLISE. During the night of 25th/26th the Field Coys. marched from ROIGLISE to following villages :-

    200th Field Coy. - PLESSIER.
    201st Field Coy. - ARVILLERS.
    202nd Field Coy. - PLESSIER.

  On the morning of 26th March 200th and 201st Field Coys. were placed at disposal of 89th and 90th Brigades to assist the Infantry prepare a position from ROUVROY to BOUCHOIR. 200th Field Coy. with 89th Brigade on the left and 201st Field Coy. with 90th Brigade on the Right. 202nd Field Coy. remained in reserve at PLESSIER. About midday 202nd Field Coy. was moved up from PLESSIER to HANGEST and remained in reserve. At 4-30pm 202nd Field Coy. was moved back from HANGEST to PLESSIER for work on defences in front of that village. On morning of 26th the 23rd Entrenching Battalion was placed under 202nd Field Coy. for work on defences in front of PLESSIER.

                      On night.

On night of 26th all roads leading into our position from direction of enemy were blocked to Armoured Cars. On morning of 27th the 200th and 201st Field Coys. were still in the line from ROUVROY to BOUCHOIR working with their affiliated Brigades. 202nd Field Coy. with the 23rd Entrenching Battalion were working on Defences in front of PLESSIER but about 10-0am they were moved further South in front of the wood one mile South of PLESSIER where they remained until the evening. On the night of 27th/28th the 30th Division was relieved by the 133rd French Division and that night 200th and 202nd Field Coys. moved to ROUVREL. 201st Field Coy. did not arrive there until night of 28th/29th. On the morning of the 29th 200th and 202nd Field Coys. dug trenches on the West bank of the River AVRE to defend the bridges and crossings of the river at MOREUIL. They returned to ROUVREL in the evening. On the morning of the 30th the three Field Coys. marched to SALEUX and entrained there for the ST.VALERY Area, arriving in their new area on the morning of 31st.

Headquarters R.E. remained with Divisional Headquarters during the whole period of operations.
R.E. Stores were pushed up by lorry but usually arrived too late to be of much use. In future I would recommend one lorry with picks and shovels being placed at C.R.E's disposal as a movable reserve to be sent where required.

Lieut-Colonel R.E.
C.R.E. 30th Division.

1-4-18.

Copy to :- 30th Division "G".
         C.E. XVIII Corps.
         War Diary (2).

SECRET.

WAR DIARY

of

HEADQUARTERS, 30TH DIVISIONAL

ENGINEERS.

FROM 1st APRIL 1918.   TO   30th APRIL 1918.

(Volume 30.)

SECRET.

VOLUME 30. APRIL 1918.

WAR DIARY
※
HEADQUARTERS 30th DIVISIONAL INTELLIGENCE SUMMARY.
ENGINEERS.

Army Form C. 2118.

Reference Maps.
```
                Scale   Sheets 27 N.E.    Abbeville 14.
                1/20,000        28 N.W.   1/100,000.
                        20 S.W. & S.E.    Sheet 27.1/40,000
                            (parts of.)   Sheet 28.
```

Instructions regarding War Diaries and Intelligence Summaries are contained in F. S. Regs., Part II. and the Staff Manual respectively. Title pages will be prepared in manuscript. *(Erase heading not required.)*

Place	Date	Hour	Summary of Events and Information	Remarks and references to Appendices
ST.VALERY-SUR-SOMME.	1st		Divisional Headquarters at ST.VALERY-SUR-SOMME. Field Companies located as follows :- 200th Field Company at VANDRICOURT. 201st " " TILLOY. 202nd " " WATHIEHURT.	Fld.Coys. refitting & resting.
	2nd		C.R.E. visited the Companies.	
PROVEN.	5th		Divisional Headquarters moved from ST.VALERY-SUR-SOMME to PROVEN.	
	6th		30th Divl.Engineers Order No.12 issued.	
	7th		Carried out Reliefs as in Appendix A.	Appendix A.
CANAL BANK	8th		Divisional Headquarters moved from PROVEN to CANAL BANK (B.24.b.9.1.)	
	11th		30th Divl.Engineers Order No.13 issued.	Appendix B.
	12th		The following Officers & O.R. were killed by a stray shell which landed in the H.&R.E.Office: T/Lieut.(A/Capt.) C.J.BARKER, Adjutant. T/2nd Lieut. F.H.CHIDGEY, Assistant Adjutant. 1 Office Staff. 1 Batman. and 1 O.R. was wounded. A certain amount of Office correspondence was also destroyed. T/2nd Lieut.R.J.LANNON, 200th Field Coy.R.E., temporarily took over duties of Adjutant.	
ELVERDINGHE CHATEAU.	13th		Divisional Headquarters moved from CANAL BANK to ELVERDINGHE CHATEAU.	
	15th		Orders re demolitions issued to Field Companies	Appendix C. (a)(b) &(c).
	15th		Further orders re demolitions issued to 202nd Field Coy.	(d)
	16th		The Line was withdrawn to the line of the STEENBEEK during the night. All demolitions were satisfactorily carried out by Field Companies.	
MOONTA CAMP. Sheet 28 G.16.c.4.0.	18th		Divisional Headquarters moved from ELVERDINGHE CHATEAU to MOONTA CAMP, near BUSSEBOOM and was transferred to XXII Corps. Field Companies and 11th South Lancs. Regt.(Pioneers) moved to BRANDHOEK-BUSSEBOOM area and took over work on the DRANOUTRE-OUDERDOM (3rd Reserve)Line. The C.R.E. reconnoitred the line with O's C.Field Companies and Pioneers.	
	19th		Distribution of work as follows :- 200th Field Coy. on Forward Line of Posts. Pioneers on Intermediate Line of Strong Points. 201st & 202nd Field Coys on 3rd Reserve Line.	

Sheet 2.

Army Form C. 2118.

WAR DIARY
or
INTELLIGENCE SUMMARY.

(Erase heading not required.)

Instructions regarding War Diaries and Intelligence Summaries are contained in F.S. Regs., Part II. and the Staff Manual respectively. Title pages will be prepared in manuscript.

Place	Date	Hour	Summary of Events and Information	Remarks and references to Appendices
CATTERICK CAMP Sheet 28. G.11.d.5.4.	20th		202nd Field Coy. joined the 21st Brigade at DICKEBUSCH for work under the 21st Division. The 201st Field Coy. took over the whole of the work on the 3rd Reserve Line.	
	21st		Divisional Headquarters moved to CATTERICK CAMP in the evening. Lieut (A/Capt.) E.N.CLIFTON,R.E., joined for duty and took over duties as Adjutant. T/2nd Lieut.R.J.LANNON,R.E., remained with H.Q.R.E. as Assistant Adjutant.	
	21st to 23rd	24th	200th & 201st Field Coys. & 11th South Lancs.Regt.(Pioneers) worked on the 3rd Reserve Line. A Report on work done by Field Coys. & Pioneers during period 18.4.18 to 23.4.18 sent to Chief Engineer, XXII Corps.	Appendix D.
	25th		The enemy attacked French Corps & 9th Division (British) on the WYTSCHAETE-KEMMEL front at 5 a.m. 200th & 201st Field Coys & 11th South Lancs.Regt.(Pioneers) were ordered to remain in Camp & to be prepared to move at half an hours notice. In the afternoon they moved with Transport to LAWRENCE CAMP (Sheet 28. G.11.a.& b.) In the evening Divisional Headquarters rear Echelon moved back to BROXEELE (Sheet 27.G.23.b.1.9.) The C.R.E. remained with Advanced Headquarters in CATTERICK CAMP.	
BROXEELE Sheet 27. C.23.b.1.9.	26th 27th		Field Coys & Pioneers resumed work on the 3rd Reserve Line. The 200th & 201st Field Coys & 11th South Lancs.Regt.(Pioneers) were transferred to the 49th Division for work. Advanced Divisional Headquarters moved back to BROXEELE, re-opening at 12 noon. Divisional Headquarters were transferred to VIII Corps. Instructions to take over work on the WATOU Line from C.R.E. 59th Division were received in the evening.	
Chateau at P.2.c.5.3. (Sheet 27.)	28th 29th		The C.R.E. reconnoitred and took over the WATOU Line & visited VIII Corps. "G" Office & C.R.E's Office moved to Chateau at P.2.c.5.3. (Sheet 27.) C.R.E. visited Chief Engineer,VIII Corps in the morning re the question of Stores and reconnoitred the WATOU Line from WATOU to HAANDEKOT later. 200th & 201st Field Coys returned to the Division for work on the new line & established Headquarters between HOUTKERQUE & HERZEELE. The 557 A.T.Coy was attached to C.R.E. for work, also 70th Labour Coy, 759,832 & part of 754 Area Employment Coys & 3 Field Engineers. 30th Division "G" issued Appendix E. and sectors for work were allotted as follows :- 557 A.T.Coy, with Labour Coy.&) Sector 5 & 6. Area Employment Coys.) Sector 7. 201st Field Coy. Sector 8. 200th " " Cntd.	Appendix E

Sheet 3.

WAR DIARY
or
INTELLIGENCE SUMMARY.

(Erase heading not required.)

Army Form C. 2118.

Place	Date	Hour	Summary of Events and Information	Remarks and references to Appendices
	30th		33rd Divl.R.E. working under G.O.C. 30th Division were to do Sectors 1 - 4. In the evening the Corps Commander decided to put 33rd Divl.R.E. on other work & Sectors were re-allotted as follows :- 557 A.T.Coy, with Labour Coy) & Area Employment Coys.) Sectors 1 - 4. (They had previously been working on this Sector.) 201st Field Coy.) Sectors 5 & 6. 200th " ") Sectors 7 & 8. Companies started work as above. C.R.E. visited O.C's Labour & Area Employment Coys & went round the Line. NOTE. Appendix F. shows list of Honours & Awards to the Field Coys during the month of APRIL.	Appendix F
	4.5.18.			

Lieut.Colonel.R.E.
C.R.E. 30th Division.

COPY

SECRET.   APPENDIX A.   Copy No.

30TH DIVISIONAL ENGINEERS ORDER NO. 12.

1. The 30th Division is relieving the Left Brigade of the 1st Division in the line on April 7th/8th.

2. The Field Companys will be located as follows:-

    200th Field Coy. R.E. at CALEDONIA AVENUE, C.9.c.
    201st Field Coy. R.E. at CALEDONIA FORT,   C.15.a.
    202nd Field Coy. R.E. at CANAL BANK.

    Os.C. Field Coys will send officers ahead to Area Commandant, Lieut-Colonel GRANT, Canal Bank (B.12.d.4.0.) who will supply guides to shew Company officers their billets.

3. Transport Lines of Field Coys will be located as follows-

    200th Field Coy. R.E. at SOLFERINO CAMP, B.22.b.
    201st Field Coy. R.E. at SOLFERINO CAMP, B.22.b.
    202nd Field Coy. R.E. at ARRACOURT CAMP, B.22.b.

    Os.C. Field Coys will send Officers ahead to Area Commandant ELVERDINGHE who will direct Transport to their lines.

4. O.C. 200th Field Coy. R.E. will take over the work in the front system of the forward zone from 26th Field Coy. R.E. who are located at KEMPTON PARK (C.27.b. 15.d.)

5. O.C. 201st Field Coy. R.E. will take over the work in the support system of the forward zone from the 23th Field Coy. R.E. who are located at ENGLISH FARM (C.27.b.)

6. Moves and reliefs to be carried out as early as possible but not later than night of 7th/8th. All details to be arranged direct between Os.C. Field Coys. and relieved Field Coys. as regards work and Area Commandants as regards accommodation and moves.

7. Headquarters 30th Divisional Engineers will move to CANAL BANK on 8th instant.

8. Field Coys to acknowledge receipt.

                            Signed   G.W.Dennison
                                         Lieut Col.
                                       for Captain R.E.
6-4-18.   Adjt. 30th Divl. Engineers.

Copy No. 1. to O.C. 200th Field Coy. R.E.
  "   " 2   " O.C. 201st Field Coy. R.E.
  "   " 3   " O.C. 202nd Field Coy. R.E.
  "   " 4   " O.C. 30th Divl. Signal Coy. R.E.
  "   " 5   " 30th Division "G"
  "   " 6   " 30th Division "Q"
  "   " 7   " 21st Infantry Brigade.
  "   " 8   " 89th Infantry Brigade.
  "   " 9   " 90th Infantry BRigade.
  "   " 10   " C.E. 11 Corps.
  "   " 11   " C.R.E. 1st Division.
  "   " 12   " War Diary.
  "   " 13   " War Diary.
  "   " 14   " File.

C O P Y.   APPENDIX B.   Copy No.

30TH DIVISIONAL ENGINEERS ORDER NO. 13.

On the order "MAN BATTLE STATIONS" the bridges and other works prepared for demolition by you will be manned by your Company.

Os.C. Field Companys will submit their plans for doing this.

                            Signed   C.J. Barker   Captain R.E.
11/4/18.   Adjt. 30th Divl. Engineers.

Copy No. 1 to O.C. 200th Field Coy. R.E.
  "   " 2 " O.C. 201st Field Coy. R.E.
  "   " 3 " O.C. 202nd Field Coy. R.E.
  "   " 4 " 30th Division "G".
  "   " 5 " 30th Division "Q".
  "   " 6 " 21st Infantry Brigade.
  "   " 7 " 89th Infantry Brigade.
  "   " 8 " 90th Infantry Brigade.
  "   " 9 " C.E. 11 Corps.
  "   " 10 " War Diary.
  "   " 11 " War Diary.
  "   " 12 " File.

COPY.　　　　　　　APPENDIX.　C(a)

To O.C. 200th Field Coy. R.E.

R 86.　　　　　　　13 th.

In addition to mining the cross roads at LANGEMARCK, please take in hand at once the mining of the cross roads at PILCKEM (C.2.C.88.) and the cross roadsat 5 CHEMINE (C.14.A. 8.8.) You will be responsible for firing the charges when the enemy come into sight, and our infantry have retired. All charges to be fired by fuze.

　　　　　　　　　　　　Signed　G.W.Dennison .　Lieut Col: R.E.
　　　　　　　　　　　　　　　　　　　C.R.E. 30th Division.

COPY.   APPENDIX C(B).

To O.C. 201st Field Coy R.E.

    R89   13th.

You will be responsible for preparing all bridges over the STEENBEEK in our Divisional Area for demolition. You will also be responsible for firing charges and blowing bridge on the approach of the enemy.

                                    Signed   G.W.Dennison Lieut Col: R.E.
                                                      C.R.E. 30th Division.

COPY.   APPENDIX C(c)

To O.C. 202nd Field Coy R.E.

      R87   13th.

You will be responsible for firing charges on all the bridges across the YSER Canal in our Divisional Area, except the broad gauge railway bridge at (B.12. b.4.4.) which will be prepared and fired by Railway Engineers. Bridges will be blown under orders of Brigadier commanding forward troops, or in default of such orders, they are to be blown when enemy attackn bridges in force.

                                  Signed G.W.Dennison. Lieut Col: R.E.
                                            C.R.E. 30th Division.

COPY.   APPENDIX C(d)

    To O.C. 202nd Field Coy. R.E.

      R112   15th.

The BOESINGHE Railway bridge has been prepared for demolition by
the 120 Railway Coy R.E. The demolition party are living in a
dugout 30 Yards south of the railway bridge on the West side of the
Canal. You will relieve this party tomorrow morning at 10am and
will be responsible for the destruction of this bridge from that
date and time. Acknowledge.

From C.R.E. 30th Division½

                              Signed G.W.Dennison.   Lieut Col: R.E.

APPENDIX D

[Stamp: COMMANDING ROYAL ENGINEERS 23 APR 1918 (COUNTY PALATINE) ENGINEERS]

C.E.
XXII Corps.

Your No. E.3/2/10 of 20.4.18.

The 30th Division arrived in the XXII Corps Area on the 18th instant and during that day the Field Company and Pioneer Officers reconnoitred the work, and the following morning work was commenced as follows:-

200th Field Company R.E. and 1 Battalion Infantry on 4 Forward Posts at H.16.a.5.8., H.16.d.3.3., H.22.c.3.8., and H.27.c.6.7.
11th Bn. South Lancs. Regt. (Pioneers) and 1 Battalion Infantry on 4 Intermediate Posts at H.8.c.6.0, H.14.d.0.2., H.15.c.6.9 and H.26.c.2.8.
201st Field Company R.E. and 2 Battalions Infantry on Northern portion of G.H.Q. 3rd Reserve Line from G.6.c.6.1. to G.18.c.9.0.
202nd Field Company R.E. and 2 Battalions Infantry on Southern portion of G.H.Q. 3rd Reserve Line G.18.c.9.0 to H.25.c.2.2.

The Infantry had just arrived on the work when orders were received for them to stop work and return to Camp. The Field Companies and Pioneers continued work on repairing trenches and wire.

On the morning of the 19th the whole of the Infantry and 202nd Field Company were taken off the work and sent up into the line. The 2 Field Companies and Pioneers continued work as shown above on the 19th and 20th.

On the 21st our Northern Boundary was altered and work was allotted as follows:-

201st Field Company R.E. on the G.H.Q. 3rd Line of Defence from G.24.a.9.7. to H.25.c.2.2.
Pioneers on 2 Intermediate Posts at H.26.c.2.8. and H.32.c.5.7.
200th Field Company R.E. on 3 Forward Posts at H.22.c.3.8., H.27.c.6.7., and H.32.d.6.2.

Work consisted in digging out and repairing old trenches and repairing old wire, except at Post at H.22.c.3.8. which is a new work for all round defence.

On the 23rd two Battalions of Infantry were employed on the work, one with 200th Field Company R.E. on the Forward Posts and one with 201st Field Company R.E. on the Main Line.

On the 22nd a Support Line to the Main Line was taped out by 201st Field Company R.E. and work commenced on it on the 23rd.

Very little new wire has been put up owing to the small supply of barbed wire from the Army Park, but a considerable amount of work has been done in repairing existing belts of wire.

Lieut.Col. R.E.
C.R.E., 30th Division.

23.4.1918.

APPENDIX E

30" Div.G/263/413.

S E C R E T.   Copy No......

Reference Map. Sheet 27.N.E.
Scale 1/20,000.   28th April, 1918.

INSTRUCTIONS FOR WORK ON THE WATOU - CAESTRE LINE
North of the STEENVOORDE - ABEELE Road.

1. The work on the WATOU - CAESTRE LINE, North of the STEENVOORDE - ABEELE Road will be carried out under the direction of G.O.C., 30th Division.

2. Work on the above line will be confined for the present to:-
   (a). The Line of Resistance, which is to be made continuous.
   (b). Observation Line.
   These will be worked on concurrently.

3. Between the STEENVOORDE - ABEELE Road and HAANDEKOT the line will be subdivided into eight Sectors as follows:-
   No.1.Sector: STEENVOORDE - ABEELE Road to CROSS ROADS K.29.c.9.8.
   No.2.Sector: K.29.c.9.8. to CROSS ROADS K.23.a.1.9.
   No.3.Sector: CROSS ROADS K.23.a.1.9. to CROSS ROADS K.16.b.9.9.
   No.4.Sector: CROSS ROADS K.16.b.9.9. to ROAD JUNCTION K.4.b.4.9
   No.5.Sector: ROAD JUNCTION K.4.b.4.9. to CROSS ROADS E.22.d.8.3
                (WATOU DEFENCES).
   No.6.Sector: CROSS ROADS E.22.d.8.3. to CROSS ROADS E.22.d.9.6.
   No.7.Sector: CROSS ROADS E.22.d.9.6. to CROSS ROADS E.16.b.8.1.
   No.8.Sector: CROSS ROADS E.16.b.8.1. to HAANDEKOT.

4. Each Sector will be organised approximately as in the attached Sketch.

                                                Lieut.Colonel,
28-4-18.   General Staff, 30th Division.

Copies No. 1 to 6. to C.R.E., 30th Division for distribution to
                    units working on the line.
   "   No. 7. to VIII.Corps.

GROUP POST
　　　O　　　　　　　　　　　　　　　　　　　　O
←————————— OBSERVATION LINE —————————→
　　　▭　　　　　　　　　　　　　　　　　　▭
　1 PLATOON　　　　　　　　　　　　　1 PLATOON

　　(▭ ▭ ▭ LINE OF RESISTANCE ▭ ▭ ▭)
　　　3 PLATOONS　　　　　　　　　　　　
　　　1 COMPANY　　　　　　　　　　1 COMPANY

←————————— LINE OF STRONG POINTS —————————→
　　　▭　　　　　　　　　　　　　▭　　　　▭
　2 PLATOONS　　　　　　　　1 PLATOON　1 PLATOON

　　　　　▭　　　　　　　　　　　　　　　▭
←————————— RESERVE LINE —————————→
　　▭　　　　　　　　　　　▭
　　　　　　1 COMPANY

BN HQ IN RESERVE LINE

APPENDIX F.

LIST OF AWARDS TO N.C.Os. & MEN OF THE 30th DIVISIONAL ENGINEERS DURING APRIL.

No.	Rank.	Name.	Unit.	Award.	Authority.
521939	L/Cpl.	JONES, G.G.	201st Fld.Coy.	Military Medal.	D.R.O.3561 dated 13.4.18.
43355	Sergt.	INGLEDEW, E.	200th " "	Bar to Military Medal.	D.R.O.3572 dated 18.4.18.
62368	C.S.M.	MORGAN, E.D.	201st " "	Distinguished Conduct Medal.	D.R.O.3574 dated 21.4.18.
311852	Pnr.	GARLICK, C.	30th Divl.Signal Coy.	Military Medal.	D.RO. 3578 dated 22.4.18.
33370	Sergt.	MAYBURY, A.	200th Fld.Coy.	Distinguished Conduct Medal.	D.R.O.3585 dated 24.4.18.

CONFIDENTIAL.

WAR DIARY

of

HEADQUARTERS, 30th DIVISIONAL ENGINEERS.

FROM 1st MAY 1918.   TO   31st MAY 1918.

(VOLUME 31.)

SECRET.

HEADQUARTERS, 30th DIVISIONAL ENGINEERS.

WAR DIARY
&
INTELLIGENCE SUMMARY

(Erase heading not required.)

VOLUME 31.   MAY 1918.

Army Form C. 2118.

Reference Maps:
Scale 1/20,000. Sheets 27 N.E.
" 28 N.W.
57E S.E., 57D S.W.,
62E N.E., 62D N.W., Pts.of.

Scale 1/100,000
Abbeville 14.
Dieppe 16.
Amiens 17.

Instructions regarding War Diaries and Intelligence Summaries are contained in F. S. Regs, Part II. and the Staff Manual respectively. Title pages will be prepared in manuscript.

Place	Date	Hour	Summary of Events and Information	Remarks and references to Appendices
Chateau at 27/P.2.c.5.3			The events for the Month of May are divided into 3 groups. 1. Work on WATOU-ABEELE Defence Lines, 1st to 13th May. 2. Work on training 35th U.S.Division in EU Area, 14th to 25th May. 3. Training of 110th U.S. Engineer Regiment & work on G.H.Q. Line North of AMIENS. PRELIMINARY. Work on WATOU Line was taken over by 30th Division on 28.4.18, the Division being transferred to the VIII Corps. Advd. Divisional H.Q. & H.Q.R.E. established at Chateau at 27/P.2.c.5.3. 200th & 201st Field Coys were located in the neighbourhood of HOUTKER UE. 202nd Field Coy was still with the 21st Brigade in the Line, attached to 21st Division. 11th South Lancs Regt.(Pioneers) remained in the Line with the 49th Division. Description of WATOU Line & work thereon is contained in Appendix "A" (Handing over Notes.) General distribution of Labour on WATOU & ABEELE Lines is shown in Appendix "B". This was subject to various changes from time to time. Orders for work were issued to O's C. Army Troops Coys. each evening & they distributed the labour at their discretion. Field Coys. were employed principally in reconnoitring & taping out new lines & wiring. There was a shortage of barbed wire, but otherwise stores were sufficient for the work. *Small scale map attached showing approximate position of Line.*	Appen. "A" Appen. "B"
	1st		C.R.E. visited the work. Received orders in the evening from Corps to start wiring ABEELE Line the next day. C.R.E. visited Coys. at once & issued orders accordingly.	
	2nd		Took over construction of ABEELE Line from 33rd Division. Labour employed on the line remained. (The ABEELE Line ran approximately East & West & joined the WATOU Line about 1000 yds.North of the STEENVORDE-ABEELE Road).	
	3rd		Work on WATOU & ABEELE Lines was continued.	
	4th		The 202nd Field Coy. rejoined the Division & camped at E.20.b.2.5.	
	5th		Advd. Divl.H.Q. & H.Q.R.E. moved into hutted Camp at K.9.a.3.9. Work continued as before.	
	6th		202nd Field Coy.moved down to billets at PAMSGAT, preparatory to starting work on a continuation of the ABEELE Line in a S.Westerly direction. Work was to have been started on this line on the 8th Inst., but orders were never issued owing to the French Corps taking over the area.	
	8th		The French Corps took over work on the Southern portion of the WATOU Line up to where the	

Army Form C. 2118.

Sheet 2.

WAR DIARY
of
INTELLIGENCE SUMMARY.

(Erase heading not required.)

Instructions regarding War Diaries and Intelligence Summaries are contained in F. S. Regs., Part II. and the Staff Manual respectively. Title pages will be prepared in manuscript.

Place	Date	Hour	Summary of Events and Information	Remarks and references to Appendices
	9th		ABEELE Line joined it. B.G.G.S.VIII Corps, B.G.C. 90th Brigade & C.R.E. reconnoitred a new line running from the Eastern end of the ABEELE Line in a North Easterly direction, as far as LA LOVE Chateau.	
	10th		Division "G" moved back to BROXEELE. B.G.C. 90th Brigade took over all work on the WATOU & ABEELE Lines. C.R.E. remained with B.G.C. 90th Brigade. 202nd Field Coy. moved back to BROXEELE preparatory to moving to EU on the 11th Inst., to arrange Camps & training grounds for the 35th American Division.	
	11th		C.R.E. attended Conference at Corps H.Q. on the new line reconnoitred by B.G.G.S. VIII Corps on the 9th Inst. It was decided that the work would not be carried out by B.G.C. 90th Brigade	
	12th		Received orders for H.Q.R.E. to rejoin Division H.Q. at BROXEELE. The Division was transferred to the XXII Corps, who also took over work on WATOU Line from VIII Corps. The French took over works on the ABEELE Line. A considerable amount of labour was withdrawn from the works. Remaining Labour, with distribution on the works, is shown in Appendix "C". Started handing over to B.G.C. 90th Brigade. O.C. 200th Field Coy. took over the administration of Stores for the WATOU Line.	Appen "C"
	13th		Completed handing over to B.G.C. 90th Brigade & moved to BROXEELE.	
	14th		Division transferred to Reserve Army. C.R.E. moved to EU. Adjutant & Office remained at Broxeele. C.R.E. took over work on ranges, camps, etc. already started by 202nd Field Coy. The following work was in hand :- 2 Rifle Ranges 300 & 600 yards. Appendix "D" shows details of them & of other work proposed.	Appen "D"
	15th		C.R.E. went round works. Adjutant & Lt.Lannon with horse transport entrained at A UDRUICQ for EU.	
	16th		Adjutant & Lt.Lannon with horse transport arrived at EU 4.30.a.m. Office Staff arrived by Lorry at 7.30.p.m.	
	17th		C.R.E. went round ranges in afternoon. 202nd Fld.Coy. moved H.Q. from EU to Mill near INCHEVILLE & established dump & workshops at Coy. H.Q. Having heard that the Division was being transferred from the Reserve to the 4th Army.C.R.E. & Adjt. visited C.E. 4th Army to make arrangements re Stores. Nothing however was definitely settled, as C.E. 4th Army knew nothing of the transfer.	
	18th		C.R.E. reconnoitred sites for Bath Houses.	

Cntd.

Sheet 3.

Army Form C. 2118.

WAR DIARY
INTELLIGENCE SUMMARY.

(Erase heading not required.)

Instructions regarding War Diaries and Intelligence Summaries are contained in F.S. Regs., Part II. and the Staff Manual respectively. Title pages will be prepared in manuscript.

Place	Date	Hour	Summary of Events and Information	Remarks and references to Appendices
	18th		The Divisional Commander decided that on the arrival of the U.S. Engineer Regiment the C.R.E. should hand over the R.E. work in the Area to O.C.202nd Field Coy. & move to the vicinity of the H.Q.American Engineer Regiment, so as to be in close touch & devote all attention to their training.	
	19th		C.R.E. met O.C. 4th Army at H.Q.R.E. 66th Division & discussed training arrangements. The 110th U.S. Engineer Regt. arrived & opened H.Q. at TOEUFREVILLE. C.R.E. & Adjt. visited their H.Q. in the evening. Headquarters,11th South Lancs(Pioneers) Training Cadre established at TOEUFREVILLE. The Division was transferred to the XIX Corps, 4th Army.	
	20th		C.R.E. with O.C. American Engineers went ro rd work on ranges & handed over works to O.C. 202nd Field Coy. Adjt. selected site for Divl.H.Q.R.E. near TOEUFREVILLE in the morning. *Vide Appendix "B"* Stores for Ranges, etc, were difficult to obtain. Received G/512/821 stating that it was proposed that the U.S.Engrs. should be employed on the G.H.Q. Line near AMIENS during their period of training.	*Appen "B"*
THIL.	21st		H.W.R.E. opened at LE THIL, near TOEUFREVILLE. C.R.E. was put in charge of all training arrangements of American Engineers. Discussed training with C.'s C. Amn.Engrs. & Pnrs., in evening. Wrote minute to "G" asking whether U.S.Engrs. were going to be provided with their own technical equipment & if not,recommending that they be equipped in the same manner as British Fld.Coys. less Pontoon equipment.	
	22nd		C.R.E. & O.C. 110th U.S. Engrs. visited 4th Army H.Q & 19th Corps H.Q. with reference to the suggested move for work on the G.H.Q. Line. It was ecided that the move should take place on the 27th Inst., & that the work would be on the line from ARGOEVES - COISY approx. The 19th Corps would make all arrangements for the move. The Coys not being instructed in Gas or Musketry were employed instruction per Coy per week, The pioneers on a scale of 4 hours Gas & 2 hours musketry on steady drill,Bombing & physical training. Owing to the move on the 27th it was decided th at no engineering training could be started,as stores could not b obtained in time. Arrangements wer made for instruction in Pontooning to be given by 202n Field Coy. on lake near their H.Q. (The 110th U.S. Engrs. having had no previous experience in this work & it as thought that, although their pontoon equipment differs from that used by the British, yet it was essential that a proportion of the men would be taught to row.)	

Sheet 4.

Army Form C. 2118.

WAR DIARY

INTELLIGENCE SUMMARY

(Erase heading not required.)

Instructions regarding War Diaries and Intelligence Summaries are contained in F.S. Regs., Part II. and the Staff Manual respectively. Title pages will be prepared in manuscript.

Place	Date	Hour	Summary of Events and Information	Remarks and references to Appendices
	23rd 24th		C.R.E. gave lecture to the Officers of the 2nd Battn. on work on Defence Lines. Party of U.S. Engrs. started Pontoon instruction.	
	25th		C.R.E. lectured the 2nd Battn. on work on Defence Lines. Instruction in pontooning continued. Confidential report on training sent to 30th Div. "Q" (Not attached.)	
ST.VAST.	26th		H.Q.R.E. moved by lorry to St.VAST en AMENOIS, starting at 9.a.m. Horse transport left at 7 p.m. & staged at ALLERY for the night. C.R.E. visited C.R.E. "A" Sector, G.H.Q. Defences & discussed works to be carried out by the U.S. Engrs. *Appendix E attached* Appendix "F" shows programme of works which had been arranged. American Advanced parties left by lorries independently. Adjt. arranged billets of H.Q. 110 U.S.Engr.Regt. with Area Commandant.	Appen.'E' Appen. "F"
	27th		H.Q.R.E. opened at St.VAST in the evening. C.R.E. went round portion of the works in the morning with C.R.E. "A" Sector.Adjt.visited Camp of 1st Battn near COISY & R.E.Dump at BERTANGLES. H.Q.R.E. transport arrived in the afternoon. American Engrs. arrived in the evening, having entrained at EU in the morning. 1st Battn camped just N. of COISY. 2nd Battn camped near ARGOEUVRES.	
	28th		C.R.E. & O.C. Amn.Engrs. went round proposed new switch in front of COISY with C.E.19th Corps. Adjt. & Amn.Stores Officer chose site for Battn dump near ARGOEUVRES. 1 Coy. of 1st Battn.started work on Trenches & dugouts in Line in front of Coisy.	
	29th		1 Coy. of 2nd Battn.started work on trenches near ARGOEUVRES. C.R.E. & O.C. Amn.Engrs.visited 1st Battn in morning & 2nd Battn. later.	
	30th		C.R.E.visited works with O.C. Amn.Engrs. & in the afternoon visited sites of proposed Infantry & Artillery crossings over SOMME with C.R.E. "A" Sector & decided to start work on Infantry crossing 1 & 2 & Artillery Crossing No.1. on Monday.(See Appendix "G".) 2 Coys from each Battn carried on work on trenches, the remaining Coy from each Battn. being trained in Musketry & Gas by the Pioneers. This was made a standing arrangement. A Dump party of 1 Master Engineer & 6 O.R. was sent to BERTANGLES to work on trench & camp stores.	Appen "G"
	31st		C.R.E. went round works. Adjt. & Amn.Stores Officer reconnoitred Infantry & Artillery crossings. Artillery crossing appeared to need no work except marking out the track & making approaches to bridge. A dry	

Sheet 5.

Army Form C. 2118.

WAR DIARY
or
INTELLIGENCE SUMMARY
(Erase heading not required.)

Place	Date	Hour	Summary of Events and Information	Remarks and references to Appendices
			track across the swamp was discovered which would eliminate building a bridge over the lagoon.	
			Stores for works were sufficient, but great difficulty was experienced in obtaining technical tools & also stores for construction of camp accessories.	
			List of Awards for the month attached as Appendix "H".	Appen "H".
			(signed) Lt.Col. R.E. C.R.E. 30th Division. 5.5.18.	

War Diary   APPENDIX. A.

HANDING OVER NOTES OF WORK ON THE WATOU LINE.

1. Attached is a map showing work completed & proposed. (Not attached)

2. The WATOU Line extends from about K.22.central to HAANDEKOT (E.4.central) & joins up with the French on the South & with the Belgians on the North. The line to the South has been dug, but nothing has yet been done by the Belgians on the North.

   For work purposes the line has been divided into three portions :-
   Southern Portion from K.22.central to K.4.d.3.5., Centre portion from K.4.d.3.5. to E.22.b.7.5., Northern portion from E.22.b.7.5. to HAANDEKOT.

3. The line consists of

   (a) Outpost (or Observation) Line.
   (b) Line of Resistance.
   (c) Line of defended localities or strong points.
   (d) Reserve Line.

   The line of Resistance & the reserve Line have been made continuous. The Outpost Line & the Strong Points are isolated works sited with a view to mutual support. (see Appendix A.)

4. Machine Gun emplacements have been sited & constructed as shown on plan.

5. There are two Communication Trenches from the Line of Resistance to the Reserve Line, in each Battalion Front. Some of these could be used as "Switches" if necessary.

6. The greatest care has been taken as regards siting & construction of the trenches to conceal them from ground observation.

7. The form of trench was at first made as shown in sketch A, & afterwards modified to that shown in sketch B.

   except in marshy places, when the depth of the trench was lessened & the parapet built up. Some of the parapets still need thickening.

8. A certain amount of clearing of hedges & woods has been done, but considerably more is yet required.

9. Some of the trenches are very difficult to drain & a good deal of work is still necessary

10. A portion of the Line has been wired, as shown on plan.

11. At present the following labour is being employed on this work:-

Cntd.

-2-

NORTHERN PORTION.

200th Field Coy. R.E.
121st Labour Coy.
719th   "   "

Centre Portion.

201st Field Coy. R.E.
66th Labour Coy.
9th Bn. Seaforth Highlanders.

SOUTHERN PORTION.

134 Army Troops Coy. R.E.
20 Labour Coy.
70 Labour Coy.

Average working strength & Map location of Units are attached (see Appendix B.)

12. All stores are obtained from No.3. Advanced R.E. Park at ABEELE on indent from O.C.R.E. Coys, with the exception of wiring material, which is allotted by C.E. XXII Corps as available. Pickets are usually obtained from the Park without reference to Corps.

13. Corps have been informed that O.C. 200 Field Coy. will officiate in all questions regarding stores & all allotments of stores for WATOU Line will be sent to O.C. 200 Field Coy. c/o B.G.C. 90th Brigade.

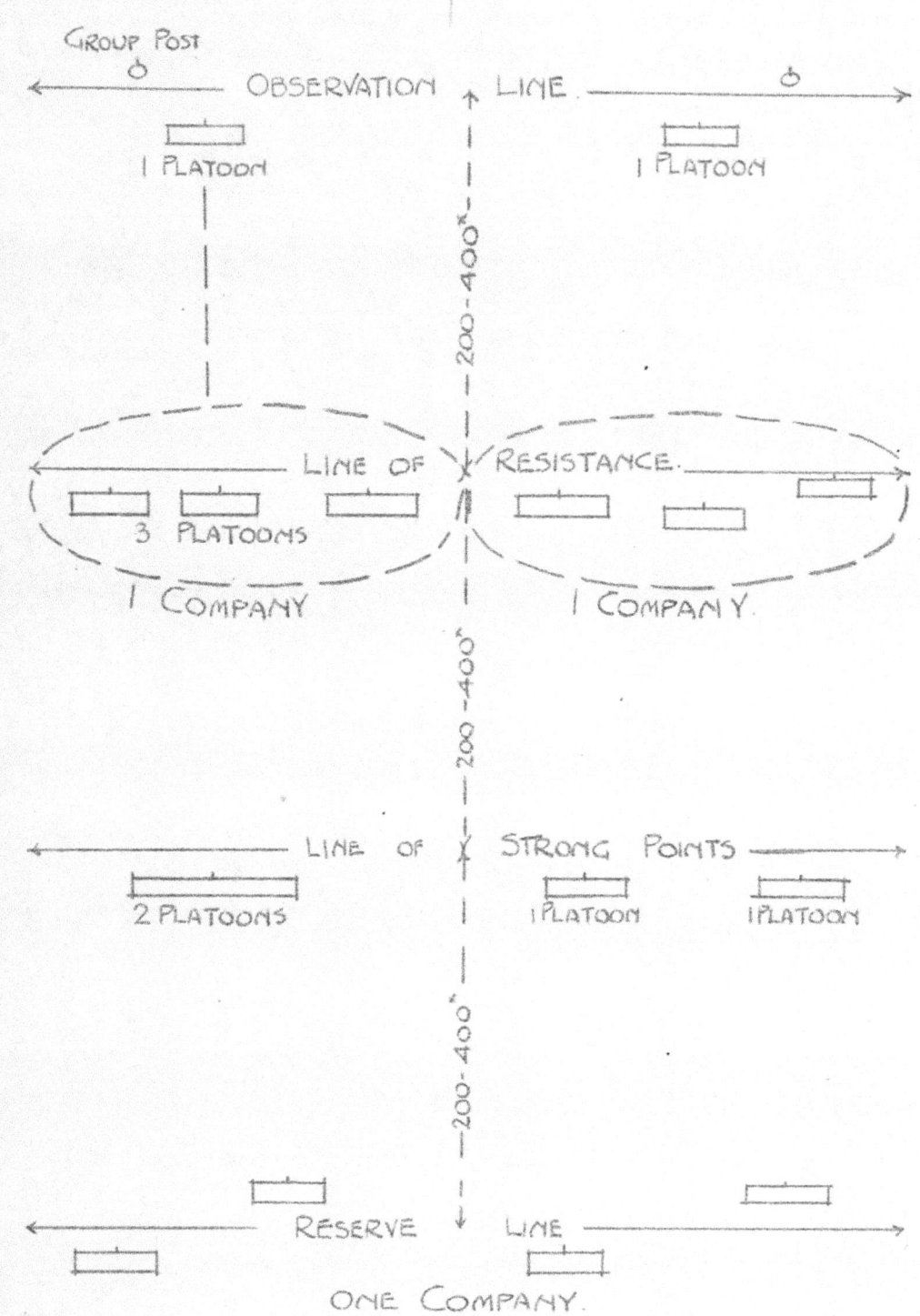

APPENDIX B.

LOCATIONS etc of UNITS.

UNIT.	Location of H.Q.	Average working strength.	Work engaged on.
30 Divl Engrs. H.Q.	K.9.a.3.9.		
200 Field Coy.	E.7.a.7.7.		
201 Field Coy.	D.18.c.2.3.		
101 Bde.(34 Div.)	E.20.b.2.6.(Shrine Camp.)		
134 Army Troops Coy.	E.25.b.6.4.	66.	WATO Line ; N.of Watou.
121 Lab Coy.	E.26.b.9.8.	250	ditto.
719 Lab.Coy.	ditto	300.	ditto.
66. Lab Coy.	K.II.b.6.8.	250.	ditto.
15.Royal Scots.	to Bde	300.	ditto.
16.Royal Scots.		150.	ditto.
557.Army Troops Coy.	K.26.d.8.8.	80.	WATOU Line, S. of Watou.
70 Lab Coy.	K.6.c.8.5.	280.	ditto
20 Lab Coy.	K.II.b.6.8.	260.	ditto.
9th Bn.Seathforth Highrs. (Pioneers.)	E.26.d.5.3.	200	ditto.
832 Area Employ. Coy.	K.27.e.4.9.	280.	ditto.
759 ditto	K.27.d.8.4.	100.	ditto.
11th .Suffolks. (to Bde)		340.	ditto.
235 Army Troops Coy.	K.11.b.6.8.	90.	ABEELE Line.
17 Lab Coy.	L.9.a.9.3.	290.	ditto.
19 Lab Coy.	L.9.a.8.6.	340.	ditto.
185 Lab Coy.	L.9.c.3.3.	290.	ditto.

APPENDIX C

) LOCATIONS etc of UNITS. (

UNIT.	Location of H.Q.	Average working strength	Work engaged on.
30 Div:Engrs:H.Q.	K.9.a.3.9.		
200 Field Coy;	E.7.a.7.7.	100	WATOU Line (G.&H.Sectors.)
~~201 Field Coy;~~	~~D.18.c.2.3.~~		
121 Lab:Coy:	E.26.b.9.8.	250	ditto
719 Lab:Coy:	ditto	300	ditto
201 Field Coy;	D.18.c.2.3.	120	WATOU Line (E.&F.Sectors.)
9th Bn:Seaforth Highs. (Pioniers)	E.26.d.5.3.	200	ditto
66 Lab:Coy:	K.11.b.6.8.	250	ditto
134 A.T.Coy:	E.25.b.6.4.	66	WATOU Line (C.&D.Sectors.)
20 Lab:Coy:	K.11.b.6.8.	260	ditto
70 Lab:Coy:	K.6.c.8.5.	280	ditto

Appendix D

30th Division G./250/708

Reserve Army.

LABOUR FOR RANGES.

1. The following Long Rifle Ranges have been sited in my Divisional Area:-
    (i). ½ Mile North of T. in PONTS ET MARAIS.
    (ii). At the T. in BOUVRINCOURT.
    (iii). At the R. in LE VERT PIGNON. (Near BAZINVAL).
    (iv). At the R. in VAL DU ROI. (Near VILLY LE BAS.)

It is proposed to construct these Ranges for firing at 300 yds. and 600 yds. according to your instructions and the wishes of the 35th American Division.

2. Two Machine Gun Ranges have also been sited at a point ½ mile South of the M. in SEPT MEULES. (On the South side of the VILLY LE BAS - SEPT MEULES Road).

3. (a). Work can be started on all the above at once provided labour is available. The following labour is required:-
    Nos. (i), (iii), (iv) Rifle Ranges .... 50 Men. each
    No. (ii). Rifle Range ....100 Men.
    Each Machine Gun Range .... 50 Men.

(b). It is estimated that 100 R.E. are necessary to superintend the work if it is all put in hand simultaneously. I have only one Field Coy. (strength approximately 6 Officers, 50 other ranks) at my disposal for R.E. work in the whole Area and should be glad if another two Sections R.E. could be allotted to me for a time.

4. Work is being commenced at once on Nos. (ii), (iii) Rifle Ranges. Prisoners of War working on the former and American Troops on the latter superintended by my Field Company.

Major General,
Commanding 30th Division.

14th May, 1918.

Copies to:- "Q".
C.R.E.
Divl.Musk:Officer.
D.M.G.O.

Appendix E.

<u>CONFIDENTIAL.</u>

30th Division No. A/8031.
C.R.E. No. 147.

30th Division "Q".

Can you please insert the following in Divisional Orders:-

" The C.R.E. & Adjutant are moving with the 110th American Engineer Regiment to area North of AMIENS. O.C. 202nd Field Coy. R.E. will remain in charge of all works in the EU Area.
All correspondence relating to Works & Stores in the EU Area should be addressed to O.C. 202nd Field Coy. R.E. All other correspondence to be addressed to C.R.E. 30th Division. "

                              (Sd). E.H.CLIFTON, Captain R.E.
25.5.18.   for C.R.E. 30th Division.

                 2.

Forwarded for information.

                                       Lieut. Colonel.
26.5.1918.   A.A. & Q.M.G., 30th Division.

Issued as per Divisional Routine Orders.

APPENDIX F.

To. C.R.E. 30th DIVISION.

The following are items of work arranged to give the American Engineers some practice on the G.H. Line.

A. Battalion at ARGOEUVES.

1. Digging of trenches (limited.)
2. Breastworks with revetting & U Framing.
3. Infantry & Artillery Crossings, over River SOMME.
4. Splinter proof shelters in the trench system.
5. Wiring.
6. Brushwood work (Parties to be sent by lorry to Forests)
7. Concrete Pill-boxes.

B. Battn. at COISY.

1. Digging trenches.
2. Wiring.
3. Tunnel dugouts.
4. Splinter proof shelters in trench system.
5. Possibly some Brushwood work.

There is plenty digging work at COISY, but there is only just sufficient to keep Battn. at ARGOEUVRES going for one day. We must therefore organize other work under the other headings for the 30th Inst.

                sd.......... Lt.Col.R.E.
28.5.18.   C.R.E. "A" Sector.

APPENDIX G.

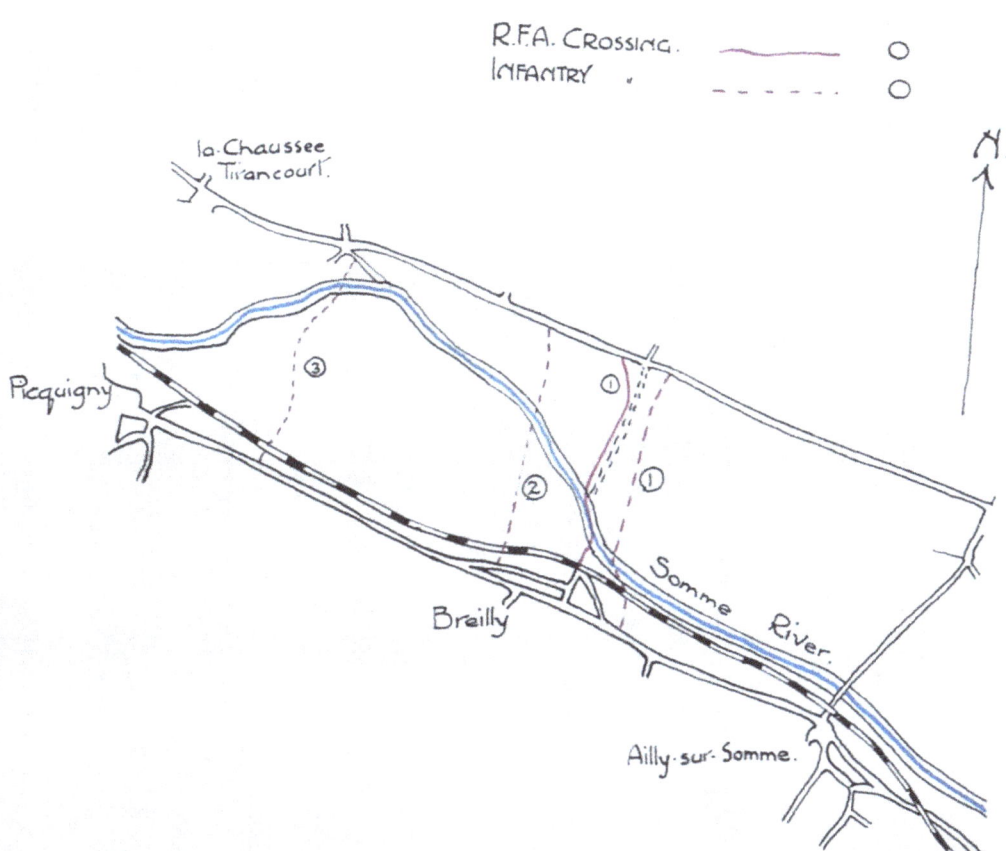

SCALE. 1:40,000.

APPENDIX H.

LIST OF AWARDS DURING THE MONTH OF MAY.

		Awarded.
T/Lieut. J.W.WRIGHT.	30th Divl. Signal Coy.	M.C.
No.16380. Sergt. G.H.Kent.	" "	M.M.
No.142800 Corpl. FERGUSON.D.C.	" "	M.M.
No.81427 Spr. F.NAYLOR.	" "	M.M.
No.312768 Corpl. G.H.CLARKSON.	" "	M.M.

SCALE. 1:100,000.   APPENDIX

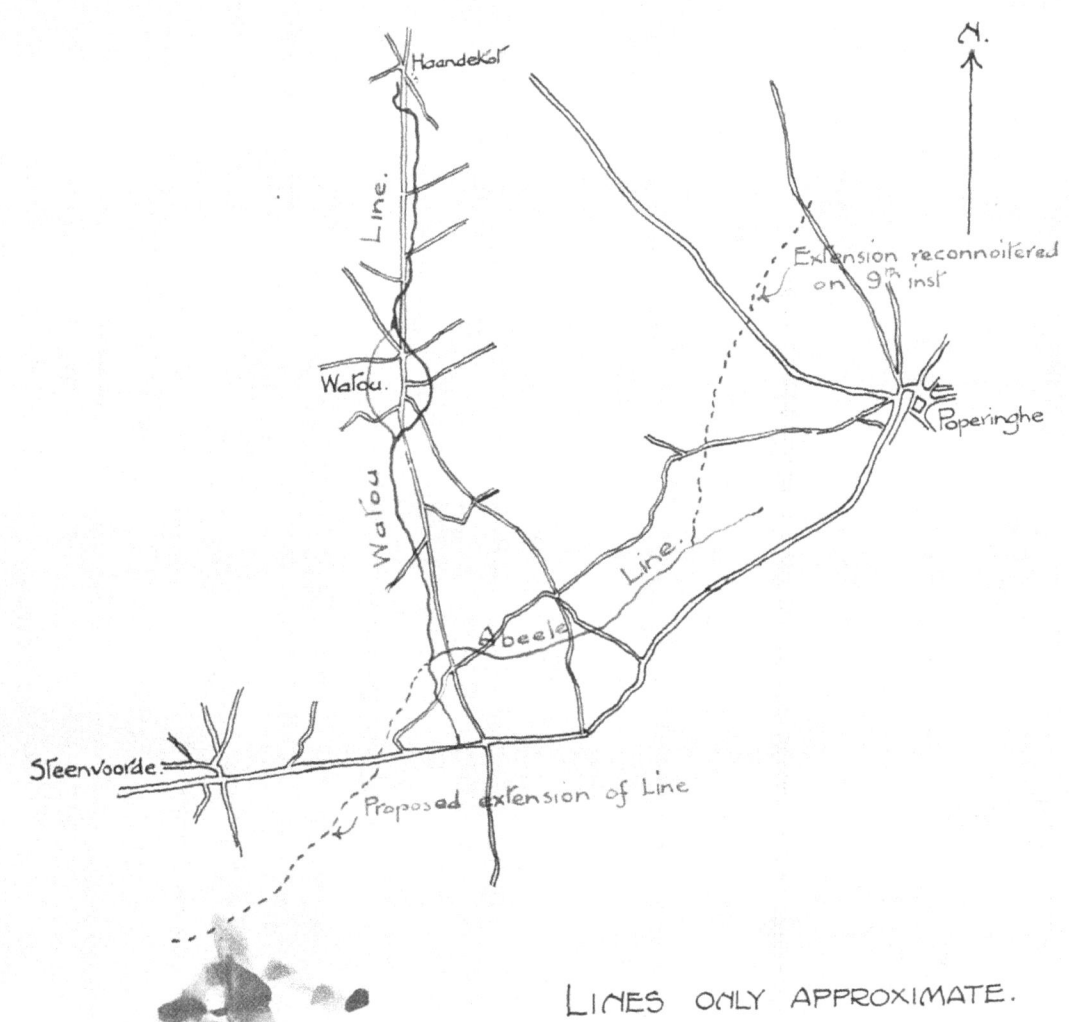

LINES ONLY APPROXIMATE.

CONFIDENTIAL.

WAR DIARY

of

HEADQUARTERS, 30th DIVISIONAL ENGINEERS.

From 1st JUNE 1918. to 30th JUNE 1918.

VOLUME 32.

VOLUME 32.

Army Form C. 2118.

WAR DIARY
or
INTELLIGENCE SUMMARY.

(Erase heading not required.)

Instructions regarding War Diaries and Intelligence HEADQUARTERS, 30th
Summaries are contained in F. S. Regs., Part II. DIVISIONAL
and the Staff Manual respectively. Title pages ENGINEERS.
will be prepared in manuscript.

June 1918.

Place	Date	Hour	Summary of Events and Information	Remarks and references to Appendices
ST VAAST EN CHAUSSEE.			**PRELIMINARY.** The Division was engaged in training the 35th and 33rd U.S. Divisions. Divisional Headquarters were at EU. Headquarters R.E. were at ST VAAST-EN-CHAUSSEE where the 110th U.S. Engineer Regiment (35th U.S. Div.) were being employed daily on the work in "A" Sector, G.H.Q. Defence line. Three Companys per Battalion were employed daily on the works, the fourth Company being trained in Musketry and Gas by Training Cadre of 11th S. LANCS. REGT.(Pioneers). The 1st Battalion was located near GOISY, and the 2nd Battalion in ARGOEUVRES. The following works were in hand. 1st Battalion. Digging, Wiring, eight Dugouts and M.G. Emplacements. 2nd Battalion. Digging, Wiring, Breastworks.	
	1st.		Reconnoitred one Artillery and two Infantry Crossings over the SOMME.	
	2.		All works between the ST VAAST - AMIENS Road and the R. SOMME were handedover to the C.R.E. by C.R.E. "A" Sector.	
	3.		C.R.E. lectured Officers of 1st Battalion on Interior Economy of a Field Company in the Line. Work was started on the Infantry and Artillery Crossings by the 2nd Battalion.	
	4.		C.R.E. lectured the Officers of the 2nd Battalion on Interior Economy of a Field Company in the Line. Part of 2nd Battalion had practice in laying 20lb track. U.S. Engineer Regt: received orders to be prepared to move imediately. Orders to cease work were issued.	
	5.		G.E. 4th Army visited American Engineers, and was asked that the supply of tool carts to the American Engineers might be expedited. The Pioneers were instructed to carry o with Gas and Musketry within the limits of the camps.	
	6.		C.R.E. wired Division to find out whether Headquarters R.E. and Pioneers would move with the U.S. Engineers, and received a reply in the negative. D.A.Q.M.G. 4th Army arrived to make arrangements for the move of the U.S. Engineers, and arranged three trainsat 6pm, 9 pm, and 12 midnight on the 7th inst. British Transport Personnel attached to the U.S. Engineers was returned to the Base.	
	7.		Received wire from 30th Divl: "G" saying that Headquarter R.E. and Pioneers would remain in	

Army Form C. 2118.

SHEET 2.

WAR DIARY
or
INTELLIGENCE SUMMARY.
(Erase heading not required.)

Instructions regarding War Diaries and Intelligence Summaries are contained in F. S. Regs., Part II. and the Staff Manual respectively. Title pages will be prepared in manuscript.

Place	Date	Hour	Summary of Events and Information	Remarks and references to Appendices
		8.	present location as it was expected that the 108th U.S. Engineers Regt: (33rd U.S. Division) would be sent up to carry on the work left by the 110th U.S. Engineer Regt. Move of the 110th U.S. Engineer Regt was posponed 24 hours and details altered slightly.	
		9.	The 110th U.S. Engineer Regt: left ST VAST area. C.R.E. visited Divisional Headquarters at EU and discussed the training of American Engineers with the G.O.C.	
		13.	Received Appendix A from 30th Divl: "G". Appendix B shows action taken.	Appendix A Appendix B
			Copy of orders to Pioneers to move is shown in Appendix C.	Appendix C
		14.	Pioneers moved to CONTAY.	
		15.	Received G.342 from 30th Division saying H.Q. R.E. would return to EU. (Appendix D) C.R.E. visited C.E. 3rd Corps where he found O.C. Pioneers and made final arrangements re training etc.	Appendix D
EU.			It was ascertained that the 1st Battalion was with the 3rd Corps and not the 2nd Battalion.	
		16.	C.R.E. and Office Staff moved by lorry to EU.	
		17.	Wrote to "G" asking that 200th and 201st Field Companys be returned to the Division so as to give them opportunity to train.	
		18.	Received Divisional Order No 177 saying that 30th Division, less Training Cadres, would move to the RUE area on 20th inst.	
		19.	Arranged with C.E. XIX Corps that 202nd Field Company should leave behind a small party to hand over Works and Dump to the incoming Division expected about the 21st inst.	
		20.	Divisional Headquarters moved to RUE.	
RUE.			Handing over notes (Appendix E) were sent to Corps and 21st Divisional C.R.E.	Appendix E
		26.	Division transferred to XXII Corps.	
		27.	Received 30th Div: Order No 178, saying Division will move to EPERLEQUES on 27th inst. Division transferred to VII Corps, Second Army., and moved to EPERLEQUES.	
EPERLEQUES		28.	Call on 202nd Field Company for Training programme. Reconnoitred sites of Gas Chambers near MOULLE, WESTROVE.	
		30.	202nd Field Company submitted programme of training for period 1st to 6th July. Arranged for them to have the use of the Range on July 1st.	
			Appendix F shows list of Honours and Awards to 30th Divisional Engineers.	Appendix F

Lt Col.R.E.
C.R.E. 30th Division.
2-7-18.

APPENDIX A.

SECRET.   30th Division G/515/R.E.2

33rd American Division.

1. The 108th Engineer Regiment will entrain tomorrow at AIRAINES and will detrain at POULAINVILLE, under arrangements that are being made by Fourth Army Headquarters.

2. It is understood that they will work in 2 parties, one under the Chief Engineer of the III Corps and the other under the Chief Engineer of the Australian Corps; and it is probable that they will be camped in two places to fit in with the work, but no definite information about this has yet been received.

3. On arrival in the new area Regimental Transport as under will be issued under Fourth Army arrangements:

    10 wagons G.S. (horsed).
    2 Water Motor Lorries.

4. The C.R.E. 30th Division will make preliminary arrangements regarding tools and engineering stores.

5. The 11th Bn South Lancs Regt (Pioneers) Training Cadre will be attached to 108th Engineer Regt in the new area and will assist them in musketry, gas and other training, as may be required. The 11th Bn South Lancs Regt. will be prepared to move from their present camp, so as to be in close touch with 108th Engineer Regiment.

[signature] Lieut Col

Major General
Commanding, 30th Division.

12-6-18.

Copies to 21st Infantry Brigade)
         ✓ C.R.E. (Adv. Hdqrs.)) For information and
         11th Bn South Lancs R.) necessary action.
         "Q"   )

30th Division "G".

On receipt of your letter C/515/372 dated 12.6.18, I went across & saw the Chief Engineer's Australian & 3rd Corps. C.E. Australian Corps informed me that the 1st Battalion of the 108th Engineer Regiment was being split up into Camps several miles apart, one Company being put under each C.RE. working on the Army Line & will be working along with an Army Troops Coy.R.E. Each C.R.E. is undertaking the technical training of, and the supply of stores & Tools to, the Engineer Coy attached to him.

C.E. 3rd Corps informed me that the 2nd Battalion is also being split up, two Companies to be attached to a Siege Coy.R.E. & the other Company to be under a Field Engineer. Tools & stores will be provided by the C.R.E. 3rd Corps Troops

Both C.Es. agreed to allow one platoon of each Company off work each day for Training in Musketry & Gas. The C.E. Australian Corps agreed to supply Instructors & did not require the services of the 11th South Lancs. The C.E. 3rd Corps asked for all the 11th South Lancs Instructors for the training of the Engineer Coys. attached to them. I have therefore ordered the whole of the 11th South Lancs to move to the Camp of the H.Q. 2nd Battalion American Engineers in 3rd Corps Area tomorrow, but some of them can easily be moved to the Australian Corps Area if desired.

Seeing that the 108th Engineer Regiment is being split up into several Camps many miles apart & working under four different C.R.E's, who have Army Troops Coys, Siege Coys, Tunnelling Coys etc. working on the same portion of the line along with the American Engineers, I do not consider it of any advantage my staying up here & request that I may return to EU.

Lt. Col. R.E.
C.R.E. 30th Division.

13.6.18.

"A" Form
MESSAGES AND SIGNALS.

Army Form C. 2121
(In pads of 100.)

APPENDIX C

HEADQUARTERS,
R.E.
30TH DIVISION.

TO: OC 11 S Lancs Regt Pernois

Sender's Number.	Day of Month.	In reply to Number.	AAA
KM	13		

You will move to-morrow to the HdQrs of the 2nd Battalion of the 105th American Engineer Regt and take in hand the training of that Battalion in Musketry Gas etc. aaa The 3rd Corps are sending one Lorry to be at your camp at ARGOEUVES at 2 P.M. to-morrow to convey Baggage. You are to report above lorry to report to area commandant at BEAUCOURT at 3 P.M.
(near la Hallue)

From
Place
Time

The above may be forwarded as now corrected (Z)

Censor. Signature of Addressor or person authorised to telegraph in his name
* This line should be erased if not required.

Order No. 1625. Wt. W3253/ P 511 27/2 H. & K., Ltd. (E. 2634)

"A" Form
MESSAGES AND SIGNALS.

Army Form C. 2121
(In pads of 100.)

No. of Message..........

Prefix....Code.....m.	Words	Charge.	This message is on a/c of:	Recd. at......m.
Office of Origin and Service Instructions	Sent		HEADQUARTERS, R.E. ...Service.	Date..........
	At ....m.		30TH DIVISION.	From..........
	To			
	By		(Signature of "Franking Officer")	By..........

TO {

Sender's Number.   Day of Month.   In reply to Number.   A A A

where it will pick
up tents. aaa Guides
will be at area
commandant office BEAUCOURT
at 3.00 pm to
guide your men and
lorry to set up
camp. aaa Report your
arrival by wire to this
there H.Q. ... ...
shelter etc should be struck & ready
by ... hours

C.E. Devenny
Lt. Col.
C.R.E. 30

From
Place
Time
The above may be forwarded as now corrected (Z)

Censor.   Signature of Addresser or person authorised to telegraph in his name
* This line should be erased if not required.

APPENDIX D

"C" FORM.
MESSAGES AND SIGNALS.

Army Form C. 2123.
(In books of 100.)

No. of Message ....

Prefix......Code......Words......	Received.	Sent, or sent out.	Office Stamp.
£ s. d.	From......	At......m.	
Charges to Collect	By......		
Service Instructions		To......	
		By......	

Handed in at............Office............m. Received............m.

TO CRA 30 Div
    via Signals Regiment

*Sender's Number.	Day of Month.	In reply to Number.	AAA
A 942	14	R1425	

30 Div AC HE
will return to EU
as soon as convenient

30 Div

FROM
PLACE & TIME

* This line should be erased if not required.
(19629) Wt528/M1970. 300,000 Pads. 4/17. McC. & Co., Ltd. (E1213).

War Diary. Appendix E

HANDING OVER NOTES ON WORK IN THE AU AREA.

Ranges.

1. Long range completed for each Regtl. Area except at BAZINVAL, where there is 2 days work to finish the 500 & 600 yds. point.

2. Field firing range. Work commenced. Three targets ready in R.E. Dump BOUVAINCOURT. Estimate this work could be finished in 7 days, but it has not yet been finally settled on what scale the range would be - whether for Batn. or Coy. The whole work could however be done in a week by getting sufficient men, as the work is all scattered & sufficient men on the job could do this in a week. No stores on site.

3. M.G. Range. Work on Machine Gun range is finished. 6 spare 7' x targets in shops.

Water Supply.

1. EPT HEULES. Completed. The pump has not yet been tested.

Bath Houses.

AU.   Completed.
LE LIEU DIEU. In farm next to Munition Factory. Two days work required to complete. All materials on site.
GAMACHES.   In foundry. (Area Commandant knows location). Work started on 17th Inst. 3 or 4 days work required to complete. All material on site.
VILLY LE BAS. Last farm on N.W. corner of village. Work started on 18th Inst Most of material on site. Remainder on Bouvaincourt Dump.

Gas Training Grounds.

1. Northern Area. Gas dugout. Gas curtains to be fixed, about ½ days work finishing off.

2. Southern Area. 1½ days work to finish. 200ft. mm boarding & 12 yards Union Cloth required.

Bayonet Course.

One Bayonet Course has been erected by each Batn. in the Divl. Area. For sites of these, please see attached map.

A handing over party consisting of 1 Officer & 6 O.R. of the 202nd Field Coy. are located at Bouvaincourt Mill, 1 mile N.E. of Bouvaincourt, & just North of the H. in HALTE.

Stock sheets attached, showing (a) Material handed over to 66th Divl. R.E. at BOINCOURT Station & (b) Stores left under charge at Workshops at Bouvaincourt.

20.6.18.

Lt. Col. R.E.
C.R.E. 30th Division.

KING'S BIRTHDAY LIST OF HONORS AND AWARDS.

Bt. Lt. Col.
Major, (./Lt. Col.) C.F.DUNSON. D.S.O.

M.C.

T/Lt,(A/Capt.) F.H.DALLICON.   30th Divl: Signal Coy.RE
T/Lt,(A/Capt.) F.B.COOLEY.   201st Field Company R.E.

D.C.M.

512762. S/Cpl,(./Cpl.) G.H.CLIFTON.   30th Divl: Signal Coy.R.E.
                                       (Attached 148 Bde: R.F.A.)

M.S.M.

81860.   Sgt: J.LYNCH.   201st Field Company. R.E.
81647.   Sgt: T.PEACOCK.   200th Field Company. R.E.
33104.   2/Cpl,(A/Cpl.) A.J.WARD.   202nd Field Company. R.E.

CONFIDENTIAL.

WAR DIARY

of

HEADQUARTERS, 30TH DIVISIONAL

ENGINEERS.

From. 1st JULY 1918.   to   31st JULY 1918.

VOLUME 33.

Army Form C. 2118.

WAR DIARY
~~INTELLIGENCE SUMMARY~~

(Erase heading not required.)

HEADQUARTERS, 30th DIVISIONAL ENGINEERS.

VOLUME 33.

July 1918.

Reference Maps.
1/40000 Sheet 27A
" " 27
" " 28
1/20000 Sheet 27S.E.
& 28 S.W. (combined)

Instructions regarding War Diaries and Intelligence Summaries are contained in F. S. Regs., Part II. and the Staff Manual respectively. Title pages will be prepared in manuscript.

Place	Date	Hour	Summary of Events and Information	Remarks and references to Appendices
EPERLECQUES			**PRELIMINARY.** The Division was at EPERLECQUES under the VIIth Corps 2nd Army, and was in process of being reformed. The 200th and 201st Field Companies were working under the XVth Corps on the LE PEUPLIER SWITCH. The 202nd Field Company was with the Division, and was training. A little work was also being done in connection with Water Supply.	
	3rd.		Received notification that the Division would be transferred to the Xth Corps about July 8th and that the 200th and 201st Field Companies would rejoin the Division on reaching the new area.	
	6th.		Received Divisional Order No. 179 with reference to transfer to Xth Corps at Mid-night 7/8th. During this period the 6th Bn. South Wales Bdrs. joined the Division as Pioneers, but were attached to the 21st Brigade, pending the arrival of the 3rd Battn. to that Brigade.	
	7th. 9th.		Received the 30th Division Defence Scheme No. 1 (Provisional) Division moved to CASSEL, the Division being in Xth Corps Reserve. The C.R.E. went round the Army (BERTHEN) Line with the G.O.C. and visited the C.R. Corps. It was arranged that the 202nd Field Company should go forward and work on a sector of the Army line under C.R.E. Corps Troops and that the 200th and 201st Field Companies should be withdrawn from work on the LE PEUPLIER SWITCH, and be given opportunity for training, carrying out at the same time work on preparing roads for demolitions.	
CASSEL.	10th.		Received C.E. Xth Corps 999/17 re demolitions and sent copies to 200th and 201st Field Coys. for necessary action. (See Appendix A.)	Appendix A.
	11th. 12th.		The 200th and 201st Field Companies rejoined the Division. The 202nd Field Company moved forward for work on the Army (BERTHEN) Line. A small Divisional R.E. Workshop was established in CASSEL (SeeAppendix B.)	Appendix B.
	13th.		Received C.E. Corps 1008/28, saying that the C.R.E. would be appointed C.R.E. Army Line and would take over from the Controller of Mines, 2nd Army on the 15th inst. ~~(Appendix C.)~~	~~Appendix C.~~

Army Form C. 2118.

SHEET NO. 2

WAR DIARY
or
INTELLIGENCE SUMMARY.
(Erase heading not required.)

Instructions regarding War Diaries and Intelligence Summaries are contained in F.S. Regs., Part II. and the Staff Manual respectively. Title pages will be prepared in manuscript.

Place	Date	Hour	Summary of Events and Information	Remarks and references to Appendices
			This was arranged verbally on the 11th inst.	
	14th		Received instructions from C.E. Corps to make 2 Battle Tracks from the STEENVOORDE-ECKE Road to the Army Line, in each of the forward Divl. Areas. 200th Field Coy. detailed to take on tracks in S. Divl. Area, 201 Field Coy. detailed to take on work in N. Divl. Area. Tracing of completed tracks is shown in Appendix D.	Appendix D.
	15th		Saw Controller of Mines 2nd Army re taking over work on the Army Line. Visited the Tunnelling Coys and Army Troop Coys employed on the Line and went round portion of line. Took over Appointment of C.R.E. Army Line. Received G.185/6/247, saying that Units working on Army Line, with the exception of attached Infantry,would form a Nucleus Garrison of the Line in case of an Alarm, until relieved by Infy. of 30th Divn; they would be under Orders of Xth Corps.	
	16th 17th		Instructed Units on Army Line to give wiring precedence of all other work. Received G.185/280 -- Divl. Defence Scheme No.2.(Appendix E)	Appendix E
	18th 19th		Issued 30th Divl. Engineers Order No.14. Received G.185/313 re "Battle Stations" and "Test Orders". Received G.485 from Divn.G. saying that work on construction of 3 Brigade Hqrs. was to be started at once. Each Field Coy. was instructed to do one, also 49 large English Shelters in each. Received C.E. Corps 1008/52 saying that Battle Tracks would be extended back to West of the St SYLVESTER CAPPEL-STEENVOORDE road. Arrangements were made accordingly. Arranged for 12 G.S. Wagons to be attached to Units working on the Army Line to assist in drawing Stores. Instructed units to be working on Army Line to erect notice boards as below,-according to instructions received from C.E. Corps:-	BATTLE

| Army Line. Front Line. | Army Line. Support Line | Army Line Reserve Line. |

			points, such as where trenches crossed roads &c. Map references to be added at important Received 30th Div. G.185/B/348. instructions on receipt of command "Battle Stations". Received "Test Orders". For details see Appendix F.	Appendix F.
	22nd	11.24 p.m.	Received instructions from C.E. Xth Corps to start work on an advanced Divl. Hqrs. in W. HOKERBELE.	
		11.55 A.M.	Received "Test Orders". For details see Appendix. F	Appendix F.

SHEET No.3.

WAR DIARY
or
INTELLIGENCE SUMMARY.
(Erase heading not required.)

Army Form C. 2118.

Instructions regarding War Diaries and Intelligence Summaries are contained in F. S. Regs., Part II. and the Staff Manual respectively. Title pages will be prepared in manuscript.

Place	Date	Hour	Summary of Events and Information	Remarks and references to Appendices
	24th		The 202nd Field Coy. were withdrawn from work on the Army Line and started work on the Divl. Hqrs. on MT. POKEREKIE with a working party of 100 Infantry. The 6th Battn. South Wales Bdrs. took over the whole of the LEFT SECTOR of the Army Line, and had a Battn. of Infantry from the 29th Divn.to work under them.	
	30th		G.O.C. Division inspected the 200th and 201st Field Companies, R.E. Received 30th Divn. C.185/6/670.	
			NOTES: Copies of Progress Reports for work on the Army Line and on works on preparing road demolitions are attached as Appendix G & H. and List of Honours and Awards not shown on last months War Diary are shown as Appendix I.	Appendix I.

[signature]
Lt. Col. R.E.
C.R.E. 30th Division.

5.8.18.

Appendix A

C.E. Xth Corps, 999/17

Controller of Mines, Second Army,
C.R.E. 30th Division,

   A map shewing proposed demolitions to be prepared in Xth Corps area is attached.

   The demolitions in the area from ST. SYLVESTRE CAPEL inclusive eastwards will be prepared by Controller of Mines, Second Army, and those westwards by C.R.E. 30th Division.

   Please inspect and report on these proposals, adding any further demolitions you consider necessary, and arrange to carry out the work.

   Please report progress by 6 p.m. on Fridays weekly.

Headquarters,
Xth Corps,
9th July 1918.

Captain, R.E.,
for Chief Engineer, Xth Corps.

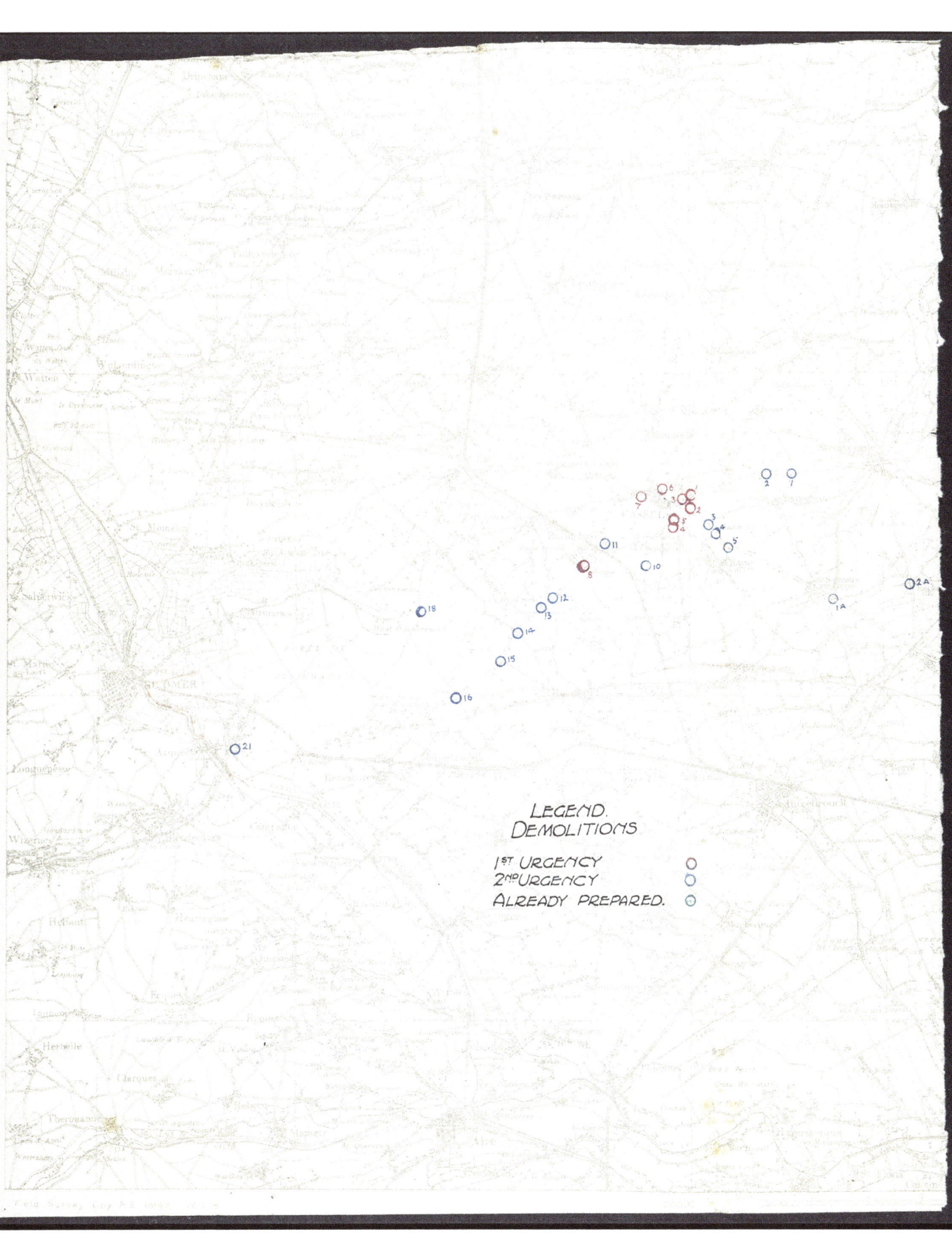

APPENDIX. B

On 12.7.18. a small Divisional R.E. Workshop was established in CASSEL, to which units could send men to construct Sanitary Appliances, under the supervision of the R.S.M.

These men on arrival were attached to the Divl, Employment Coy. for accomodation and rations, and were returned to their units, as soon as they had completed the work required by the unit.

This arrangement proved a great success, and eliminated the necessity of withdrawing skilled men from the Field Coy's to do the work and also resulted in considerable economy in material.

Men were sent in by 19 different units and the following articles were made and issued:-

45	5 Seater Latrines.	
45	2 " "	Total 335 seats
20	1 " "	
5	Meat safes.	

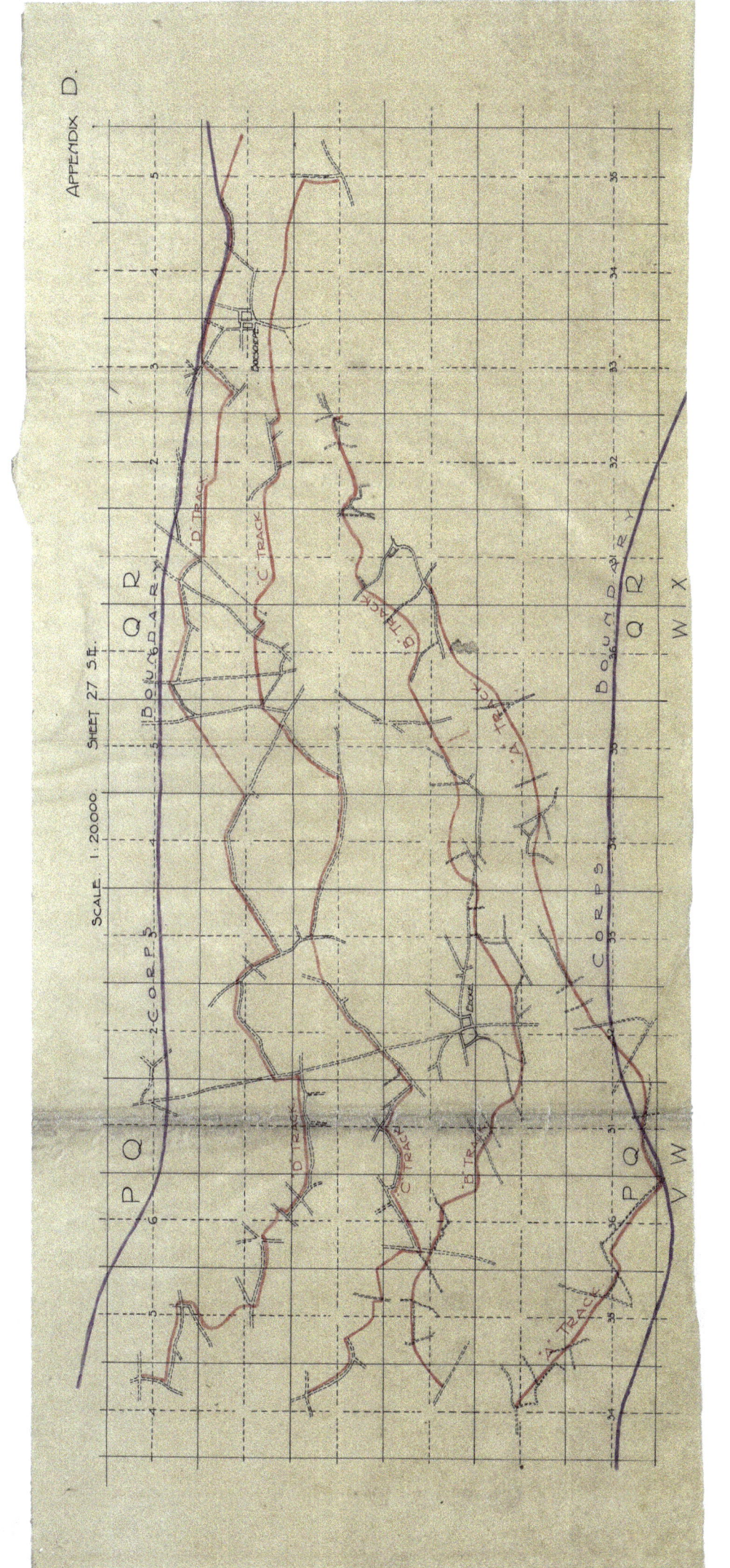

SECRET   Appendix E   Copy No 13

30th DIVISIONAL ENGINEERS ORDER NO 14.

1. In event of an enemy's attack the Divisional R.E. will be employed as follows:-

(a) 200th Field Coy R.E. will detail one section to assist the 77th Artillery Brigade to repair tracks for getting guns into position. This section will report at the H.Q. 77th Artillery Brigade at J.34.b.
    201st Field Coy R.E. will detail one section to assist the 148 Artillery Brigade and one section to assist the 149 Artillery Brigade to repair tracks for getting guns into position. These sections will report at the H.Q. 148 Artillery Brigade at P.2.Cent and at the H.Q. 149 Artillery Brigade at P.11.Cent respectively.
(b) 200th Field Coy R.E. (less one section) and 201st Field Coy R.E. (less two sections) will move to the GODEWAERSVELDE area and remain in Divisional Reserve.
    Billets will be allotted by 21st Infantry Brigade.
(c) 202nd Field Coy R.E. will man a portion of the Army Line under order of O.C. 6th S.W.B.(Pioneers).
(d) H.Q. 30th Divisional R.E. will move to K.32.b.

2. O.C. Field Companies will notify this office of their exact map locations immediately they arrive in their new billets.
3. The above moves will take place on the alarm being given or on opening of enemy's bombardment.
4. Field Companies will acknowledge.

Capt R.E.
Adjt: 30th Divl: Engineers.

17-7-18

Copy No.1 to O.C. 200th Field Coy R.E.
  -   - 2 - O.C. 201st Field Coy R.E.
  -   - 3 - O.C. 202nd Field Coy R.E.   )
  -   - 4 - O.C. 6th Bn: S.W.B. (Pioneers)   )
  -   - 5 - C.R.A. 30th Division.   )
  -   - 6 - O.C. 77th Artillery Brigade.   )
  -   - 7 - 30th Divisional "G"   )
  -   - 8 - 30th Divisional "Q"   )
  -   - 9 - 21st Infantry Brigade.   ) For information.
  -   -10 - 89th Infantry Brigade.   )
  -   -11 - 90th Infantry Brigade.   )
  -   -12 - C.E. Xth Corps.   )
  -   -13 - War Diary.   )
  -   -14 - War Diary.   )
  -   -15 - File.   )

Appendix ..... F.

TEST ORDERS.

			Estimated.	
			Ready to move.	Reach Battle Stations.
July. 19th.	Received at H.Q. R.E.	at 11.24am.	—	—
"	Received at 200th Field Coy. R.E.	at 11.50pm.	1.20 am.	2.5 am.
"	Received at 201st Field Coy. R.E.	at 11.42pm.	12.42 am.	—
20th.	Received at 202nd Field Coy. R.E.	at 12.12am.	1.15 am.	2.20 am (Redoubt Line)
22nd.	Received at H.Q. R.E.	at 11.55am.	—	—
"	Received at 200th Field Coy. R.E.	at 12.24pm.	1.54pm.	2.39pm.
"	Received at 201st Field Coy. R.E.	at 12.25pm.	1.25pm.	—
"	Received at 202nd Field Coy. R.E.	at 12.26pm.	1.29pm.	2.34pm.

C.E., Xth Corps.

PROGRESS REPORT - ARMY LINE, from 15-7-18 to 18-7-18.

Map showing progress of work in the line up to 18-7-18 is attached. Can this be returned after perusal so that it can be corrected and brought up to date in time for next week's Progress Report, please.

I am having the line surveyed and hope by next week to have a corrected map, the present map being incorrect in many places. In this respect it would be a great help if air photos could be obtained.

During the week a considerable amount of work has been done in clearing the crops in front of the front line, and also on drainage which was found necessary after the heavy rains.

I have been unable to carry on the percentage system of Progress Report as the percentages given by the Companies differ very considerably from those handed over to me by the Controller of Mines, and in consequence it will be impossible to estimate progress thereby.

Will you please say if you wish this system adopted.

Details of work carried out are as follows.

RIGHT Sector (Q.36.cent to FONTAINE - BERTHEN Road)
Average No of men on works (R.E. 56.
(Infantry 180.
(Labour 410.

Front Line

Trench parapet thickened, trimmed, and fire bays revetted from Q.36.a.9.2. to R.31.b.1.5., and draining od trenches practically completed within these boundaries.

Field of fire cleared to 40 yards in front of wire from R.26.a.2.5. to R.26.b.3.8. and from R.19.d.4.1. to R.20.c.7.4., also from R.31.a.4.0. to R.25.b.4.1.

Spider wire at Q.25.b.5.1.

Support Line.

Trench parapet thickened and trimmed from R.31.a.5.3. to Q.36.a.1.7. also from R.19.d.3.1. to R.20.c.7.3. 80 yards C.T. to front line completed at Q.36.a.6.6.

First belt of wire completed at Q.36.b.cent. Field of fire cleared to front line from R.19.d.3.1.to R.20.c.7.3.

CENTRE Sector. (FONTAINE - BERTHEN Road to BANGLE FARM exclusive)
Average number of men on works (R.E. 75.
(Infantry 175.
(Labour 370.

Front Line.

Trenches deepened and revetted from R.16.c.0.3. to R.22.a.8.8.
600 yards of wire put out in front of R.16.c.0.1.and 400 yards in front of R.16.c.9.0. Trench completed (preliminary stage) from R.16.d.8.8. to R.17.c.3.9.

Support Line.

Work pn clearing field of fire only.

C.T. No work done. Practically all the R.Es where employed on wiring.

LEFT Sector. (BANGLE FARM inclusive, to M.2.c.1.3.)
Average number of men on works R.E. 63.
Pioneers. 480.

Working and deepening of trenches and drainage R.18.a., R.12.c. and R.17.b. Drainage was particularly necessary at R.12.c.

Front Line.

Trenches completed to 2nd stage in R.18.a., 900 yards in all.
500 yards Reserve Line trench in R.11.c.completed to 1st stage.
800 yards of wire erected from R.11.d.2.1. to R.11.b.8.0. in front & all of front and support lines from R.17.c.6.7. to R.12.c.9.8. (along the
Hedges thinned in front of reserve line from R.11.d.3.7. to R.11.b.7.2. and from R.11.c.9.5. to R.11.d.05.oo.

Crops cleared over belt of 100 yards of wire from R.18.a.4.3. to R.18.a.9.8., and from R.17.b.4.9. to R.18.a.2.8.

The practice manning on the morning of the 18th Inst. would appear to have lasted very much longer than was intended, with the result that little work was done on that morning.

PROGRESS REPORT.

C.E. Xth. Corps.

Herewith tracing of Army Line corrected up to 24.7.18. Work carried out during the preceding Week is shown in Yellow in the case of trenches, and ordinary pencil in the case of wire (Vide Legend). May this tracing be returned please in time to correct and forward with next weeks Progress Report.

Apart from work shown on the map a considerable amount of work has been done on clearing the field of fire in front of the front line, on drainage and on strengthening existing wire. Notice boards have also been erected marking the Front, Support, Reserve Lines.

Changes in Labour.

1. 202nd. Field Coy.R.E. was withdrawn from work on the Army Line, on the 24th. inst; and started work on Divl. R.E. vide your 1010/62 dated 22.7.18. The whole of the Left Sector of the Line has now been taken over by the 6th. Battn. South Wales Borderers (Pnrs).

2. The 5 Infantry Companies for 30th Division working on the Army Line were withdrawn on the 25th. inst.

3. One Infantry Battn. of the 29th. Division is starting work on the Army Line on the 26th. inst. on the Left Sector under O.C.6th. Battn. South Wales Borderers (Pnrs).

4. 200 men of the 121 Labour Coy, working on the Right Sector under the O.C.141st. Army Troop Coy. were withdrawn from work on the Army Line on 24th. inst. vide your 619/36 dated 23.7.18.

5. A small party of the 141st. Army Troop Coy. are being detailed to cut gaps in wire on Le Peuplier Switch vide your 1008/69 dated 23rd inst.

6. Labour is now distributed as follows:-

		Aver. Strength.
Right Sector.	141st. Army Troop Coy.	72.
	121st. " " "	50.
	135th. " " "	100.
Centre Sector.	214th. Army Troop Coy.	61.
	46 th. Labour Coy.	148.
	110th. " "	199.
Left Sector.	6th. Battn. S.W.Bds. (Pnrs)	480.
	Infantry Battn.	

Lt.Col. R.E.
C.R.E. 30th. Divl. Engineers. R.E.

25.7.18.

Chief Engineer Xth Corps.

PROGRESS REPORT.   Week ending 31.7.18.

2nd Position.

The attached tracing shows work carried out on the 2nd Position, during the last week. New work shown in Yellow, in the case of trenches, and in black lead pencil, in the case of wire. Vide Legend.
Will you please return this tracing in time for corrections and inclusion in next weeks report.
The following work has been carried on with but is not shown on the map.

      Clearing Crops and Trimming Hedges.
      Drainage.
      Repairing of trenches damaged by rain and shell fire.
      Making Concertina barbed wire and placing it in position in the gaps in the wire.
      Road screened from Lilt Farm (R.24.d.0.8.) to CANTA Corner (R.19.a.5.2.).

Labour employed on the Line is as follows:-

			Aver. Strength.
Right Sector.	141	Army Troop Coy.	72.
	121	" " "	50.
	185	" " "	100.
Centre Sector.	214	Army Troop Coy.	61.
	46	Labour Coy.	148.
	110	" "	199.
Left Sector.	6th Battn. S.W.Bds. (Pnrs)		480.
	Infantry Battn.		450.
			1560.

Lt. Col. R.E.
C.R.E. 30th Division.

1.8.18.

C.E., Xth Corps.

REPORT ON DEMOLITIONS.

Reference your G99/17, dated 9-7-18.

The sites of all these demolitions have been reconnoitred (except No 21) and plans have been submitted and approved.

Endeavours have been made to get 8" earth augers for this purpose in order to demolish long lengths of road with a series of charges, in preference to one big crater, but these have only arrived at No.3. R.E. Park today.

In the meantime work was started on the more urgent places, as shown on the attached tracing.

At P.7.a.5.9. the road is too broad to blow up with one crater, so six smaller craters are being made. Four 10' vertical shafts have been dug and the other two are half finished.

At O.12.d.5.8. the same method is being adopted as at P.7.a.5.9. Five shafts have been started and are 25% completed.

At P.15.c.7.3. a 9' shaft has been sunk. Some preliminary drainage was necessary here.

At P.14.d.3.8. Shaft 6' deep, dug.

All men have now been taken off these demolitions and are now working on the Battle Tracks. They will return on completion of the latter.

19-7-18.

Lt: Col: R.E.
C.R.E., 30th Division.

PROGRESS REPORT FOR WEEK ENDING 25.7.18.

Location.	Nature of Work.	No. on Work R.E.	INF.	Remarks.	
				Shaft.	Gallery.
				Completed.	Completed.
Group "A".	Road Mines.				
	No. 1 Mine.	aver.	Nil.	60%	Nil.
	No. 3 "	26 per day.		100%	5%.
	No. 5 "			90%	Nil.
Group "B".	No. 1 Mine.	aver. 12 per day.	Nil.	50%	Nil.
	No. 2 "			50%	Nil.
	No. 4 "			Nil.	Nil.
	No. 5 "			Nil.	Nil.
Group "C".	No. 1 Mine.	AVER. 20 per day.	Nil.	100%	100%
	No. 2 Mine.			100%	100%
	No. 3 Mine.			90%	Nil.
O.5.d.13.	Demolitions.	24 O.R.	10	Vertical shaft 4'x 3' sunk 15 feet and close cased. Timber removed and shaft filled in on account of water. Second shaft sunk 6 feet and closed cased. Bored to 12 feet to test for water. Shaft covered in and temporarily closed on account of water.	
O.6.c.7.6.				Vertical shaft 4'x 3' sunk 12'6" after site prepared. Shaft closed cased. Gallery 5'x 2'9" opened and mined for 10 feet. Framed, roof lagged, sides revetted and strutted	

Sketches of proposed demolitions at the undermentioned spots are attached. These have not been started yet.

    Sheet 27.   O.26.b.2.9.   O.26.a.4.2.
      "   "   T6.b.7.8.   O.31.a.8.7.
               T1.a.7.8.

                                               Capt. R.E.
25.7.18.   for C.R.E. 30th. Divl. Engineers. R.E.

Demolitions

1^a

Sheet 27.
O.6.c.7.[illegible]

Demolitions.

of fuse is prepared and

Sheet 27.
O.10.b.35.10.

1.6.16.

To. C.E. X Corps.

Appendix 1.

MENTIONS.

London Gazette 20th May 1918.

Maj.(A/Lt. Col.) G.W. DENISON. D.S.O. R.E.   C.R.E. 30th Division.
Capt.(A/Maj.) O.D. ATKINSON. M.C. R.E.   200th Field Coy. R.E.
Capt.(A/Maj.) J.E. CHIPPINDALL. M.C. R.E. 202nd Field Coy. R.E.

CONFIDENTIAL.

WAR DIARY

OF

HEAD QUARTERS. 30th DIVISIONAL

ENGINEERS.

FROM 1st August 1918.   TO. 31st August 1918.

-o-o-o- -o-o-o-o-o

(VOLUME   ).

Army Form C. 2118.

HEADQUARTERS, 30th DIVISIONAL ENGINEERS.

WAR DIARY

VOLUME 34. August 1918.

INTELLIGENCE SUMMARY. Reference Maps:- 1/40,000 Sheet 28 " 27 1/20,000 Sheet 27.S.E & 28 S.W.(combined)

(Erase heading not required.)

Instructions regarding War Diaries and Intelligence Summaries are contained in F. S. Regs., Part II. and the Staff Manual respectively. Title pages will be prepared in manuscript.

Place	Date	Hour	Summary of Events and Information	Remarks and references to Appendices
EPPLECQUES. CASSEL.			**Preliminary.** The Division was at EPPLECQUES CASSEL. C.R.E., Army Line (2nd Position) and had the following Units under him. The C.R.E. held the appointment of C.R.E. in Xth Corps Reserve.	
			RIGHT SECTOR. Average Strength	
			141 Army Troops Coy. 72.	
			121 Labour Coy. 50.	
			185 Labour Coy. 100.	
			CENTRE SECTOR. 214 Army Troops Coy. 61.	
			46 Labour Coy. 148.	
			110 Labour Coy. 199.	
			LEFT SECTOR. 6th Bn S.W. Bdrs (Pnrs) 480.	
			Infantry Battalion. 400.	
			1510.	
	1st.		Field Companies of the Division were employed as follows :- 200th & 201st Field Coys R.E. 1 section of each preparing demolitions on roads west of ST SYLVESTRE CAPEL. 3 Sections of each on Training. 202nd Field Coy. R.E. 3 Sections making Advanced Divisional Headquarters on MONT KOKEREELE, and 1 Section on Advanced Brigade Headquarters.	
			C.E., Army and C.E., Corps went round the Army Line.	
	2nd.		Received 30th Division Order No 181 saying that the Division would relieve the 35th Division in the LOGRE Sector commencing on the night 5th/6th August. Received 30th Division "G389 and G391 postponing and cancelling Order No 181respectively.	
	3rd. 4th.		The 202nd Field Coy. R.E. handed over work on Advanced Divisional Headquarters on MONT KOKEREELE to C.R.E., 35th Division and withdrew the 3 Sections to their Headquarters for training. The 6th Bn S.W. Bdrs handed over work on the LEFT SECTOR of the ARMY LINE (2nd Position) to the 214th Army Troops Coy. R.E.	
	5th		The C.R.E. handed over the appointment of C.R.E., Army Line to O.C. 214th A.T. Coy. R.E.	Appendix A.
	6th.		Received 30th Division Order No 182 saying that the 30th Division would relieve the 35th Division in the LOGRE Sector commencing on the night 8th/9th August.	

Army Form C. 2118.

WAR DIARY
INTELLIGENCE SUMMARY.
(Erase heading not required.)

Instructions regarding War Diaries and Intelligence Summaries are contained in F. S. Regs., Part II. and the Staff Manual respectively. Title pages will be prepared in manuscript.

Place	Date	Hour	Summary of Events and Information	Remarks and references to Appendices
	6th contd.		Received C.R.E., 35th Division,No 57 with reference to the relief.	
	7th		Issued 30th Divisional Engineers Order No 15.	
			Received 30th Divisional Defence Scheme No 3 (Provisional) and sent extracts to the Field Companies. In the case of alarm the Field Companies would and Pioneers would 'Stand to' at their billets. Received 30th Division G185/891 - 'Instructions for work on Defences, LOCRE Sector' - The C.R.E. would be responsible for all work in and in rear of the BLUE LINE with the exception of communication trenches.	Appendix B
	9th		The Field Companies relieved the three Companies of the 35th Division in the line and took over the same work. Completed handing over with C.R.E., 35th Division. Copy of handing over Report is attached.	Appendix C.
TERDEGHEM.	10th		Divisional Headquarters moved to TERDEGHEM. Appendix D shows how the Field Companies and Pioneers were distributed for work as soon as the necessary changes could be arranged and Appendix E shows actual works in hand on the 14th inst.	Appendix D. Appendix E.
	13th		Received 30th Division Order No 183 saying that the Division front would be changed from a 2 Brigade to a 3 Brigade front on the night of the 14th/15th inst.	
	17th		Received 30th Division Order No 184 saying that the Division would attack the DRANOUTRE RIDGE at a date to be notified later- the Brigades would use the R.E. already with them (one Section to each Brigade).	
	18th		Received G129/306 giving code words for denoting zero day and zero hour for the attack on DRANOUTRE RIDGE. The 204th Field Coy. R.E. and 2 Companies of the 19th Bn Northumberland Fusiliers(Pnrs) were attached to this Division from the 35th Division - work taken over by them is shown in Appendix F. Received 30th Division G129/239.	Appendix F.
	20th		Received Division Code wire G373 saying the attack on DRANOUTRE RIDGE would take place at 2-5 a.m. on the 21st inst. Advanced Divisional Headquarters opened at LA MONTAGNE at 6.p.m. C.R.E. remained with rear Headquarters.	

Army Form C. 2118.

SHEET 3.

WAR DIARY
or
INTELLIGENCE SUMMARY.
(Erase heading not required.)

Instructions regarding War Diaries and Intelligence Summaries are contained in F. S. Regs., Part II. and the Staff Manual respectively. Title pages will be prepared in manuscript.

Place	Date	Hour	Summary of Events and Information	Remarks and references to Appendices
	21st		The Division attacked the DRANOUTRE RIDGE and captured all objectives. A report on work done by the R.E. is attached as Appendix G. Advanced Divisional Headquarters closed at LA MONTAGNE at 2-15.p.m.	Appendix G
	23rd		Received Divl G.262/482 - proposals to change the Divisional front from a 3 Brigade to a 2 Brigade front.	
	24th		Appendix F shows work done during the week ending 23-8-18. Received Divl G.129/518.	
	27th		The 204th Field Coy. R.E. and the 19th Bn Northumberland Fusiliers (Pnrs) reverted to the 35th Division.	
	30th		The Germans started to withdraw in front of the LOCRE Sector. Received G.123/705 and G.262/689. Work on the BLUE LINE was stopped and parties on dug-outs reduced to a minimum. During the night 30th/31st the Field Coys were employed in clearing the following roads:- CANADA CORNER - LOCRE - DRANOUTRE thence along the DAYLIGHT CORNER Road and along the NEUVE-EGLISE Road. Road from M.34.c.2.6. to M.35.d.2.3. thence via HORBURY VILLA to the CLAPHAM Road and down towards CRUCIFIX CORNER. The Pioneers were also employed on these roads.	
LA. MONTAGNE.	31st		Work on Roads continued. Headquarters, 30th Divisional Engineers moved to LA MONTAGNE. Following are attached:- Appendix H, Report on Stores and Dump Party. Appendix I. Honours and Awards.	Appendix H Appendix I

August 5th 1918.

LT. COL. R.E.
C.R.E., 30th DIVISION.

Handing over Notes.
2nd Position.

APPENDIX A

1. The attached tracings, show works on 2nd Position corrected up to 30.7 30.7.18.

2. (a) C.E. Xth Corps requires a weekly Progress Report to reach his office by the first D.R. each Friday.
   (b) O's.C. Sectors have been sending in their Weekly Progress Reports to reach my office by noon on Thursdays.

3. M.G. Dug-outs and MOIR Pill Boxes are being constructed on the 2nd Position by the 171 and 255 Tunnelling Coy. They are working directly under the Controller of Mines, 2nd Army.

4. Stores are drawn from Xth Corps advanced R.E. Dump GOUDEZAER VELDE on authority of O'sC. Sectors working on the 2nd Position. Stores Officer to C.E. Xth Corps keeps this Dump stocked, but if special Stores are required or a special rush on certain stores is expected, he should be notified. Wires for such Stores should reach him by 2pm on the day p previous to that on which they are required.

5.

6. The following are enclosed:-

    1. Trench Maps&c handed over to me by Controller Of Mines 2nd Army.
    2. Daily Works Reports for preceeding week.
    3. Copy of my Progress Report to Corps for week ending 30.7.18.
    4. Correspondence relating to work on the 2nd Position.

SECRET. Copy No. 14

30th DIVISIONAL ENGINEERS ORDER NO. 15.

1. The 30th Division will be relieving the 35th Division in the LOCRE Sector commencing on the night 8/9th August.

2. (a) The 200th Field Coy.R.E. will take over the work in the Right Sub-sector from the 204th Field Coy.R.E.
   (b) The 202nd Field Coy.R.E. will take over the work in the Centre & Left Sub-sector from the 203rd Field Coy.R.E.
   (c) The 201st Field Coy.R.E. will take over the work in the Back area from the 205th Field Coy.R.E.
   (d) The 6th South Wales Borderers (Pioneers) will take over the work of the 19th Northumberland Fusiliers (Pioneers).

3. (a) The 200th Field Coy.R.E. will hand over their present work & billet to the 203rd Field Coy.R.E.
   (b) The 201st Field Coy.R.E. will hand over their present work & billet to the 204th Field Coy.R.E.
   (c) The 202nd Field Coy.R.E. will hand over their present work & billet to the 205th Field Coy. R.E.

4. (a) The 200th & 202nd Field Coys. R.E. & the 6th South Wales Brdrs. (Pioneers) will take over the billets & transport lines of the Unit they are relieving.
   (b) The 201st Field Coy.R.E. will take over the billets of 2 Sections of the 205th Field Coy.R.E. about BANGLE FARM & will find accommodation for the remaining 2 Sections as near as possible, vide my wire R.690 dated 6.8.18. They will take over the present Transport lines of the 205th Field Coy.R.E.

5. The Field Coys. & Pioneers of the 35th Division are located as follows

	H.Q.	Trans.Lines.
203rd Field Coy. R.E.	M.15.a.7.	Q.11.a.1.1.
204th Field Coy. R.E.	M.21.c.1.1.	Q.18.a.4.8.
205th Field Coy. R.E.	R.8.d.5.1.	Q.10.a.5.8.
19th Northumberland Fus.(Pnrs.)	R.12.b.2.2.	

6. O's.C.Field Coys.R.E. & Pioneers will send an Officer on the 8th to the Headquarters of Unit they are relieving to take over the work.

7. Relief to be completed by midnight of 9/10th August.

8. All details to be arranged direct between O'sC. concerned.

9. H.Q. 30th Divisional R.E. will open at TERDEGHEM on August 10th at 10 a.m. at which hour G.O.C. 30th Division is taking over charge of the LOCRE Sector from G.O.C. 35th Division.

10. Field Companies & Pioneers will acknowledge receipt.

Phillips
Capt. R.E,
Adjt. 30th Divl. Engrs.

7.8.18.

Copy No.1, to O.C. 200th Field Coy. R.E.
" No.2, to O.C. 201st Field Coy. R.E.
" No.3, to O.C. 202nd Field Coy. R.E.
" No.4, to O.C. 6th Bn.Sth.Wales. Brdrs.(Pnrs.)
" No.5, to 30th Division "G".
" No.6, to 30th Division "Q".
" No.7, to H.Q. 21st Brigade.
" No.8, to H.Q. 89th Brigade.
" No.9, to H.Q. 90th Brigade.
" No.10.to O.C. 30th Divl.Signal Coy.
" No.11.to Chief Engineer,X Corps.
" No.12. to C.R.E. 35th Division.
" No.13. War Diary.
" No.14. " "
" No.15. File.

APPENDIX C

HANDING OVER REPORT.

From C.R.E., 30th British Division to C.R.E., 35th British Division.

The following works are in hand:-

DEMOLITIONS.

Roads to be prepared for demolition at places shown on plan "A".   A File.

Copy of my Progress Report to Corps dated 8.8.18 and map is enclosed, also copies of handing over reports from 200th and 201st Field Companies.

Each of these Companies were employing one Section on the work.

Corps were asked to supply labour for the work but none was obtainable.

It is understood that C.E., Xth Corps only requires you to complete demolitions already in hand.

A Progress Report is required by C.E. Corps each Friday morning.

ADVD. BRIGADE HEADQUARTERS.

Two of these have been completed, one at R.2.a. and the other at Q.17.c.9.8.   B File.

The remaining one at R.2.a.5.9. is completed except for 25% of the Burster Course and camouflage.

Copy of handing over report by O.C. 202nd Field Coy. is enclosed. One section only was employed.

TRAINING.

The remaining 3 sections of each Field Coy. are employed in training.

DEFENCE SCHEME &c.

Secret file containing the following sub-files is enclosed:- Secret File.
1. 30th Divl. Defence Scheme No.1.(Provl) with maps and amendments.
2. 30th Divl. Defence Scheme No.2. with maps and amendments.
3. 30th Divl. G. Counter Attack Scheme with map.
4. Miscellaneous.

STORES.

A small dump and workshop has been established in CASINO CAMP. This was made to enable units to send in men to make latrines, meat safes &c, for their units. The men were attached to the D.E.C. for accommodation and rations.

This proved successful in that it saved taking Sappers away from the Field Companies, to do the same work, and enabled them to train. It also saved a considerable amount of material.

I do not think much more sanitary work is required.

Stores for the dump were drawn by Lorry from the Xth Corps dump at LA CLOCHE, and No.3 R.E. Park, BAUDECQUE, authority to draw being obtained from Stores Officer for C.E. Corps in the usual manner.

All indents for material on Xth Corps Main Dump, LA CLOCHE are cancelled if not drawn in 5 days from the date of the voucher.

Any stores required for work in connection with the Army Line (Gun Emplacements, Dressing Stations, T.M. Emplacements &c) can be drawn on your own authority from Xth Corps advanced dump R.E. Dump GODE. The N.C.O. in charge can be got on the phone by ringing up the Stores Officer 35th Division who lives on the dump and asking him to send for the N.C.O.

I also have a Battle Reserve of stores there consisting of the following:-

```
        750 Coils      Barbed Wire.
         50 Bdles      French concertina
       1150 Shovels    G.S.
        350    "       French
        400 Picks
      10000 Sandbags
       1000 Screw pickets  long
       2000    "      "    short
```

(2).

I have informed the N.C.O. in charge that you will take this over on the 10th inst.

RETURNS.

List of Stores Returns required by C.E. Corps are shown on his letters No. 733/15/1. dated 8.7.18 and No.733/132 dated 6.8.18.

List of other returns required is shown in C.E. Xth Corps 1002/18 dated 8.7.18.

A Progress Report on Demolition Work is required each Friday morning.

A Narrative Report on Engineer Work during the preceding week is required by C.E. Xth Corps each Saturday.

Lt. Col. R.E.
C.R.E. 30th Division.

9.8.18.

APPENDIX D

NARRATIVE REPORT ON R.E. WORK.

for week ending 16-6-17.

C.E., 7th Corps.

On taking over from the 35th Division on the 8th inst, the Field Coys and Pioneers took over the work being done by the corresponding Units of the 35th Division, but as soon as possible they were distributed as follows :-

RIGHT Brigade Sector Area.

With Brigade on forward work, One Section of 200th Field Coy R.E.
Under C.R.E. (R.A. and Medical work) One Section of 200th Field Coy R.E.
With Brigade on C.Ts, One Company of Pioneers.

LEFT Brigade Area.

With Brigade on forward work, 2 Sections of 202nd Field Coy R.E.
Under C.R.E. (R.A. and Medical work) 2 Sections of 202nd Field Coy R.E.
With Brigade on C.Ts, One Company of Pioneers.

BLUE LINE.

Under C.R.E. 4 Sections of 201st Field Coy R.E.

BACK AREA.

Under C.R.E. 2 Sections of 200th Field Coy R.E.
Under C.R.E. (On roads) 1 Company of Pioneers.

6th LEFT Brigade Area becoming a 2 Brigade area, 1 Section of the 202nd Field Coy was attached to each Brigade, remaining in the same areas as previously.

By the end of the week the following works were in hand :-
201st Field Coy   BLUE LINE, with 250 Infantry.
200th & 202nd Field Coys.   COTTAGE. O.P.
                                PAUL. O.P.
                                8 Dug-outs.
                                5 Shelters(improving & enlarging)
                                Mule Track from K.20.d.7.5.to K.28.c.7.7
                                Well being sunk at K.16.c.7.3.
                                Gas Proofing Dug-outs.
                                Road Screening.

Pioneers. 2 Companies with Brigades on C.Ts.
           1 Company on roads from WESTOUTRE to CANADA CORNER, and
           from K.9.c.5.2. to K.20.d.0.0.

(sd)
Lt. Col. R.E.
C.R.E., 30th Division.

PROGRESS REPORT.

Week ending, noon, 14th inst.

BLUE LINE.
    Labour.   82. R.E.   247 Infantry, (average).
    Trenches.
        Trenches dug to 3 feet.   370 yards.
        Five Fire Bays built about M.27.c.31.45. - 95% complete.
    Wiring.
        300 yards Apron Fence erected.
        New trenches taped out.

MULE TRACK.   (M.20.d.7.5. to M.28.c.7.7. (Coy.Hqrs))
    Labour. 24 R.E.
    Progress. 1160 yards - 2 Bridges built.
    Estimated time to complete, 3 days.

WATER.
    Well sunk at U.10.c.7.3.   80% complete.

LOCATION.	R.E.	OTHERS	REMARKS.
O.P's			
COTTAGE O.P. M.22.b.0.5.	23.		Tunnelled entrance, 10' progress. Work delayed by water and bad air and absence of labour prior to R.E.'s relief. 34' required to complete. Estimated time 15 days.
PAUL O.P. M.30.d.3.3.	26.	27 R.A.	Gallery, Observing Chamber & Accommodation Chamber. Gallery Progress. 15'. Chamber. 11'. Estimated time to complete, 3 weeks.
DUG-OUTS.			
M.G. M.22.b.7.7.			Tunnelled passage, 100 c.ft. excavated.
Coy. Hqrs. M.23.a.5.6.	5.	5.Inf.	300 c.feet excavated. 4% complete.
Coy Hqrs. M.17.d.2.3.	6.	-	400 c.feet excavated. % complete.
2 Dugouts. M.10.c.9.8.			45% complete.
1 Dugout. M.10.c.8.8.	6.		25% complete.
Coy Hqrs. M.23.a.9.2.			2% complete.
Mined Dug-out. M.21.a.2.2.	23.		2 Shafts. Progress 16' each. Estimated time to complete, about 6 days.
SHELTERS.			
M.G. Shelter & Emplacement M.17.c.9.3.			2 Shelters, 95% complete, open emplacement.
ditto. M.17.c.7.1.			Excavation to 2 Shelters complete. Total 30% complete.
Coy Hqrs. M.23.a.7.0.	5.	12 Inf.)	
ditto M.22.b.3.2.	5.	5.Inf.)	Strengthening & enlarging.
ditto. M.21.c.1.6.	5.	18.Inf.)	

ROADS.
    Labour. 1 Coy, 8th Bn. S.W.Bdrs: (Pioneers).
    Road opened from M.15.b.9.0. to CANADA CORNER.
    Road from N.9.a.5.0. to M.20.d.0.0.,
    All shell holes filled in.
    Drains cleared down to about M.15.a.4.6.
    The Company was also employed on moving their camp.

6 Sappers have been employed permanently on gas proofing dugouts.
Map is attached.

(signed)
Lt. Col. R.E.
C.R.E., 30th British Divl. Engineers.

16-8-18.

NARRATIVE REPORT ON R.E. WORK

for week ending 26-8-17.

On 18-8-17 the 204th Field Coy. R.E. and 2 Companies of the 19th Bn: Northumberland Fusiliers (Pioneers) were attached to this Division from the 35th Division.

The 204th Field Coy R.E. took over work on Artillery H.Q., 2 other dug-outs and some shelters for I.O. arrange onto from Field Companies of this Division.

60 Infantry and about 25 R.A. were attached to them for the work.

The 2 Companies of the 19th N.F. (Pioneers) took over work on forward roads from the Company of the Pioneer Bn: of this Division, which was then put on to work on the BLUE LINE.

A report on the work carried out by the R.E. during the attack on the DRAHOUTEN RIDGE was forwarded on 25-8-17.

The work during the week was somewhat disorganised by this attack, particularly the work on the BLUE LINE, as no working parties were supplied by the Infantry for the 3 days previous to the attack, and work on the BLUE LINE was stopped during the 24 and 25th inst also.

During these 2 days the 3 Rec Field Companies moved to forward billets in F.15.

Despite the above 1100 yards of double apron fence were erected in front of the BLUE LINE, and 666 yards of new trench was dug to a depth of 3 feet.

Report on work on H.Q., Flood Dug-outs, Baths & stables completed during the week was forwarded on 25th inst.

The 2 Companies of 19th N.F. (Pioneers) took over work on roads from the Company of the Pioneer Battalion of this Division which was then distributed for work as follows:-

2 Sections to each Brigade in the line for work on C.Ts.
2 Sections to rest of the Battalion on forward roads.

On 25th inst the BLUE LINE was divided into 2 Sections & work was re-organized as follows:-

Each Field Coy 1 Section attached to Inf: Brigades for work
                1 Strong Section on BLUE LINE, with 2 Platoons Pioneers
                & 1 Coorpy Infantry to each Section.
                2 Sections on dug-outs with Infantry labour as required.

6th Bn: S.W. Bdrs (Pnrs) had besides 2 platoons attached to each Brigade in the line.

204th Field Coy R.E.   ) as before.
19th Bn: N.F. (Pioneers))

Lt. Col. R.E.
C.R.E., 30th Division.

26-8-17.

APPENDIX "G"

REPORT ON WORK CARRIED OUT BY THE R.E. DURING THE ATTACK ON THE DRAMOUTRE RIDGE ON 21-8-18.

The Sections R.E. were attached to Brigades as under.

1 Section of 200th Field Company R.E. to 89th Brigade on the RIGHT.
1 Section of 202nd Field Company R.E. to 90th Brigade on the CENTRE.
1 Section of 202nd Field Company R.E. to 21st Brigade on the LEFT.

1. The Section of the 200th Field Company R.E. under 2/Lt F. THURLBY, R.E. attached to 89th Brigade was detailed to open up a track from the head of LOCRE CHATEAU Drive to PIGOT FARM, M.35.c.3.7.

   3 Sections of the 5th Bn: S.W. Borderers (Pioneers) were attached to them to assist, but no officers came with the party.

   The Section R.E. was divided into 3 squads, and 1 Section of Pioneers was attached to each squad.

   The party assembled at M.21.a.2.2. at midnight 20/21st inst in working formation, and arrived at M.28.a.7.5. at 1.a.m.

   The O.C. Field Company was at Bn: H. Qrs, 2nd E. Lancs Regt.

   At about 3-30.a.m. walking wounded reported that MOWBRAY WOOD had been taken (this was the first intimation of the fact) and shortly after the Party was instructed to start work. The whole party had started work by 4-15.a.m.

   At 5-30.a.m. the fog started to lift and the Party were instructed to stop work and return independently.

   The track (tracing attached) was made passable for men in single file, and for mules in single file in bright weather.

   Notice Boards were erected in prominent places.

   There were no casualties.

2. The Section of the 202nd Field Company R.E. under 2/Lt GARRARD, R.E., attached to the 90th Brigade, was split up into 4 Parties (2 men each) with Bangalore torpedoes, and 2 Parties for tracks.

   Each Torpedo Party was attached to a Company of the assaulting Infantry, to whom they reported at 10.p.m. 20th inst, with the object of blowing up any uncut wire encountered. They were not required as eventually turned out.

   These parties had two men wounded from M.G. fire, one somewhat badly - both were successfully evacuated.

   The first 'Track' Party cleared a track running approximately from M.26.d.45.85, through M.28.d.65.80, and M.28.d.55.75. to M.29.c.75.45.

   The ground was somewhat marshy in one place and could have been improved greatly if Trench Boards had been available. The worst places were bridged with Infantry Bridges.

   This party succeeded in capturing 7 Germans in a shell hole who had been passed over by the Infantry. This was effected by Cpl. CLOUGH, who discovered them, and having his rifle slung, assaulted them with a felling axe.

   The 2nd 'Track' Party cleared a track from approximately M.28.d.45.85. to approx: M.35.a.0.0. This Party met with some difficulty owing to the enemy barrage dropping on the line of the track, and also a number of fallen trees had to be contended with.

   The 'Track' Parties reached their assembly positions about 1½ hours before zero, and started work soon after zero.

   No Infantry Carrying Parties were provided, otherwise the tracks could have been improved considerably by laying trench boards.

   No casualties were incurred.

3. The Section of the 202nd Field Company R.E. under Lt. L.C. ALLERTON, R.E. attached to 21st Brigade, was detailed to work in front of our old front line as soon as the Infantry went forward.

   They assembled at 10-30.p.m. in shell holes immediately behind our Front Line trench, and spent the time between then and zero hour in carrying down wiring materials from the Advanced Brigade Dump at M.29.b.20.85. This was successfully laid out in 'No man's land' before zero hour.

   On the assaulting Infantry going forward at zero hour, this party occupied our old front line trench, but on the enemy putting down a

(barrage

3. cont.

barrage on the trench, and also about 100 yards to the rear, this party was withdrawn from the trench and they got shell holes between the two lines of barrage.

At about 5.a.m. (the shelling having died down) the party started back.

Wire was shot at from about 1.20.a.m. to 2.45.a.m., overlapping gaps being made every 25 yards. The gaps consisted of a single belt of French Barbed concertina or Medium Apron in the with 3 horizontal strands of barbed wire fastened on it.

The party arrived at about 5.30.a.m. with no casualties.

23-3-18.

APPENDIX H.

R.E. DUMP AND WORKSHOPS.   AUGUST 1918.

1st to 9th.

Work was carried out at CASSEL as during the previous month.

10th to end.

The Dump was situated on the GODEWAERSVELDE - BOESCHEPE road at R.2.c. centl:. A good supply of R.E. stores of all kinds was maintained with the exception of Scantling and Long Screw Posts which were practically unobtainable. Barbed Wire made up in large coils weighing about 1cwt each were supplied in lieu of small coils towards the end of the month.
A double windlass for rewinding these by hand was made but it was found to be exceedingly slow work.
The large coils were of no use for night wiring over bad ground.
A Dump Party was obtained of 24 O.R. from the Xth Corps Labour Commandant.
2 Sappers from each Field Company were employed in the workshops making up the articles required by Units. A large number of Notice Boards were sent out for erection on the various defensive lines.

APPENDIX I.

30th DIVISIONAL ENGINEERS.

LIST OF HONOURS & AWARDS FOR THE MONTH OF AUGUST 1918.

Regt No.	Rank.	Name.	Unit.	Honour or Award.
83035.	Sergt.	CRYSTAL, J. D.C.M.	202nd Field Coy.	Military Medal.
113722.	Cpl.	REECE, E.	202nd Field Coy.	Military Medal.
81561.	2/Cpl.	ROBERTS, W.	200th Field Coy.	Military Medal.
81320.	L/Cpl.	HOOTEN, J.	200th Field Coy.	Military Medal.
966661.	L/Cpl.	BEECH, E.L.	Divl: Signal Coy.	Military Medal.
311851.	Pioneer.	WOOD, W.H.	do do do.	Bar to Military Medal.
64871.	Sapper.	McKENZIE, R.J.	do do do	Military Medal.

WD 35

CONFIDENTIAL.

WAR DIARY.

OF

30TH DIVISIONAL ENGINEERS.

FROM SEPTEMBER 1st 1918.   TO SEPTEMBER 30th 1918.

VOLUME 35.

Army Form C. 2118.

WAR DIARY
HEADQUARTERS, 30th DIVISIONAL ENGINEERS.
INTELLIGENCE SUMMARY.

VOLUME 35.

September 1918.

Reference Maps. 27/1/40,000.
28/1/40,000.
HAZEBROUCK. 1/100,000.
28.S.W.1. 1/10,000.
28.S.W.2. 1/10,000.
28.S.W.3. 1/10,000.
28.S.W.4. 1/10,000.

(Erase heading not required.)

Instructions regarding War Diaries and Intelligence Summaries are contained in F.S. Regs., Part II. and the Staff Manual respectively. Title pages will be prepared in manuscript.

Place	Date	Hour	Summary of Events and Information	Remarks and references to Appendices
			Preliminary. The Germans had started to withdraw from the Divisional Front on 30-8-18. Advanced Divisional Headquarters were at N.20.d.2.2. C.R.E. was with 200th Field Company N.21.a.1.1. Headquarters R.E. were at LA MONTAGNE. The Field Companies and Pioneers were employed on rushing forward the Roads. Report on work done by the R.Es and Pioneers between 30-8-18 and 5-9-18 is shown in Appendix A.	Appendix A.
LA MONTAGNE.	1st.		Received 30th Divisional Order No 186.	
N.20.d.2.2.	3rd.		Headquarters, R.E. moved to N.20.d.9.2.	
	5th.		Received 30th Division Operation Order No 2/123/827 - Warning Order for attack on MESSINES - WYTSCHAETE Ridge.	
			Received 30th Division Operation Order No 188 ordering attack on MESSINES-WYTSCHAETE Ridge and G.985 cancelling same.	
			Received 30th Division Order 189.	
	6th.		Received 30th Division Order 190. Major P.T. STOKY, D.S.O. R.E. reported for duty to take over temporarily the appointment of C.R.E., 30th Division. Headquarters, R.E. moved to N.21.a.1.1.	
N.21.a.1.1.	7th.		Received 30th Division Order No 191.	
	10th.		Major P.F. STORY, D.S.O., Lt.Col. S. IRVINE, D.S.O. R.E., A.E. completed taking over the appointment of C.R.E., 30th Division from Lt.Col. S. IRVINE, D.S.O. R.E. Conference held with Field Company Commanders at 200th Field Company Headquarters.	
	12th.		Received 30th Division Operation Order No 192.	
	14th.		Advanced Divisional Headquarters moved to MONT NOIR CHATEAU. Headquarters R.E. remained as before.	

Army Form C. 2118.

WAR DIARY
or
INTELLIGENCE=SUMMARY.
(Erase heading not required.)

Instructions regarding War Diaries and Intelligence Summaries are contained in F. S. Regs., Part II. and the Staff Manual respectively. Title pages will be prepared in manuscript.

Place	Date	Hour	Summary of Events and Information	Remarks and references to Appendices
	15th.		Received 30th Division G185/6/112 - Instructions for work on Defences - WULVERGHEM Sector.	
	17th.		Received 30th Division C123/86 saying that the Division might have to take over the 36th Division Front in addition to its own.	
	18th.		Received 30th Division G123/109 - Warning Order re relieving the 36th Division. Received 30th Division Operation Order No 193 re above. Arrangements were made for the 200th Field Company to take over the Forward Area work and the 202nd Field Company R.E. the Back Area work of the Field Companies of the 36th Division - The Pioneers took over from the Pioneers of the 36th Division.	
	19th.		Completing taking over work from the R.Es of the 36th Division.	
	20th.		Received 30th Division Operation Order No 194 - Brigade Relief.	
27/R.24.c.6.3.	21st.		Headquarters, R.E. moved to 27/R.24.c.6.3. Received C.E., Xth Corps No 1027/2/61	Appendix B.
	22nd.		Received 30th Division Order No 196.	
	23rd.		Received 30th Division Order No 195 saying that the enemy were likely to withdraw in front of the Division. No	
	24th.		Issued 30th British Divisional Engineers Order/16.	Appendix C.
	26th.		Issued 30th British Divisional Engineers Order No 17.	Appendix D.
	28th.		The enemy started to with-draw on the Division Front. Received 30th Division Order No 197. C.R.E. established Advanced Headquarters at K.31.a.6.7.	
	29th.		The Field Companies and Pioneers started work on Roads at dawn in accordance with Appendix D. Main Road cleared for lorries as far as MESSINES by 5.pm. Received 30th Division Orders Nos 198 and 199.	
	30th.			

Army Form C. 2118.

WAR DIARY
of
INTELLIGENCE SUMMARY
(Erase heading not required.)

Instructions regarding War Diaries and Intelligence Summaries are contained in F. S. Regs., Part II. and the Staff Manual respectively. Title pages will be prepared in manuscript.

Place	Date	Hour	Summary of Events and Information	Remarks and references to Appendices
			APPENDIX.E. Deals with Stores. APPENDIX.F. Gives List of Honours and awards since the list submitted with the War Diary for August.	
			Lt. Col. R.E. C.R.E., 30th (B) Division.	

APPENDIX A.

NARRATIVE REPORT ON WORK CARRIED OUT BY THE ROYAL ENGINEERS DURING OPERATIONS BETWEEN 30.8.18 & 5-9-18.

On 30.8.18 it became evident that the enemy was starting to withdraw on the Division front and orders to the following effect were issued on that date to the Field Companies.

1. All work on the BLUE LINE to be stopped and Infantry Working Parties cancelled.

2. Parties working on dug-outs to be reduced to a minimum.

3. 200th Field Company to employ 1 Section on clearing the road from N.34.c.2.6. to N.35.d.2.3., thence via NORBURY VILLA to the CLAPHAM Road and down towards CRUCIFIX CORNER. They were to be assisted by 2 platoons of Pioneers working under them on the BLUE LINE.

4. 201st Field Company to employ 1 Section on clearing roads the LOCRE - BAILLEUL Road with 2 platoons of Pioneers.

5. 202nd Field Company to employ 1 Section on clearing the CANADA CORNER - LOCRE - DRANOUTRE Road with 1 Company of Pioneers. Barrier at N.17.c.4.1. to be removed.

6. Lt LANNON, attached H.Q. R.E. to reconnoitre the LOCRE - DRANOUTRE Road for Land Mines and 'Booby Traps' as soon as the Infantry had occupied DRANOUTRE.

7. Field Companies to keep the remainder of their men in reserve.
Note :- The 3rd Company of the Pioneers was attached to Infantry Brigades.

On 31st August and 1st Sept work was carried on on these roads in continuous shifts. C.E., Xth Corps took over responsibility for roads up to the old German Front Line on 31-8-18, but parties were left to complete work in hand.
201st Field Company took the DRANOUTRE - NEUVE EGLISE Road.
202nd Field Company took the DRANOUTRE - DAYLIGHT CORNER Road.

On 2-9-18 2 Sections Field Companies were employed on repairing Advanced Divisional Headquarters, and 2 Sections on opening up Wells in DRANOUTRE - 6 Wells were opened in all.
Each Company had one Section on building accomodation for Brigades. The remaining Sections were employed on roads.
From the 2nd to the 5th the Pioneers had 2 platoons with the forward Brigade, 1 platoon resting and the remainder on forward roads and tracks.
From the 3rd onwards Field Companies were employed chiefly on work in connection with accomodation, water supply and erecting Baths at N.34.b.25.60.
Rates of progress on roads are shown below :-

Midnight 31st/1st.
CANADA CORNER - LOCRE - DRANOUTRE Road, clear for wheeled transport to DRANOUTRE.

Midnight 1st/2nd.
LOCRE - DRANOUTRE - NEUVE EGLISE Road, clear for wheeled transport to about T.1.c.4.2., where demolished bridge was being repaired - from T.1.c.4.2. road was cleared to T.7.a.8.5. DAYLIGHT CORNER.
DRANOUTRE - DAYLIGHT CORNER - DAYLIGHT CORNER Road clear for H.T. to DAYLIGHT CORNER and for Lorries up to AIRCRAFT FARM.
Road from N.34.c.2.6. - N.35.d.2.3. - NORBURY VILLA thence to CLAPHAM Road and down to CRUCIFIX CORNER, clear for H.T.
Road from NORBURY VILLA to LOCRE - BAILLEUL Road at S.6.a.7.7., clear for H.T.

Sheet #2.

Midnight 2nd/3rd.

Bridge at R.1.c.4.2. requires to take 1dwd tons (Gunner of a ty of 45) and NIEUPORT - NEUVE EGLISE Road for lorry transport to R.14.b.3.9.

Midnight 3rd/4th.

BAILLEUL CORNER - QUEN TRIEN Road cleared to C.A.L.T.S. for R.E.
DAYLIGHT CORNER - LACK EAGLE Road cleared to R.E.A.L.S.

Midnight 4th/5th.

DAYLIGHT CORNER - NEW ROAD Road clear for M.T.
DAYLIGHT CORNER - MILLBRIDGE Road clear for M.T.

Work on upkeep of roads was carried on throughout. This was particularly necessary in DRANOUTRE and the screening of the DRANOUTRE-NEUVE EGLISE Road was put in hand.
Casualties to R.Es. N I L.

Lt. Col. R.E.
C.R.E., 36th (B) Division

September 5th 1918.

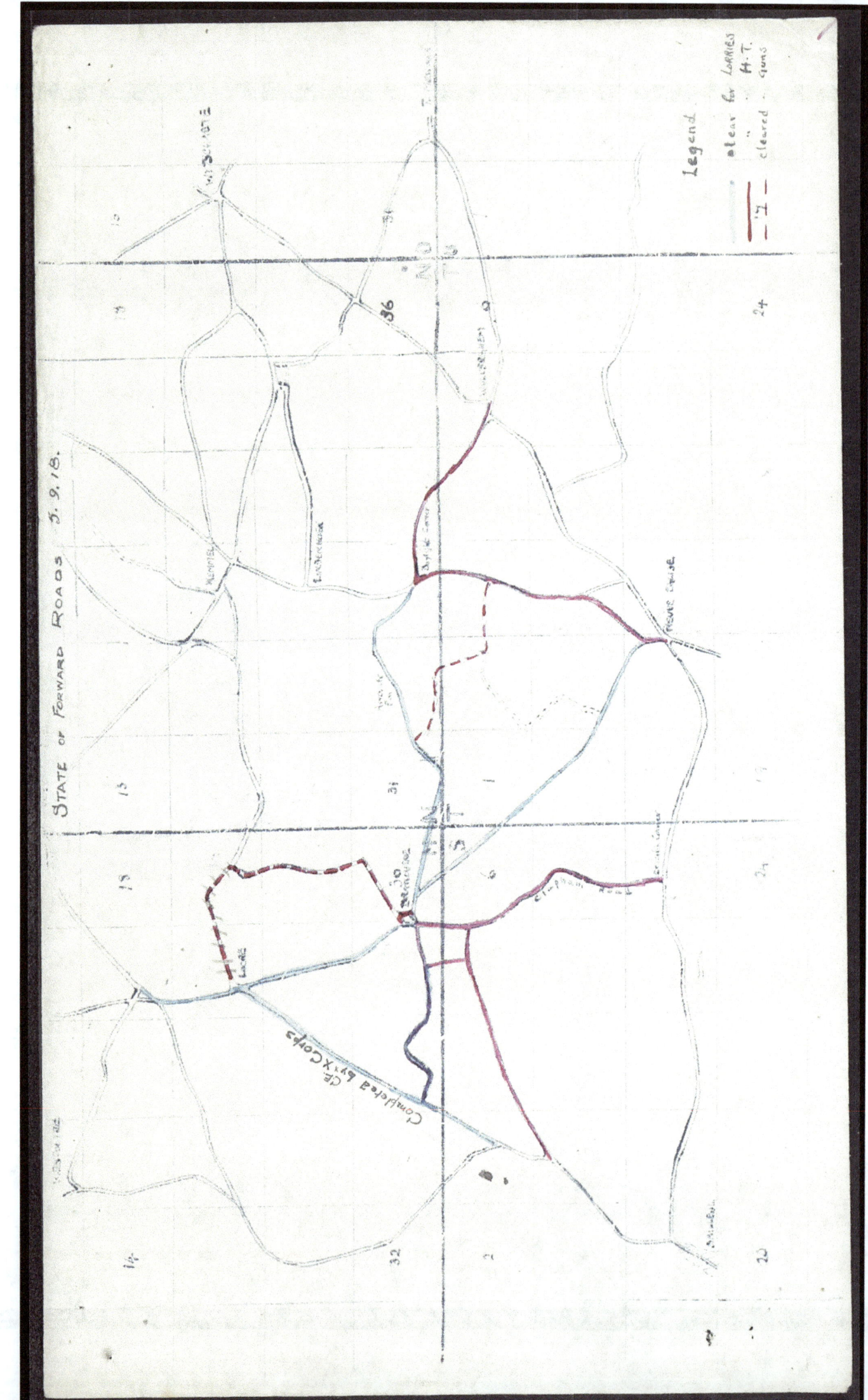

S E C R E T.   APPENDIX. B.

C.R.E., 30th Division.

      For your information the following is copy of minute received from Chief Engineer, Second Army, dated 20-9-18,-

      In accordance with Second Army Artillery Instruction No.1,- it is intended that the Guns shall follow the advancing Infantry in the forthcoming operations within half an hour of ZERO.

      It is therefore of importance that R.E. Road Parties and Material should be ready to move up immediately behind the Infantry so that they may be able to bridge any craters or remove obstacles at once and prevent the guns being delayed.

Headquarters,   (Sd) C.E. MUSGRAVE. Capt. R.E.
Xth Corps.   for C.E., Xth Corps.
21-9-18.

SECRET.

30th (BRITISH) DIVISIONAL ENGINEERS ORDER NO 16.

Copy No. 11.
Appendix "C"

1.   The following moves and exchanges of work will take place on the 25th inst.
     200th Field Coy R.E. will take over work of the 202nd Field Coy. R.E. in intermediate area.
     201st Field Coy R.E. will take over forward billets of the 202nd Field Coy R.E. and move its Transport Lines to Asylum at BAILLEUL, S.14.b.1.8. taking over charge of the Dump from 202nd Field Coy. R.E.
     201st Field Coy. R.E. will take over work from 200th Field Coy. R.E. in forward area.
     202nd Field Coy. R.E. will take over billets and work of the 201st Field Coy. R.E. in Rear Area.
     (Note. Locations and distribution for work after the move are shown in Appendix A.)

2.   Companies will arrange details of move between themselves, so as to cause least disturbance possible to work.

3.   Parties moving backwards or forwards should do so in small groups only.

4.   Report completion of moves by wire.

5.   Field Companies will ACKNOWLEDGE.

                                            Capt. R.E.
     24th Sept. 1918.   Adjt. 30th (B) Divl. Engineers.

Copy No.1. to O.C. 200th Field Coy. R.E.
     No.2. to O.C. 201st Field Coy. R.E.
     No.3. to O.C. 202nd Field Coy. R.E.
     No. 4. to 30th Division "G".
     No.5. to 30th Division "Q".
     No.6. to O.C. 6th Bn S.W. Bdrs.(Pioneers).
     No.7. to H.Q., 21st Inf. Brigade.
     No.8. to H.Q., 89th Inf. Brigade.
     No.9. to H.Q., 90th Inf. Brigade.
     No.10. to O.C. 30th Div. Signal Coy. R.E.
     No.11. to War Diary.
     No.12. to "   "
     No.13. to File.

APPENDIX A.

LOCATIONS AND ZONES OF WORK FOR FIELD COMPANIES AFTER MOVE ON 25-9-18.

UNIT.	Forward Hdqrs.	Transport Lines.	Zone of Work.
200th Field Coy. R.E.	N.31.d.1.7.		Intermediate.
201st Field Coy. R.E.	N.31.a.9.8.	S.14.b.1.8.	Forward.
202nd Field Coy. R.E.	M.9.d.0.7.	M.9.d.0.7.	Back.

Appendix "D"

SECRET.   Copy No. 18

30th BRITISH DIVISIONAL EXAMPLE ORDERS No. 17

1. Enemy Withdrawal.
Information has been obtained pointing to the probability of the enemy withdrawing in the near future from his present front to positions beyond the MESSINES to WYTSCHAETE Ridge or still further East. The day on which this withdrawal may commence will be known as J Day.

2. Advance of Division.
On J Day at H Hour fighting patrols will be pushed forward against the 4 most northerly points within Divisional Area marked in Blue circles on Map A. Later at L Hour Right Brigade in co-operation with 31st Division will attack the 2 most southerly points shown on plan. Further advance beyond this general line will not take place without further orders.

3. Boundaries.
The Boundaries of the Division from a night to be notified will be as shown on attached Map.
Infantry Brigades will advance within the boundaries shown on Map.

90th Inf. Brigade on the RIGHT.
89th Inf. Brigade on the LEFT.
The objectives of Brigades are shown on the Map.

4. R.E. & Pioneers.
The main tasks allotted to the R.E. and Pioneers are :-
(a) Repair of the WULVERGHEM - MESSINES Road, hereinafter referred to as X Road for heavy traffic.
(b) Repair of the WULVERGHEM to WYTSCHAETE Road, hereinafter referred to as Y Road for limbers only.

5. Reconnaisance.
Reconnaisance reports will be submitted as quickly as possible on the condition of following Roads and Tracks.

(a) 200th Field Coy. R.E.   X Road.
(b) 6th Bn. S.W. Bdrs.(Pioneers)   Y Road.
(c) 202nd Field Coy. R.E. Road from WULVERGHEM, through T.5.H. & T.11.b. to LA PLUS DOUVE FARM, thence through T.12.a.c.b. - U.7.a.c.b. to North of STINKING FARM through U.2.c.&. to X Road at U.2.a.0.3.
(d) 202nd Field Coy :- Track or Road from Y Road Eastwards through T.6.a. N.36.c.c.d. O.31.c.c.b. O.32.a. to O.32.b.2.4., thence North through O.26.c.c.a. to Divisional Boundary.
These Roads and Tracks are marked GREEN on Map.

6. Method of Repair.
1. In event of the Roads being found in a condition to be easily and quickly repaired, 200th and 201st Field Companies and 2 Companies of Pioneers will work on X Road.
One Company of Pioneers will work on Y Road.
202nd Field Company will be in reserve.

-2-

7. Method of Repair.	In event of a plank road deviation or any other special work being found necessary, the 3 Field Coys will work in 6 hour shifts continously until the work has been completed.
2.	The Pioneers will work as detailed in 6.

8. Transport.
200th 201st & 202nd Field Companies will each detail 3 pontoon wagons
6th S.W. Bdrs(Pioneers) will detail 4 G.S. Wagons and 2 Limbers.
O.C. D Troop, Capt. CALVERT, R.E., No 7 Pontoon Park, will detail 6 Pontoon Wagons.
Each Unit will detail at least 1 N.C.O.
202 ~~200th~~ Field Coy. will detail Capt. C.C. LINDSAY R.E. to take charge of the above transport.
Transport will report to Capt LINDSAY at Road Junction Sheet 28, I.34.c.2.5. on BAILLEUL-LOCRE Road at 9.a.m. on J Day, with rations and forage for J Day and J + I Day.

9. R.E. Stores.
A Dump of the following Material is being formed at DAYLIGHT CORNER N.33.c.8.8.

Artillery Bridges	Pit Props, Pointed.
Infantry Bridges.	Hurdles, Brushwood.
Sandbags.	Fascines.
Road Slabs.	Plain Wire.
Wheelbarrows.	Shovels.
6" Nails	Picks.
	Cutting Tools.

Lt LANNON R.E. will be responsible for issuing Stores at Dump.
201st Field Coy. will detail Capt. WOOLLEY, R.E. to regulate delivery at Forward End and to send back indents.
A loading and unloading party consisting of 3 Platoons of Infantry will be provided by 21st Inf. Brigade. They will report to 200th Field Company on 26th September.

10. Notice Boards.
Notice Boards will be fixed indicating direction of Roads and Tracks and names with Map locations, of prominent points and buildings.
200th Field Coy. will detail an Officer and party for RIGHT Brigade Area.
201st Field Coy. will detail an Officer and party for LEFT Brigade Area.

11. Booby Traps.
171st Tunnelling Coy will detail No 3 Section, O.C. Capt. DANIELL to deal with enemy Booby Traps.
The following parties will be provided :-
(a) Party to specially search X Road for Tank Traps and Mines - Specially old British Dugouts at U.4.b.75.70. and U.5.a.2.8.
(b) Party to search Y Road for Tank Traps and Mines.
(c) Parties to search Dugouts for Booby Traps North and South of X Road within Divisional Boundaries.

12. Locations on J Day.
200th Field Coy, R.E. will be at N.31.d.1.7.
201st Field Coy, R.E. will be at N.31.a.9.8.
6th Bn S.W. Bdrs (Pnrs) will be at N.25.b.1.0.
No 3 Section 171st Tunnelling Coy at N.5.d.8.4.
202nd Field Coy. will move up to neighbourhood of BEAVER HALL, N.31.a.9.4. by 9.a.m. ~~on J Day.~~

Appendix "T"

-3-

12.(contd) O C
Locations. He will establish his Headquarters with 201st Field Coy.

13. The 3 Field Companies, 1 Tunnelling Section and Pioneers
Messengers. will each send a messenger with bicycle and rations for
J and J+1 Day to report to C.R.E. by H Hour on J Day at
N.31.a.central.

14. Units will be prepared on J Day to move off immediately
Move on receipt of orders.
forward.

15. Watches will be synchronised as follows :-
Time.
R.A. & M.G. Bns at 2.p.m. at Divl H.Q. MONT NOIR.
89th Inf. Bde. at 3.p.m. at TYRO FARM.
90th Inf. Bde. at 3-30.p.m. at S.18.a.

16.
Headquarters. Headquarters will be established as follows by H Hour
on J Day.

Divl. Battle H.Q. (G.S. & R.A.) at TYRO FARM M.36.a.
R.E. and M.G. Batts at N.31.a.central.
89th Inf. Brigade at ARMOUR FARM N.33.d.
90th Inf. Brigade at KENNEDAY SIDING. T.4.c.

17. H & L Hour and J Day will be notified later.

18. ACKNOWLEDGE by wire. Copies 1 to 5

E.N.Scott.
Capt. R.E.
Adjt. 30th (B) Divl. Engineers.

September 26th 1918.   G

X Copy No 1. to O.C. 200th Field Coy. R.E.
X   No 2. to O.C. 201st Field Coy. R.E.
X   No 3. to O.C. 202nd Field Coy. R.E.
X.   No 4. to O.C. 6th Bn S.W. Bdrs (Pioneers).
X   No 5. to O.C. 171st Tunnelling Coy. R.E.
       No 6. to 30th Division "G".
       No 7. to C.R.A.
       No 8. to 30th Division A & Q.
       No 9. to 21st Inf. Brigade.
       No 10. to 89th Inf. Brigade.
       No 11. to 90th Inf. Brigade.
       No 12. to O.C. 30th Divl. Signal Coy. R.E.
       No 13. to O.C. 30th Bn M.G.C.
       No 14. to A.D.M.S.
       No 15. to C.E., Xth Corps.
       No 16. to C.R.E., 31st Division.
       No 17. to C.R.E., 34th Division.
       No 18. to War Diary.
       No 19. to   "   "
       No 20. to File.
       No 21. Spare.
       No 22.   "

Note Only those marked X, Map sent to.

APPENDIX.

STORES.   SEPTEMBER. 1918.

The supply of Stores during the month of September was satisfactory though owing to the amount of work required in connection with accommodation the supplies of Roofing Felt and Corrugated Iron were at times insufficient.

A new dump was established near WESTOUTRE at N.9.a.3.3., the Main Divisional Dump at BOESCHEPE being too far back. Much labour would have been saved if a siding could have been constructed to run Stores from the railway to near the road. The matter was referred to Army but they would not undertake the work.

On 19-9-18 a new Dump was taken over from the 36th Division in BAILLEUL but was of very little use as it was so far from all transport lines.

On 24-9-18 an operation Dump was started at DAYLIGHT CORNER in view of the expected withdrawal of the enemy. The following Stores were available there when the German withdrawal started:-

	20 Artillery Bridges.
	10 Infantry "
	10,000 Sandbags.
X	1,500 Road Slabs.
X	20 Wheelbarrows.
X	15 Cwt 6" Nails.
X	300 Fascines.
X	300 Brushwood Hurdles.
X	2000 Shovels.
	500 Picks.
	Cutting Tools.
X	Pumps.

Items marked X were largely drawn.

Two large German Dumps were taken during the advance, one in U.l.b. and one at HOUTHEM, but no small stores such as Shovels, Tools, Nails were found. There were very large stocks of Trench Boards and Artillery Bridges on wooden rollers.

APPENDIX. F.

30th DIVISIONAL ENGINEERS.

LIST OF HONOURS & AWARDS FOR THE MONTH OF SEPTEMBER 1918.

No.	Rank.	Name.	Unit.	Honour or Award.
	2/Lt.	C.P. GARRARD.	202nd Field Coy. R.E.	Military Cross.
139643.	Cpl.	S.R. SLOUGH.	202nd Field Coy. R.E.	D.C.M.
83537.	Driver.	B.T. LINES.	200th Field Coy. R.E.	Military Medal.

WAR DIARY.

30th DIVISIONAL ENGINEERS.

FROM 1st OCTOBER. TO 31st OCTOBER.
1918.

VOLUME 36.

H.Q.

Army Form C. 2118

WAR DIARY
or
INTELLIGENCE SUMMARY
(Erase heading not required.)

HEADQUARTERS 30th DIVISIONAL ENGINEERS. OCTOBER 1918.   VOLUME 36.

Instructions regarding War Diaries and Intelligence Summaries are contained in F. S. Regs., Part II. and the Staff Manual respectively. Title Pages will be prepared in manuscript.

Ref. Maps. HAZEBROUCK 1/100,000. Sheet 28. 1/40,000.
TOURNAI 1/100,000. " 29. 1/40,000.

Place	Date	Hour	Summary of Events and Information	Remarks and references to Appendices
MONT NOIR CHATEAU.	1st		The Germans had just withdrawn in front of the Division and were holding approximately the line of the LYS from COMINES to WERVICQ. Advanced Headquarters Divl. Engineers were at N.31.a.6.7. and Rear Headquarters at MONT NOIR Chateau. Field Companies and Pioneers were employed principally on roads and accommodation.	
28/P.14.a.2.0. 28/0.26.a.3.5.	2nd.		Advanced Divisional Headquarters moved to KORTEWILDE in the afternoon and back to LUNN FARM in the evening. Field Companies moved forward to the HOUTHEM OUSTERVERNE area and worked on the WYTSCHAETE-OUSTERVERNE-HOUTHEM Road.	
28/0.19.c. central.	2nd.		Advanced Divisional Headquarters moved to LAMPOST CORNER, O.19.c.central. Work on roads continued.	
	3rd.		Work on roads continued. 200th Field Company were instructed to construct bridges at P.13.d.7.0., P.19.b.9.7., and P.20.a.4.0. Instructed the Pioneers to carry on with Repair of road from HOUTHEM Bridge, east of the Canal to TENBRIELEN and onwards.	
	4th.		Issued instructions for work to be started,collecting material for plank road from P.13.c.05.50. to P.13.b.60.35. - Pioneers and 202nd Field Company to work on the road, and 201st Field Coy to construct the Bridge.	
	5th.		Parties taken off the WYTSCHAETE - OUSTERVERNE - HOUTHEM Road as responsibility for upkeep of this road was with Corps.	
	6th.		Opened up track for Infantry along the railway line from O.21.c.5.8. to just south of HOUTHEM.	
	7th.		Work on roads continued.	
	8th.		Captain E.N. CLIFTON left for leave to the U.K. 2/Lt R.J. LANNON took over the duties of Adjutant.	
	9th.		200th Field Company was withdrawn to N.29.a.5.7. to undertake back area work. 201st and 202nd Field Companies started work on HOUTHEM avoiding road from P.13.c. to P.13.b.6.2., 201st Field Company building the bridge over Canal and constructing the road East of the Canal.	

1875 Wt. W593/826 1,000,000 4/15 J.B.C. & A. A.D.S.S./Forms/C. 2118.

Army Form C. 2118.

WAR DIARY

~~INTELLIGENCE SUMMARY~~

(Erase heading not required.)

Instructions regarding War Diaries and Intelligence Summaries are contained in F. S. Regs., Part II and the Staff Manual respectively. Title pages will be prepared in manuscript.

Place	Date	Hour	Summary of Events and Information	Remarks and references to Appendices
	10th & 11th		-2-	
	12th		Work, as on the 9th, was continued.	
			Jumping off line for attack on WERVICQ was pegged out by 201st and 202nd Field Companies on night 12th/13th.	
	13th		The same line was taped out on the night of 13th/14th.	
	14th		Division attacked in conjunction with Second Army and Belgian Army. R.E. were employed as in Operation Order attached, and taped out defended localities after the Infantry moved forward.	APPENDIX A.
	15th		1 Section of 201st Field Coy. R.E. attached to 21st Brigade assisted in crossing the LYS. On night 15th/16th, 200th Field Company put pontoon bridge across the LYS at Q.28.c.8.2. near BOUSBECQUE. All 6 pontoons were employed in this. APPENDIX B is a copy of the Divisional Commander's appreciation of this work.	APPENDIX B.
TRALEE FARM	16th		R.E. H.Q. moved from WYTSCHAETE to TRALEE FARM, 2.14.d.4.4.	
	17th		201st and 202nd Field Companies were engaged in constructing footbridges across the LYS. 201st Field Company constructed a floating raft bridge at R.19.a.1.2., and 202nd Field Coy, a barrel bridge at about Q.30.central. R.E. Headquarters moved in the afternoon to Q.13.d.8.7. 200th Field Company commenced work repairing one trestle bridge at Q.27.b.0.5.	
Q.13.d.8.7.	18th		R.E. Headquarters remained at Q.13.d.8.7. 200th Field Company continued work on bridge at Q.27.b.0.5. 201st and 202nd Field Companies completed footbridges and moved Transport forward from MORTEMUDE. 1 Section 201st Field Company was attached to forward Brigade for work.	
BOUSBECQUE CHATEAU.	19th		R.E. Headquarters moved to BOUSBECQUE CHATEAU, Divisional Headquarters going on to RONCQ. 200th Field Comanpy completed trestle bridge for ~~heavy transport~~ lorries at Q.27.b.0.5. 201st and 202nd Field Companies with pioneers commenced preparing for superheavy pontoon bridge at R.19.c.3.8. 30 pontoons were sent up to site.	

Army Form C. 2118.

WAR DIARY
INTELLIGENCE SUMMARY.
(Erase heading not required.)

Instructions regarding War Diaries and Intelligence Summaries are contained in F. S. Regs., Part II. and the Staff Manual respectively. Title pages will be prepared in manuscript.

-3-

Place	Date	Hour	Summary of Events and Information	Remarks and references to Appendices
STERHOEK.	20th		R.E. Headquarters moved from BOUSBECQUE CHATEAU to STERHOEK, rejoining Divisional Headquarters. 200th Field Company dismantled pontoon bridge. The whole of the pontoon equipment was pooled and placed in charge of Captain HILL, M.C. R.E. The Company and pontoon gear moved to ROLLEGHEM. 201st and 202nd Field Companies continued on super heavy pontoon bridge, the superstructure arriving during the day.	
	21st		R.E. Headquarters remained at STERHOEK. 200th Field Company moved with pontoon train to DOTTIGNIES, and remained in readiness to move forward to bridge the L'ESCAUT. Super heavy pontoon bridge at R.19.c.3.8. was completed, and opened for traffic at noon. It took an 8" howitzer with about 9" freeboard. Major O.D. ATKINSON. M.C. R.E., 200th Field Company, was wounded. 200th Field Company put pontoon bridge across at C.5.a.3.5. and blew a sluice near by to allow drainage of Southern Area to proceed.	
COYGHEM.	22nd		R.E. Headquarters moved to COYGHEM. 201st Field Company less 2 Sections and 202nd Field Company moved from MENIN to ROLLEGHEM area. 1 Section of 200th Field Company attached to forward Brigade 21st remained to assist Infantry to cross on rafts. Pontoon Bridge at C.5.a.3.5. was destroyed by shell fire.	
	23rd		200th Field Company, on evening of 23rd, erected 2 footbridges across the L'ESCAUT River at C.4.a.8.3. and C.5.a.4.4. One of these was afterwards destroyed by shellfire (See APPENDIX C). Major A.J. FAWCETT reported to command 201st Field Company.	APPENDIX C.
	24th		201st and 202nd Field Companies moved from ROLLEGHEM to RUDDERVOORDE Area in T.11. 1 Section of 202nd Field Coy relieved Section of 200th Field Coy with 21st Brigade, Remainder resting.	
	25th		Sections attached to Brigades constructed rafts to ferry Infantry across L'ESCAUT to raid enemy posts. APPENDIX D is a summary of work done by the Divisional Engineers during fortnight ending 25-10-18.	APPENDIX D.
	26th		202nd Field Coy prepared material for proposed H.T. bridge across L'ESCAUT at HELCHIN. 1 collapsible boat sent up to 21st Brigade was sunk while attempting to cross the River.	

Army Form C. 2118

WAR DIARY

~~INTELLIGENCE~~ SUMMARY

(Erase heading not required.)

Instructions regarding War Diaries and Intelligence
Summaries are contained in F. S. Regs., Part II.
and the Staff Manual respectively. Title Pages
will be prepared in manuscript.

Place	Date	Hour	Summary of Events and Information	Remarks and references to Appendices
	26th contd.		Captain E.N. CLIFTON returned from leave. Major E.O. ALABASTER reported to take over command of 200th Field Company.	
	27th		C.E., Second Army visited these Headquarters, and discussed the site and erection of bridge at HELCHIN, with C.R.E. Major O.D. ATKINSON. M.C. R.E. died of wounds received on the 21st instant.	
	28th		Work started on diversion for new H.W. bridge at U.12.b.3.6. (Lock 5' Bossuyt Canal) Lieut. LANNON rejoined the 200th Field Company.	
	29th		Work on preparations for Bridge at HELCHIN were stopped owing to leaving that area. Received minute from "G" saying that Infantry were to be trained in launching and carrying rafts and light bridges for crossing the SCHELDT. Materials for mule bridge across the SCHELDT dumped in BOSSUYT at night.	
	30th		Work on new bridge for lorries at KOEN started. Lieut BENNETT, 201st Field Company made reconnaissance of the Landbeek from 0.30.a.2.0. to U.24.b.6.3. to endeavour to find sluice by which inundations could be lowered. ~~Bridge for mule transport at U.13.3.6~~ completed	
ROLLEGHEM.	31st		Divisional Engineers moved to ROLLEGHEM. Work started on new bridge for lorry traffic over Bossuyt Canal at U.6.a.3.1. 3 Trench Bridges were thrown across the dyke running from V.14.c.6.8. and V.14.b.4.0. Note During the last week the Field Companies were employed in constructing light bridges and barrel piers at COYGHEM. The Pioneers were employed on roads, filling in shell holes and mine craters, and clearing trees. The 171st Tunnelling Coy. R.E. carried on reconnaissance of roads, railways, and bridges in the area, removing any charges found.	

November 5th 1918.

Lieut- Col. R.E.
C.R.E., 30th (British) Division.

APPENDIX A.   War Diary.

S E C R E T.   (1).   COPY NO .....17....

30th DIVISIONAL ENGINEERS ORDER NO. 18.

Reference 1/10,000 Sheet WERVICQ Edition 7b.

1. **Attack.** The Division will attack and capture enemy position on the front CRUCIFIX FARM (P.30.b) to Q.9.c.0.5. on a day J and at an hour H to be notified.
   34th Division is attacking on left of 30th Division.
   This operation is the Right Flank of an attack by the 2nd British Army and the Belgian Army.

2. **Objectives.**
   (a) The objectives of attack are shown on attached Map X.
   (b) In the event of success, fighting patrols will be pushed forward to the River LYS on the line HOOGEMOTTE - WERVICQ - BOUSBECQUE - LE MALPLAQUET - QUATRE MONDES.
   They will not cross the LYS without further orders.

3. **Boundaries.**
   (a) The Divisional Boundaries are shown on Map X.
   (b) The Inter-Brigade Boundary is shown on Map X.
   21st Infantry Brigade will be on the RIGHT.
   90th Infantry Brigade will be on the LEFT.

4. **R.E. & PIONEERS.**
   The tasks allotted are :-
   To R.E. (a) Marking out of Infantry forming up line.
          (b) Organising a Main Line of Resistance.
   To PIONEERS. (a) Clearing and repairing of Roads forward.
   201st Field Company will work in LEFT Brigade Area.
   202nd Field Company will work in RIGHT Brigade Area.
   200th Field Company will be in Reserve.

5. **Forming up Line.**
   (a) On the night of 12th/13th October the Infantry forming up line shown with a firm R E line on Map X will be marked out with pegs. The definite points shown will be adhered to.
   Representatives of Battalions concerned will accompany the R.E. parties.
   (b) On the night of J-1/J day a line of tracing tape will be laid down by R.E. on the line in (a) above.
   (c) On the night of J-1/J day short lines of direction parallel to direction of attack will be taped out by R.E. at intervals of about 200 yards from behind the forming up line forwards. Lines giving general direction of attack are shown on Map, but Brigades should be consulted.

6. **Main Line of Resistance.**
   (a) A Main Line of Resistance consisting of 5 Company Localities (3 in RIGHT Brigade Area and 2 in LEFT Brigade Area) will be marked out with tape by R.E. in the positions approximately marked in GREEN on Map X. Approximately 1 Section of Machine Guns will be allotted to each Locality.
   As many Concrete Pill-boxes as possible will be included in each post. The tape will indicate the front of each Locality.
   (b) Notice Boards indicating RIGHT and LEFT of each Locality with name and MG. positions numbered from RIGHT to LEFT, will be fixed.
   (c) Lines of approach to each Locality will be arranged with Brigades and will be clearly marked with ample sign boards.

(2)

6. contd.
(d) Taping out will be commenced as soon as conditions permit on J Day. Touch should be kept with Brigades.

7. Clearing of Roads. (probably not before dusk on J Day)
(a) The Pioneers as soon as conditions permit will repair, and clear the Roads of obstacles, marked BROWN on plan.
(b) A report will be submitted as soon as possible on the condition of the Roads.

8. Locations on J Day.
200th Field Company will be at N.29.a.5.7.
201st Field Company will be at P.19.b.7.7.
202nd Field Company will be at O.23.b.2.8.
6th Bn. S. . Bdrs.(Pioneers) will be at O.21.central.

9. Messengers.
One orderly from each Company will report to C.R.E. on evening of J-1 Day with 2 days rations.

10. Time.
Watches will be synchronised as follows :-
(a) At Divisional Headquarters at 10.49 on J-1 Day.
(b) At 21st Inf.Bde. Headquarters at 15.00 on J-1 Day.
(c) At 90th Inf.Bde. Headquarters at 15.30 on J-1 Day.

11. Headquarters.
Divisional Battle Headquarters will remain at WYTSCHAETE.
21st Infantry Bde. Headquarters will be at P.20.d.3.6.
90th Infantry Bde. Headquarters will be at TRALEE FARM
(P.14.b.4.4.).
89th Infantry Bde. Headquarters will be at TORREKEN FARM
(O.20.d.2.3.)

12. ACKNOWLEDGE BY WIRE.

2/Lt. R.E.
A/Adjt. 30th (B) Divisional Engineers.

October 12th 1918.

    Copy No 1. to O.C. 200th Field Coy. R.E.
X   No 2. to O.C. 201st Field Coy. R.E.
X   No 3. to O.C. 202nd Field Coy. R.E.
X   No 4. to O.C. 6th Bn S. . Bdrs (Pioneers).
X   No 5. to 30th Division "G".
    No 6. to C.R.A.
    No 7. to 30th Division "A" & "Q".
    No 8. to 21st Inf. Brigade.
    No 9. to 89th Inf. Brigade.
    No10. to 90th Inf. Brigade.
    No11. to O.C. 30th Divl. Signal Coy. R.E.
    No12. to O.C. 30th Bn. M.G. Coy.
    No13. to A.D.M.S.
    No14. to C.E., Xth Corps.
    No15. to 31st Division C.R.E.
    No16. to 34th Division C.R.E.
    No17. to War Diary.
    No18. to War Diary.
X   No19. to File.
    No20. Spare
    No21. Spare.

Note Only those marked X as sent to.

Copy No ...7....

AMENDMENT NO 1 TO 30th DIVISIONAL ENGINEERS ORDER NO 18.

Reference 1/20,000 Sheet 28 S.E. (revised to 6.9.18.)

1. **EXPLOITING SUCCESS.**
   The 21st and 90th Infantry Brigades will have Advanced Guards ready to cross the LYS and capture PAUL BUCQ HILL and BOUSBECQUE.
   The XVth Corps are preparing to cross the River LYS at COMINES.

2. **DIVISIONAL BOUNDARY.**
   The Southern Divisional Boundary to South of River on West Side of PAUL BUCQ will be the BECQUE DES BOIS in Q.31.and W.1.

3. **INTER-BRIGADE BOUNDARY.**
   Inter-Brigade Boundary will be amended as follows :-
   Boundary as laid down to Cottages at Q.21.a.2.1. - NEERBRUGGE FARM to Right Brigade - House at Q.27.b.5.2. to Left Brigade - House Q.33.b.0.6. to Left Brigade - KITH HOUSE W.4.a.0.0. to Left Brigade.
   It is intended that Bridge at Q.27.b.5.0. will be inclusive to Left Brigade.

4. **GAS BOMBARDMENT.**
   Attention of all troops advancing beyond the Divisional Objective is to be drawn to the fact that certain areas will be shelled with "BB" shell (mustard gas) on J-1/J night.
   Details of the areas affected is attached in Appendix A.

5. **INFANTRY BRIDGES.**
   (a) Cs.C. 201st and 202nd Field Companies will each hold one Section in reserve ready for attachment to Advanced Guards of 21st and 90th Infantry Brigades for the purpose of assisting the Infantry to cross the LYS in the event of the Advanced Guards being ordered forward.
   (b) A plan showing latest information as to existing condition of Bridges and known Timber Dumps, is attached.
   (c) Air photographs affecting portion of River to be bridged by each Company, are enclosed.

6. **PONTOON BRIDGE.**
   200th Field Coy R.E. will be prepared to move forward to construct a pontoon bridge for Field Guns and horse transport at Q.31.c.1.8.

7. **PONTOON TRANSPORT AND EQUIPMENT.**
   (a) O.C. 200th Field Coy. R.E. will detail Capt HILL to take charge of the whole of the Bridging Transport and Equipment.
   (b) The Bridging Wagons of the 3 Field Companies will report fully equipped with 2 days forage and rations to Capt. HILL at N.29.a.5.7. at 10.00. hours on J Day
   (c) O.C. Transport will be prepared to move forward to a point to be notified later.

8. **DAY.**
   J Day will be 14th October. This date will not be communicated to the troops till the latest possible hour.

(2)

9. ACKNOWLEDGE BY WIRE 1 to 4.

October 13th 1918.   2/Lt. A...
                              A/Adjt. 50th (B) Divl. Engineers.

Copies 1 to 21 to all recipients of 50th Divisional Engineers Order No 18.
Copy No 22 to O.C. Detachment 171st Tunnelling Coy. R.E.
Appendix A with copies 1 to 4 and copy 22 only.

APPENDIX A.

The following are the targets which will be gas shelled :-

3rd. Divisional Artillery.

1. PAUL BUS, from H.2.c.8.7. - H.2.a.8.6.-
   H.2.b.3.6. - H.2.d.7.0.
2. H.34.a.0.0.
3. Manor Farm - H.26.a.0. and c.
4. Battery - H.29.c.15.40.
5. " H.23.b.9.8.
6. " H.31.d.45.60.
7. " H.3.c.0.9.
8. " H.9.b.50.44.
9. " H.9.b.70.57.

24th Divisional Artillery.

1. Cross Roads, CRUCO Village - H.17.d.2.6.
2. SCOUT Farm - H.23.b.3.4.
3. Houses - H.13.d.15.30.
4. RATES Junction - H.13.c.6.8.
5. CLUSTER Farm - Q.22.d.0.1.
6. Houses - H.23.a.2.2.
7. Houses - H.24.a.1.7.
8. DOMNIELL Bridge - H.19.c.4.3.

5th Corps Heavy Artillery.

1. Battery - H.29.c.15.40.
2. " H.34.a.55.10.
3. " H.35.a.90.15-40.15.
4. " H.35.b.35.50.
5. " H.35.c.90.55.
6. " H.35.d.45.60-30.50.
7. " H.3.c.0.9. From.
8. PAUL BUS, from H.2.c.8.7. - H.2.a.8.6.
   H.2.b.3.6. - H.2.d.9.0.

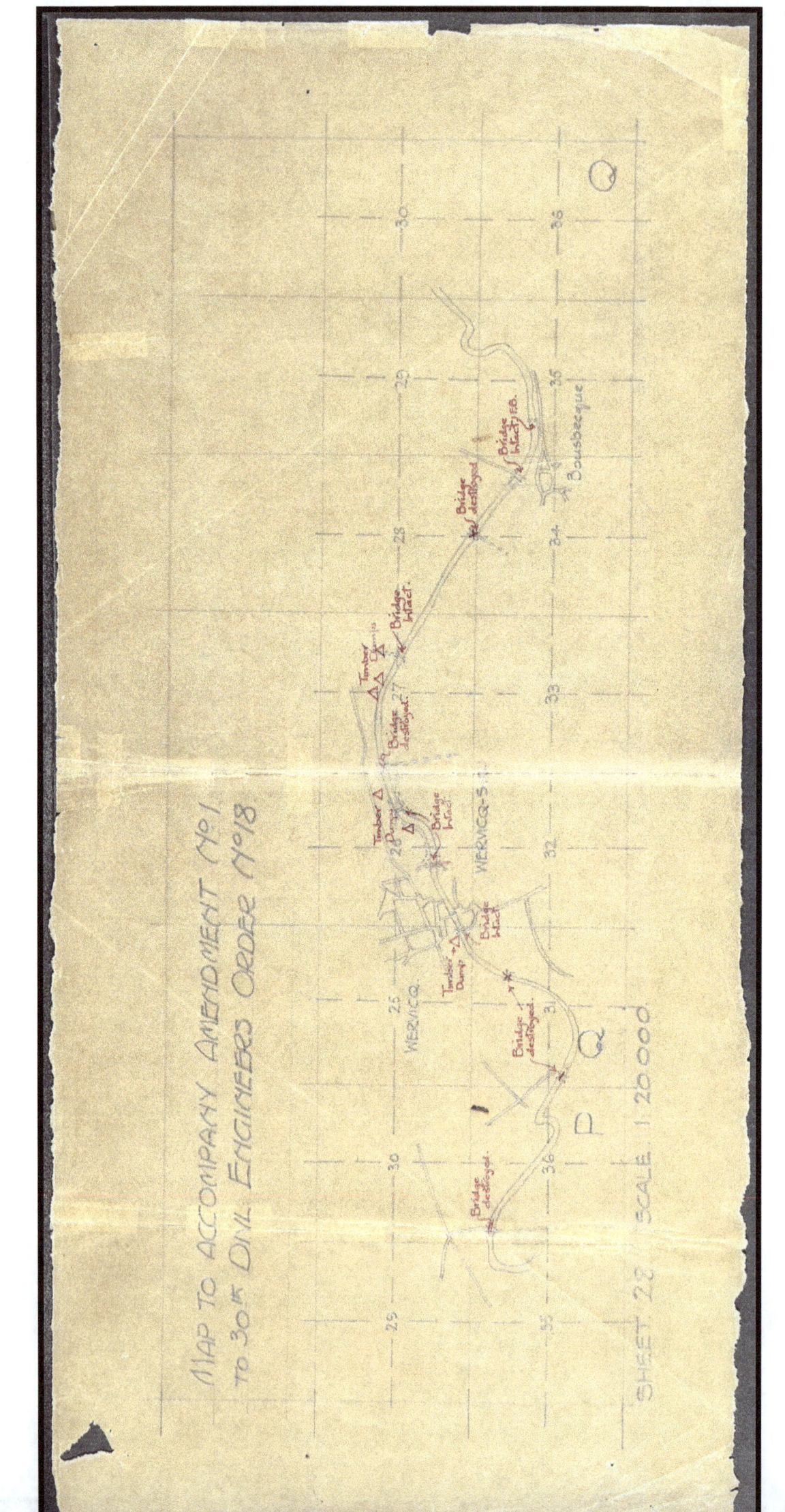

APPENDIX B

30th Division G./129/32.

C.R.E.

The G.O.C. wishes to congratulate Lieut. Col. STORY and 200th Field Company. R.E. on the fine work carried out last night in bridging the LYS under fire, in close touch with the enemy.
It was a fine feat of which any Company can be proud. It shows good training and a fine soldierly spirit throughout the Company, and reflects great credit on all concerned.

16-10-18.

(Sd) P. NEAME. Lt. Col.
General Staff, 30th (British) Division.

O.C. 200th Field Coy. R.E.

In forwarding the above copy of letter from the G.O.C. of the Division, I would like to add my very sincere congratulations to the 200th Field Company R.E.
The Bridge was built at short notice and without previous reconnaissance. The material had to be sent up in the dark a distance of some 12 miles by unknown roads.
One cannot but look with pride on such a fine performance. It is the greatest honour to have such a fine Company under ones command.

24-10-18.

(Sd) P.F. STORY. Lieut. Col.RE.
C.R.E., 30th (British) Division.

C.R.E., 30th Division.

Report on two Infantry Bridges built across the SCHELDT at C.4.a.8.3. and C.5.a.4.4., on night of 23/24th October, 1918.

C.4.a.8.3.

Work started at 9-30.pm, and finished at 12-45.am. Eleven Men were employed. The span was approximately 75 feet.

C.5.a.4.4.

Work started at 9-30.pm, and finished at 1-45.am. Ten Men were employed.

The proximity of the site desired to an enemy post rendered it advisable to construct the Bridge 300 yards up stream, and float it down. This was done and the Bridge floated down at right angles to the shore by means of two lashings fixed ¼ way from either end and taken on to the towpath. A capable man was placed at each end on the Bridge with a boathook to find.

It is considered that if the Bridge had been built on the final site the work, including the offloading of the wagons, could have been completed by ten men in three hours.

Attached is a sketch showing the type of Bridge constructed. It is very stable and required no anchorage. Owing to the play of the structure and the desirability of avoiding noise, it was found that lashings were more suitable than nails.

A handrail was added consisting of 3"X 2" uprights on each pier and a rope rail.

STORES required.

Piers (prepared)	8.)	
Trenchboards. 9'	9.)	
3"X 2" Timber. f.r.	100.)	1½
Shore Transomes. 12'X 9"X 3"	2.)	pontoon
Wooden Pickets round 3'X 3"	12.)	wagon
Lashings (2 fathoms) 1¼"	18.)	loads.
Handrail Cordage 2" fathoms	16.)	
Other " 16 fathoms 2"	2.)	

TOOLS required.

Mauls. ... 1.
Saws Hand. ... 2.
Hammers. Claw. ... 2.
Axes. Hand. ... 1.
Nails. 4". lbs...14.

=============

24-10-18.

(Sd) L. HILL. Capt. R.E.
O.C. 200th Field Coy. R.E.

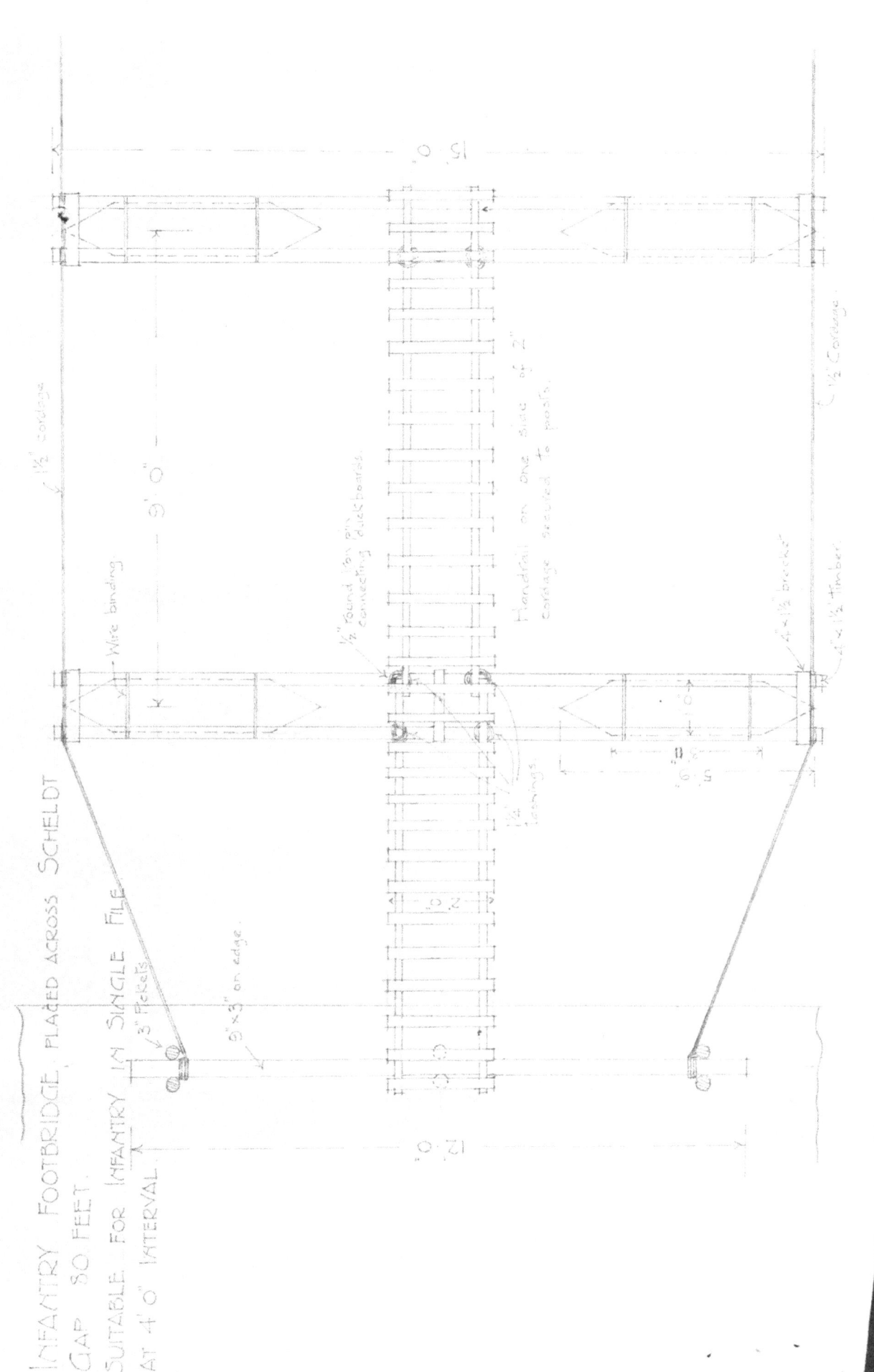

Appendix C

C.E., Xth Corps.

    I enclose a report on some floating Infantry Bridges constructed by 200th Field Company, R.E. of this Division, showing a method of making use of German cylindrical floats found by us. They make a very compact and light form of Bridge.
    Each pier can easily be carried by 2 men.
    Timber available was used, but lighter scantling could have been employed with advantage.

P. L. Story

Lieut. Col. R.E.,
C.R.E., 30th (British) Division.

October 25th 1918.

APPENDIX D.

NARRATIVE REPORT.

For fortnight ending 25-10-18.

During the past fortnight the Field Companies have been almost exclusively employed on bridging operations consequent upon the Division advancing over the LYS to the L'ESCAUT River.
The following are a list of bridges erected by the various Companies :-

Date.	Place.	River.	Nature of Bridge.	Traffic.	Company employed
15/16th.	Q.28.c.8.2.	LYS.	PONTOON (Medium)	M.T.	200th Field.
17th.	R.19.a.1.2.	"	FLOATING RAFT.	Inf.(Single file).	201st Field.
17th.	Q.30.central.	"	Barrel Pier.	do.	202nd Field.
17-19th.	R.27.b.0.5.	"	Heavy Trestle.	L.T.	200th Field.
20-21st.	R.19.c.3.8.	"	Super Heavy Pontoon.	All Transport	201st & 202nd
21st.	C.5.a.3.5.	L'ESCAUT.	PONTOON (Medium)	Infantry.	200th Field.
23rd.	C.4.a.8.3.	"	FLOAT PIER (Foot).	Inf.(Single file).	200th Field.
23rd.	C.5.a.4.4.	"	" " "	" "	200th Field.

In addition to the above, the R.E. taped out assembly positions for the attack on the 14th inst, and also taped defended localities immediately after the attack was launched.
Parties of R.E. also assisted patrols and raiding parties to cross the LYS and L'ESCAUT Rivers on several occasions by means of improvised rafts and foot bridges.

October 26th 1918.

for Lieut. Col. R.E.
C.R.E., 30th (British) Division.

HEAD QUARTERS,
R.E.,
30TH DIVISION.

SECRET.

WAR DIARY.

30TH DIVISIONAL ENGINEERS.

FROM 1ST NOVEMBER, 1918.   TO 30TH NOVEMBER, 1918.

VOLUME 37.

Army Form C. 2118.

HEADQUARTERS, 30th DIVISIONAL ENGINEERS. WAR DIARY. Reference Maps Sheets 30. 38. 29. 37. & 28.
1/40,000. TOURNAI. VOLUME. 37.

or

~~INTELLIGENCE SUMMARY.~~

(Erase heading not required.)

Instructions regarding War Diaries and Intelligence Summaries are contained in F.S. Regs., Part II. and the Staff Manual respectively. Title pages will be prepared in manuscript.

Place	Date	Hour	Summary of Events and Information	Remarks and references to Appendices
			PRELIMINARY.	
			Divisional Headquarters were at ROLLEGHEM. 200th Field Company was employed on constructing a bridge for single way lorry traffic across the BOSSUYT Canal at 29/U.6.a.3.1. (Started on 31-10-18) The 201st and 202nd Field Companies were employed on preparing floating bridges and barrel piers for the SCHELDT crossings. The 6th Bn S.W. Borderers (Pioneers) were employed on repairs to roads, and a detachment of the 171st Tunnelling Coy R.E. on road, railway, and bridge reconnaissance for mines.	
			The Field Companies and Pioneers were very short of officers and men owing to influenza. Major LEE and Lieut. FROST of 202nd Field Company were in hospital, and other officers confined to bed. The average working strength of the Pioneers was reduced to about 100.	
ROLLEGHEM. 29/T.1.b.85.85.	1st.		Work carried on as above.	A2
	2nd.		Work carried on as above. Lieut THURLBY, 200th Field Coy. R.E. evacuated to C.C.S. with influenza.	A2
	3rd.		Bridge for single way lorry traffic across the BOSSUYT Canal at 29/U.6.a.3.1. was completed by 200th Field Coy. R.E. Lieut BENNETT, 201st Field Coy. R.E. was admitted to hospital accidentally injured. Reconnoitred for billets for Field Companies and Pioneers at 29/O.16. and 17.	A2
BELLEGHEM. 29/I.7.a.0.1.	4th.		Divisional Headquarters moved to BELLEGHEM. C.R.E. reconnoitred for suitable bridge sites near AVELGHEM.	A2
	5th.		Held conference of Company Commanders in the morning at Headquarters R.E., and discussed bridging arrangements for the passage of the SCHELDT. Visited C.E. 4th Corps in the afternoon, and discussed bridging arrangements with C.E. Corps and C.E., Second Army. It was decided at the above conferences that :- (a) The Infantry would cross the old river bed and the main stream by means of a series of light floating bridges to be erected by the R.E. The Infantry patrols would then carry forward a further supply of these bridges to cross the GRAND COURANT, LA HATE River, and any further water obstacles. These would be put over by the Infantry	A2

WAR DIARY
or
INTELLIGENCE SUMMARY.
(Erase heading not required.)

Army Form C. 2118.

Sheet 2.

Place	Date	Hour	Summary of Events and Information	Remarks and references to Appendices
	5th contd.		themselves (parties had already been trained for this work)	
			(b) A pack mule bridge would be pushed over as soon as possible at about 29/V.15.a.4.3., the routes to and from the river from this point having been ascertained to be passable as far as could be found out from reconnaissance, information from civilians and air photos.	
			(c) The AVELGHEM - CELLES Road would be the main lorry route. On the day of the advance a bridge would be erected at 29/V.9.b.7.8. to take lorries, a medium pontoon bridge would then be put over at V.10.c.05.55. and super heavy pontoon bridge for 'A' loads would be erected at V.10.c.5.7.	
			Lieut-Col. P.F. STORY. D.S.O. R.E. awarded a Bar to the D.S.O. for gallantry in the Field on 14-10-18 (Authy D.R.O. 2922 dated 5-11-18).	
			Major FAWCETT, O.C. 201st Field Coy. R.E. evacuated to hospital with influenza.	
	6th.		The Field Companies and Pioneers moved their billets to the neighbourhood of KNOKKE (29/O.15.d.) ~~the Division Front was reduced to run from~~	
			Instructions issued to Capt. HILL., 200th Field Company to take over the command of the 201st Field Company, pending Major FAWCETT'S return from hospital (Capt. WOOLLEY. R.E., 2nd in command of 201st Field Coy was on leave to U.K.).	kw
			Instructions issued to O.C. 201st Field Company to be prepared to assist 89th Inf. Brigade in crossing the old river bed and DEN RITTGRACHE on the night of the 7th inst.	
			12 G.S. Wagon loads of road slabbing sent forward for road diversion for lorry bridge.	
	7th.		Held conference of Field Company Commanders at 201st Field Coy. Headquarters in the morning. Instructed Companies to take on bridging as follows :-	kw
			(a) 201st Field Company to carry out all bridging in connection with the passage of the river by the Infantry, including the pack mule bridge.	
			(b) 202nd Field Coy. to construct the bridge for lorries at 29/V.9.b.7.8., after/they would carry on with the Super Heavy Pontoon Bridge.	which
			(c) 200th Field Company to construct medium pontoon bridge at V.10.c.05.55.	
			Floating bridges were tested on canal by KNOKKE R.E. Dump after the conference. G.E., Second Army was asked to provide temporary replacements for 6 Officers who were in hospital.	
			Lieut. J.B. FROST. R.E. rejoined the 202nd Field Coy. from hospital (Influenza)	

Army Form C. 2118.

WAR DIARY
or
INTELLIGENCE SUMMARY.
(Erase heading not required.)

Instructions regarding War Diaries and Intelligence Summaries are contained in F. S. Regs., Part II. and the Staff Manual respectively. Title pages will be prepared in manuscript.

Place	Date	Hour	Summary of Events and Information	Remarks and references to Appendices
	7th contd.		12 G.S. wagon loads of road slabbing sent forward for road diversion for lorry bridges. Pioneers worked on repairs to craters at V.3.b.2.9. The whole of the 171st Tunnelling was handed over to the C.R.E. for work. The 201st Field Coy. R.E. threw a floating Infantry Bridge across the old river bed at V.3.a.8.8. in conjunction with a minor operation carried out by the 89th Inf. Brigade. The Division Front was reduced to run from V.14.d.0.0. to V.5.c.0.0.	
	8th.		The C.R.E. attended conference at 89th Brigade Headquarters. Gauge for measuring rise and fall in water level was fixed in the canal at 29/V.13.c.85.45. by 200th Field Company R.E. (Appendix. A.) Pioneers worked on road craters at V.3.B.2.9. 12 G.S. wagon loads of road slabbing sent forward for road diversions for lorry bridges. Working Parties Transport arranged for the 9th inst, as in Appendix. B.	APPENDIX "A" APPENDIX "B"
	9th.		On the night 8th/9th the 201st Field Coy. R.E. threw 4 Infantry Bridges and 2 rafts across the SCHELDT and subsidiary streams, to enable a battalion of the 89th Inf. Brigade to cross the river. Locations and lengths of bridges are as follows :-	
			(1) 29/V.15.a.1.6. (30 feet).	
			(2) V.15.a.4.4. (30 feet).	
			(3) V.9.b.7.0. (50 feet).	
			(4) V.4.c.5.9. (30 feet).	
			Total 190 feet.	
			Rafts were launched at V.9.a.9.5. and V.14.d.9.9. - at this latter point the stream was too swift to enable a crossing to be made. The 202nd Field Coy started work on abutments for the bridge at V.9.b.7.9. Information was received that the enemy had started to withdraw from the river opposite the Division.	
		03.00 hours approx.		
		04.30 hours	Capt. LINDSAY. R.E. 202nd Field Coy. carried out detailed reconnaissance of the bridge at V.9.b.7.8., and reported to Headquarters. R.E. at 09.00 hours. It was decided that a heavy trestle bridge would be necessary, the span being 86 ft (Approx). Work on constructing the trestles forthwith on KNOKKE R. . Dump, and wagons containing completed bridge left the Dump	

Army Form C. 2118.

WAR DIARY
or
INTELLIGENCE SUMMARY
(Erase heading not required.)

Instructions regarding War Diaries and Intelligence Summaries are contained in F. S. Regs., Part II. and the Staff Manual respectively. Title pages will be prepared in manuscript.

Place	Date	Hour	Summary of Events and Information	Remarks and references to Appendices
			Sheet. 4.	
HEESTERT		15.00 hours	Work was started as soon as bridge arrived on site. The 200th Field Company by 15.00 hours. threw an Infantry Float Bridge across the SCHELDT at V.10.c.8.8. during the morning. Advanced Divisional Headquarters moved to HEESTERT. The Super Heavy Pontoon Bridge was ordered to report at V.3.d.4.4. at 13.00 hours, 10th inst. Pioneers constructed a plank road diversion round the craters on the main road at V.3.d.5.6. The 171st Tunnelling Coy. R.E. worked on the plank road diversion for the bridge.	
	10th.	02.00 hours.	Barrel Pier Bridge for pack animals over the SCHELDT at V.15.a.9.7. completed by 201st Field Coy. at 02.00 hours. This bridge broke twice in swinging into position, which caused considerable delay.	R.
		02.30 hours.	Heavy Trestle Bridge and road diversion at 29/V9.d.7.8. completed by 202nd Field Coy. R.E. at 02.30. hours. The 200th Field Coy. R.E. then started work on the medium pontoon bridge	
		08.45 hours.	across the main stream at V.10.c.05.55. - this with approaches was by 08.45. hours. 6 pontoons were used.	
		12.30 hours.	The Super Heavy Pontoon Bridge started to arrive at 12.30. hours - the last Pontoons arrived at 22.00. hours - no superstructure arrived till 11.00 hours on the 11th inst, so work was held up for 13.hours. Work on plank road diversion started by 2 Field Companies of 36th Division and 1 Labour Coy. Advanced Divisional Headquarters moved to WATRIPONT. 200th and 202nd Field Companies moved to ESCANAFFLES, 201st Field Company to 37/E.14.a.0.3, and Pioneers to 29/V.4.a.2.8. 201st Field Coy. R.E. was made responsible for repairs to road from ESCANAFFLES to RENAIX.	
WATRIPONT	11th.		Received notification that hostilities would cease at 11.00. hours. Advanced Divisional Headquarters moved to ELLEZELLES.	
ELLEZELLES		11.00 hours.	Superstructure for Super Heavy Pontoon Bridge started to arrive at 11.00 hours and 202nd Field Coy. R.E. started work on Bridge, working in 6 hour shifts - 202nd Field Coy. took over the Bridging Convoy (9 Pontoon Wagons) from Capt. HILL. R.E. The 200th Field Coy. R.E. moved to 37/E.14.a.0.3. The 201st Field Coy. R.E. " " " RENAIX leaving one Section on detachment at WATRIPONT to repair 3 partially destroyed bridges on WATRIPONT - RENAIX Road. One Section 201st Field Coy. was attached to 89th Brigade. Pioneers moved to GAILLARD. 29/N.26.b. 256th A.T. Coy. R.E. joined for work and was billetted in WATRIPONT.	R.

Army Form C. 2118.

WAR DIARY
or
INTELLIGENCE SUMMARY.
(Erase heading not required.)

Instructions regarding War Diaries and Intelligence Summaries are contained in F. S. Regs., Part II. and the Staff Manual respectively. Title pages will be prepared in manuscript.

Place	Date	Hour	Summary of Events and Information	Remarks and references to Appendices
	14th contd.		Sheet. 5. 171st Tunnelling Coy. R.E. (less one detachment working on reconnaissances for mines) reverted to C.E., Xth Corps.	
	14th.	11.00 hours 12.00. 12.04.	Super Heavy Pontoon Bridge completed by 202nd Field Coy. R.E. at 11.00. hours. First lorry crossed the bridge. 202nd Field Coy. was instructed to remain at ESCANAFFLES to maintain the 2 pontoon bridges. Section of 201st Field Coy. attached to 89th Brigade rejoined its Unit. 200th Field Coy. worked on roads. 201st Field Coy. worked on removing a steel girder Railway Bridge which had been dropped across the main RENAIX - BLESSINES Road at 29/X.22.b.7.4. - Their detachment at WATRIPONT worked on the bridges, but was held up through lack of material. The Pioneers worked on the road from JONCQUOIS through HAUT, HAUT CHEMIN to 57/E.9.a. 256th A.T. Coy worked on roads and reverted to C.E., XXI Corps in the evening.	k k
	15th.		Work continued as on 13th inst.	
	14th.		Work as on 13th inst. Received information that the Division would move back to MOUSCRON Area on the 14th but that the R.E. & Pioneers would remain behind to carry on with work on bridges and roads. Issued Appendix "C".	k APPENDIX "C".
RENAIX.	15th.		Divisional H.Q. moved to MOUSCRON. Headquarters R.E. moved to RENAIX. Took over repair of bridges at 37/E.12.b.8.1., F.19.c.0.8., &E.30.6./5.40. from C.R.E. 29th Div.	k
	16th.		Pioneers worked on main AMBERGFUL - RENAIX Road. 200th Field Coy. started work on bridges taken over from C.R.E., 29th Division. Received orders to rejoin Division, staging at HERSTERT on night 17th/18th. Issued Appendix "D".	k APPENDIX "D".
HERSTERT.	17th.	23.00	Headquarters R.E., 200th., 201st Field Coys.R.E. moved to Herstert. 202nd Field Coy. remained at ESCANAFFIES. Detachment attached from 171st Tunnelling Coy reverted to its Unit.	k
MOUSCRON	18th.		Headquarters,R.E. moved to MOUSCRON. Field Coys rejoined their Brigade Groups and were located as follows :- 200th Field Coy. LUINGNE. 201st Field Coy. 29/N.9.d.3.2. and 202nd Field Coy at ROLLEGHEM.	k

Sheet. 6.

Army Form C. 2118.

WAR DIARY
or
INTELLIGENCE SUMMARY.

(Erase heading not required.)

Instructions regarding War Diaries and Intelligence Summaries are contained in F. S. Regs., Part II. and the Staff Manual respectively. Title pages will be prepared in manuscript.

Place	Date	Hour	Summary of Events and Information	Remarks and references to Appendices
	18th contd.		Pioneers were billetted by 90th Infantry Brigade at AELBEKE.	
	19th.			
	20th.		Held conference on Education and Recreation schemes at H.Q. R.E. Company Commanders, 2nds in Command & Unit Educational Officers were present. It was decided (1) Lt. LANNON should continue to act as R.E. Educational Officer, and that Lt. PEARSON, Lt. PETSCHLER and Lt. FROST should represent their respective Field Coys. (2) That Capt. HILL should form a Recreation Committee composed of 1 Officer, 1 N.C.O. and 1 O.R. from each Field Coy. to deal with all matters of outdoor and indoor recreation. Lt. EVANS, 1l/Lt. EDGAR and Lt. FISHER were chosen as the Officer Representatives for the 3 Field Coys. (3) That a further meeting should be held on the 25th inst, by which time Capt. HILL and Lt. LANNON would formulate definite schemes, and OsC. Coys would find out necessary details about the men in their Companies.	
	21st.		The Division was transferred to the XIXth Corps.	
	22nd.		Lt. A.W. MADGER reported for duty with 201st Field Coy R.E., to replace Lt. BENNETT, to ENGLAND (accidentally injured).	
	23rd.		Companies employed in training and refitting.	
	24th.		Companies resting.	
	25th.		Held 2nd meeting on Education and Recreation. The Divisional Education Officer was also present. (See APPENDIX "E").	APPENDIX "E".
	26th.		Lt. LANNON attached to H.Q. R.E. as Education Officer for Divl. Engineers. 2/Lt. R.C.P. JAMES, R.E. reported for duty with 200th Field Coy, to replace Lt. THURLBY, R.E. to ENGLAND (Sick). 2/Lt. H.L. FORSTER reported for duty with the 201st Field Coy, to replace Lt. H.E. APPS, to Assistant Inspector Searchlights, Third Army. Medium pontoon bridge at 29/V.9.b.7.8. was picked up By 202nd Field Coy.	
	27th.		Issued Appendix, F, orders for move to AIRE Area.	APPENDIX "F".
	28th.		201st Field Coy. R.E. moved to LAURE.	
	29th.		Field Coys started to march with the 21st Inf. Brigade in ARMENTIERES Area.	
	30th.		Field Companies staged first night in LINCEILLES Area. List of Honours & Awards for month of November is shown in Appendix "G".	APPENDIX "G".

December 8, 1918

P.Y. Terry
Lieut-Col. R.E.
C.R.E., 30th (British) Division.

Appendix "A"

A.1356.

O.C. 200th Field Coy. R.E.

    A water level gauge was today fixed at BOSSUYT to a mooring post in centre of canal south of locks 1 & 2 at approximately V.13.c.85.45. The water level gauge was of the pattern drawn herewith, and the reading at 17.30. hours (the time of fixing) was -1ft.

    The water level gauge can be read from either side of the canal and is also in view from the upper storeys of houses at corner of Road at V.13.c.80.05.

                                                 (Sd) A.D. BUMPSTEAD.
8-11-18.   1/Lt. R.E.

C.R.E.

    Forwarded.

                                               (Sd) M.C. ALABASTER, Major, R.E.
8-11-18.   O.C. 200th Field Coy. R.E.

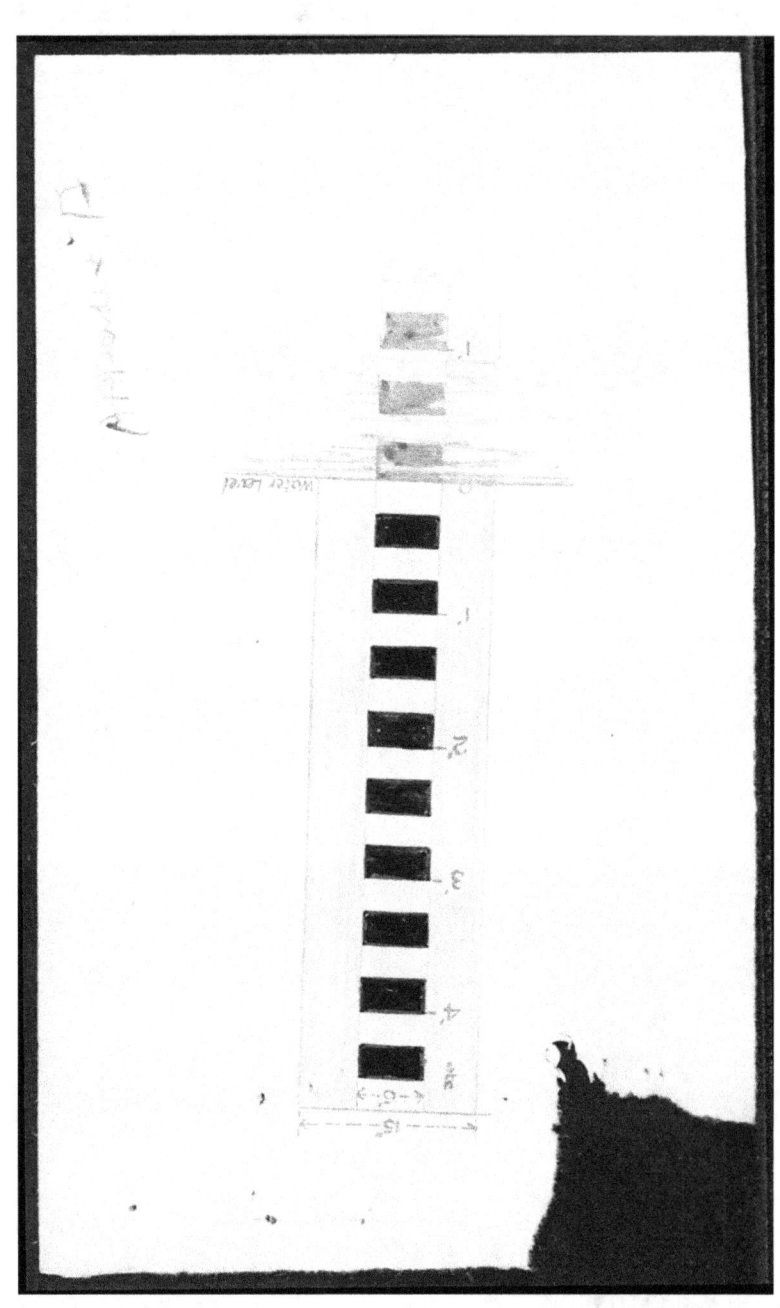

APPENDIX "E".

TRANSPORT & WORKING PARTIES FOR NOVEMBER 9th 1918.

1. 40 men and 7 Limbered wagons to report to N.C.O. of 202nd Field Coy R.E. at the office of INCHY R.E. Dump at 13-00 hours.

2. 30 men and 12 G.S. wagons to report to Officer of 200th Field Coy R.E. at Area Commandant's Office in INCHY Dump at 14.00 hours to carry forward bridging material for 201st Field Coy. R.E.
    G.S. Wagons made up as follows :-

    (a) 6 from C.E. Corps, to be returned as early as possible
    (b) 3 from Division.
    (c) 3 (1 from each Company.)

3. 20 men and 20 G.S. Wagons to report to Officer of Pioneers at INCHY R.E. Dump at 16.00 hours.
    G.S. Wagons made up as follows :-

    (a) 14 from Division.
    (b) 6 from Pioneers.

4. 20 men to report to Officer of Pioneers at F.31.a.9.6. at 13.00. hours to unload wagons - This party will wait for the wagons if they are late.

    Note. Wagons mentioned in para 2 (a) will arrive at 13.00 hours and will probably report to N.C.O. of 202nd Field Coy. R.E. - They must however be handed over to Officer of 200th Field Coy. R.E.

5. 100 men to report to Officer of the Pioneers at V.3.b.2.9. at 18.00 hours for carrying material for road repairs.

(Sd) E.N. CLIFTON. R.E.
8-11-18. Adjt. 30th (B) Divl. Engineers.

Copies to :-
   O.C. 200th Field Coy. R.E.   ) For information and action
O.C. 201st Field Coy. R.E.   ) as regards para 2 (c)
   O.C. 202nd Field Coy. R.E.   )
   O.C. 6th Bn. C.M.Bdrs (Pioneers).For information.

APPENDIX "C"

O.C. 200th Field Coy. R.E.
O.C. 201st Field Coy. R.E.
O.C. 202nd Field Coy. R.E.
O.C. 6th Bn. S.W. Bdrs (Pioneers)

      Reference my minute delivered this morning re moves, rations, etc.
      Supply wagons should be at WATRIPONT Refilling point by 12.00 hours on the 16th inst and onwards. Ration indents will be handed to the R.S.M. R.E.

(Sd) E.H. CLIFTON, R.E.
November 15th 1918.   Adjt. 30th (B) Divl. Engineers.

APPENDIX "C".

O.C. 200th Field Coy. R.E.
O.C. 201st Field Coy. R.E.
O.C. 202nd Field Coy. R.E.
O.C. 6th Bn. S.W. Bdrs (Pioneers).

MOVE OF DIVISION.
The Division, less Royal Engineers and 6th Bn. S.W. Bdrs (Pioneers) is moving to a back area tomorrow, 15th inst.
The R.E. and Pioneers will remain at present and carry on with their present work.

HEADQUARTERS, R.E.
Headquarters, R.E. will move to RENAIX (about L.22.a.7.3.) tomorrow 15th inst.

COMMUNICATION.
O.C. Signals is arranging to have the following Units connected by telephone to Headquarters, R.E. :-
    201st Field Coy. R.E.   29/L.22.a.7.3.
    202nd Field Coy. R.E.   ESCANAFFLES.
    6th Bn. S.W. Bdrs (Pioneers). 37/R.3.b.5.2.
It is understood that the 6th Bn. S.W. Bdrs will maintain the line from their Headquarters to RENAIX. (This is being arranged direct between O.C. Signals and O.C. Pioneers.
The D.R.L.S. will probably leave H.Q. R.E. at 20.30. hours nightly. This hour will be confirmed later.
All correspondence to Divl. Headquarters should reach this Office a quarter of an hour before the D.R.L.S. is due to leave.

RATIONS.
Rations will be delivered daily at MATRIPONT at a time to be notified later, from the 16th inst onwards. They will be issued by the R.S.M. R.E.
O.C. 6th Bn. S.W. Bdrs. will please detail a butcher to cut up the meat.
202nd Field Coy. R.E. will arrange to draw from MATRIPONT on the 16th inst - after that date it may be possible to deliver direct to their Headquarters by the lorry when it returns.

14-11-18.
                                (Sd) E.M. CLIFTON. R.E.
Copies to :-   Adjt. 30th (E) Divl. Engineers.

    O.C. Detachment, 171st Tunnelling Coy. R.E.
    R.S.M.

APPENDIX "D".

O.C. 200th Field Coy. R.E.
O.C. 201st Field Coy. R.E.
O.C. 6th Bn. S.W.Bdrs.(Pioneers).

      Field Companies and Pioneers will rejoin 30th Division on 18th inst, staying night of 17th/18th at HEESTERT.

      Send billetting party to meet Adjutant R.E. at HEESTERT Church at 11.30. hours tomorrow 17th. Move early under your own arrangements.

      You will draw rations tomorrow for 18th at S.R.P. on AUTRYVE - BOSSUYT Road en route.

      Further orders will be issued on 18th.

16th November 1918.
                            (Sd) E.N. CLIFTON. R.E.
                            Adjt. 30th (B) Divl. Engineers.

APPENDIX "D".

O.C. 201nd Field Coy. R.E.

       Field Coys and Pioneers will rejoin Division, on the 18th.
       You will draw rations tomorrow for the 18th at S.R.P. on
AUTRYVE to BOSSUYT Road.
       Further orders will be issued for move on 18th.
       Be prepared to take up pontoon bridge tomorrow on receipt
of further orders.

                                                    Sd. C.H. CLIFTON. R.E.
16th November 1918.   Adjt. 30th (D) Divl. Engineers.

Appendix "E"

30th Division R.E. EDUCATION SCHEME.

At a meeting held at R.E. Headquarters on 25th inst, the following Education Scheme was approved as being likely to meet the needs of the men in the Field Companies. Each man has been personally interviewed by an Officer, and the results of these interviews were summarised and placed before the meeting. This summary is appended.

The scheme falls under 5 heads :-

(i) ELEMENTARY COURSE. A large number of N.C.Os and men desire to refresh their Elementary English, letter writing, aritmetic, and workshop calculations. Classes to meet this will be formed and teachers will be found as far as possible from the Field Companies. The D.E.O. will assist if possible with instructors from other sources.

(ii) TRADE GROUPS.
(a) Building Construction. This Group comprises Carpenters, Joiners, Bricklayers and Stone Masons. Most of these men desire a Course in Building Construction and allied subjects, including workshop practice. Lieut EVANS, 200th Field Company was asked to undertake the organization of this branch.
(b) Mechanical Engineering. Under this Group are included Fitters, Blacksmiths, Metal Turners, Engine Drivers, etc. It was pointed out that the instruction in this branch would vary much more than in (a), and would require more individual treatment. Lieut PEARSON. undertook to organize this Group.
(c) Electrical Engineering. Most of the instruction required would be in elementary theory, and practical fitting work.
It was decided to ask Lieut PETSCHLER to undertake this branch. Lieut EDGAR will assist in Groups (b) and (c).

(iii) UNRELATED SUBJECTS. Lieut LANNON undertook to make the best possible arrangements for classes in languages, agriculture, commercial subjects, vetinary science, etc, and if it was not possible to form classes in all of these, to try and arrange for the men to obtain the necessary instruction elsewhere.

(iv) PRACTICAL WORK. This will depend largely on workshop accommodation, and the supply of tools and material. The woodworking and bricklaying classes will come under Lieut EVANS, and iron work under Lieut PEARSON. Practical instruction in other trades will be given as opportunity permits. Men from other Units will be given instruction in their own trades where practicable.

(v) LECTURES, ETC. It was decided to make as much use as possible of short lectures, and every endeavour will be made to obtain lectures from the Field Companies.

November 30th 1918.

(Sd) R.J. LANNON. R.E.
E.O., 30th (B) Divl. Engineers.

SUMMARY OF COURSES.

	Field Companies.		
	506th.	508th.	512nd.
1. ELEMENTARY COURSE.	57.	56.	168.
2. TRADE GROUPS.			
(a) Building Construction.	.	40.	40.
(b) Mechanical Eng:.	10.	13.	10.
(c) Electrical Eng:.	3.	8.	1.
3. UNRELATED SUBJECTS.			
Languages. "French"	9.	15.	22.
" "Spanish"	4.	--	1.
Agriculture.	3.	19.	13.
Veterinary Science:.	11.	3.	1.
Commercial Course:.	3.	34.	17.
Drawing, Freehand.	--	3.	10.

Note. A number of men desire instruction in special subjects and trades not included in the above summary.

APPENDIX "F".

S E C R E T.   WARNING ORDER.

O.C. 200th Field Coy. R.E.
O.C. 201st Field Coy. R.E.
O.C. 202nd Field Coy. R.E.
----

1. The Division will move to an area about BLARINGHEM on 28th November, and following days.

2. For purposes of this move there will be three Brigade Groups as under :-

GOODMAN'S GROUP.	CURRIE'S GROUP.	STEVEN'S GROUP.
21st Inf. Brigade.	89th Inf. Brigade.	90th Inf. Brigade.
3 Field Coys. R.E.	30th Bn. M.G.C.	6th Bn. S.W. Bdrs.
96th Field Ambulance.	97th Field Ambulance.	98th Field Ambulance.
No.4. Coy. Div. Train.	No.2. Coy. Div. Train.	No.3.Coy. Div. Train.

3. There will be 4 staging areas as follows :-

    "H" - - - - LINSELLES Area.
    "G" - - - - ARMENTIERES Area.
    "F" - - - - ESTAIRES Area.
    "E" - - - - ST. VENANT Area.

4. GENERAL ROUTE. :- NEUVILLE - Cross Roads. Immediately N. of NEUVILLE - HALTE at LA ROUSSELLE - LA VIGNETTE - LINSELLES - LE VEAU - QUESNOY - LA PREVOTE - HOUPLINES - ARMENTIERES - MERVILLE - HAZEBROUCK - or ST VENANT.

5. For the purpose of this move all 3 Field Companies will be placed under the command of Major E.O. ALABASTER, R.E, O.C. 200th Field Coy.R.E. and will march with GOODMAN'S Group, which will probably move to "H" staging area on the 29th inst, arriving in the new are on the on the 3rd December.

6. Major ALABASTER. R.E. will get into touch with 21st Infantry Brigade in BELLEGHEM and arrange all details direct with Brigade and other Field Companies.

7. Headquarters, Royal Engineers will move probably on the 2nd December.

8. Field Coys. will acknowledge.

                                        (Sd)   E.N. CLIFTON. R.E.
November 25th 1918.   Adjt. 30th (B) Divl. Engineers.

Copies to :- 30th Div. "G"
              30th Div. "A" & "Q".
              21st Inf. Brigade.
              30th Divl. Signal Coy. R.E.

APPENDIX "D".

O.C. 200th Field Coy. R.E.
O.C. 201st Field Coy. R.E.
O.C. 202nd Field Coy. R.E.

Reference D.18. dated 25-11-18 (Warning Order).

1. Moves will take place as stated therein.

2. On arrival in the new area Brigade Groups will be located as follows :-

   <u>GOODMAN'S Group</u> - CAMPAGNE - HAZEBROUCK - RACQUINHEM.

   <u>CURRIE'S Group.</u> - LYNDE - WALLON CAPPEL - SERCUS.

   <u>STEVEN'S Group.</u> - BOESEGHEM - STEENBECQUE - THIENNES.

   <u>R.A. & R.E.</u> - AIRE.

3. Wireless communication is being arranged for by the O.C. Signal Coy. in each staging area.
Appendix "A" gives table of R.E. runs.

4. Divisional Headquarters and Headquarters R.E. will move to RENESCURE on 2nd December. Advanced D.H.Q., with representatives of A.&Q.& G. will open at the same time place on 30th November.

5. The R.E. Area will be in AIRE with the R.A.
Lieut. LANNON is going forward tomorrow to arrange billets.
Further information re this will be forwarded later.

November 27th 1918.

(Sd) E.E. CLIFTON, R.E.
Adjt. 30th (B) Divl. Engineers.

APPENDIX "G".

HONOURS & AWARDS FOR NOVEMBER 1918.

83351.	Sergt.	TURNER. C.	200th Field Coy. R.E.	D.C.M.
113722.	Corpl.	REECE. E. M.M.	202nd Field Coy. R.E.	D.C.M.
83269.	Corpl.	FIELDING. A. M.M.	200th Field Coy. R.E.	Bar to M.M.
81380.	Corpl.	BRADSHAW.	201st Field Coy. R.E.	M.M.
102062.	Sapper.	WHITEHOUSE. J.W.	171st Tunnelling Coy. R.E.	M.M.
139315.	"	GIBSON. W.I.	" " " "	M.M.
312773.	2/Cpl.	BAKER. E.	" " " "	M.M.

WAR DIARY.

OF

30TH. DIVISIONAL ENGINEERS.

FROM 1ST DECEMBER 1918.   TO 31ST DECEMBER 1918.

VOLUME 38.

Army Form C. 2118.

WAR DIARY
or
INTELLIGENCE SUMMARY.

(Erase heading not required.)

VOLUME 38.

Reference Maps:-
HAZEBROUCK 1/100,000.
Sheets 27 & 36. 1/40,000.

Instructions regarding War Diaries and Intelligence Summaries are contained in F. S. Regs., Part II. and the Staff Manual respectively. Title pages will be prepared in manuscript.

Place	Date	Hour	Summary of Events and Information	Remarks and references to Appendices
MOUSCRON.	Dec. 1st.		**PRELIMINARY.** Divisional Headquarters were at MOUSCRON. The Division was in the process of moving to the RENESCURE - AIRE Area, and the three Field Companies were moving with the 21st Brigade.	
			Field Companies staged the night in the ESTAIRES Area. Lieut. PETSCHLER. R.E. awarded the MILITARY CROSS for gallantry in action at AVELGHEM on night 7th/8th November (authy. MS.522, dated 1-12-18).	
RENESCURE.	2nd.		Divisional Headquarters moved to RENESCURE. Field Companies staged the night in the ST VENANT Area.	
	3rd.		Field Companies arrived at AIRE.	
	5th.		Took over R.E. Dump at LA LACQUE. Field Companies resting and refilling.	
	7th.		Lieut. BURFORD. R.E., 202nd Field Company. R.E. went on special leave to U.K. C.R.E. visited Brigade Commanders to discuss Hutting schemes.	
	9th.		Field Companies attached one Officer to their affiliated Brigades, to organize the Hutting schemes.	
	10th.		Held conference with Company Commanders, re hutting.	
	14th.		Chief Engineer, XIX Corps inspected Barracks at AIRE.	
	16th.		Medal Ribbons presentation by G.O.C. Division, to Field Companies and Signal Company.	
	18th.		Handed over LA LACQUE. R.E. Dump to representative of D.D.E.S. (N).	
	19th.		G.O.C., XIX Corps inspected Field Company Billets in AIRE. 1 Section of 201st Field Company attached to 90th Inf. Brigade, and 1 Section of 200th Field Company to 89th Inf. Brigade, to assist in Hutting.	

Army Form C. 2118.

WAR DIARY
or
INTELLIGENCE SUMMARY

(Erase heading not required.)

Instructions regarding War Diaries and Intelligence Summaries are contained in F. S. Regs., Part II. and the Staff Manual respectively. Title pages will be prepared in manuscript.

- 2 -

Place	Date	Hour	Summary of Events and Information	Remarks and references to Appendices
RENESCURE. (contd)	20th.		1 Section of 202nd Field Company attached to 21st Inf. Brigade for Hutting.	
	24th.		Sections of Field Companies attached to Brigades rejoined their Units.	
	25th.		Resting.	
	26th.		Resting.	
	27th.		Lieut-Colonel P.F. STORY. D.S.O. R.E. proceeded on leave to U.K. Major. E.O. ALABASTER. R.E., O.C. 200th Field Coy. R.E. assumed the duties of A/C.R.E., but remained at AIRE. Received notification that the Division had been nominated for duty at Base Ports, and that Field Companies would move very shortly. Brigades rejoined Brigades to superintend R.E. Officers previously attached to Inf. return of Huts and Stores to R.E. Dumps. See APPENDIX. A.	APPENDIX. A.
	28th.		Received orders that 2 Field Companies would move by march route to DUNKIRK, starting 29th inst, and staging night 29th/30th at WORMHOUT - this was cancelled, and Companies were instructed to be prepared to move by train at short notice. 201st and 202nd Field Companies were detailed for this move.	
	29th.		Received instructions for 2 Field Companies (less pontoon & Trestle equipment) to entrain at AIRE at 06.00 hours, 30th inst, for DUNKIRK. Issued instructions for Pontoon & Trestle equipment of these Companies to be handed over to 200th Field Coy. R.E. Received instructions that 200th Field Company would proceed to ETAPLES by march route, starting 31st inst and staging 2 nights. Major E.O. ALABASTER. R.E., A/C.R.E. joined Headquarters. R.E.	
	30th.		201st and 202nd Field Companies, less Pontoon Equipment, entrained for DUNKIRK.	

Army Form C. 2118.

WAR DIARY
or
~~INTELLIGENCE SUMMARY.~~
(Erase heading not required.)

Instructions regarding War Diaries and Intelligence Summaries are contained in F. S. Regs., Part II. and the Staff Manual respectively. Title pages will be prepared in manuscript.

Place	Date	Hour	Summary of Events and Information	Remarks and references to Appendices
RENESCURE. (Contd).	31st.		200th Field Company. R.E. proceeded to ETAPLES by march route. Pontoon & Trestle Equipment of 201st and 202nd Field Companies were attached to 6th Bn. Cheshire Regiment, with orders to proceed with them to DUNKIRK by march route, starting January 2nd. ————————o———————— APPENDIX.B. gives a Summary of the Hutting Schemes. APPENDIX.C. " " " " " Educational Work. APPENDIX.D. " " " " " Recreational Work. APPENDIX.E. " " " " List of Honours & Awards for month of December.	

January 1919.

for Lieut-Colonel. R.E.
C.R.E., 30th (British) Division.

APPENDIX. A.

O.C. 200th Field Coy. R.E.
O.C. 201st Field Coy. R.E.
O.C. 202nd Field Coy. R.E.
R.E. Officer attd 21st Inf. Bde.
R.E. Officer attd 89th Inf. Bde.
R.E. Officer attd 90th Inf. Bde.

The Division, less Artillery, has been selected for duty at a Base Port - no further details are known at present, but an early move is expected.

The policy to be adopted re works, is shewn below :-

1. No new work will be started except when specially detailed.

2. All Nissen Huts delivered to sites, but not yet erected, will be returned to No. 2. R.E. Park, RENESCURE.

3. Huts partially erected will be completed or else dismantled and returned as in 2 - whichever entails the least labour.

4. All Nissen Hut floor panels issued for tables at Christmas will be returned to LA LACQUE R.E. Dump.

5. Bath Sets collected from DENNEBROEUCQ and ARNEKE will be returned to XIX Corps R.E. Dump, RENESCURE, in complete sets, and a receipt obtained, which will be forwarded to this Office.
Spare parts and fittings will also be returned, as above, but no receipt required.

6. All other R.E. Stores will be returned to either LA LACQUE Dump or XIX Corps R.E. Dump, RENESCURE (whichever is the nearest) where possible - when this is not possible, they will be handed over to Area Commandant.

7. Tools issued to Brigades will be collected in some central spot by R.E. Works Officers attached to Brigades, and a report stating quantities will be sent to this Office. Instructions re disposal of same will be issued later.

8. A return showing number of huts newly erected, with locations, will be sent to this Office as early as possible, alsoa return showing Bath Houses which are in working order.

9. The workshop at LA LACQUE will carry on for the present, and will concentrate on making forms, which will be issued on the signature of the Staff Captain, R.A. The total requirements are about 210 - when these are completed, a report will be sent to this Office.

10. Demands for lorries required for work as above, will be submitted to this Office by O.C. R.E. Companies and R.E. Works Officers attd to Brigades by 09.00 hours on the day before they are required.
The following details are required :-

   1. Number required.
   2. Where required and to whom to report.
   3. Time at which they should report.

Until these demands are received, I am asking for 2 lorries to report daily to each Brigade Headquarters.

(Sd) E.N. CLIFTON. Capt. R.E.
December 27th 1918.   Adjt. 30th (B) Divl. Engineers.
Copies to :- Oi/c R.E. Workshops, LA LACQUE, (for action re para 9).
            Osi/c No.2.R.E.Park, XIX Corps R.E.Dump, LA LACQUE R.E. Dump
            (For information).

APPENDIX. B.

On arriving in the Area it was found that the accommodation was very bad.

It was therefore necessary to get out Hutting Schemes, and to help in this, an R.E. Officer was attached to each Brigade, and later, a Section of a Field Company.

The policy adopted was as follows :-

1. Endeavours would be made to concentrate the Troops by Companies.

2. The fullest possible use would be made of existing accommodation such as barns, etc, which could be bunked for sleeping purposes - such Troops as could not be accommodated in barns would be put into Nissen Huts.

3. As there was practically no existing accommodation for dining and recreational purposes, a type of hut larger than the Bow Nissen would have to be provided, but owing to shortage of transport and more urgent demands for decent sleeping accommodation, it was only possible to deliver and erect 6 of these.

The provision of sleeping accommodation for the Division would have been completed by the end of the month if orders to move had not been received.

APPENDIX. C.

The Adjutant. R.E.
    30th (B) Division.

- Re Education Report -

During the month all preparations were made for classes in the following subjects :-

    Building Construction.
    Carpentry (Practical).
    Fitting   "
    Plumbing   "
    French.
    Elementary Mathematics.
    Mechanical Engineering (Theory).
    Electrical   "   "

Classrooms were obtained and fitted out with desks and equipment. Workshops to accomodate at one time 40 Carpenters, 20 Fitters, 10 Plumbers were fitted with all necessary appliances and tools for the Carpenters Shop were procured. About 150 men were interviewed personally by the Instructors and placed in the stages for which they were fitted in their particular subjects.
19 O.R. from Units in the Division were attached for instruction in Carpentry and Plumbing.
All preparations were completed and it was proposed to start all the classes enumerated above on 30th December.
Orders entailing the movement of the Field Companies were received on the 28th, and in consequence no start could be made in the above classes in AIRE.

28-12-18.

(Sd) R.J. LANNON. Lieut. R.E.
Education Officer, 30th Div. R.E.

APPENDIX. D.

Recreation 30th Division R.E. for month of December 1918.

The Three Field Companies being together, it was found possible, and very suitable, to run inter-Company tournaments in various branches of sport.

Association Football was found to be 'the catch' and was taken up with enthusiasm. Rugby Football is being started on a small scale, the difficulty being to find sufficient players of Rugby Union rules. Athletic sports were to have been held on Christmas Day in the form of an inter-company tournament, but were posponed to New Year's Day.

A R.E. Institute was started to provide indoor recreation for the men. A suitable building was obtained and fitted up as Canteen, N.C.O's room, Reading Room, Games Room. The first two were got going early in the month, but the others were not used owing to the difficulty of obtaining any lighting. One or two public lectures have been given during the month, and largely attended by the R.E.

The reported move of the Division has rather cramped initiation during the last few days of the month.

28-12-18.

(Sd) L. HILL. Capt. R.E.
Recreation Officer, 30th Division R.E.

APPENDIX. E.

HONOURS & AWARDS for month of DECEMBER 1918.

Lieut.	R.F. PETSCHLER.	201st Field Coy. R.E.	MILITARY MEDAL.
83150.	Sergt. E. CALDERBANK.	201st Field Coy. R.E.	CROIX DE GUERRE (DIVISION)
99762.	Corpl. B. LLOYD.	201st Field Coy. R.E.	CROIX DE GUERRE (BRIGADE)
99756.	Corpl. W. HARROP.	202nd Field Coy. R.E.	CROIX DE GUERRE (BRIGADE)
133341.	Sapper. A.V. MUNDY.	200th Field Coy. R.E.	CROIX DE GUERRE (REGIMENT)
198178.	2/Cpl. W.H.E. BERRY.	202nd Field Coy. R.E.	MENTION.

9039

SECRET.

WAR DIARY
OF
30th Div. R.E. H.Q RES.
for
Month of Jan. 19.

Army Form C. 2118.

Sheet. 1.

WAR DIARY
or
INTELLIGENCE SUMMARY.

(Erase heading not required.)

Instructions regarding War Diaries and Intelligence Summaries are contained in F. S. Regs., Part II. and the Staff Manual respectively. Title pages will be prepared in manuscript.

Place	Date	Hour	Summary of Events and Information	Remarks and references to Appendices
	1919.			
RENESCURE.	JANUARY. 1st.		Divisional Headquarters remained at RENESCURE. 200th. Field Company arrived at HUCQUELIERS en route for ETAPLES. 201st and 202nd Field Companies were engaged in providing accommodation for themselves at DUNKERQUE.	
	2nd.		200th. Field Company R.E. arrived at ETAPLES. For work the Field Companies came under the orders of the Base C.R.E's.	
	3rd.		Major FAWCETT. O.C. 201st Field Company R.E. proceeded on leave to U.K. 201st and 202nd Field Companies commenced work on MARDYCK Demobilisation Camps.	
	4th.		200th. Field Coy. R.E. commenced work on Delousing Station.	
	7th.		Major LEE. M.C. R.E. O.C. 202nd Field Coy R.E. and Captain L.B.WOOLLEY. M.C. R.E. 201st Field Coy. R.E. left for U.K. under orders to proceed to NORTH RUSSIA.	
	10th.		Captain. HILL. M.C. R.E. 200th Field Coy. R.E. proceeded to U.K. for Course at Royal Ordnance College, WOOLWICH. Captain. H. de C.TOOGOOD. R.E. reported at H.Q. R.E. for duty, vice Captain HILL. R.E.	
LA CAPELLE.	12th.		Headquarters moved to LA CAPELLE, Near BOULOGNE. Captain. NEWTON. R.E. reported for duty at 201st Field Coy. R.E. vice Captain WOOLLEY. M.C. R.E.	
	17th.		A/C.R.E. visited 200th Field Coy. R.E. at ETAPLES.	
	21st.		Captain G.G.LINDSAY. R.E. 202nd Field Coy. R.E. left for repatriation to CANADA. Major. A.J.FAWCETT. R.E. returned to 201st Field Coy. R.E. from leave, 200th Field Coy. R.E. handed over work to Canadian R.E.	
	22nd.		Lieut-Colonel. P.F.STORY. D.S.O. R.E. returned from leave and resumed command of Divisional R.E.	
	23rd.		Captain E.N.CLIFTON. R.E. proceeded to U.K. for Course at S.M.E. CHATHAM. Lieut. R.J.LANNON. took over duties of Adjutant.	

Army Form C. 2118.

WAR DIARY
or
INTELLIGENCE SUMMARY.

Sheet. 2.

(Erase heading not required.)

Instructions regarding War Diaries and Intelligence Summaries are contained in F. S. Regs., Part II. and the Staff Manual respectively. Title pages will be prepared in manuscript.

Place	Date	Hour	Summary of Events and Information	Remarks and references to Appendices
LA CAPELLE.				
	24th.		Major. E.O.ALABASTER. R.E. left H.Q. for 200th Field Coy. R.E. which moved from ETAPLES to BERGUES by train. R.S.M. J.PENWARDEN. M.S.M. R.E. was despatched to Concentration Camp for Demobilisation.	
	25th.		200th Field Coy. R.E. located at HOYMILLE, Near BERGUES. Lieut. PETSCHLER. M.C. R.E. arrived from 201st Field Coy. R.E. to take over duties as A/Adjutant.	
	26th.		2/Lieut. H.J.EDGAR. 201st Field Coy. R.E. left for Demobilisation. Lieut. EVANS. R.E. 200th Field Coy. R.E. proceeded to U.K. on 14 days Special Leave.	
	27th.		200th Field Coy. R.E. commenced work on R.A.O.C. Depot. 2/Lieut. R.C.P.JAMES. R.E. 200th Field Coy. R.E. left for Course with a Field Survey Battn.	
	28th.		C.R.E. visited all Field Companies.	
			Appendices. Appendix "A" gives a list of Honours & Awards for month of JANUARY. 1919.	

5th February. 1919.

Lieut-Colonel. R.E.
C.R.E. 30th (British) Division.

APPENDIX. "A".

JANUARY. 1919.

HONOURS & AWARDS.

Name.	Company.	Award.
2/Lieut. F.THURLBY. R.E.	200. Field Coy. R.E.	M.C.
Lieut. G.G.COCHRAN. R.E.	30. Divnl Signal Coy. R.E.	Mention.
Major. E.O.ALABASTER. R.E.	200. Field Coy. R.E.	Croix de Guerre. (French)
Captain. L.A.HILL. M.C. R.E.	200. Field Coy. R.E.	Croix de Guerre. (Belgian)
Captain. C.C.LINDSAY. R.E.	202. Field Coy. R.E.	Croix de Guerre. (Belgian)
Lieut. G.R.J. WATKINS-PITCHFORD. R.E.	30. Divnl Signal Coy. R.E.	Croix de Guerre. (Belgian)
No. 83031. Sergt. H.WELSH.	200. Field Coy. R.E.	M.S.M.
No. 83247. Corpl. MEWS. S.A.	201. Field Coy. R.E.	M.S.M.
" 83311. Corpl. (A/Sergt) INCE. H.	30. Divnl Signal Coy. R.E.	M.S.M.
" 83124. Sapper. RIGBY. A.	201. Field Coy. R.E.	Croix de Guerre. (Belgian)
" 83136. Sapper. OLIVER. W.	30. Divnl. Signal Coy. R.E.	Croix de Guerre. (Belgian)

CONFIDENTIAL.

WAR DIARY FOR FEBRUARY, 1919.

R.E. HEADQUARTERS. 30th DIVISION.

VOLUME 40.

Army Form C. 2118.

WAR DIARY
or
INTELLIGENCE SUMMARY.   V O L U M E   40.   Sheet 1.

(Erase heading not required.)

Instructions regarding War Diaries and Intelligence
Summaries are contained in F. S. Regs., Part II.
and the Staff Manual respectively. Title pages
will be prepared in manuscript.

Place	Date	Hour	Summary of Events and Information	Remarks and references to Appendices
LA CAPELLE	Feb.1st/19.		Headquarters R.E. 30th Division- stationed at LA CAPELLE.	
			200th Field Coy. R.E. at R.A.S.C. Camp. HOYMILLE? BERGUES? nr DUNKIRK	
			201st Field Coy. R.E. " Mardyck, Dunkirk working on Demobilization Camps.	
			202nd Field Coy. R.E. " St. Malo " " " "	
	" 5th.		Lieut. Lennon proceeded to join C.R.E., Stores iii (3) Solesmes as Adjutant.	
	" 6th.		Lieut. Fitt posted from R.E. Base, ROUEN to 200th Field Coy. R.E.	
	" 7th.		Lt.Col. Story. D.S.O.,R.E. admitted to No. 14 General Hospital, WIMEREAUX.	
	" 9th.		Capt. H.T. Johnson, R.E. assumed Command 202nd Field Coy. R.E. Authy: A.G.55/6352 (O) d/28/1/19.	
	"10th.		Lieut. J.C. Fisher, 202nd Field Coy. R.E. demobilized.	
			Major E.O. Alabaster proceeded to England to take up appointment at School of Electric Lighting, Chatham. Authy: A.G./55/6738 (O) d/1/2/19.	
	"11th.		Capt. F.M.N. Newton, 201st Field Coy. R.E. assumed duties of Command 200th Field Coy. R.E. vice Major E.O.Alabaster. Authy: A.G.55/6738 (O) d/1/2/19.	
			Capt. H. de C. Toogood, 200th Field Coy. R.E. rejoined from leave.	
	" 15th.		Lieut. T.B. Frost, 202nd Field Coy. R.E. proceeded on leave.	

Army Form C. 2118.

WAR DIARY
or
INTELLIGENCE SUMMARY.

SHEET 2.

(Erase heading not required.)

Instructions regarding War Diaries and Intelligence Summaries are contained in F. S. Regs., Part II. and the Staff Manual respectively. Title pages will be prepared in manuscript.

Place	Date	Hour	Summary of Events and Information	Remarks and references to Appendices
	Feb.19th.		Lieut. R.F. PETSCHLER, M.C., R.E., appointed Adjutant to C.R.E. 30th Division, vice A/Capt E.N. CLIFTON, to England. Authy: A.G.55/6903 (O) d/16/2/19. Date of assuming duties being 24/1/19.	
	" 20th.		Lieut. P.N/ WALTON from R.E. Base Depot, Rouen-posted to 201st Field Coy. R.E. Authy: A.G.55/6871 (O) d/10/2/19.	
			2/Lieut. W.S. MANNERS from R.E. Base Depot, Rouen-posted to 202nd Field Coy. R.E. Authy: A.G. 55/6871 (O) d/10/2/19.	
	" 25th.		Headquarters, R.E., moved to CONDETTE, near BOULOGNE. C.R.E's Mess attached to "B" Mess.	
	" 28th.		Capt. H. de C. TOOGOOD proceeded to H.Q., D.E.S., VERTON. Authy: 30th Division No. A/1914.	

for C.R.E.,
Captain.R.E.,
30th Division.

WAR DIARY.

of the

30th Divisional Engineers.

for the month of

MARCH. 1919.

Volume No.

Volume No 4.

Army Form C. 2118.

WAR DIARY
or
INTELLIGENCE SUMMARY. of Headquarters 30th Divisional Engineers s.

(Erase heading not required.)

Instructions regarding War Diaries and Intelligence Summaries are contained in F. S. Regs., Part II. and the Staff Manual respectively. Title pages will be prepared in manuscript.

Place	Date	Hour	Summary of Events and Information	Remarks and references to Appendices
CONDETTE. Near BOULOGNE.	1/3/19 to 7/3/19.		Routine.	
	8/3/19.		Lieut-Colonel. P.F.STORY. D.S.O. R.E. granted sick leave to U.K.	
	8/3/19. to 29/3/19.		Major. A.J.FAWCETT. R.E. O.C. 201st Field Coy. R.E. took over duties of A/C.R.E. vice Lieut-Col. P.F.STORY. D.S.O. R.E. on Sick Leave.	
	9/3/19 to 18/3/19.		Routine.	
	19/3/19.		201st Field Coy. R.E. moved from DUNKIRK to CONDETTE, Near BOULOGNE.	
	20/3/19. to 23/3/19.		Routine.	
	24/5/19.			
	25/5/19.		Field Coy's received orders to get down to Cadre Strength "Cadre "A"	
	26/3/19 to 31/3/19.		Routine.	

Major. R.E.
A/C.R.E. 30th Divisional Engineers.

War Diary
of
C.R.E.
for
March 1919

WAR DIARY or **INTELLIGENCE SUMMARY**
Army Form C. 2118.

FINAL
Volume No 42

Headquarters of 30th Divisional Engineers

Place	Date	Hour	Summary of Events and Information	Remarks and references to Appendices
CONDETTE	1st/4		Routine	
"	5th		Lt Col P F STORY DSO RE proceeded to join as CRE VI Corps Troops auth'y AG 10223 (O)	
			Captain R F FETSCHLER M.E I RE on leave to UK 4/4/19 to 18/4/19.	
			2/Lt K FORSTER. 201 Field Coy RE joined as A/Adjt	
"	6/20th		Routine CAPTAIN R F FETSCHLER M E I RE proceeded to join SPA Sub area	
			auth'y A.G. 10336/adjts (O) dt - 26/3/19.	
"	21st 22nd		Routine	
"	23rd		MAJOR A T FAWCETT and 2/Lt K FORSTER rejoined. 2/Lt K FORSTER 201 Field Coy R.E.	
			after acting as A/CRE and A/Adjutant	
	24th		Personal Order Establishment moved with 201 Field Coy to MARRYCK	
			CAMP DUNKIRK and attached to 201 Coy awaiting orders for	
			Embarkation home.	
			Office of CRE closes & ceases to exist as from 24th April 1919.	

L B Steward Lieut.

War Diary
of
C.R.E.
for
April 1919

www.ingramcontent.com/pod-product-compliance
Lightning Source LLC
Chambersburg PA
CBHW080809010526
44113CB00013B/2349